KEKKAISHI

10

田辺イエロウ
YELLOW TANABE PRESENTS

The Story Thus Far

Yoshimori Sumimura and Tokine Yukimura have a special duty passed down through their families for generations—to protect Karasumori Forest from supernatural beings called *ayakashi*. People with their gift for terminating ayakashi are called *kekkaishi*, or "barrier masters."

The Night Troops, a group of outcasts within the Shadow Organization, have sent Gen Shishio, a half-ayakashi, to the Karasumori Site to assist Yoshimori and Tokine.

Gen's former Night Troops instructor, Atora, pays Gen a surprise visit at Karasumori. She is displeased with his inability to work with Yoshimori and Tokine as a team, and subjects them all to a rigorous training exercise to bring them up to snuff.

Meanwhile, the Kokuboro ayakashi send a reconnaissance expedition to the Colorless Marsh in hopes of unseating its master, and follow up with an assassination attempt on Heisuke Matsudo, an expert on their demon kind. But Heisuke fakes his demise, fooling not just his enemies, but his old friend, Yoshimori's Grandpa, as well.

Is all this nefarious activity a sign that Kokuboro is about to launch a full-scale attack against the Karasumori Site...!?

KEKKAISHI VOL. 10
TABLE OF CONTENTS

Chapter 86: Baby Steps

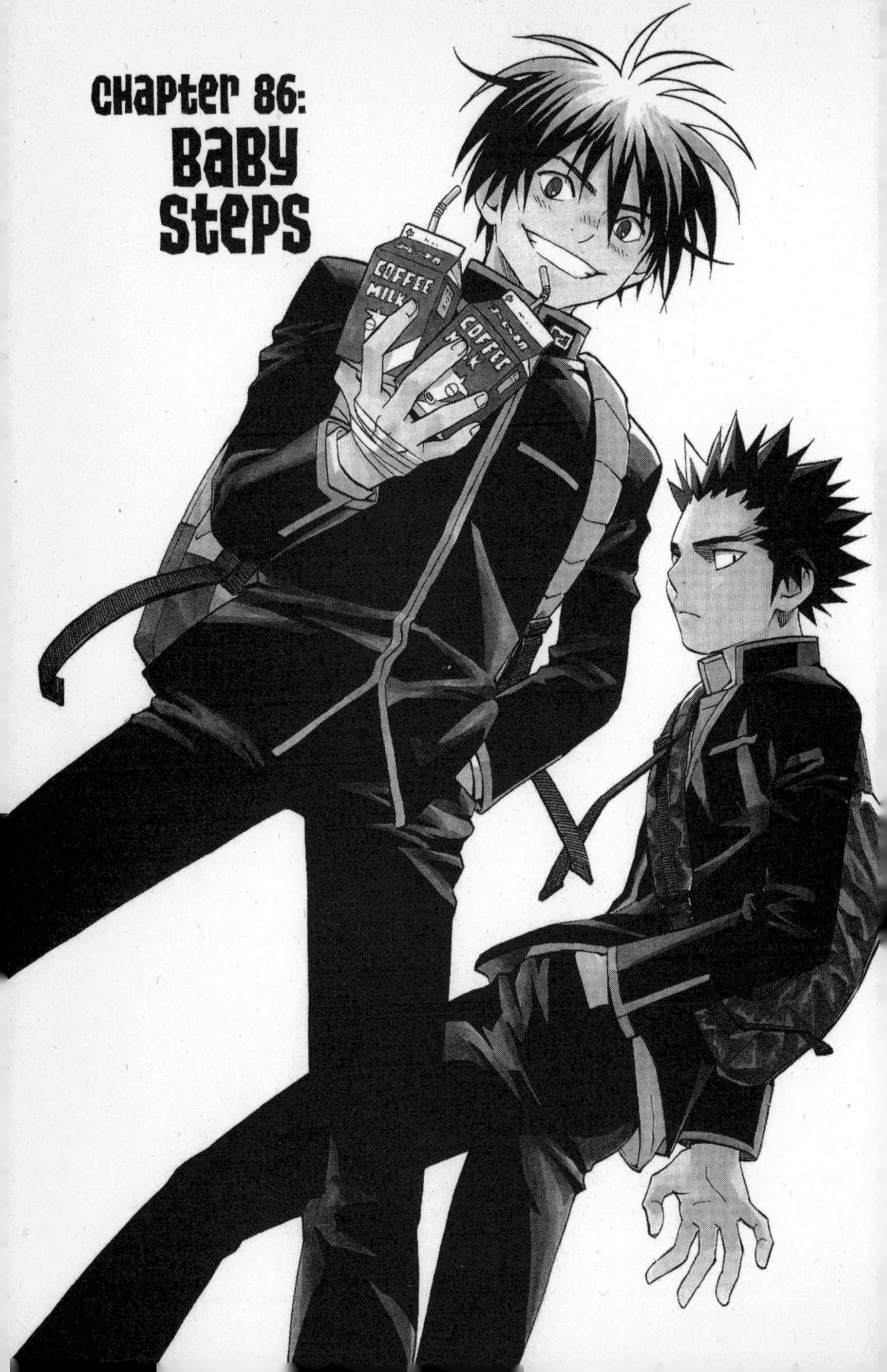
COFFEE MILK
COFFEE MILK

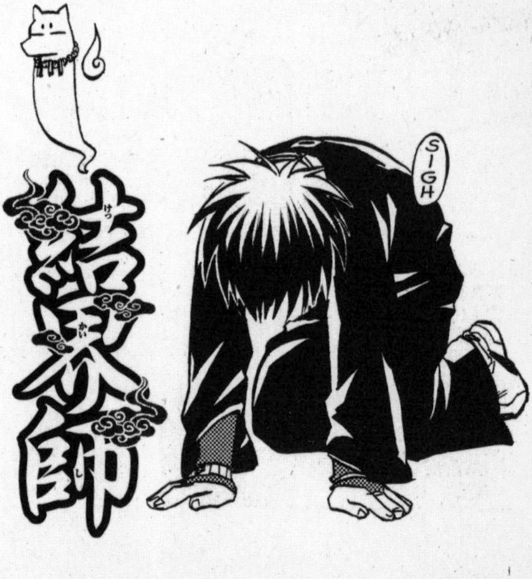
結界師
SIGH

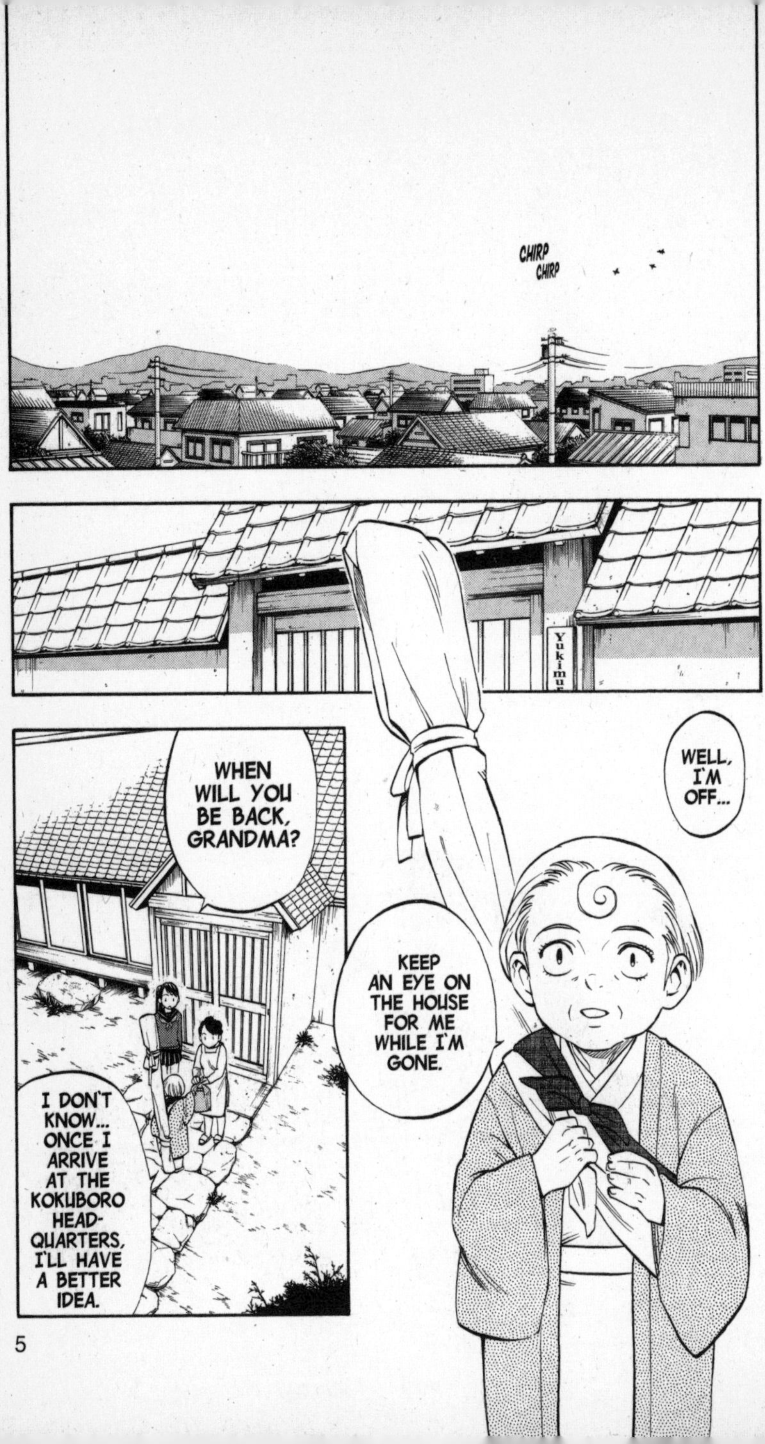
CHIRP
CHIRP
Yukimur
WELL, I'M OFF...
KEEP AN EYE ON THE HOUSE FOR ME WHILE I'M GONE.
WHEN WILL YOU BE BACK, GRANDMA?
I DON'T KNOW... ONCE I ARRIVE AT THE KOKUBORO HEAD-QUARTERS, I'LL HAVE A BETTER IDEA.

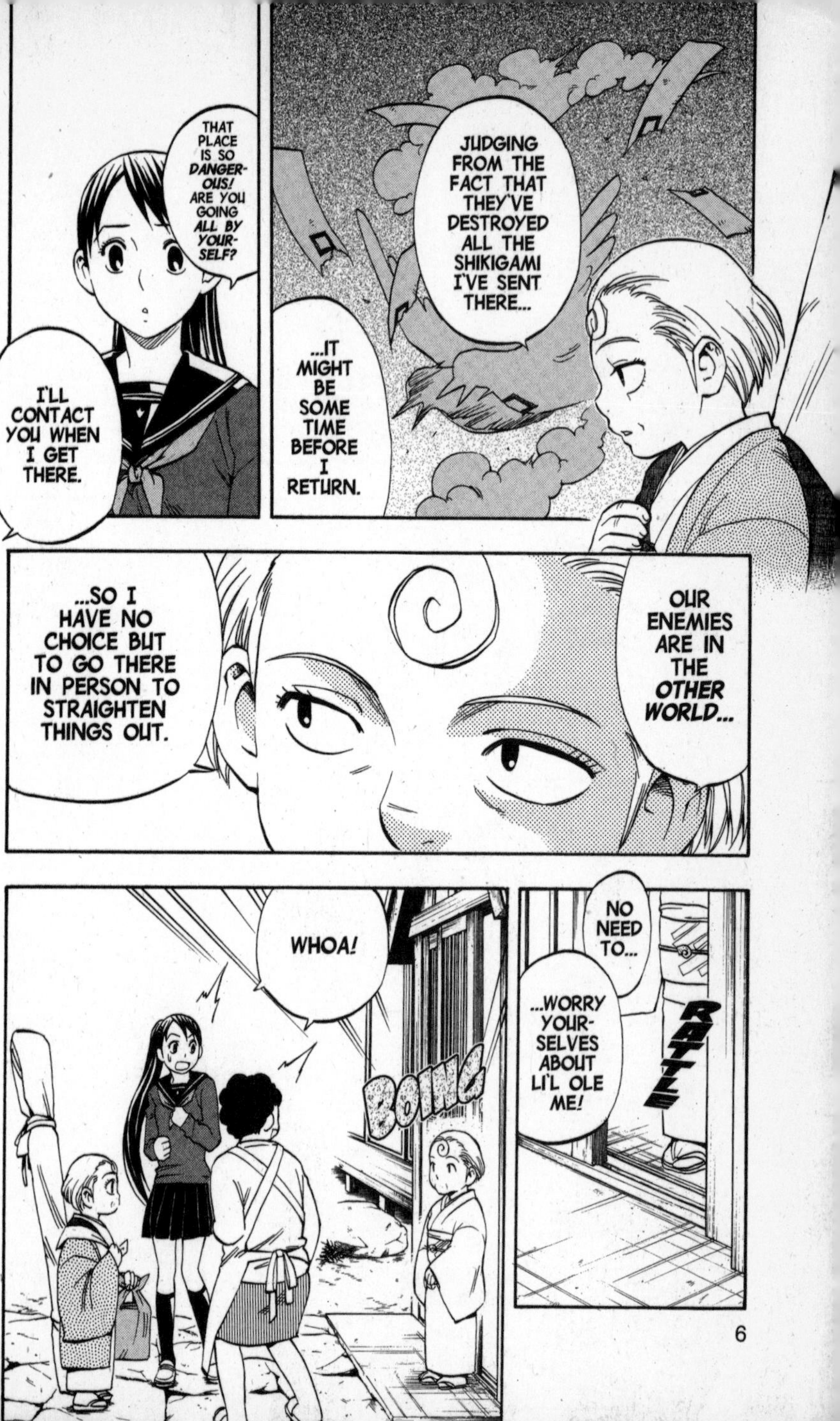
JUDGING FROM THE FACT THAT THEY'VE DESTROYED ALL THE SHIKIGAMI I'VE SENT THERE...
...IT MIGHT BE SOME TIME BEFORE I RETURN.
THAT PLACE IS SO *DANGEROUS!* ARE YOU GOING *ALL BY YOURSELF?*
I'LL CONTACT YOU WHEN I GET THERE.
OUR ENEMIES ARE IN THE *OTHER WORLD...*
...SO I HAVE NO CHOICE BUT TO GO THERE IN PERSON TO STRAIGHTEN THINGS OUT.
NO NEED TO...
...WORRY YOURSELVES ABOUT LI'L OLE *ME!*
RATTLE
WHOA!
BOING

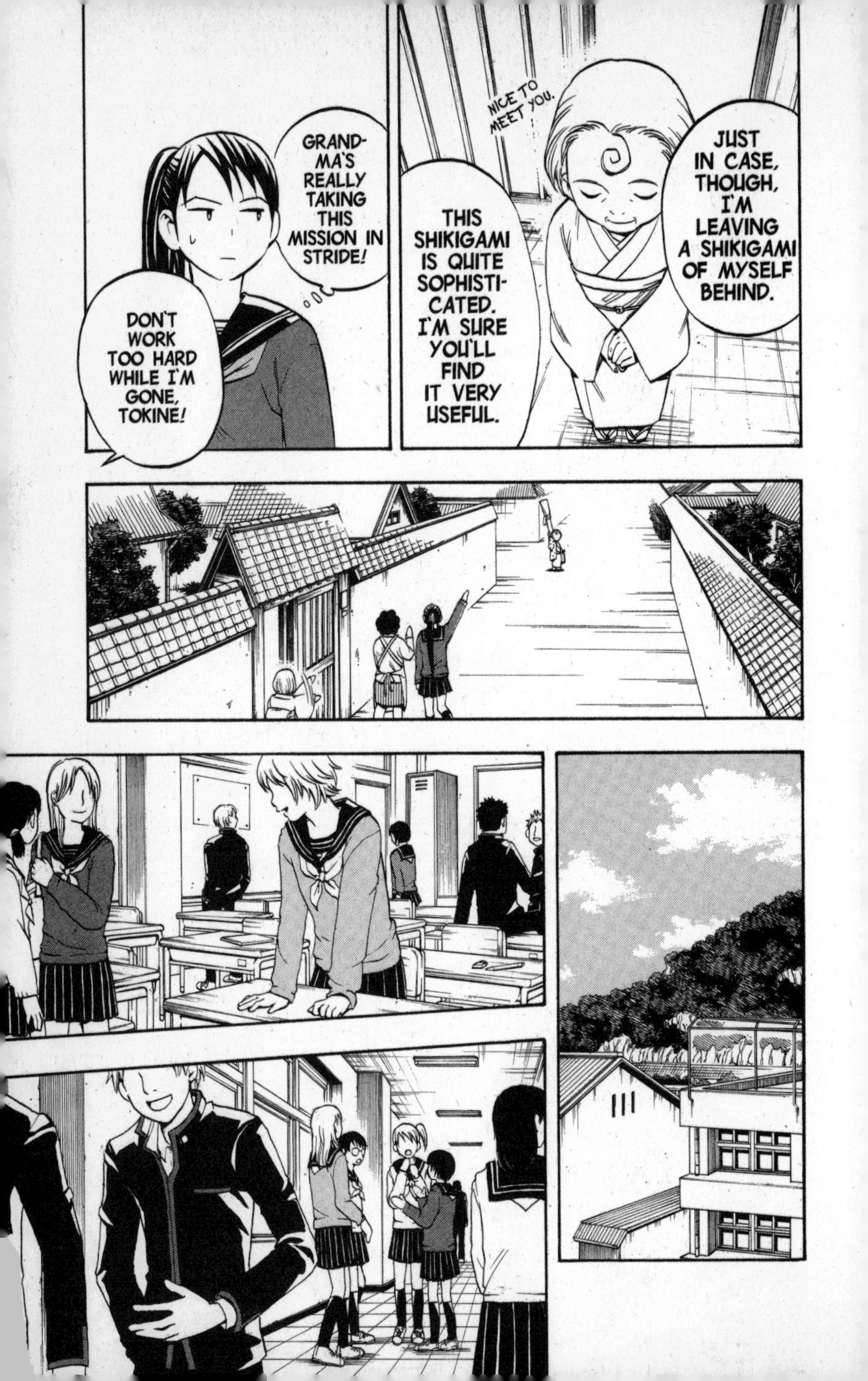
JUST IN CASE, THOUGH, I'M LEAVING A SHIKIGAMI OF MYSELF BEHIND.
NICE TO MEET YOU.
THIS SHIKIGAMI IS QUITE SOPHISTICATED. I'M SURE YOU'LL FIND IT VERY USEFUL.
GRANDMA'S REALLY TAKING THIS MISSION IN STRIDE!
DON'T WORK TOO HARD WHILE I'M GONE, TOKINE!

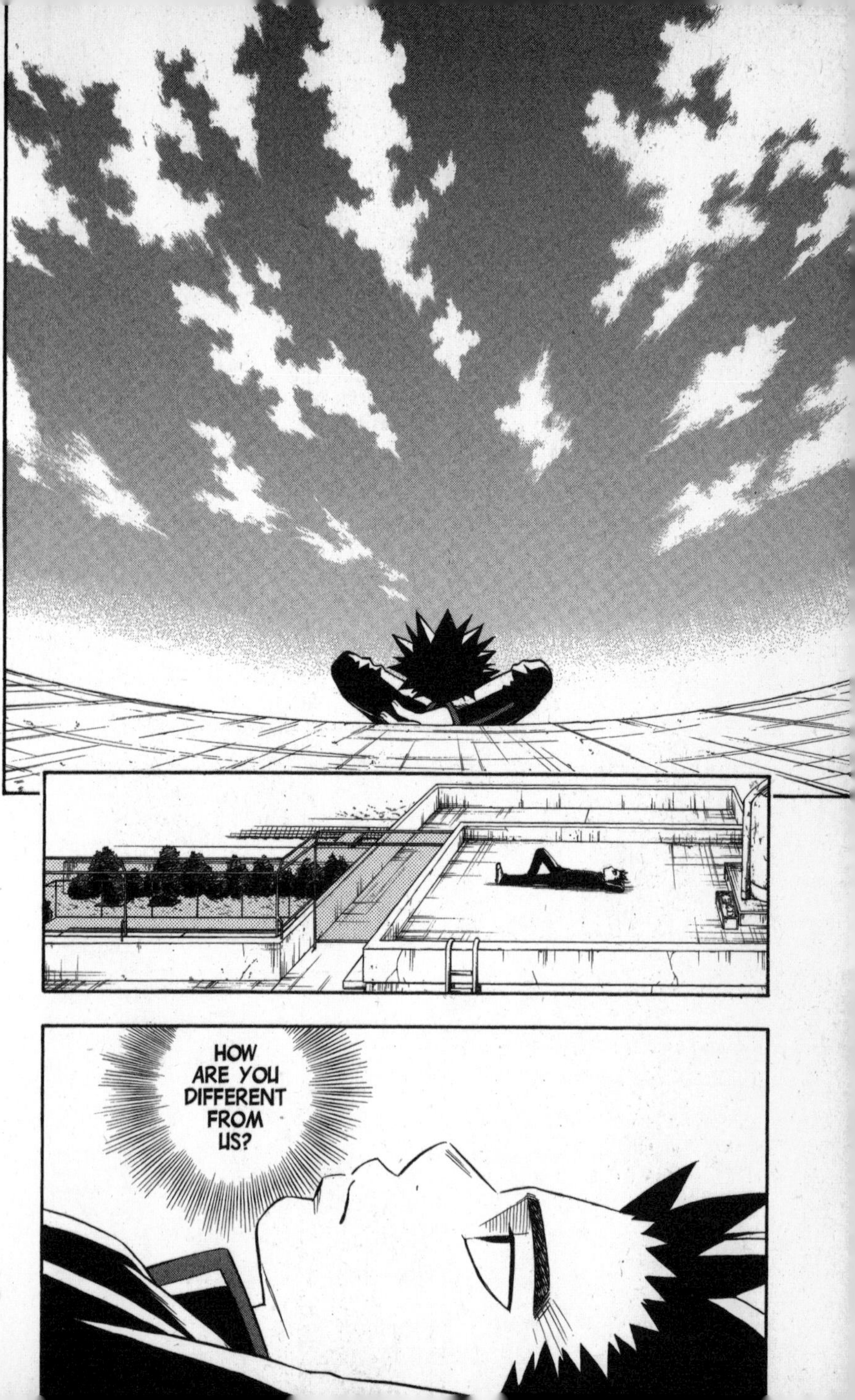
HOW ARE YOU DIFFERENT FROM US?

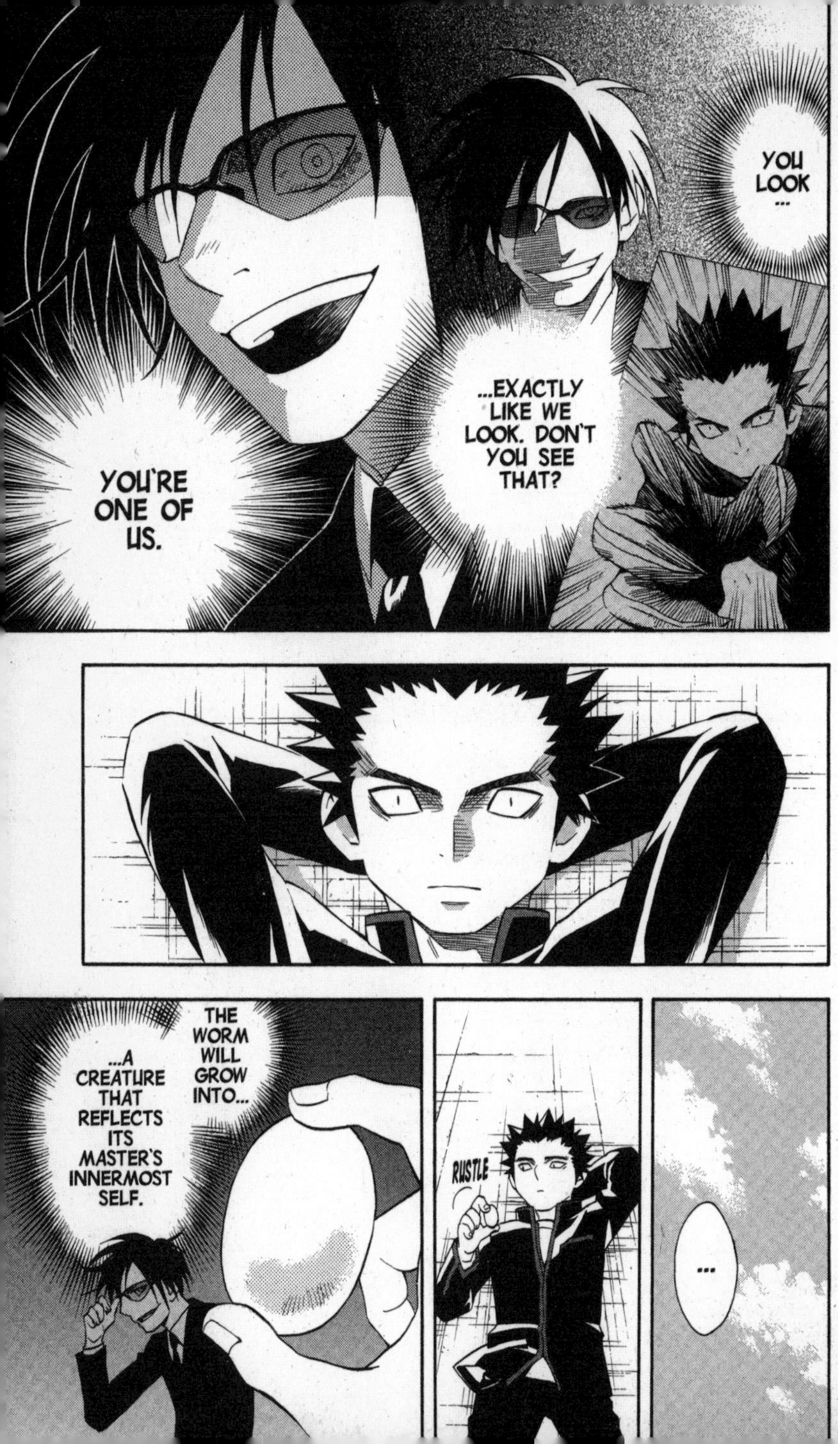
YOU LOOK ...
...EXACTLY LIKE WE LOOK. DON'T YOU SEE THAT?
YOU'RE ONE OF US.
...
RUSTLE
THE WORM WILL GROW INTO...
...A CREATURE THAT REFLECTS ITS MASTER'S INNERMOST SELF.

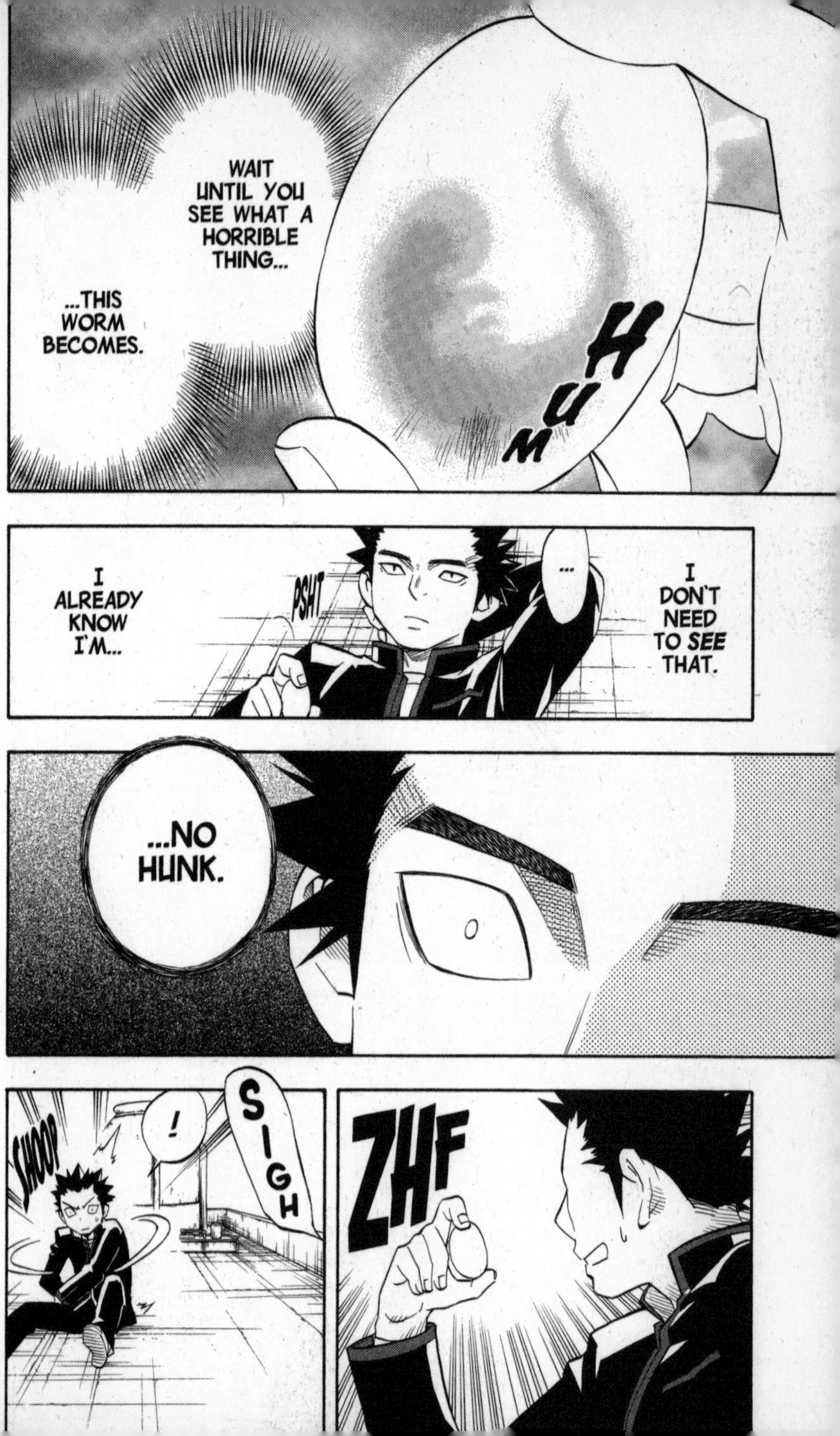
WAIT UNTIL YOU SEE WHAT A HORRIBLE THING...
...THIS WORM BECOMES.
HUM
I DON'T NEED TO SEE THAT.
...
PSHT
I ALREADY KNOW I'M...
...NO HUNK.
ZHF
SIGH
!
SHOOP

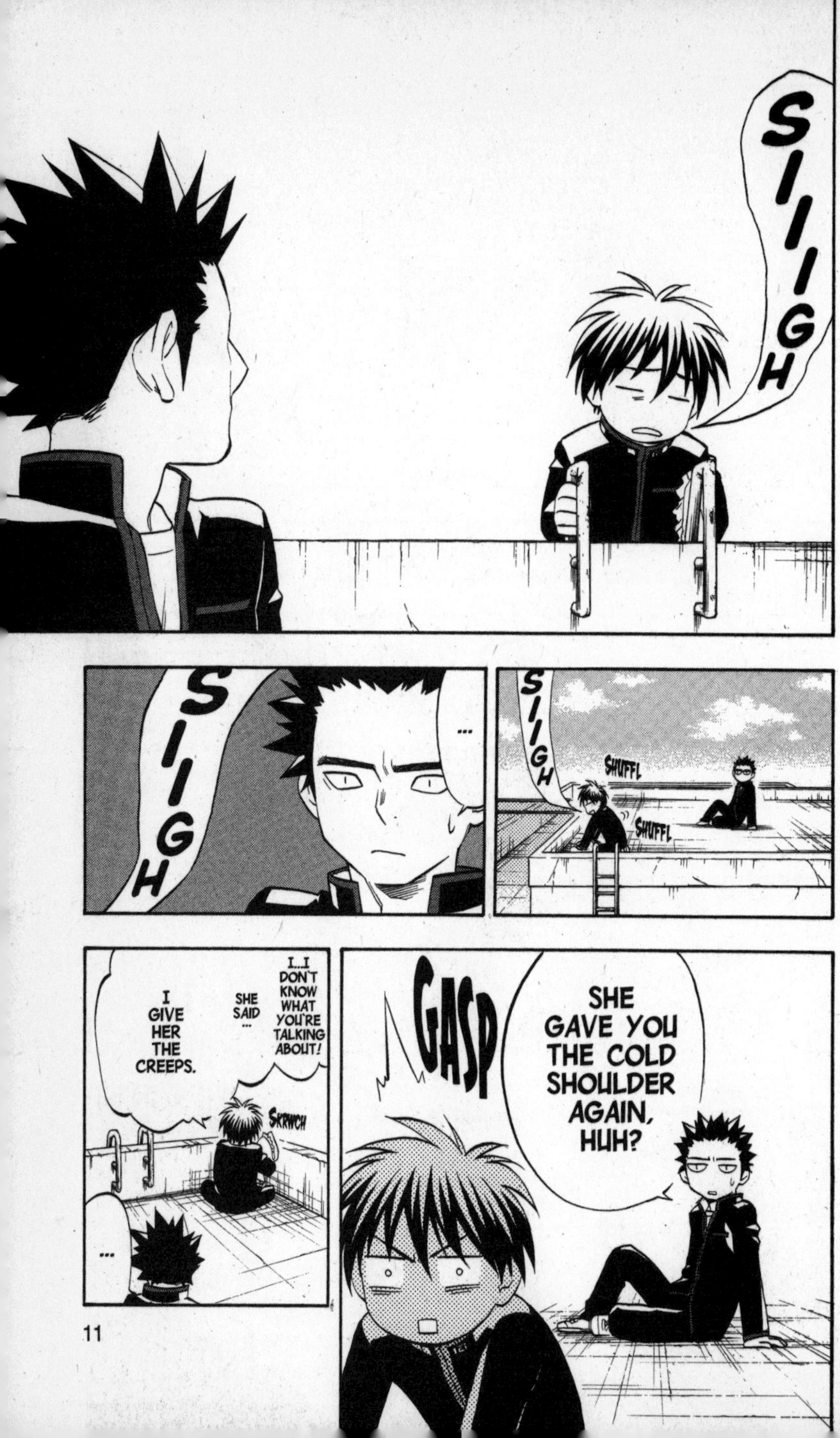

SIIIGH
SIIIGH
SHUFFL
SHUFFL
SIIIGH
...
GASP
SHE GAVE YOU THE COLD SHOULDER AGAIN, HUH?
I..I DON'T KNOW WHAT YOU'RE TALKING ABOUT!
SHE SAID ...
I GIVE HER THE CREEPS.
SKRWCH
...

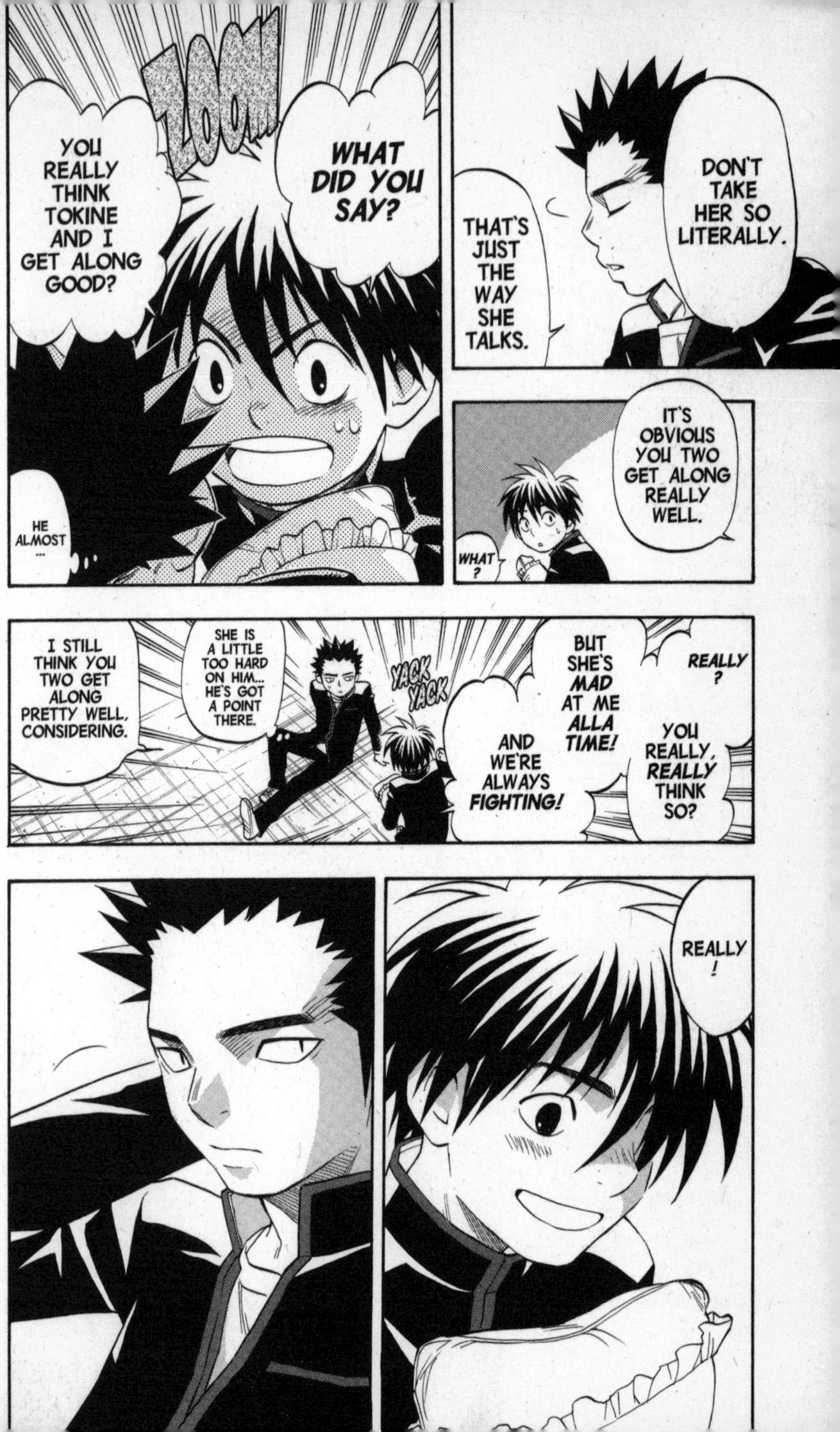

DON'T TAKE HER SO LITERALLY.
THAT'S JUST THE WAY SHE TALKS.
IT'S OBVIOUS YOU TWO GET ALONG REALLY WELL.
WHAT?
ZOOM
WHAT DID YOU SAY?
YOU REALLY THINK TOKINE AND I GET ALONG GOOD?
HE ALMOST...
REALLY?
YOU REALLY, REALLY THINK SO?
BUT SHE'S MAD AT ME ALLA TIME!
AND WE'RE ALWAYS FIGHTING!
YACK YACK
SHE IS A LITTLE TOO HARD ON HIM... HE'S GOT A POINT THERE.
I STILL THINK YOU TWO GET ALONG PRETTY WELL, CONSIDERING.
REALLY!

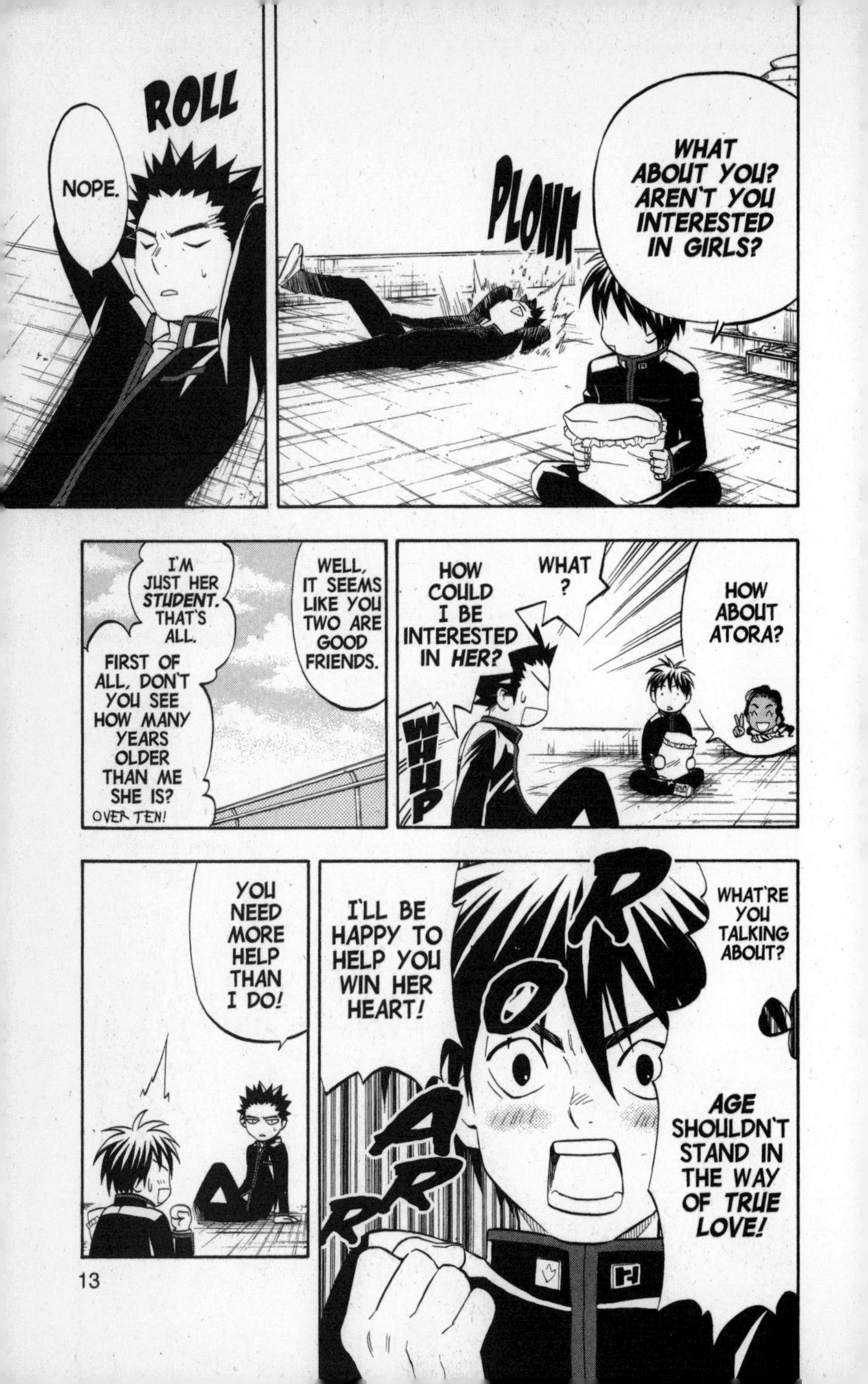
WHAT ABOUT YOU? AREN'T YOU INTERESTED IN GIRLS?
PLONK
ROLL
NOPE.
HOW ABOUT ATORA?
WHAT?
HOW COULD I BE INTERESTED IN HER?
WHUP
WELL, IT SEEMS LIKE YOU TWO ARE GOOD FRIENDS.
I'M JUST HER STUDENT. THAT'S ALL.
FIRST OF ALL, DON'T YOU SEE HOW MANY YEARS OLDER THAN ME SHE IS?
OVER TEN!
WHAT'RE YOU TALKING ABOUT?
ROAR
AGE SHOULDN'T STAND IN THE WAY OF TRUE LOVE!
I'LL BE HAPPY TO HELP YOU WIN HER HEART!
YOU NEED MORE HELP THAN I DO!

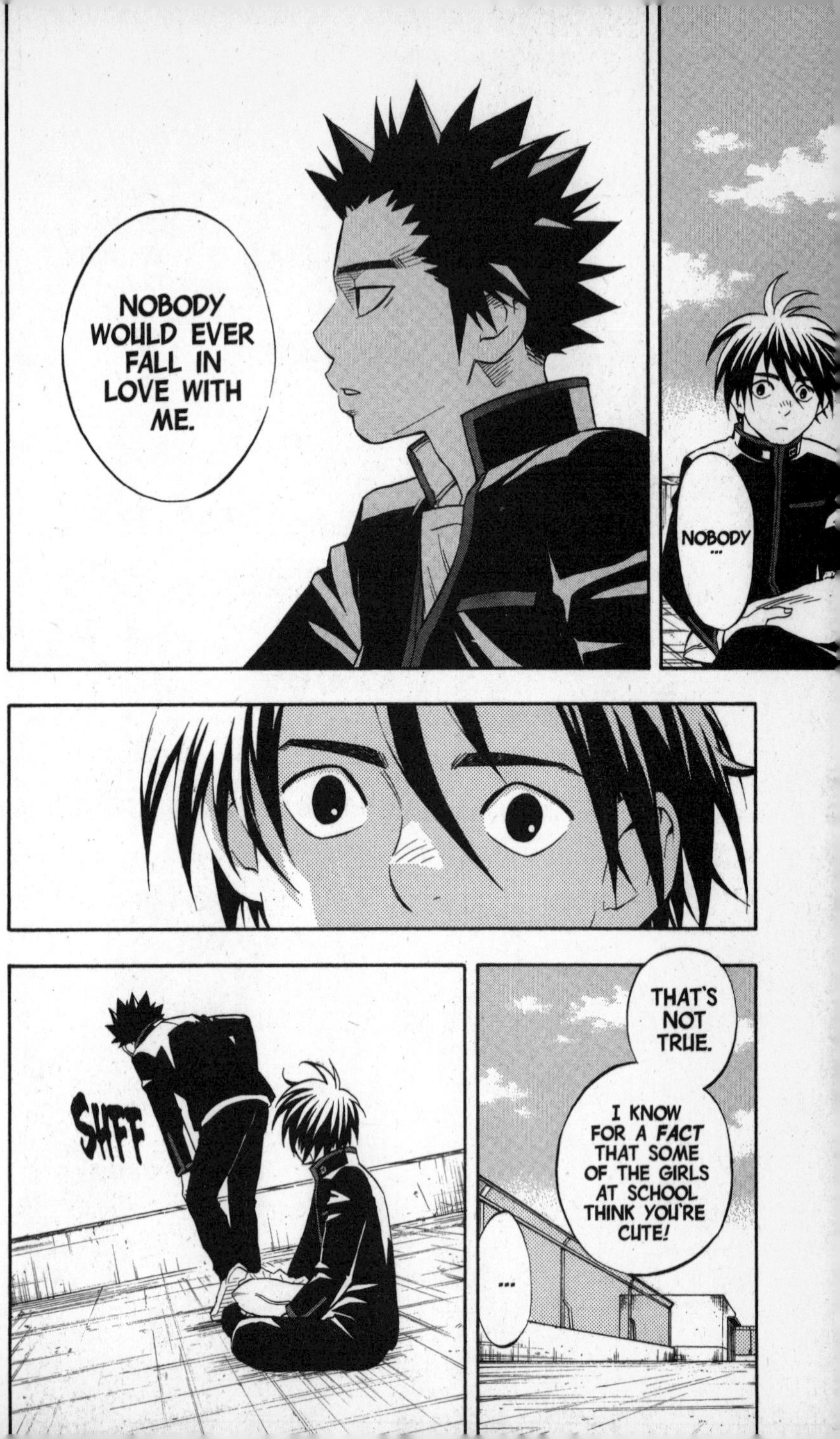
NOBODY...
NOBODY WOULD EVER FALL IN LOVE WITH ME.
THAT'S NOT TRUE.
I KNOW FOR A *FACT* THAT SOME OF THE GIRLS AT SCHOOL THINK *YOU'RE* CUTE!
...
SHFF

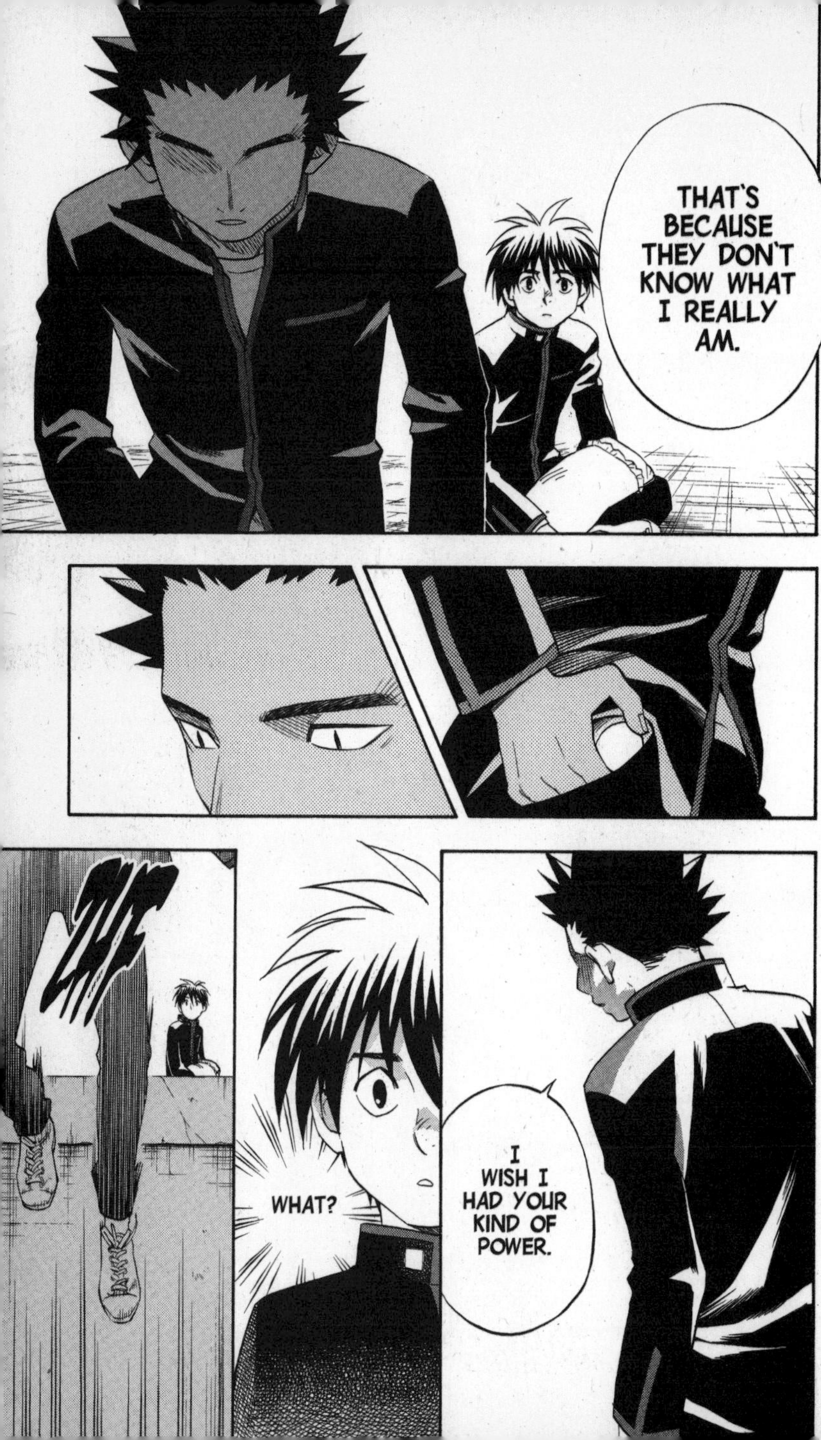
THAT'S BECAUSE THEY DON'T KNOW WHAT I REALLY AM.
I WISH I HAD YOUR KIND OF POWER.
WHAT?

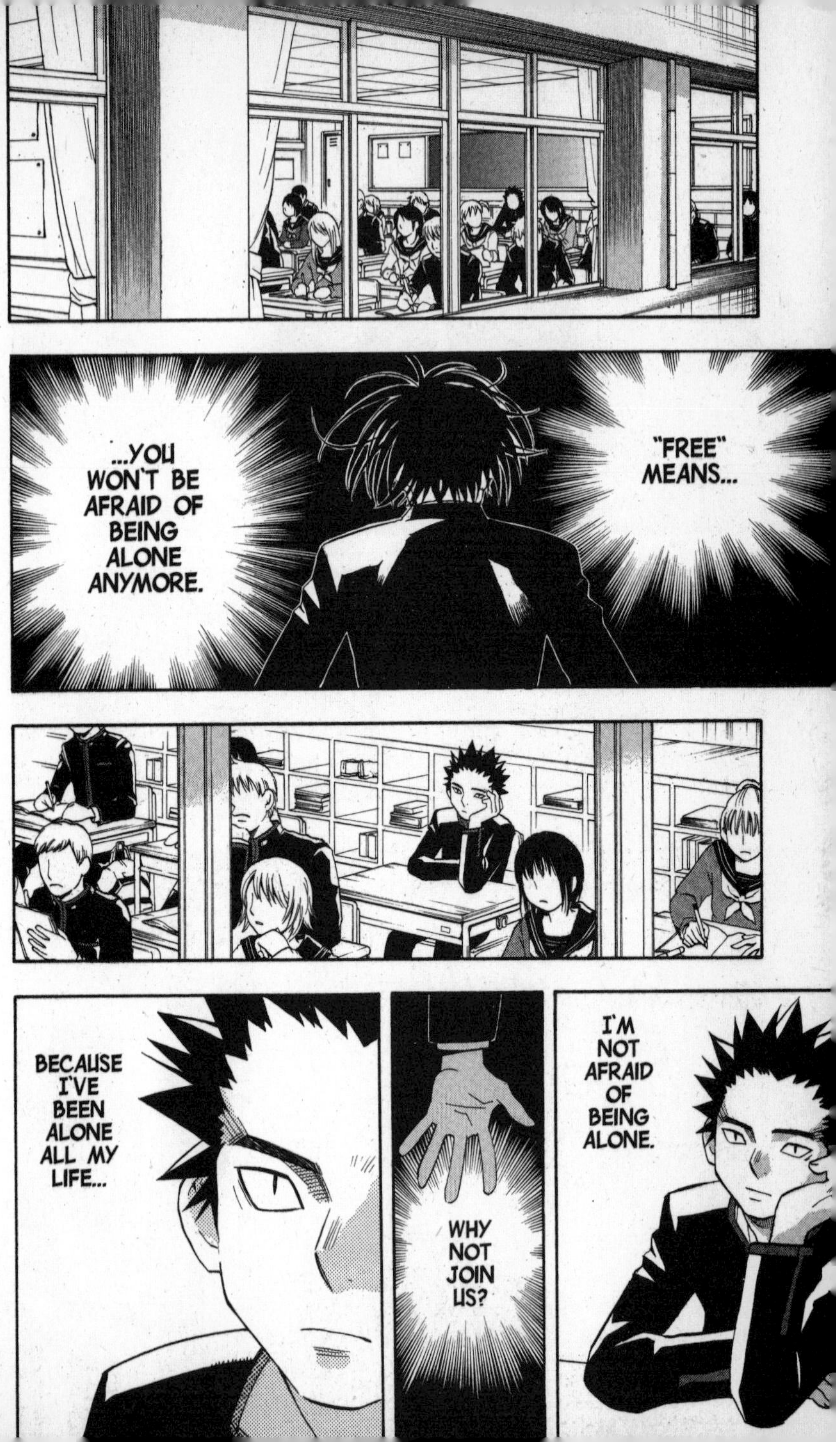
"FREE" MEANS...
...YOU WON'T BE AFRAID OF BEING ALONE ANYMORE.
I'M NOT AFRAID OF BEING ALONE.
WHY NOT JOIN US?
BECAUSE I'VE BEEN ALONE ALL MY LIFE...

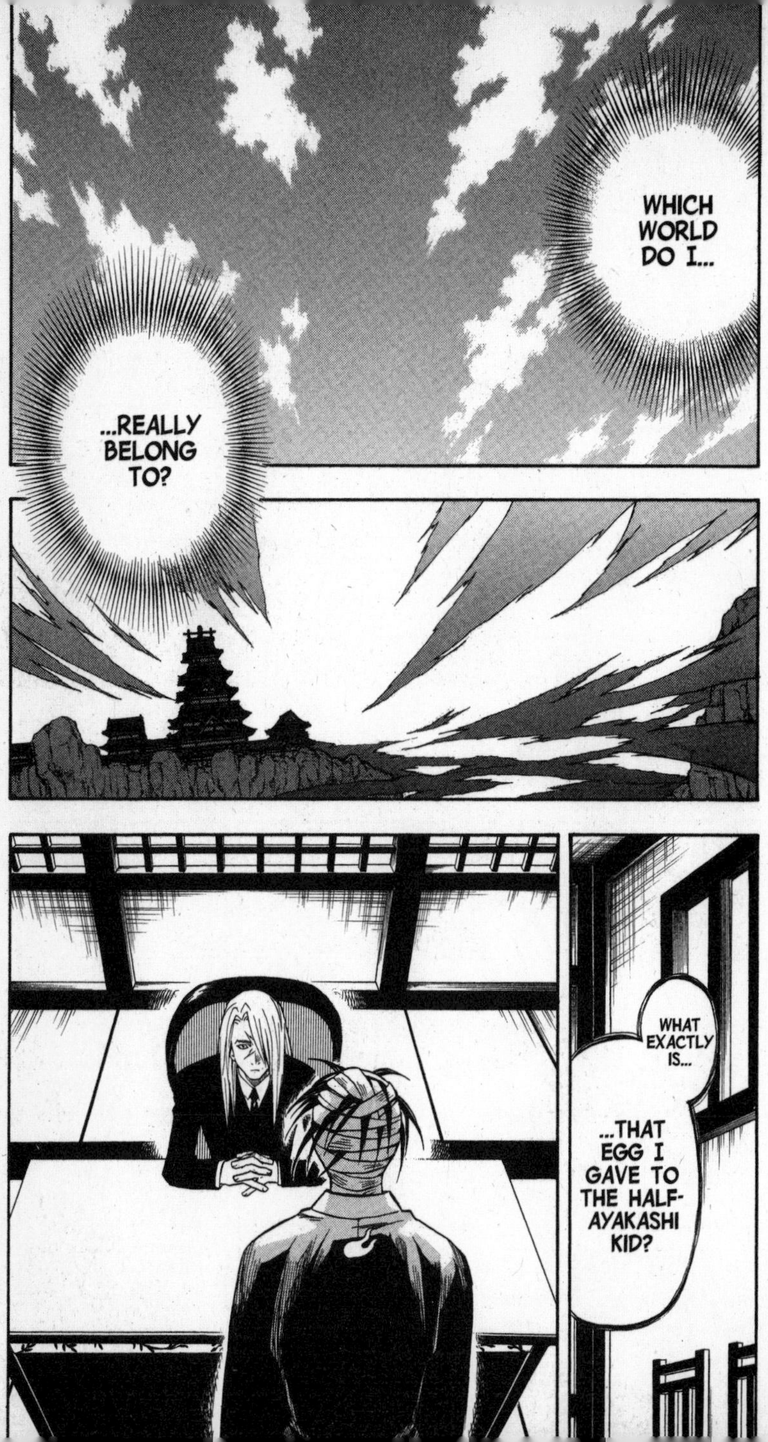
WHICH WORLD DO I...
...REALLY BELONG TO?
WHAT EXACTLY IS...
...THAT EGG I GAVE TO THE HALF-AYAKASHI KID?

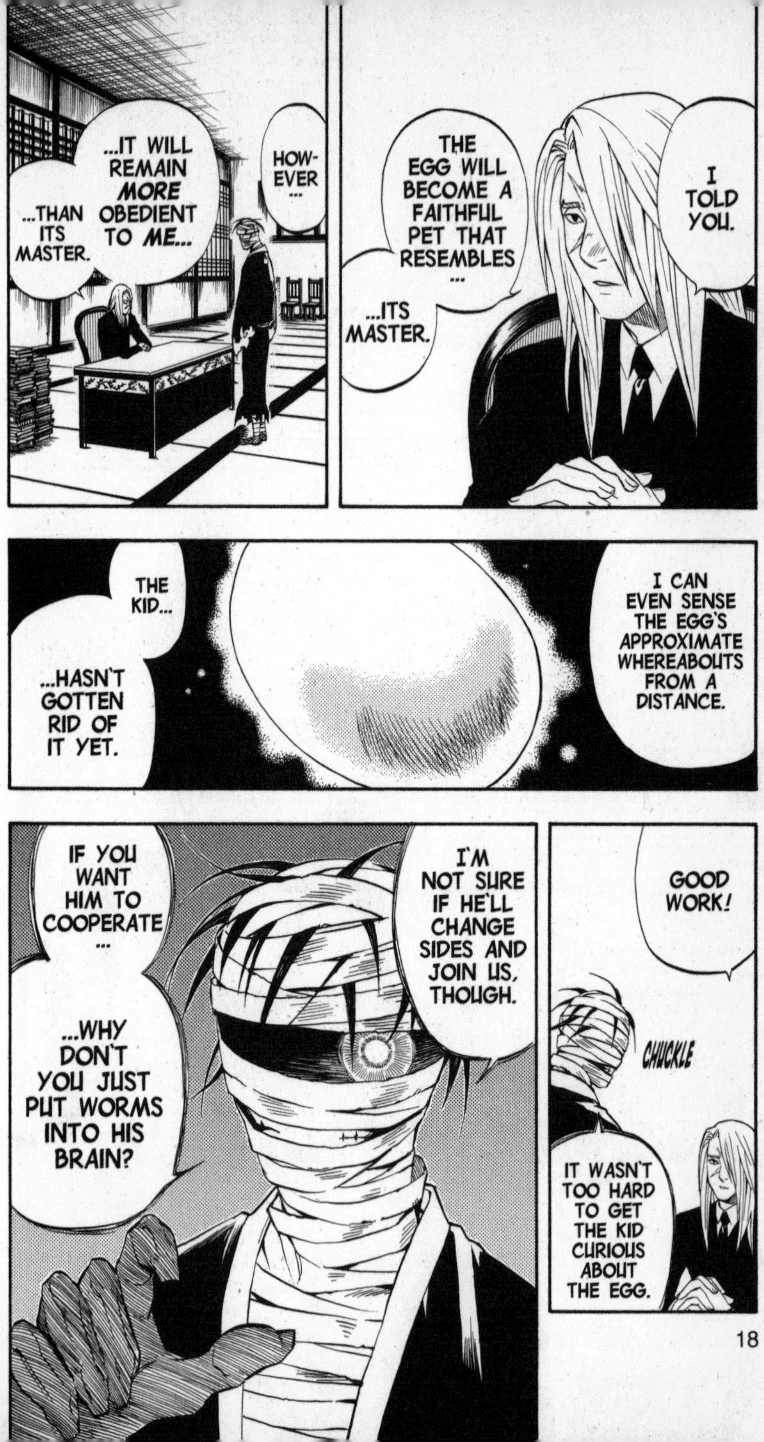
I TOLD YOU.
THE EGG WILL BECOME A FAITHFUL PET THAT RESEMBLES...
...ITS MASTER.
HOW-EVER...
...IT WILL REMAIN MORE OBEDIENT TO ME...
...THAN ITS MASTER.
I CAN EVEN SENSE THE EGG'S APPROXIMATE WHEREABOUTS FROM A DISTANCE.
THE KID...
...HASN'T GOTTEN RID OF IT YET.
GOOD WORK!
CHUCKLE
IT WASN'T TOO HARD TO GET THE KID CURIOUS ABOUT THE EGG.
I'M NOT SURE IF HE'LL CHANGE SIDES AND JOIN US, THOUGH.
IF YOU WANT HIM TO COOPERATE...
...WHY DON'T YOU JUST PUT WORMS INTO HIS BRAIN?

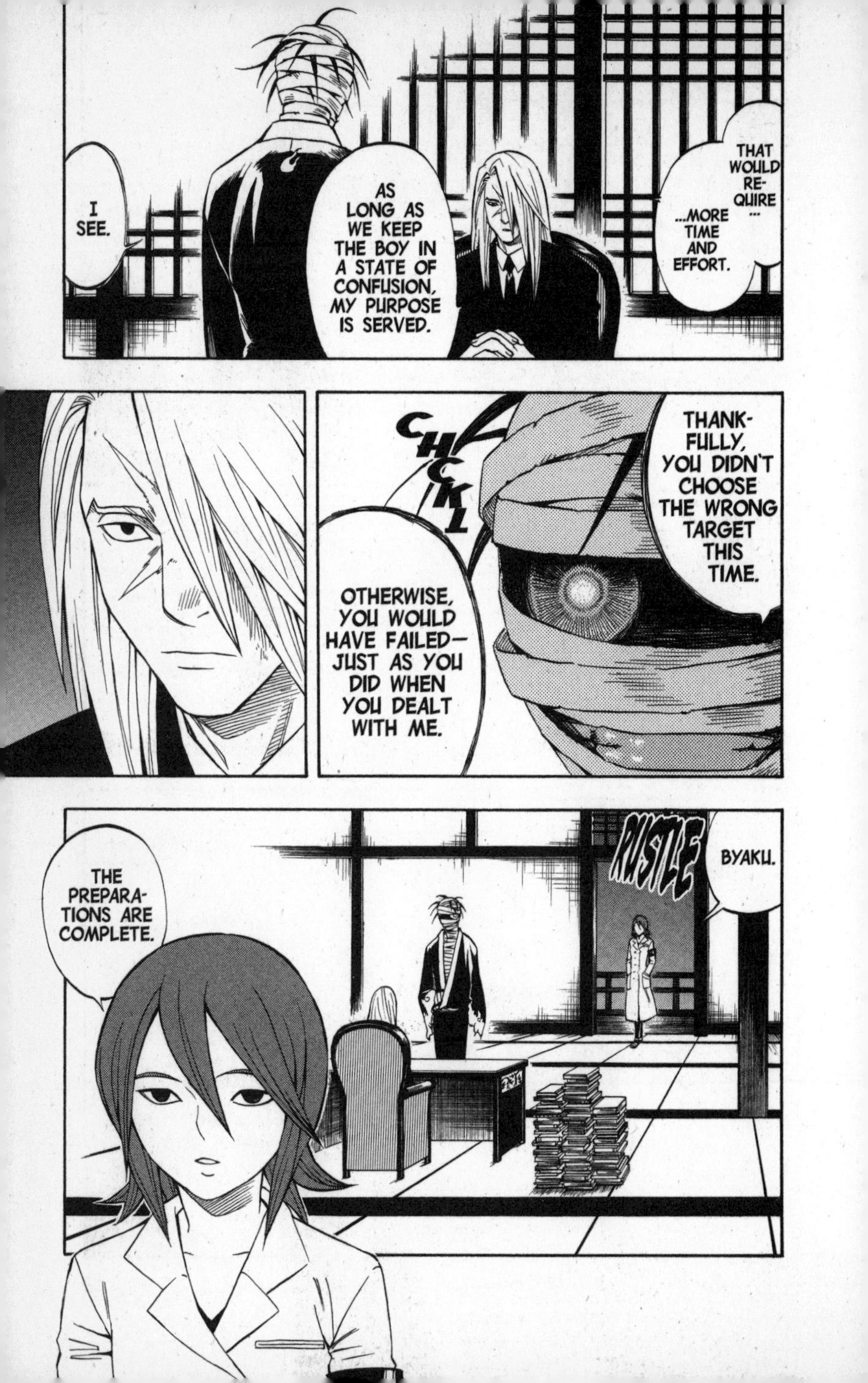
THAT WOULD RE-QUIRE ... ...MORE TIME AND EFFORT.
AS LONG AS WE KEEP THE BOY IN A STATE OF CONFUSION, MY PURPOSE IS SERVED.
I SEE.
CHCK!
THANK-FULLY, YOU DIDN'T CHOOSE THE WRONG TARGET THIS TIME.
OTHERWISE, YOU WOULD HAVE FAILED—JUST AS YOU DID WHEN YOU DEALT WITH ME.
RUSTLE
BYAKU.
THE PREPARA-TIONS ARE COMPLETE.

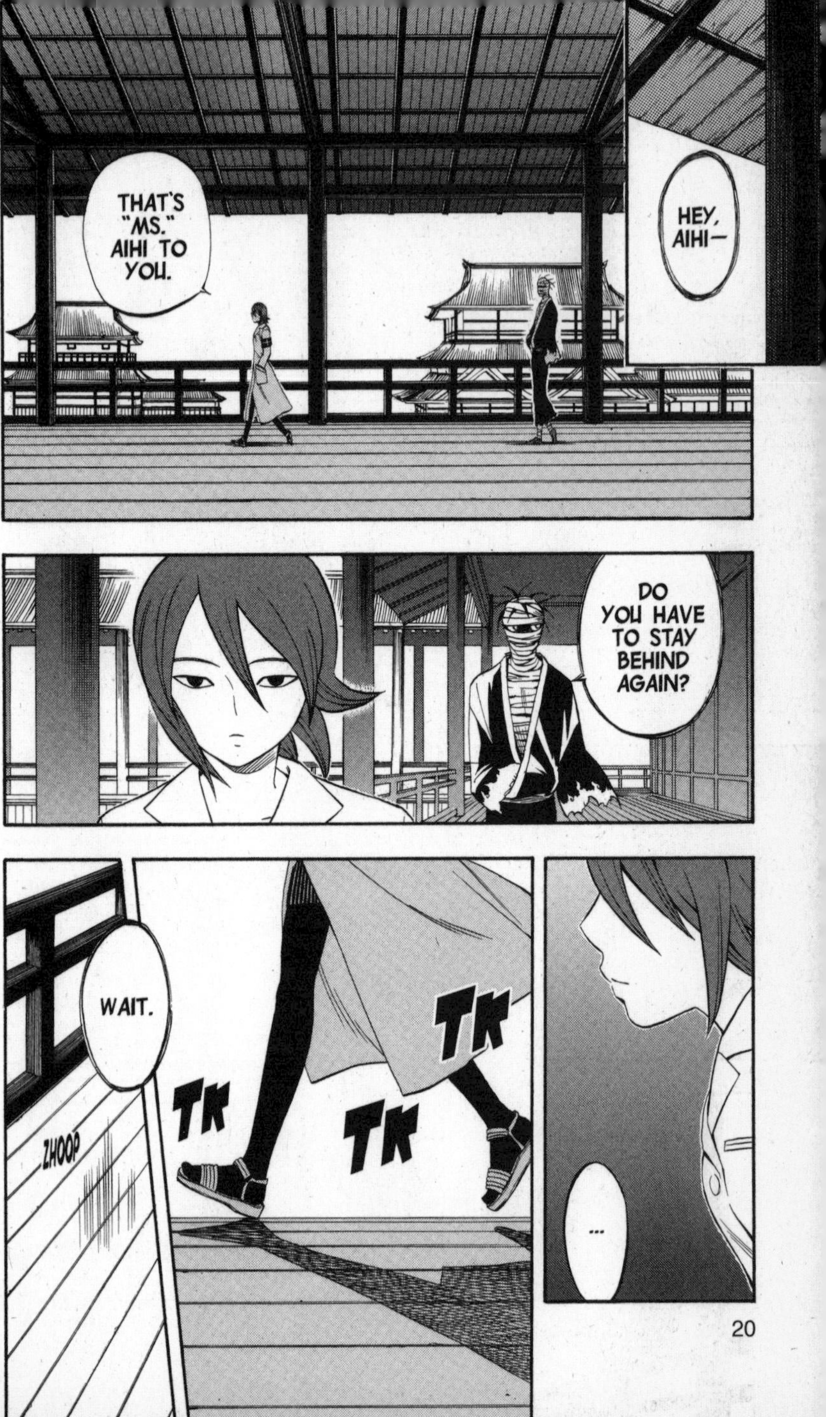
HEY, AIHI—
THAT'S "MS." AIHI TO YOU.
DO YOU HAVE TO STAY BEHIND AGAIN?
...
TK
WAIT.
TK
TK
ZHOOP

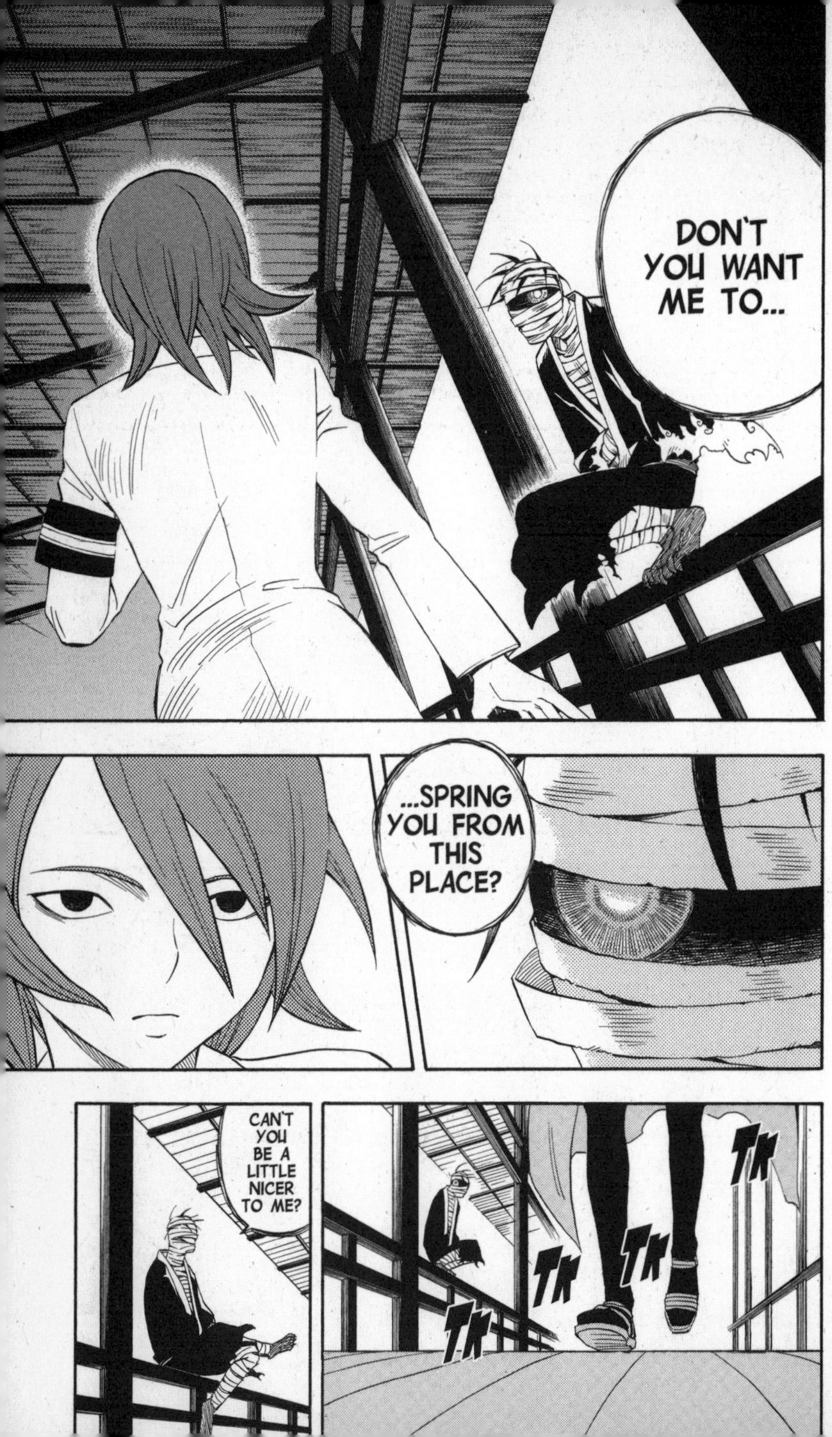
DON'T YOU WANT ME TO...
...SPRING YOU FROM THIS PLACE?
TK TK TK TK
CAN'T YOU BE A LITTLE NICER TO ME?

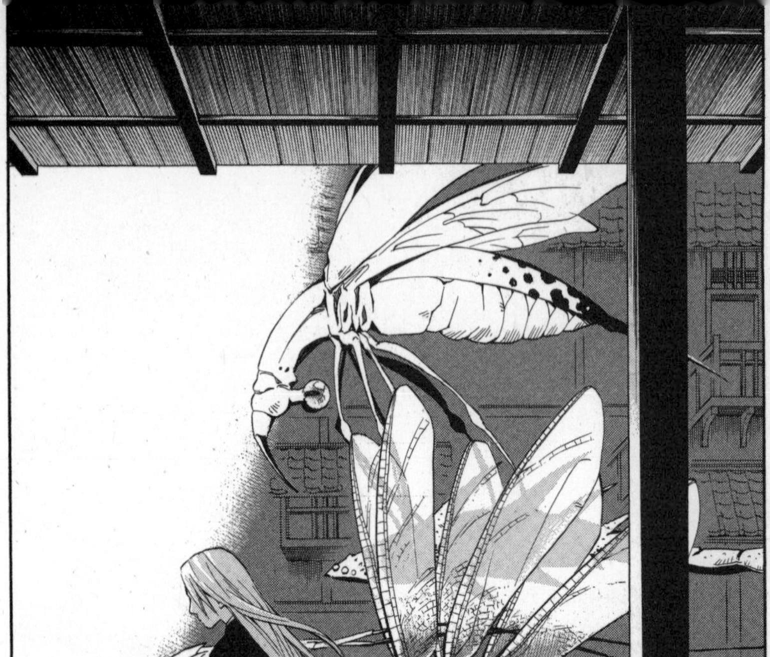

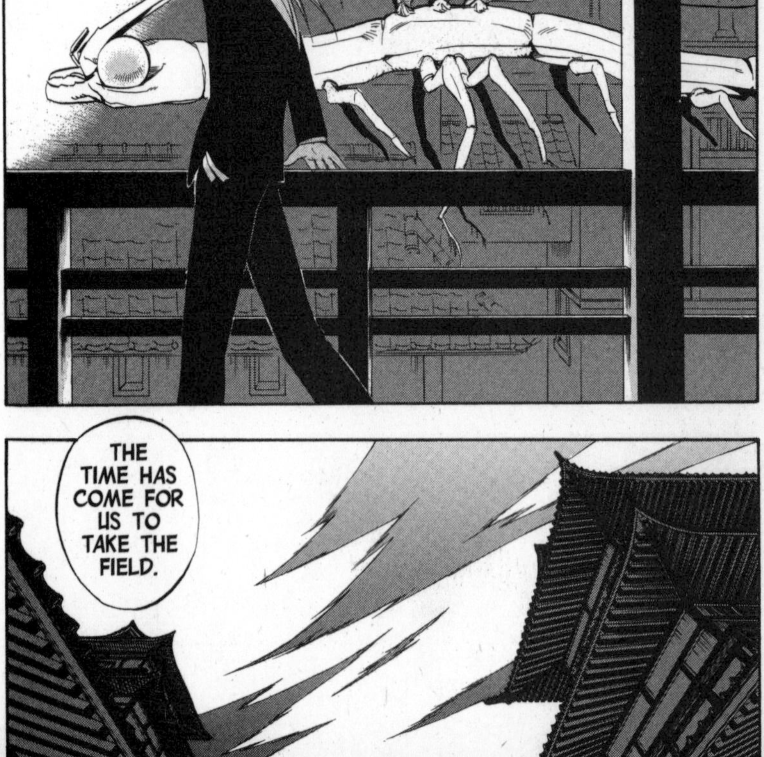
THE TIME HAS COME FOR US TO TAKE THE FIELD.

Chapter 87: Portable Throne

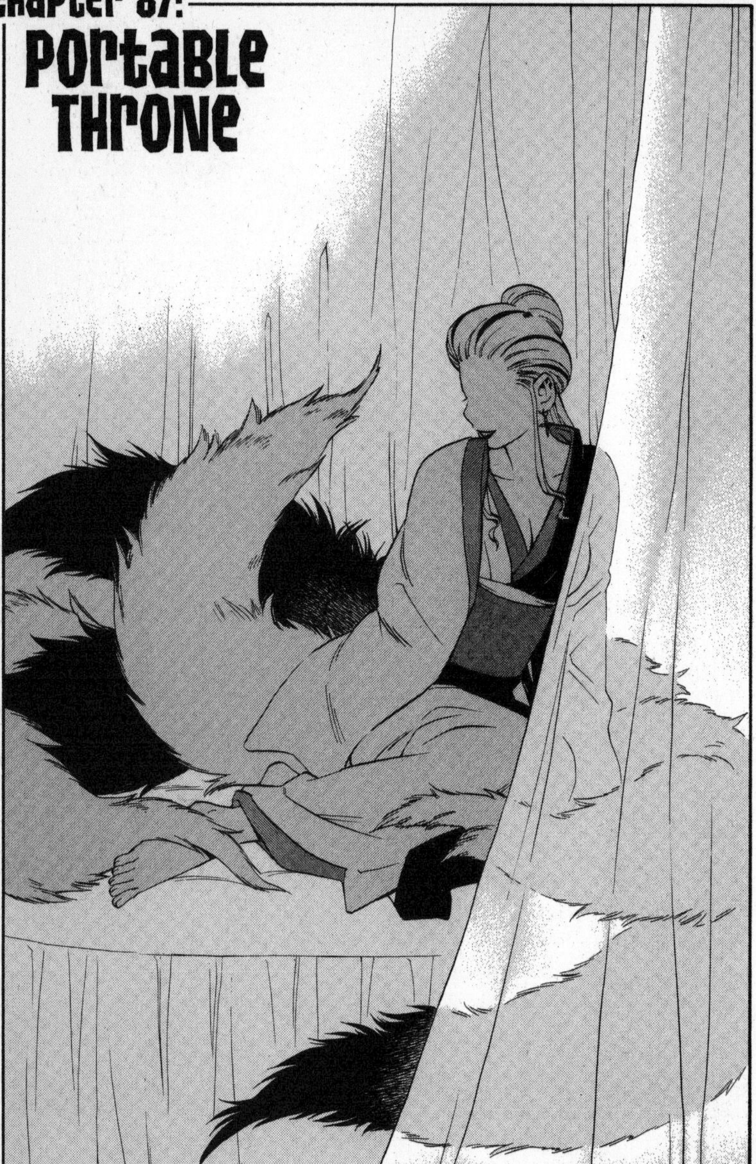

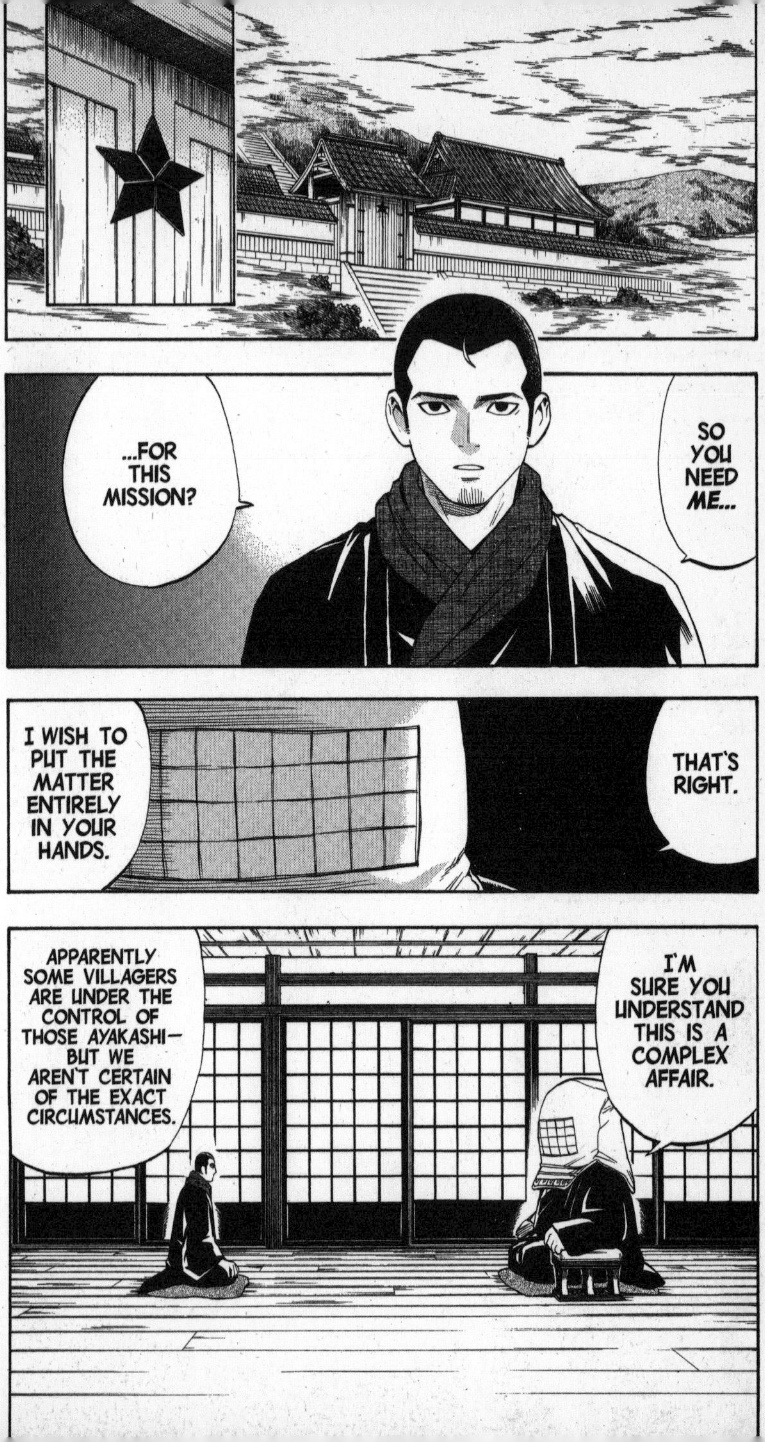
SO YOU NEED ME...
...FOR THIS MISSION?
THAT'S RIGHT.
I WISH TO PUT THE MATTER ENTIRELY IN YOUR HANDS.
I'M SURE YOU UNDERSTAND THIS IS A COMPLEX AFFAIR.
APPARENTLY SOME VILLAGERS ARE UNDER THE CONTROL OF THOSE AYAKASHI—BUT WE AREN'T CERTAIN OF THE EXACT CIRCUMSTANCES.

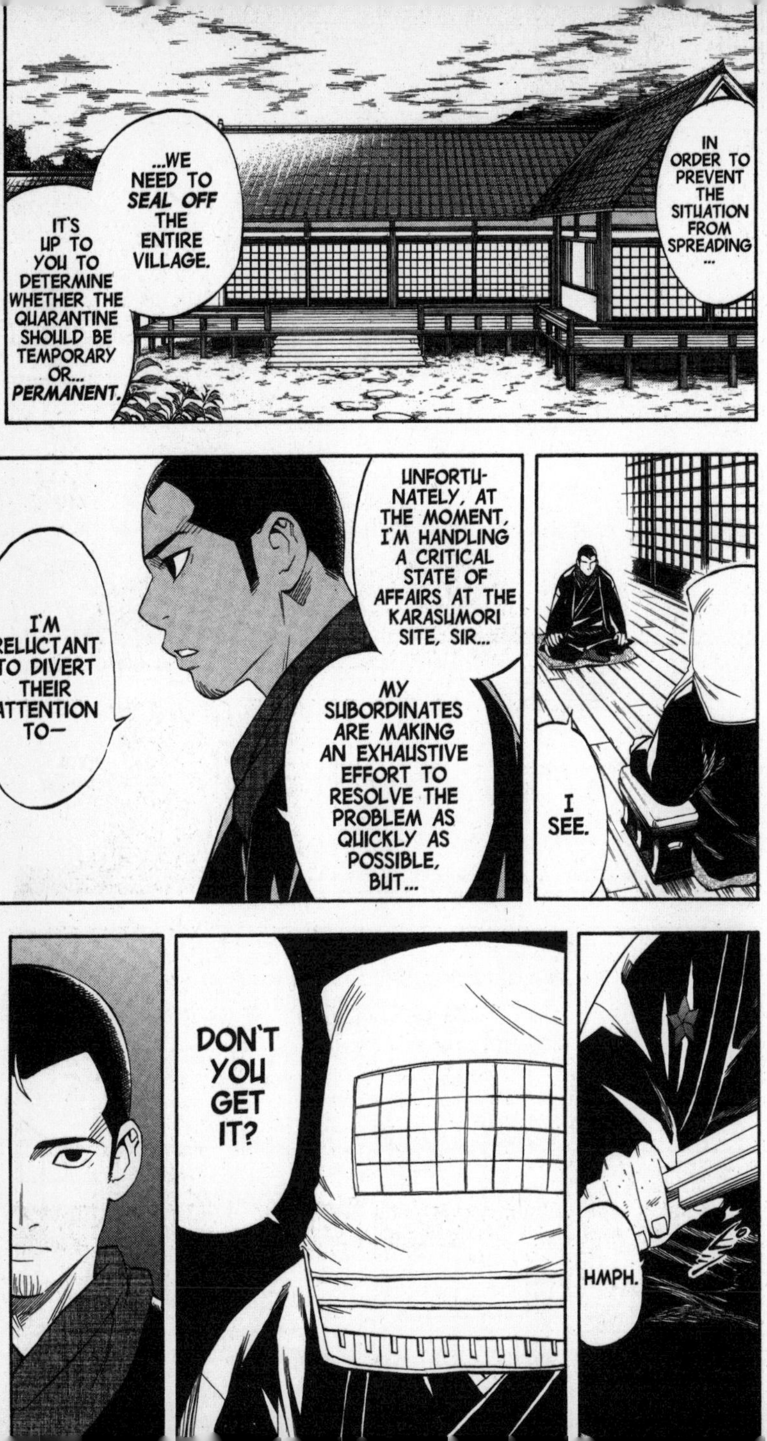
IN ORDER TO PREVENT THE SITUATION FROM SPREADING...
...WE NEED TO SEAL OFF THE ENTIRE VILLAGE.
IT'S UP TO YOU TO DETERMINE WHETHER THE QUARANTINE SHOULD BE TEMPORARY OR... PERMANENT.
I SEE.
UNFORTUNATELY, AT THE MOMENT, I'M HANDLING A CRITICAL STATE OF AFFAIRS AT THE KARASUMORI SITE, SIR...
MY SUBORDINATES ARE MAKING AN EXHAUSTIVE EFFORT TO RESOLVE THE PROBLEM AS QUICKLY AS POSSIBLE, BUT...
I'M RELUCTANT TO DIVERT THEIR ATTENTION TO—
HMPH.
DON'T YOU GET IT?

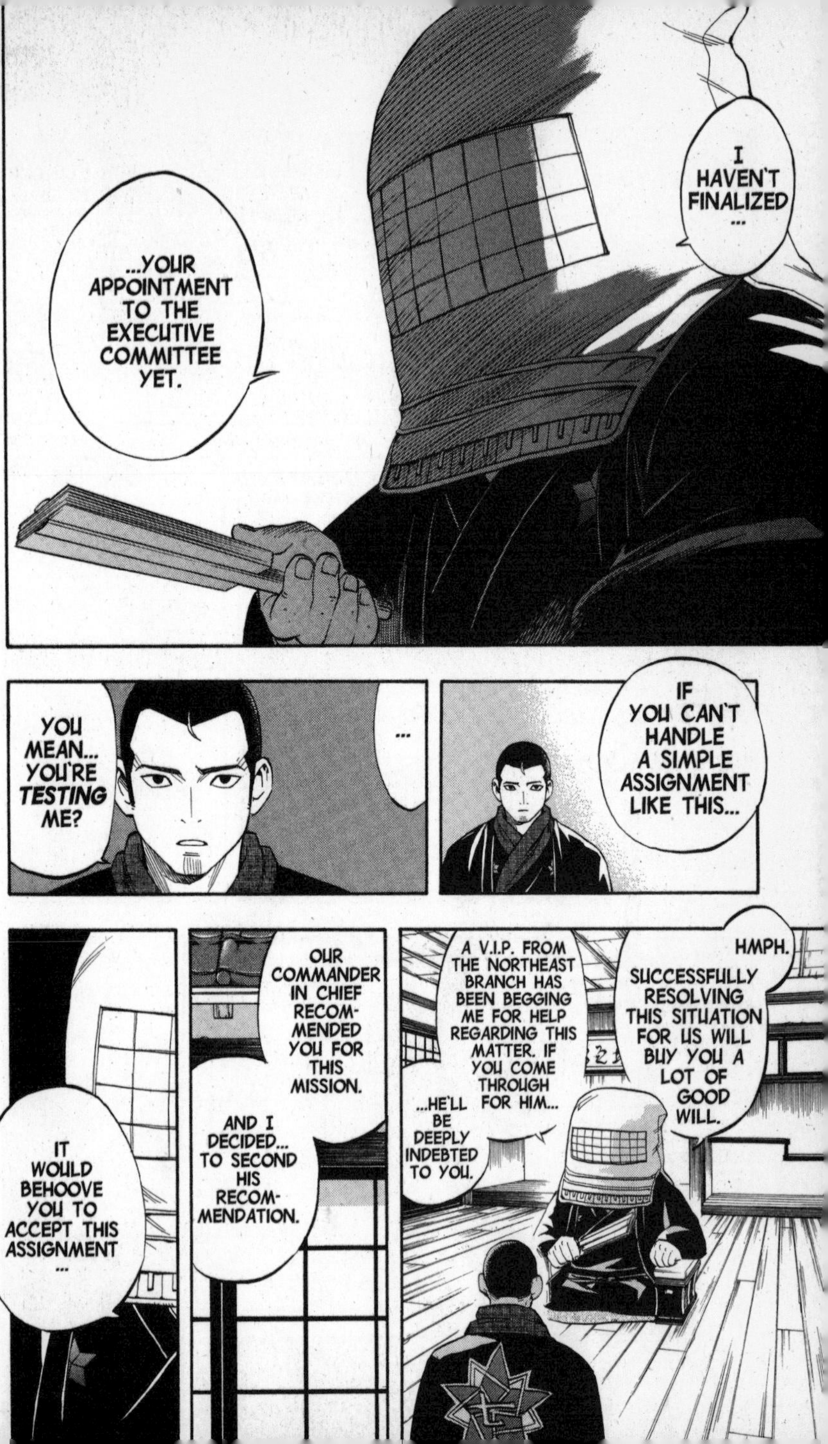
I HAVEN'T FINALIZED ...
...YOUR APPOINTMENT TO THE EXECUTIVE COMMITTEE YET.
IF YOU CAN'T HANDLE A SIMPLE ASSIGNMENT LIKE THIS...
...
YOU MEAN... YOU'RE *TESTING* ME?
HMPH.
SUCCESSFULLY RESOLVING THIS SITUATION FOR US WILL BUY YOU A LOT OF GOOD WILL.
A V.I.P. FROM THE NORTHEAST BRANCH HAS BEEN BEGGING ME FOR HELP REGARDING THIS MATTER. IF YOU COME THROUGH FOR HIM...
...HE'LL BE DEEPLY INDEBTED TO YOU.
OUR COMMANDER IN CHIEF RECOM-MENDED YOU FOR THIS MISSION.
AND I DECIDED... TO SECOND HIS RECOM-MENDATION.
IT WOULD BEHOOVE YOU TO ACCEPT THIS ASSIGNMENT ...

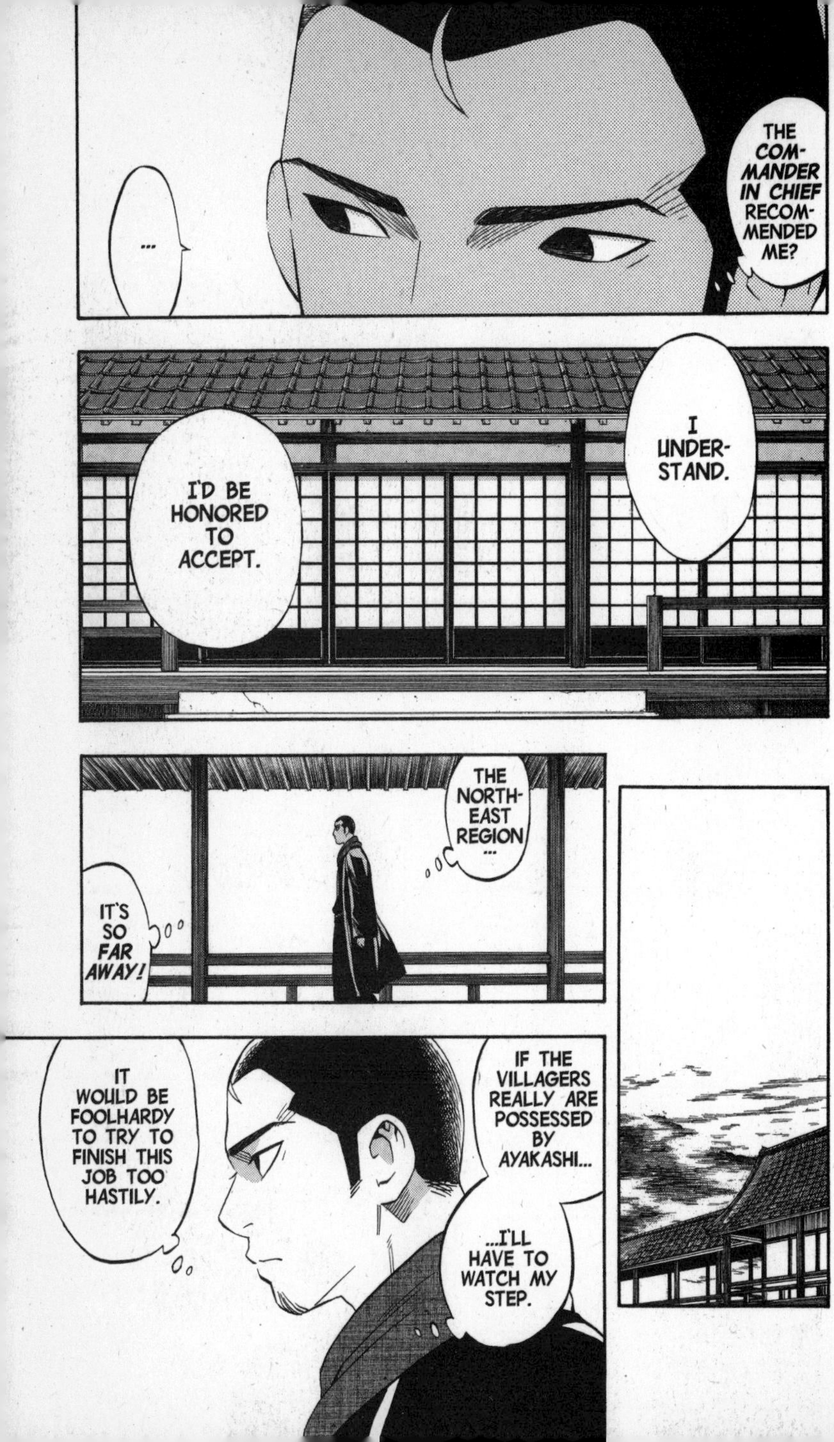
THE COMMANDER IN CHIEF RECOMMENDED ME?
...
I UNDERSTAND.
I'D BE HONORED TO ACCEPT.
THE NORTHEAST REGION...
IT'S SO FAR AWAY!
IF THE VILLAGERS REALLY ARE POSSESSED BY AYAKASHI...
...I'LL HAVE TO WATCH MY STEP.
IT WOULD BE FOOLHARDY TO TRY TO FINISH THIS JOB TOO HASTILY.

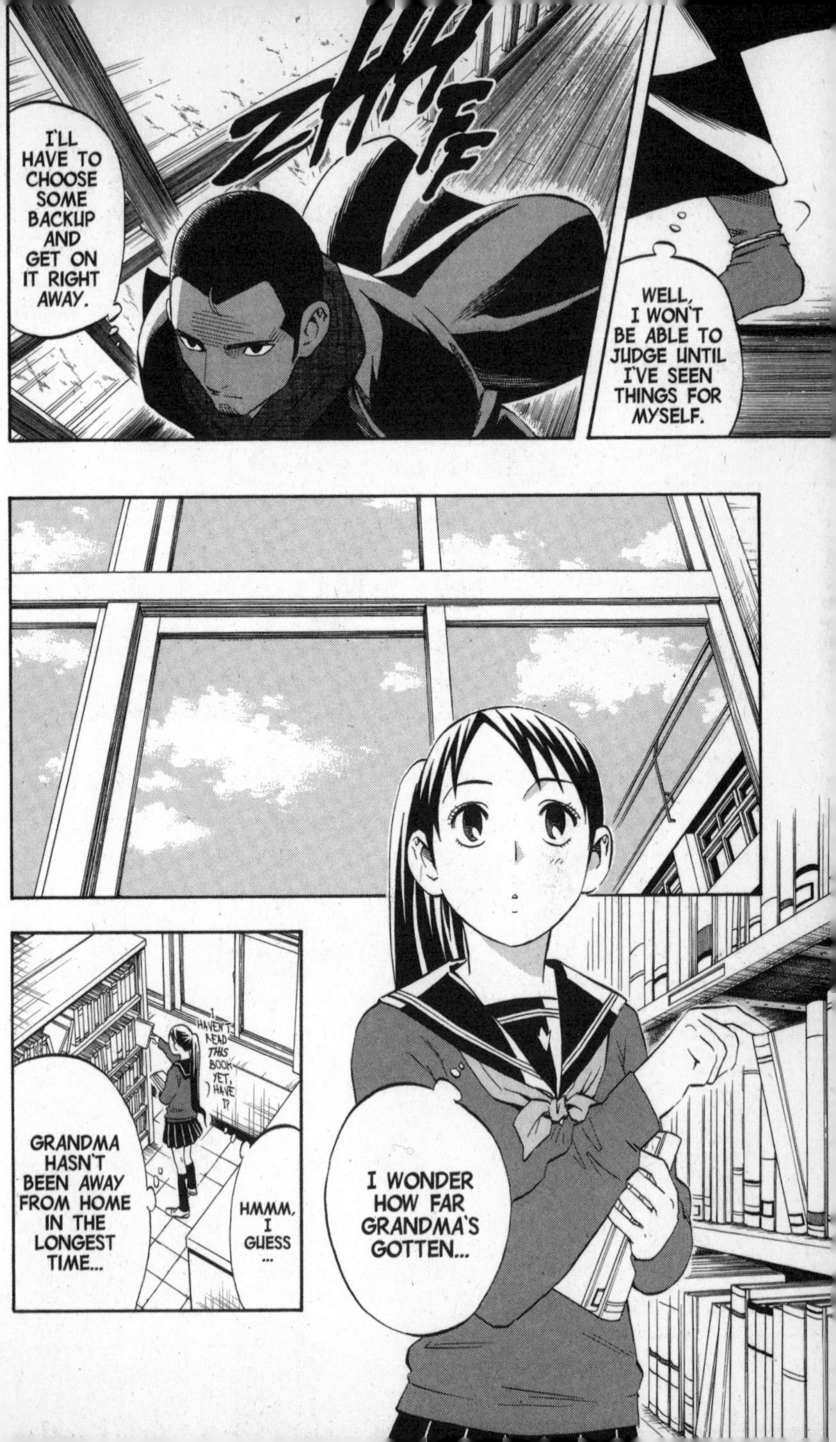
HUFF
ZHIFF
WELL, I WON'T BE ABLE TO JUDGE UNTIL I'VE SEEN THINGS FOR MYSELF.
I'LL HAVE TO CHOOSE SOME BACKUP AND GET ON IT RIGHT AWAY.
I WONDER HOW FAR GRANDMA'S GOTTEN...
I HAVEN'T READ THIS BOOK YET, HAVE I?
HMMM, I GUESS ...
GRANDMA HASN'T BEEN AWAY FROM HOME IN THE LONGEST TIME...

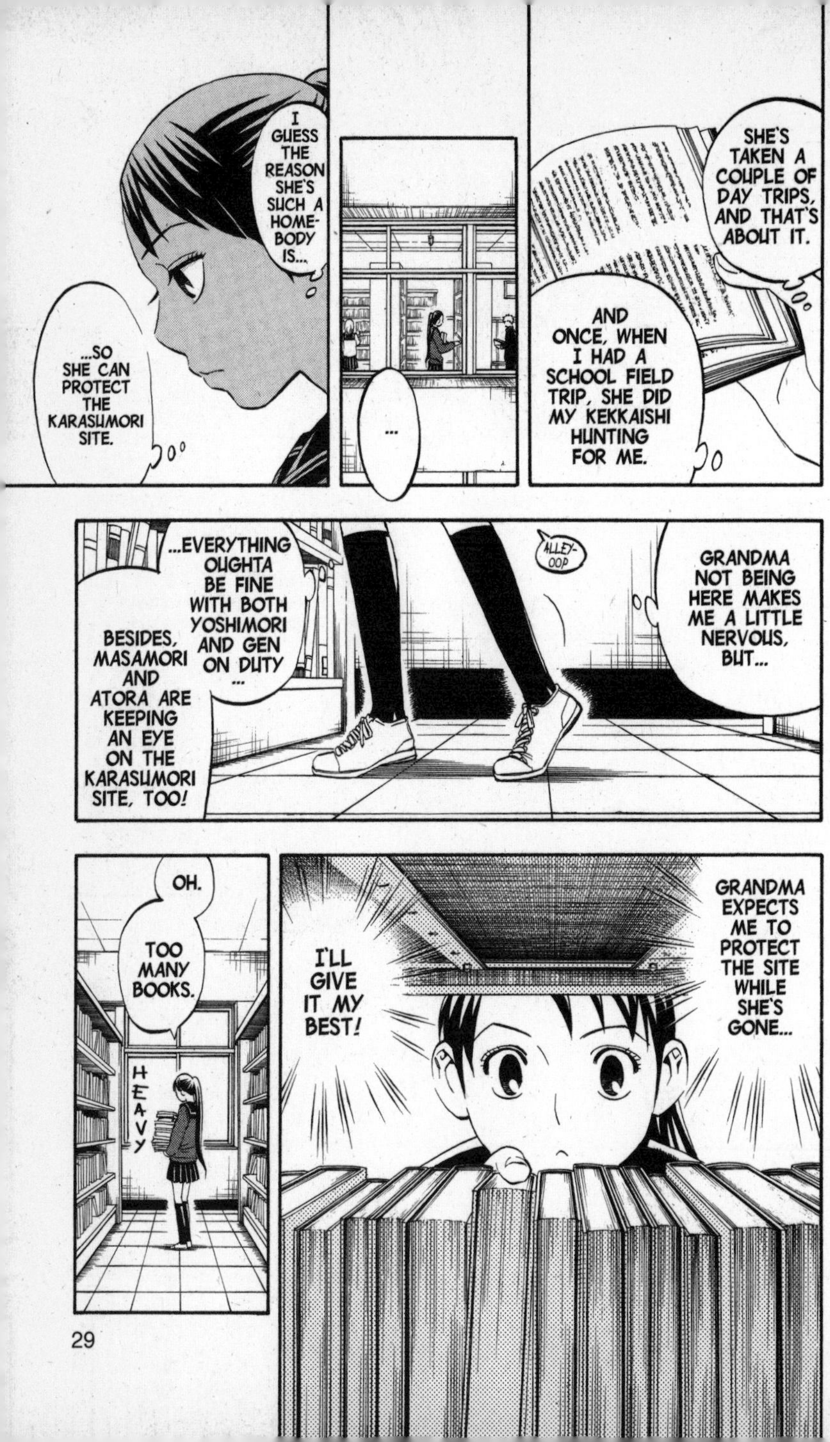
SHE'S TAKEN A COUPLE OF DAY TRIPS, AND THAT'S ABOUT IT.
AND ONCE, WHEN I HAD A SCHOOL FIELD TRIP, SHE DID MY KEKKAISHI HUNTING FOR ME.
...
I GUESS THE REASON SHE'S SUCH A HOME-BODY IS...
...SO SHE CAN PROTECT THE KARASUMORI SITE.
GRANDMA NOT BEING HERE MAKES ME A LITTLE NERVOUS, BUT...
ALLEY-OOP
...EVERYTHING OUGHTA BE FINE WITH BOTH YOSHIMORI AND GEN ON DUTY...
BESIDES, MASAMORI AND ATORA ARE KEEPING AN EYE ON THE KARASUMORI SITE, TOO!
GRANDMA EXPECTS ME TO PROTECT THE SITE WHILE SHE'S GONE...
I'LL GIVE IT MY BEST!
OH.
TOO MANY BOOKS.
HEAVY

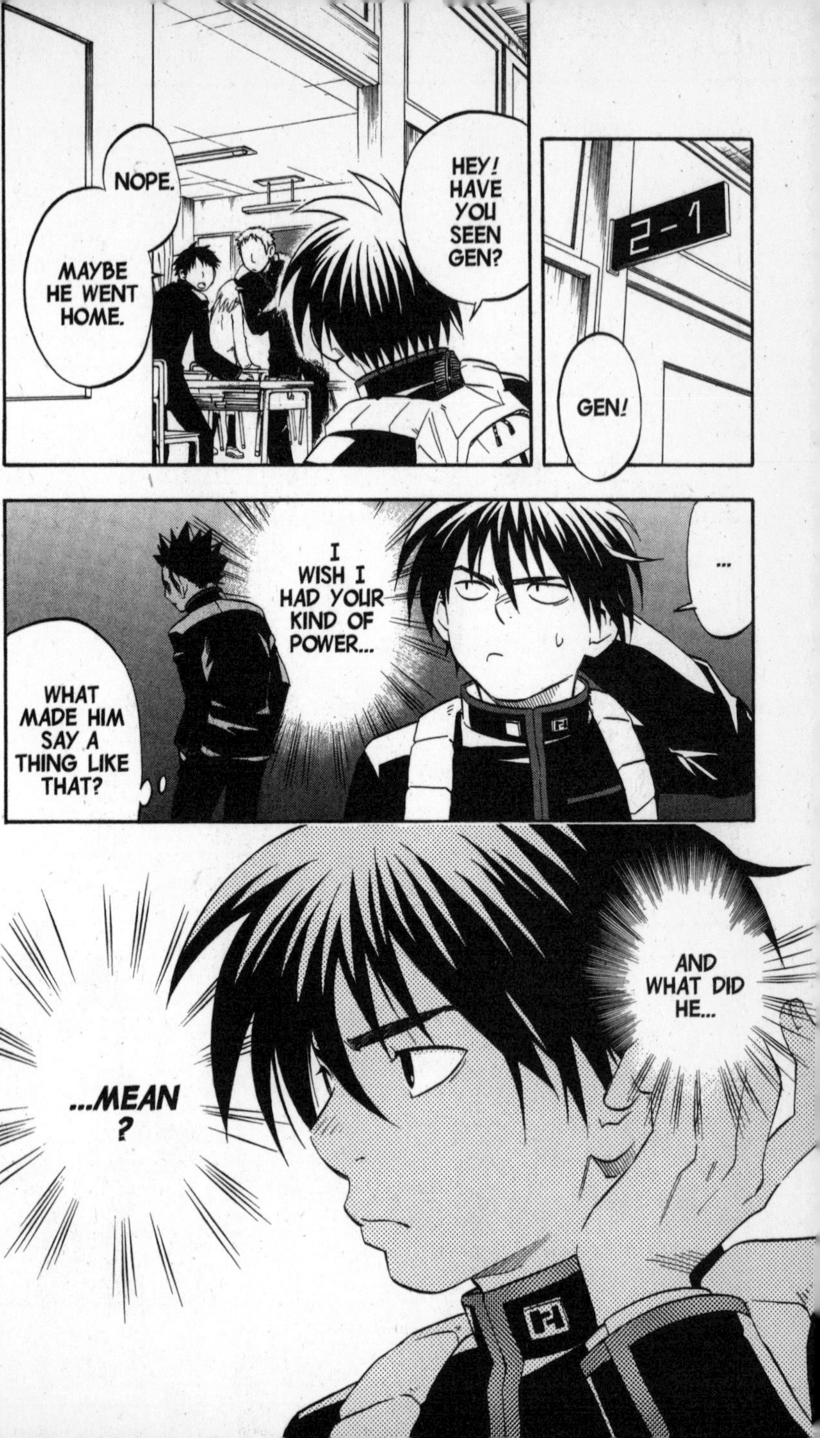
2-1
GEN!
HEY! HAVE YOU SEEN GEN?
NOPE.
MAYBE HE WENT HOME.
...
I WISH I HAD YOUR KIND OF POWER...
WHAT MADE HIM SAY A THING LIKE THAT?
AND WHAT DID HE...
...MEAN?

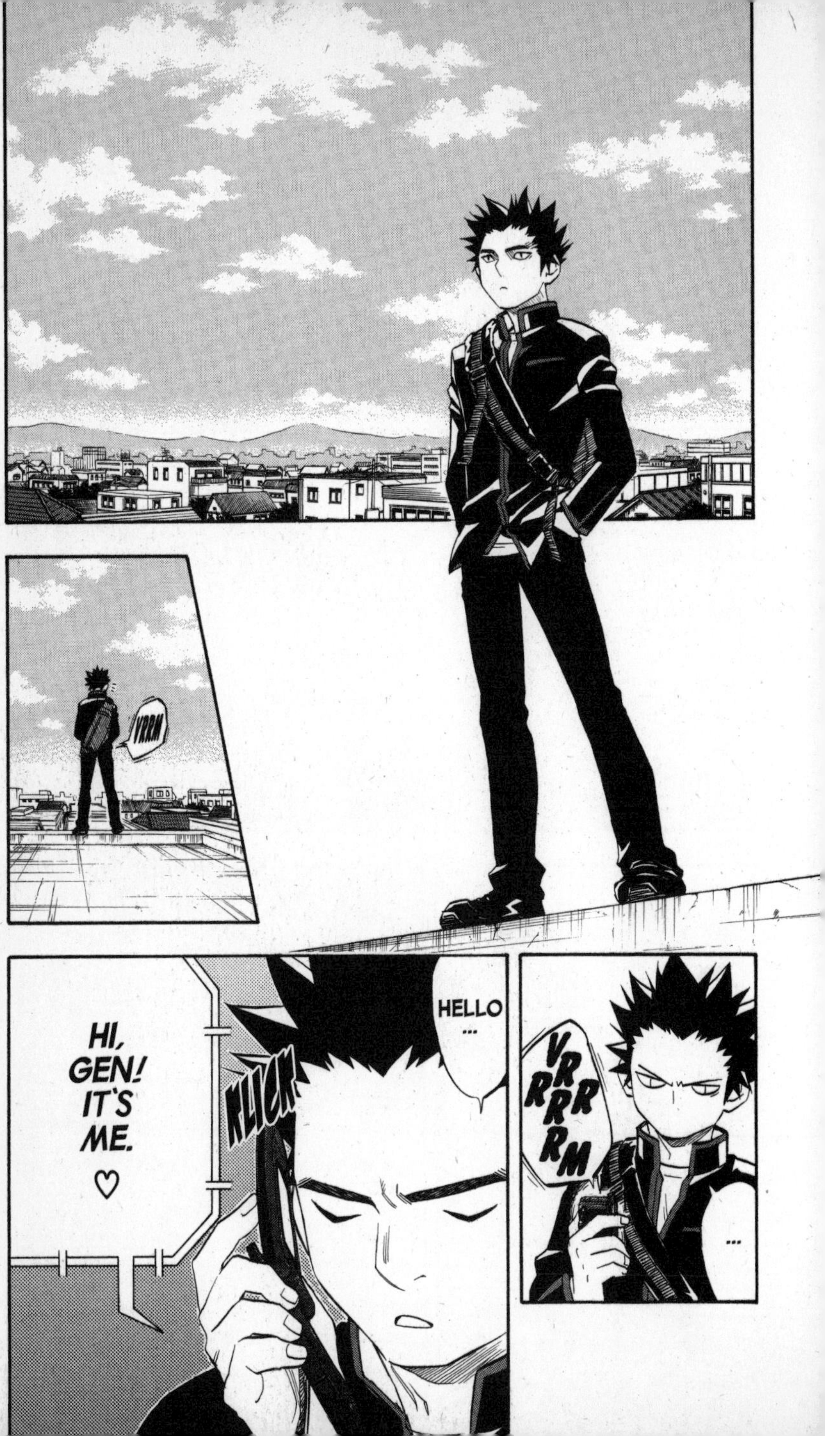
VRRM
VRRRRRM
...
HELLO...
KLICK
HI, GEN! IT'S ME. ♥

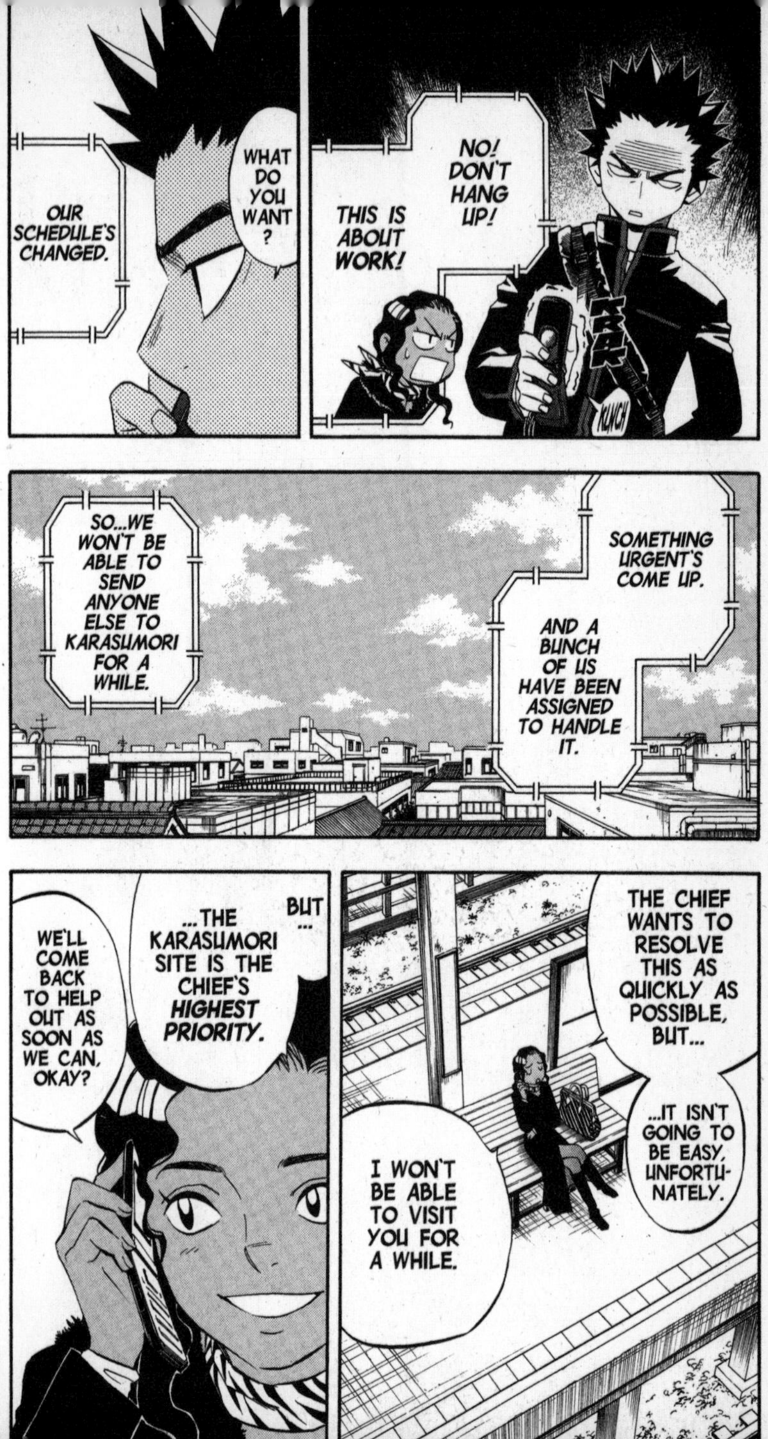
NO! DON'T HANG UP!
THIS IS ABOUT WORK!
KRAK
WHAT DO YOU WANT?
OUR SCHEDULE'S CHANGED.
SOMETHING URGENT'S COME UP.
AND A BUNCH OF US HAVE BEEN ASSIGNED TO HANDLE IT.
SO...WE WON'T BE ABLE TO SEND ANYONE ELSE TO KARASUMORI FOR A WHILE.
THE CHIEF WANTS TO RESOLVE THIS AS QUICKLY AS POSSIBLE, BUT...
...IT ISN'T GOING TO BE EASY, UNFORTUNATELY.
I WON'T BE ABLE TO VISIT YOU FOR A WHILE.
BUT...
...THE KARASUMORI SITE IS THE CHIEF'S *HIGHEST PRIORITY*.
WE'LL COME BACK TO HELP OUT AS SOON AS WE CAN, OKAY?

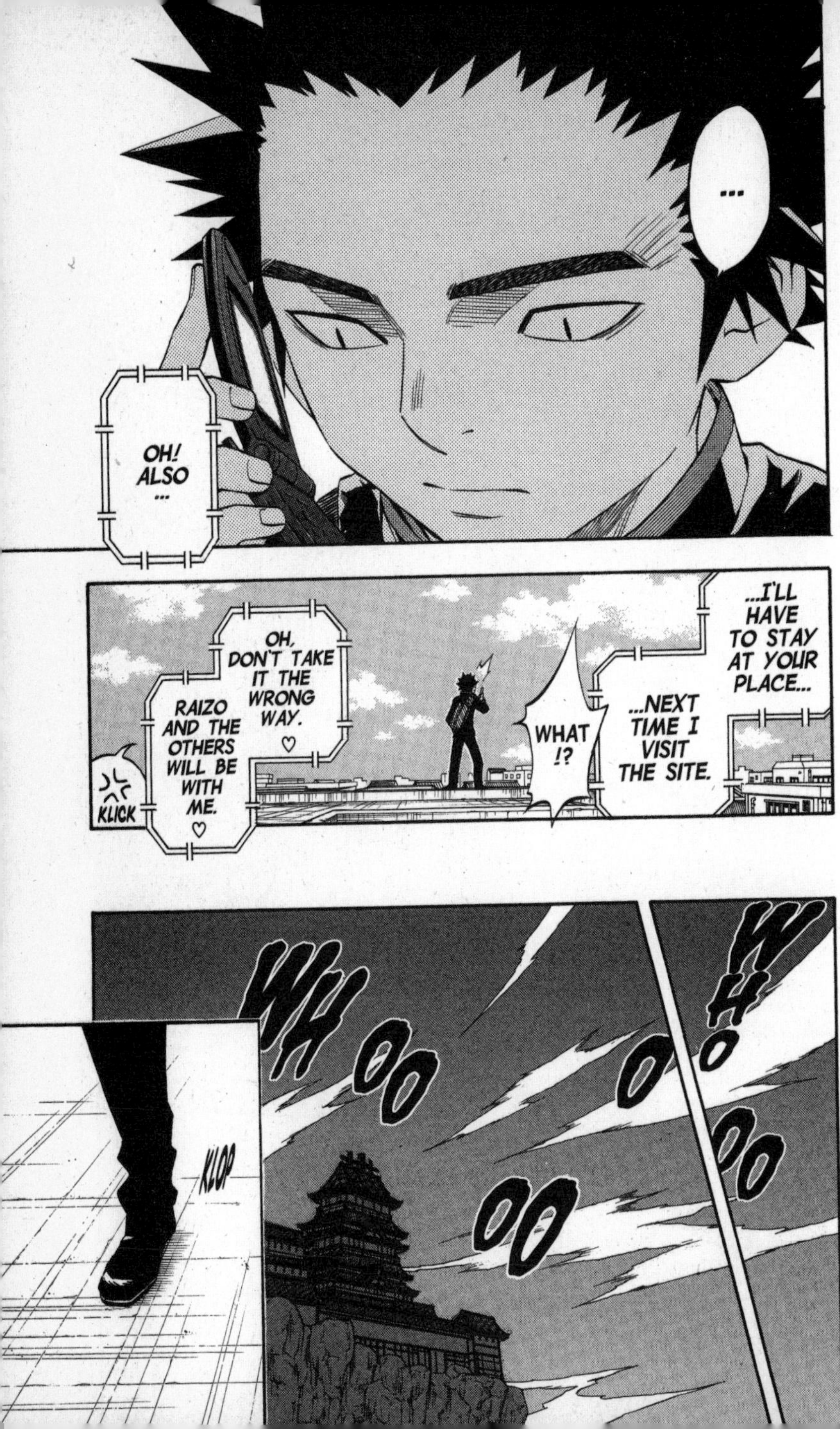
...
OH! ALSO ...
...I'LL HAVE TO STAY AT YOUR PLACE...
...NEXT TIME I VISIT THE SITE.
WHAT !?
OH, DON'T TAKE IT THE WRONG WAY. ♡
RAIZO AND THE OTHERS WILL BE WITH ME. ♡
KLICK
WHOOOO
WHOOOO
KLOP

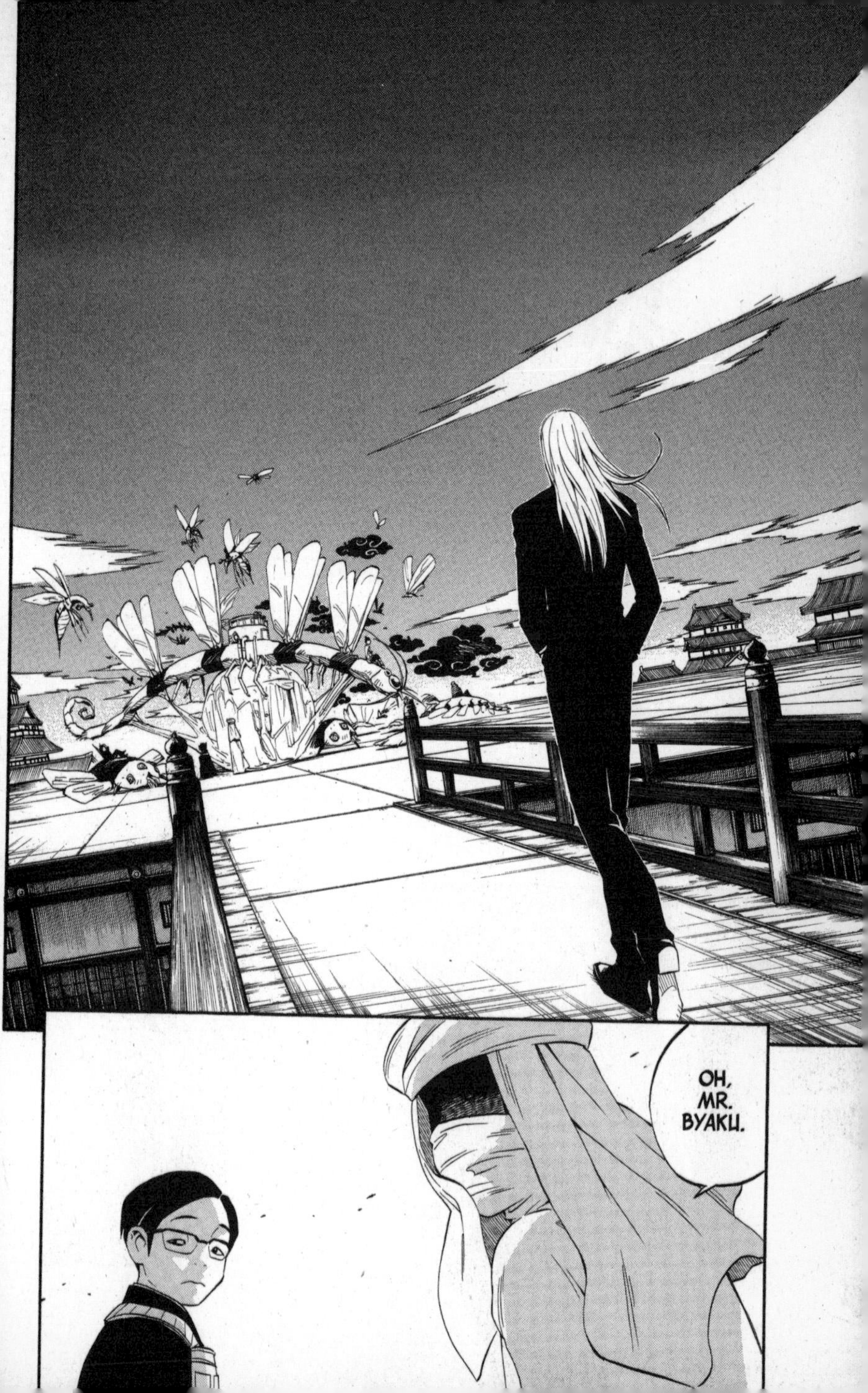
OH, MR. BYAKU.

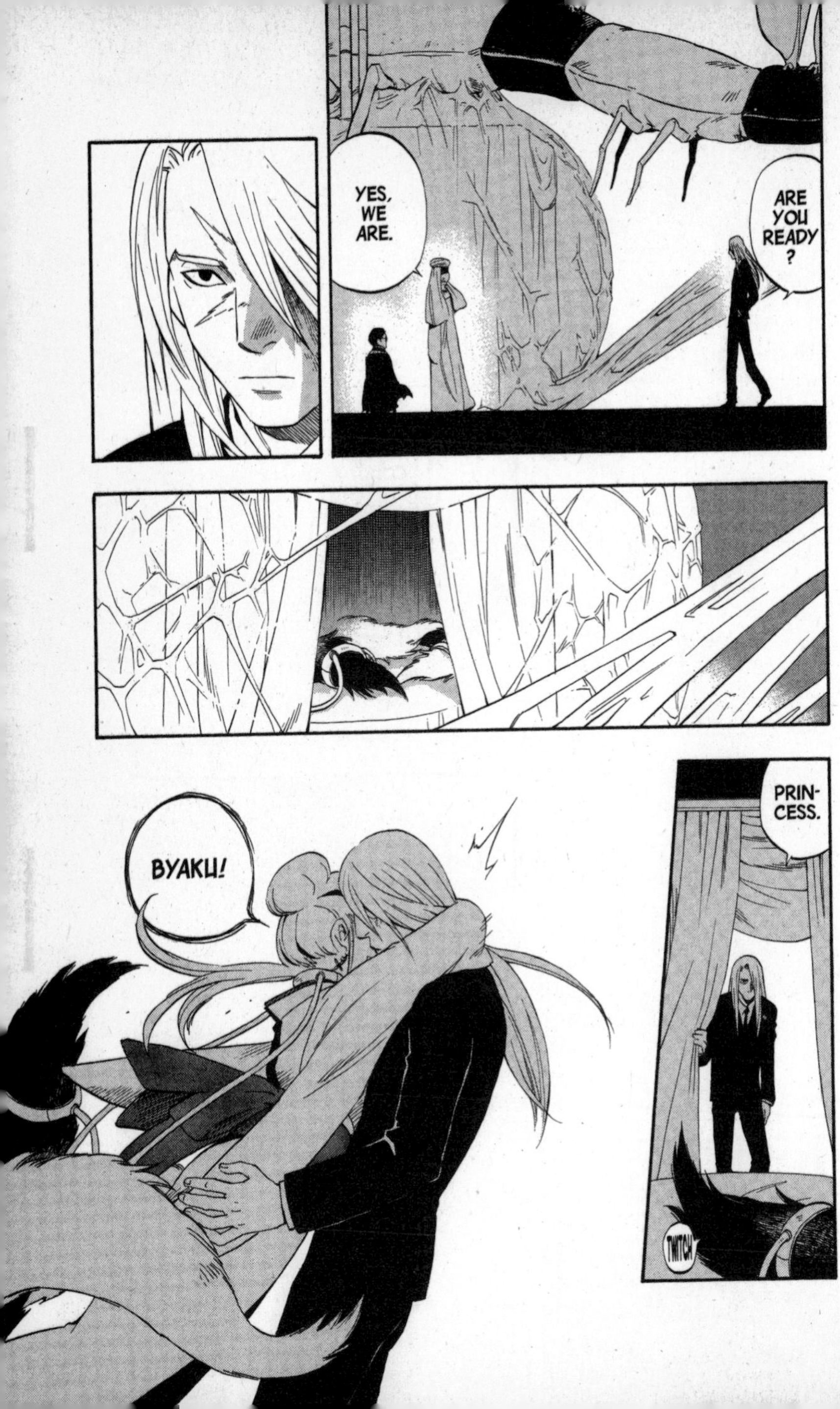
ARE YOU READY?
YES, WE ARE.
PRIN-CESS.
TWITCH
BYAKU!

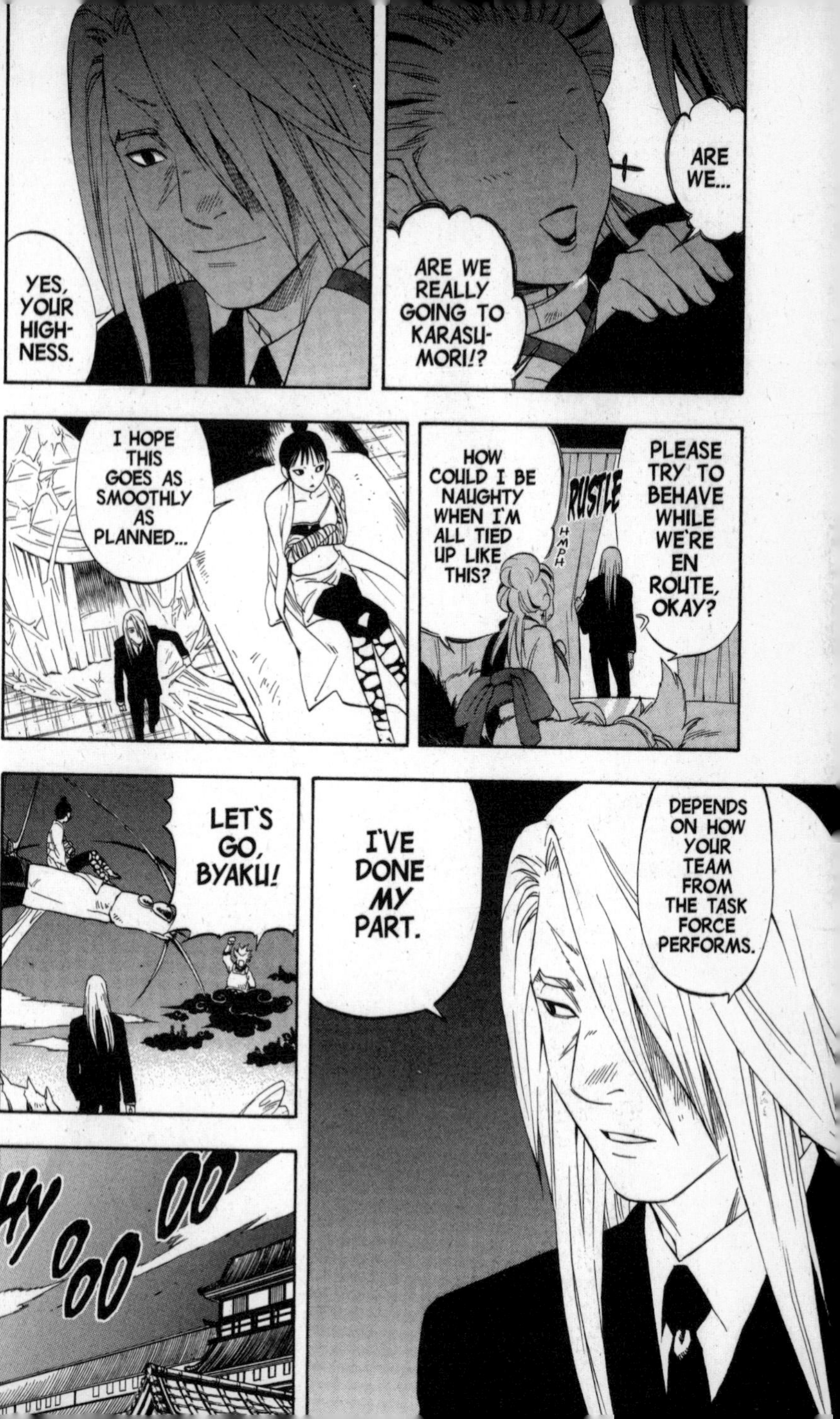
ARE WE...
ARE WE REALLY GOING TO KARASU-MORI!?
YES, YOUR HIGH-NESS.
PLEASE TRY TO BEHAVE WHILE WE'RE EN ROUTE, OKAY?
RUSTLE
HMPH
HOW COULD I BE NAUGHTY WHEN I'M ALL TIED UP LIKE THIS?
I HOPE THIS GOES AS SMOOTHLY AS PLANNED...
DEPENDS ON HOW YOUR TEAM FROM THE TASK FORCE PERFORMS.
I'VE DONE MY PART.
LET'S GO, BYAKU!
HYOOOOO

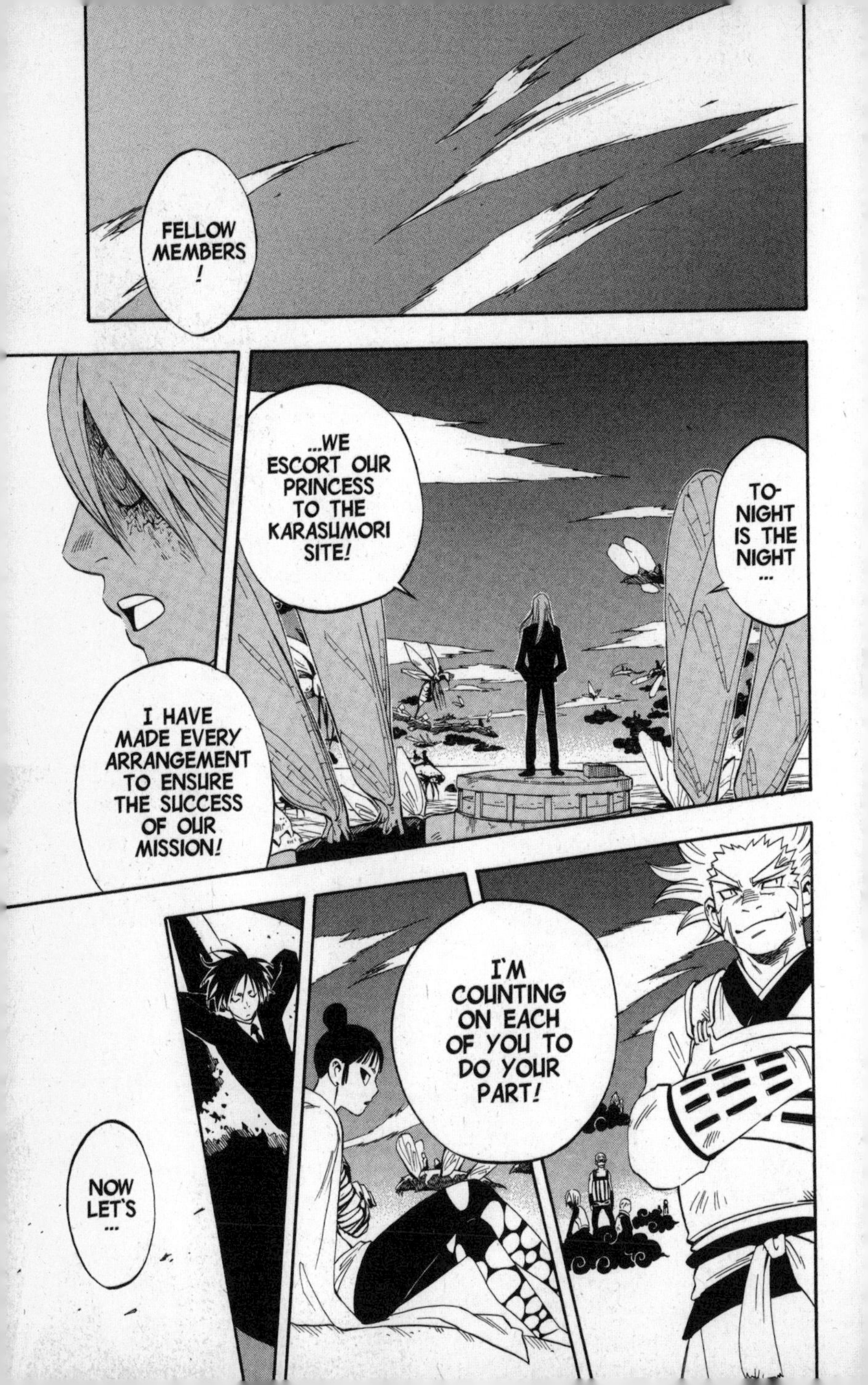
FELLOW MEMBERS!
TO-NIGHT IS THE NIGHT...
...WE ESCORT OUR PRINCESS TO THE KARASUMORI SITE!
I HAVE MADE EVERY ARRANGEMENT TO ENSURE THE SUCCESS OF OUR MISSION!
I'M COUNTING ON EACH OF YOU TO DO YOUR PART!
NOW LET'S...

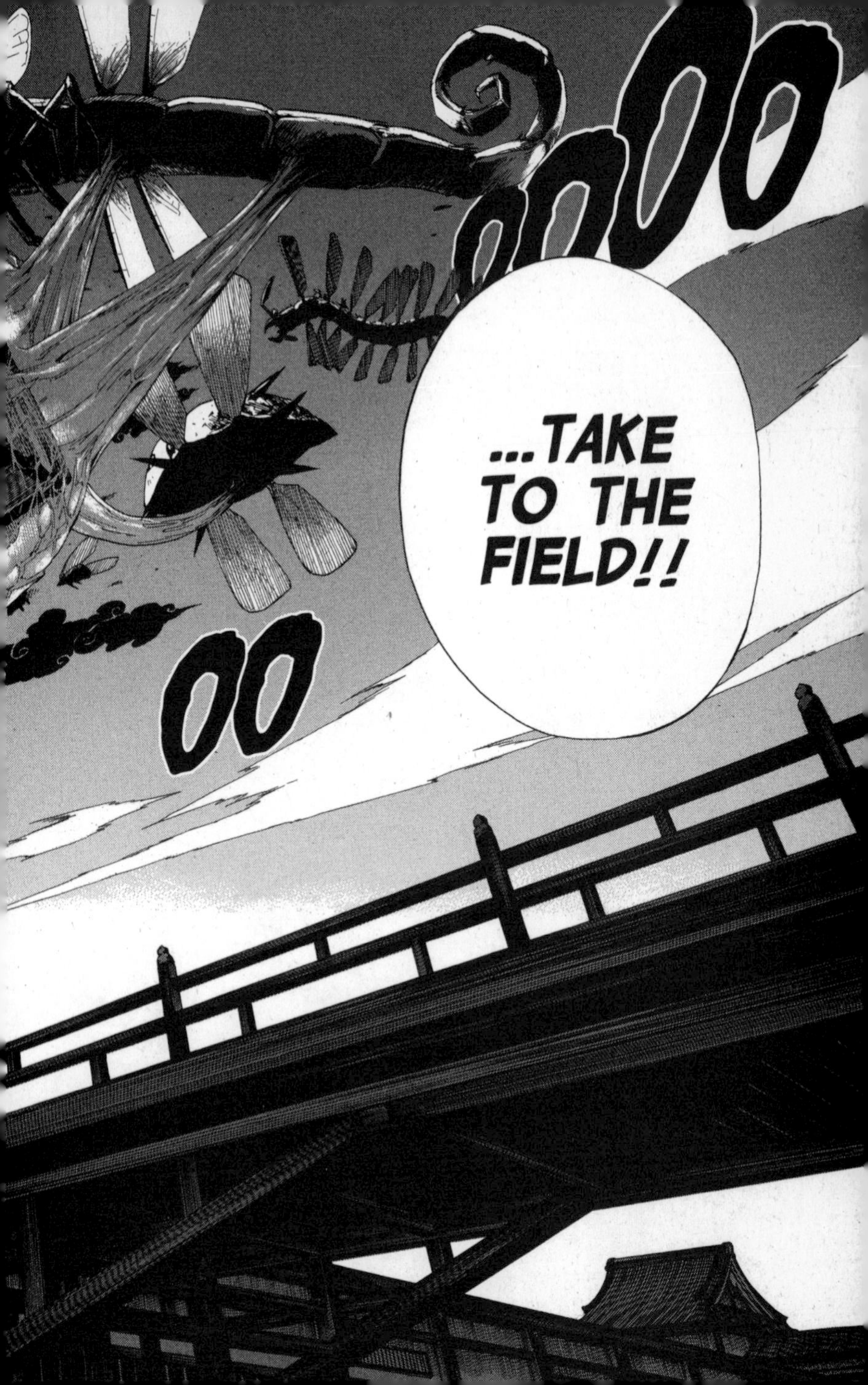
OOOOOO
...TAKE TO THE FIELD!!
OO

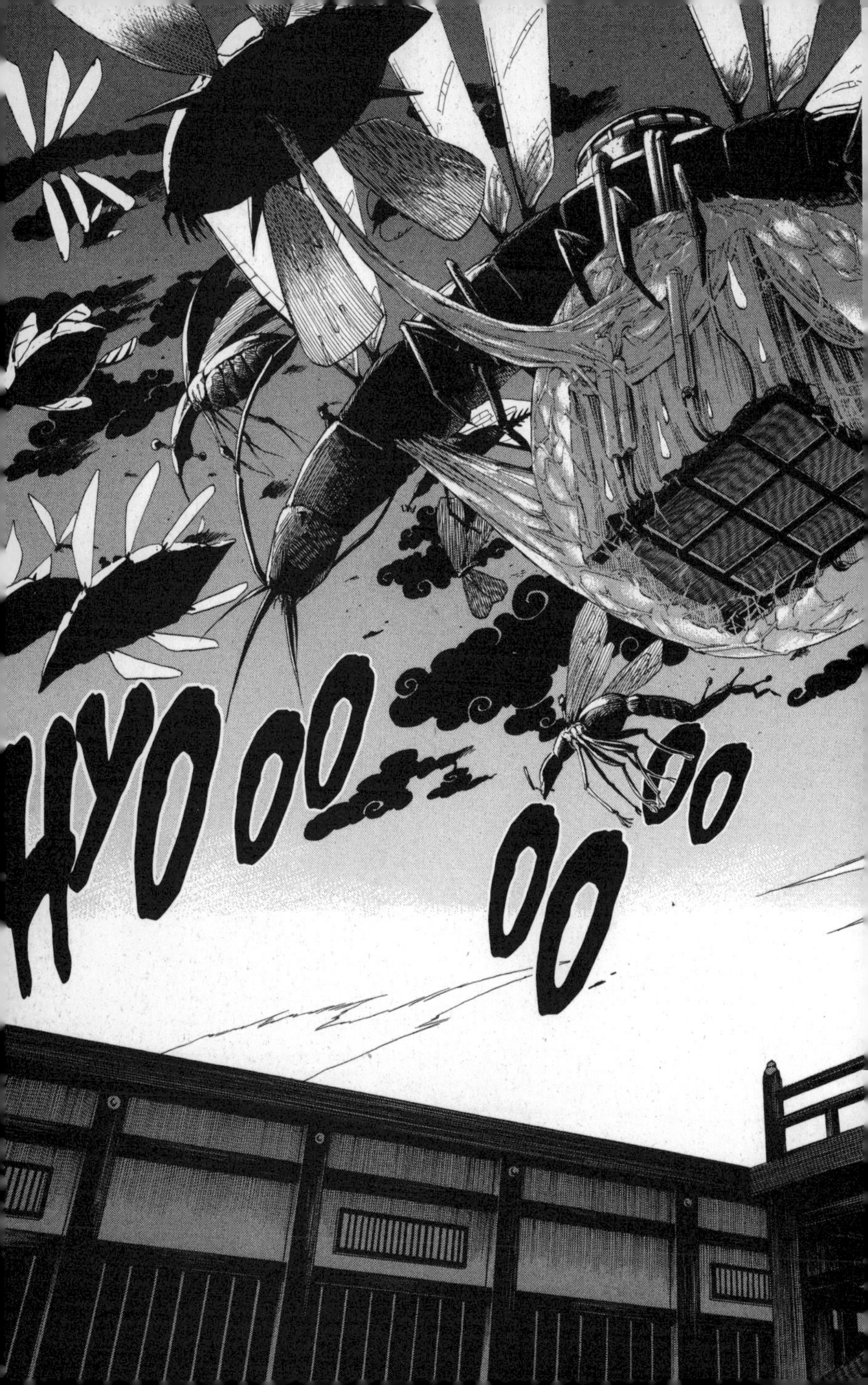
HYOOOOOOOO

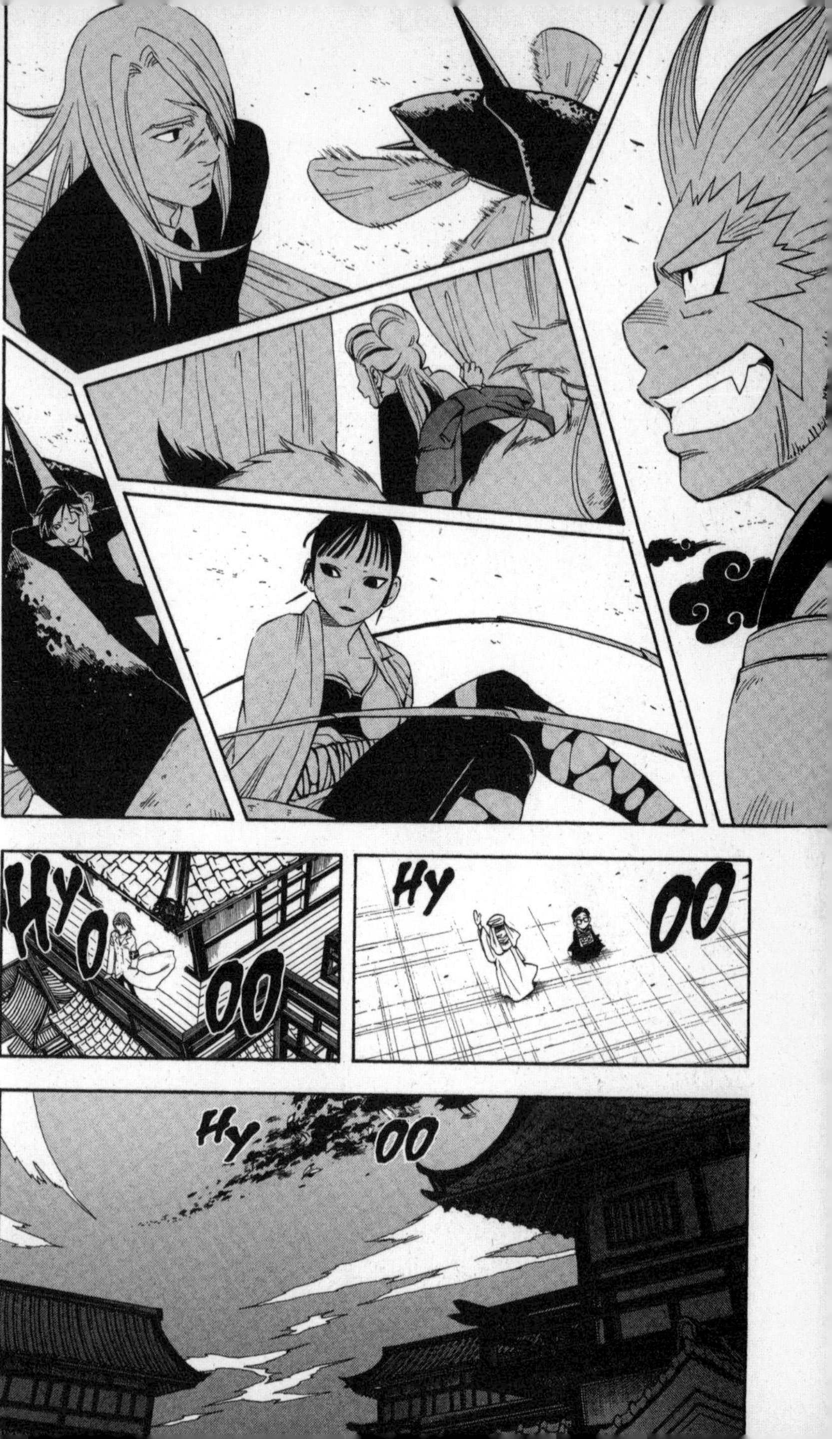
Hy
OO
HYO
OO
Hy
OO

Chapter 88: Attack of the Kokuboro

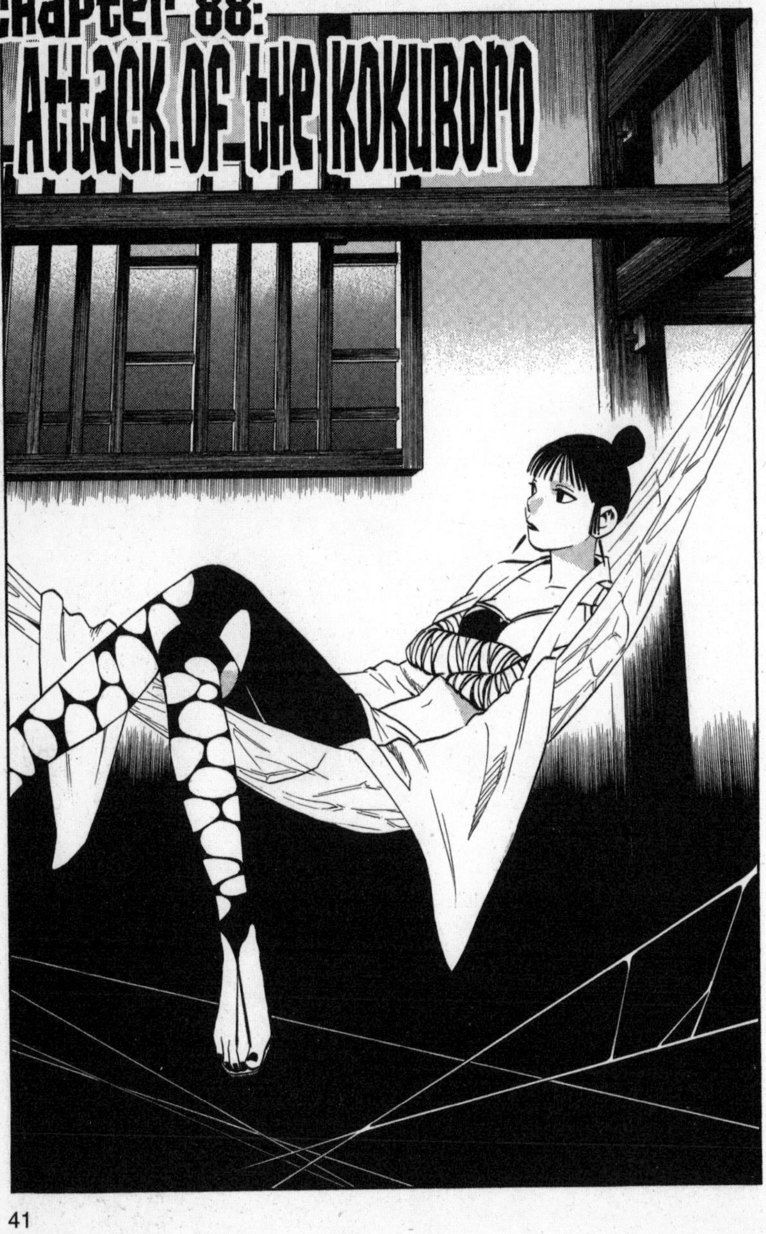

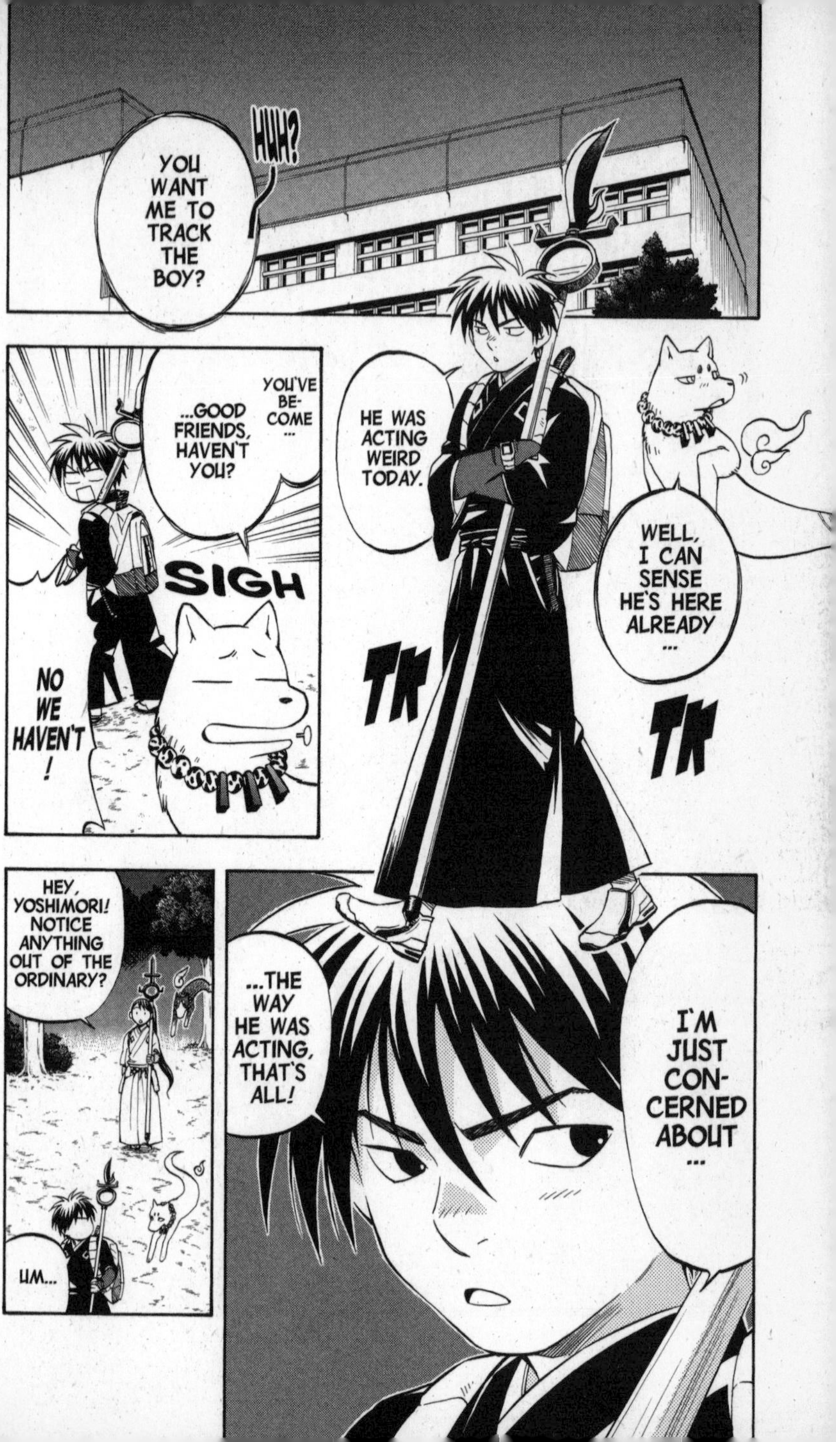
HUH?
YOU WANT ME TO TRACK THE BOY?
HE WAS ACTING WEIRD TODAY.
WELL, I CAN SENSE HE'S HERE ALREADY...
TK
TK
YOU'VE BE-COME...
...GOOD FRIENDS, HAVEN'T YOU?
SIGH
NO WE HAVEN'T!
I'M JUST CON-CERNED ABOUT...
...THE WAY HE WAS ACTING, THAT'S ALL!
HEY, YOSHIMORI! NOTICE ANYTHING OUT OF THE ORDINARY?
UM...

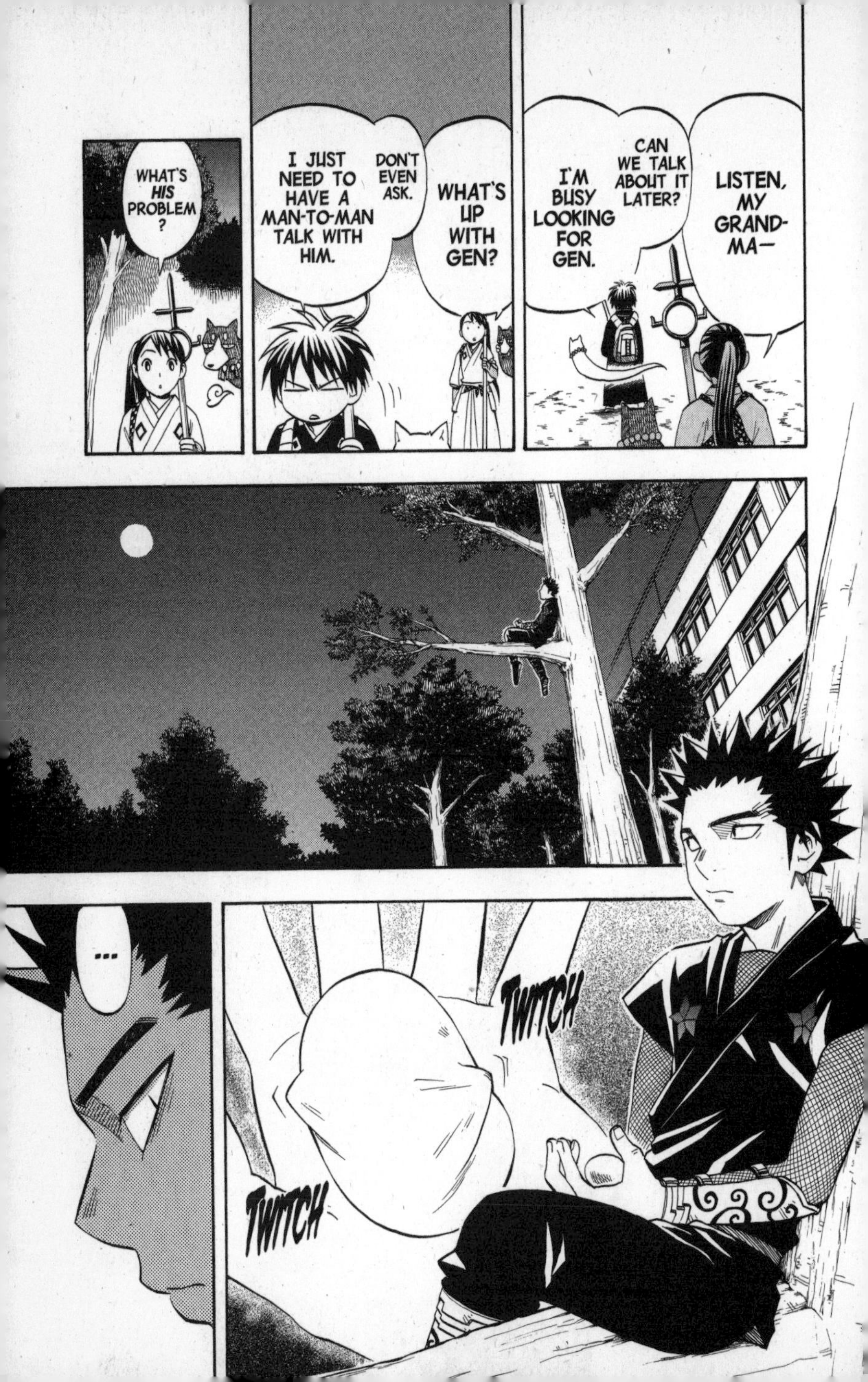
LISTEN, MY GRAND-MA—
CAN WE TALK ABOUT IT LATER?
I'M BUSY LOOKING FOR GEN.
WHAT'S UP WITH GEN?
DON'T EVEN ASK.
I JUST NEED TO HAVE A MAN-TO-MAN TALK WITH HIM.
WHAT'S HIS PROBLEM?
TWITCH
TWITCH
...

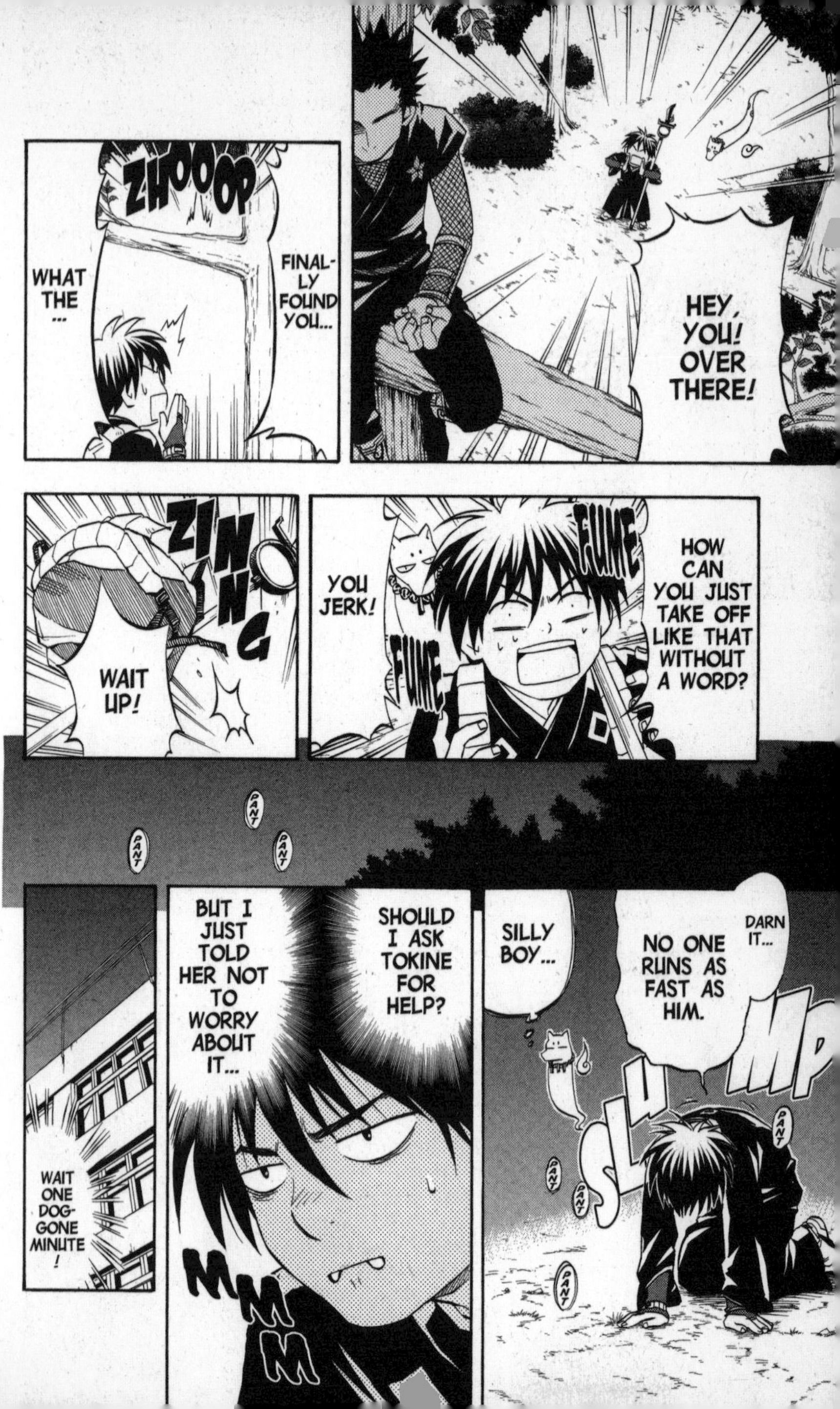
HEY, YOU! OVER THERE!
FINAL-LY FOUND YOU...
ZHOOOP
WHAT THE ...
HOW CAN YOU JUST TAKE OFF LIKE THAT WITHOUT A WORD?
FUME
YOU JERK!
FUME
ZING
WAIT UP!
PANT
PANT
PANT
DARN IT...
NO ONE RUNS AS FAST AS HIM.
SILLY BOY...
SLUMP
PANT
PANT
PANT
PANT
SHOULD I ASK TOKINE FOR HELP?
BUT I JUST TOLD HER NOT TO WORRY ABOUT IT...
MMM
WAIT ONE DOG-GONE MINUTE!

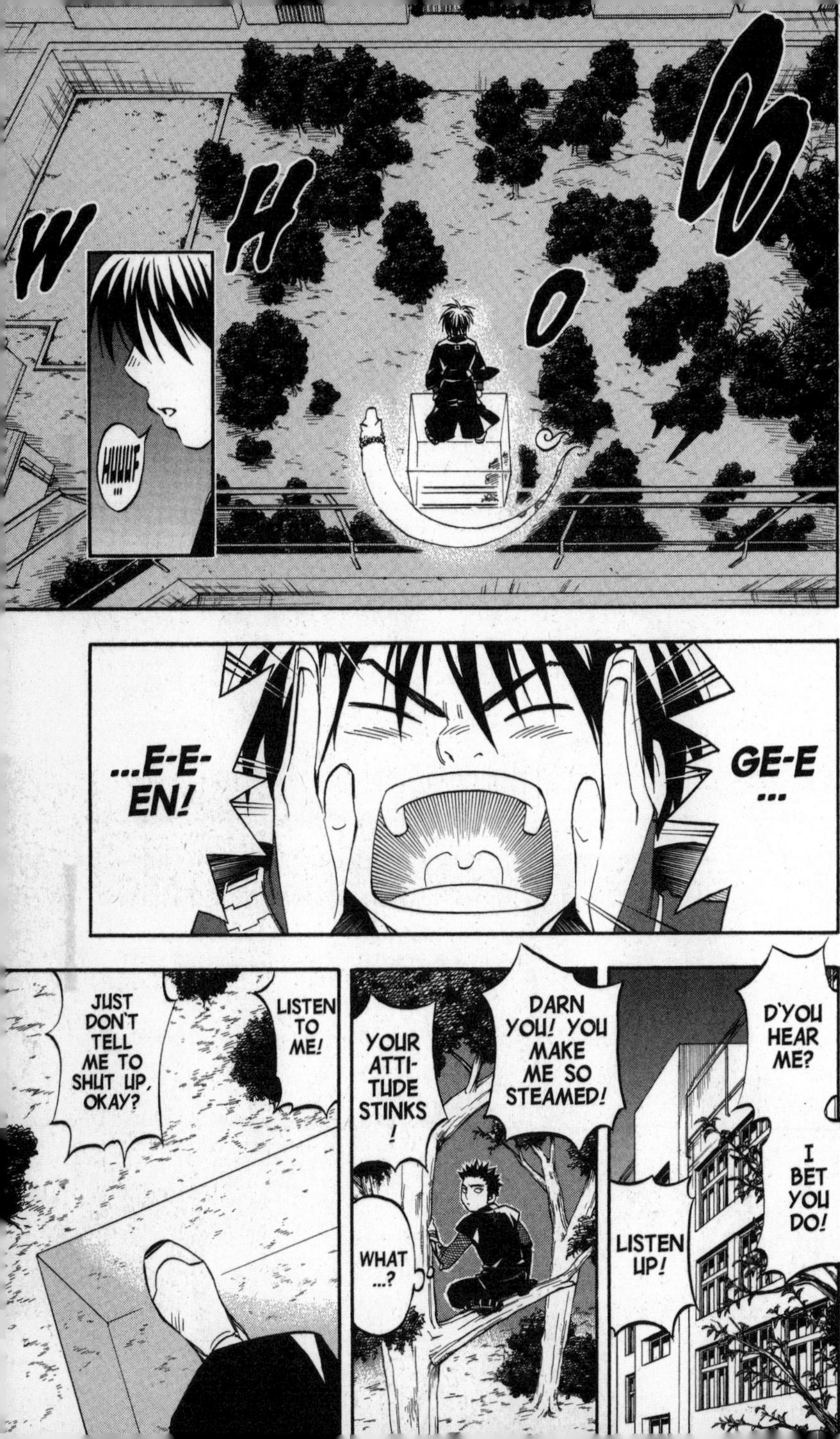
WHOOO
HUUUF ...
GE-E ...
...E-E-EN!
D'YOU HEAR ME?
I BET YOU DO!
LISTEN UP!
DARN YOU! YOU MAKE ME SO STEAMED!
YOUR ATTI-TUDE STINKS!
WHAT ...?
LISTEN TO ME!
JUST DON'T TELL ME TO SHUT UP, OKAY?

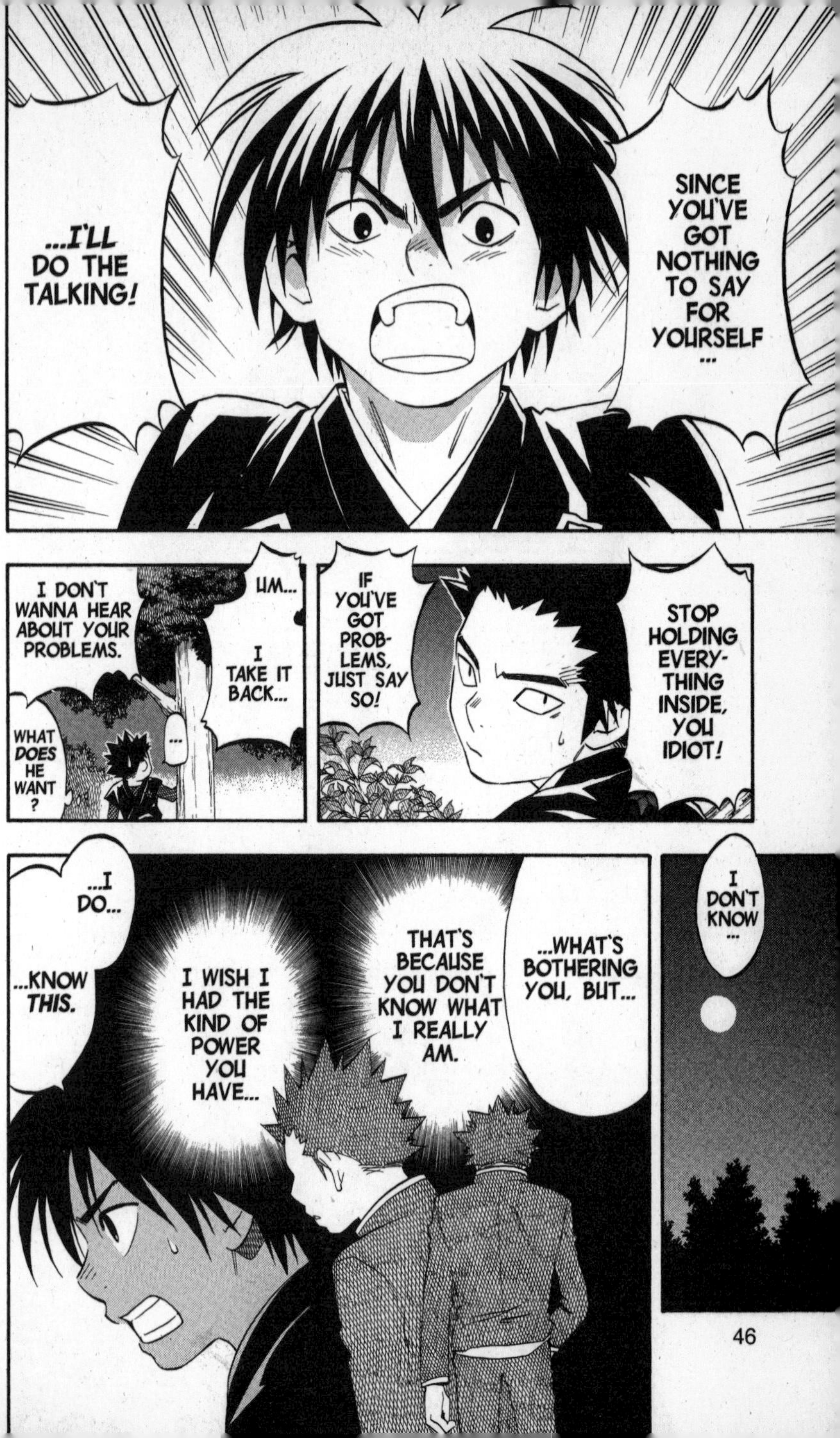
SINCE YOU'VE GOT NOTHING TO SAY FOR YOURSELF ...
...I'LL DO THE TALKING!
STOP HOLDING EVERY-THING INSIDE, YOU IDIOT!
IF YOU'VE GOT PROB-LEMS, JUST SAY SO!
UM...
I TAKE IT BACK...
I DON'T WANNA HEAR ABOUT YOUR PROBLEMS.
...
WHAT DOES HE WANT ?
I DON'T KNOW ...
...WHAT'S BOTHERING YOU, BUT...
THAT'S BECAUSE YOU DON'T KNOW WHAT I REALLY AM.
I WISH I HAD THE KIND OF POWER YOU HAVE...
...I DO...
...KNOW THIS.

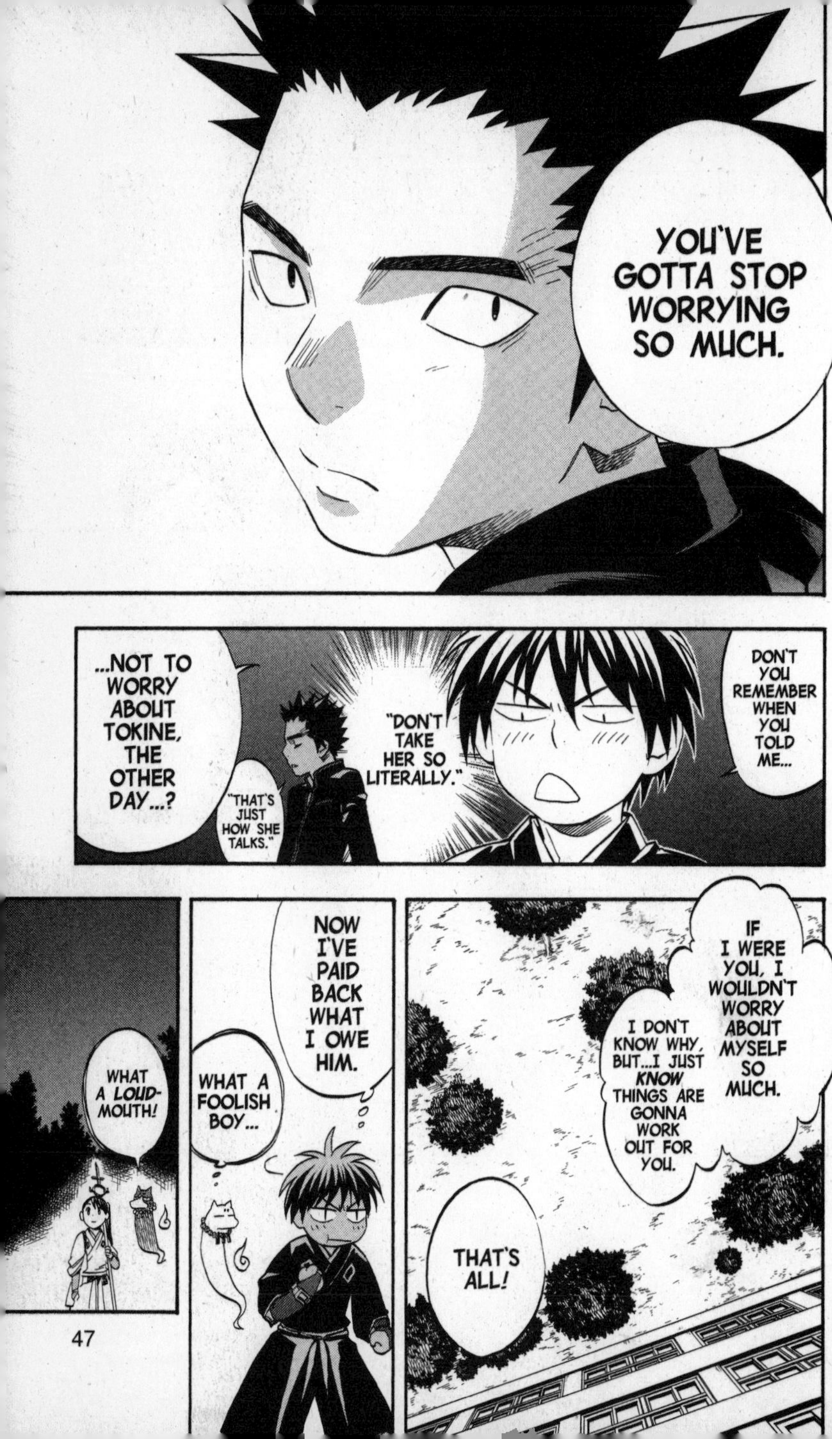
YOU'VE GOTTA STOP WORRYING SO MUCH.
DON'T YOU REMEMBER WHEN YOU TOLD ME...
"DON'T TAKE HER SO LITERALLY."
"THAT'S JUST HOW SHE TALKS."
...NOT TO WORRY ABOUT TOKINE, THE OTHER DAY...?
IF I WERE YOU, I WOULDN'T WORRY ABOUT MYSELF SO MUCH.
I DON'T KNOW WHY, BUT...I JUST *KNOW* THINGS ARE GONNA WORK OUT FOR YOU.
THAT'S ALL!
NOW I'VE PAID BACK WHAT I OWE HIM.
WHAT A FOOLISH BOY...
WHAT A *LOUD*-MOUTH!

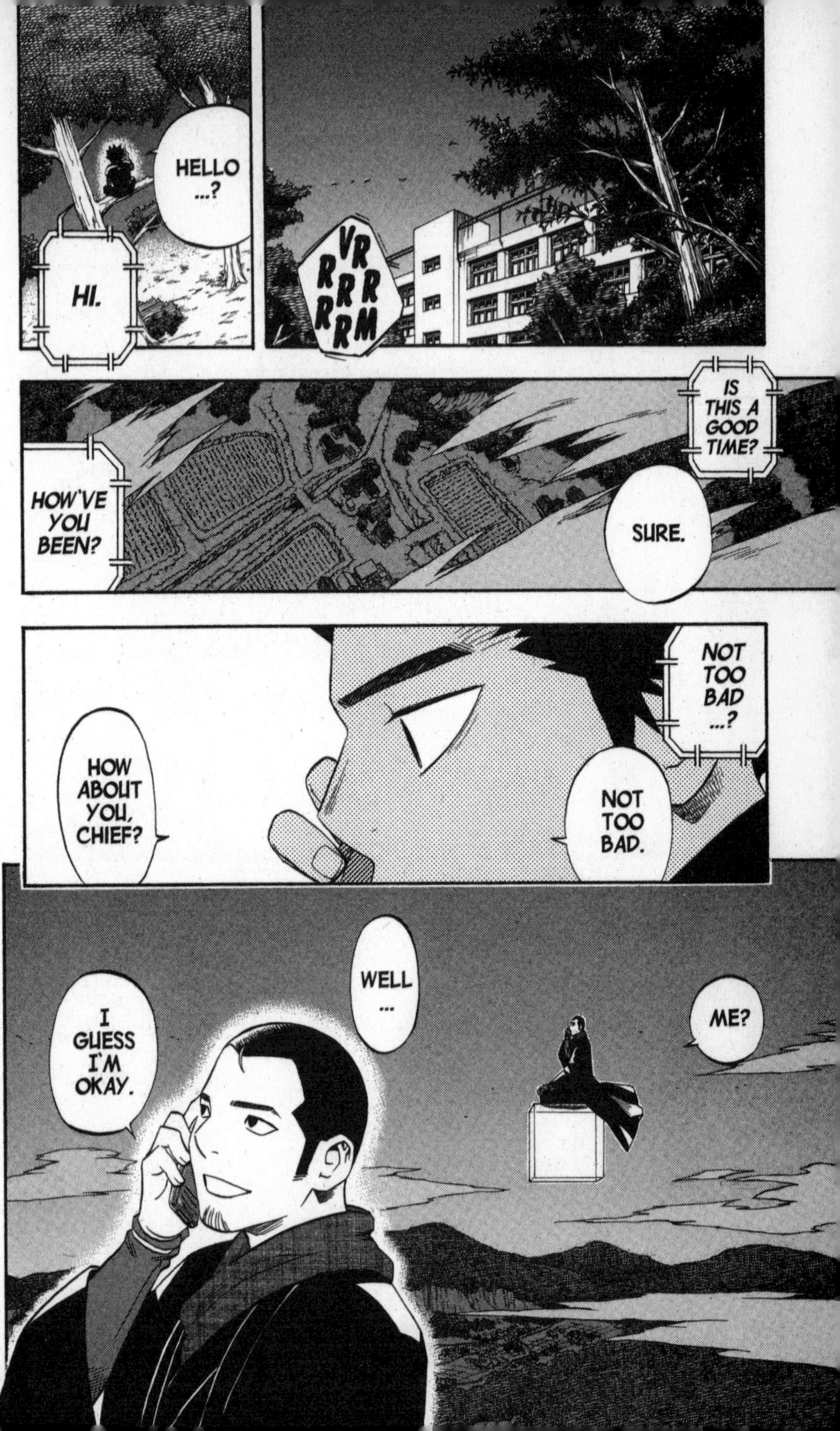
VRRRRRM
HELLO ...?
HI.
IS THIS A GOOD TIME?
SURE.
HOW'VE YOU BEEN?
NOT TOO BAD ...?
NOT TOO BAD.
HOW ABOUT YOU, CHIEF?
ME?
WELL ...
I GUESS I'M OKAY.

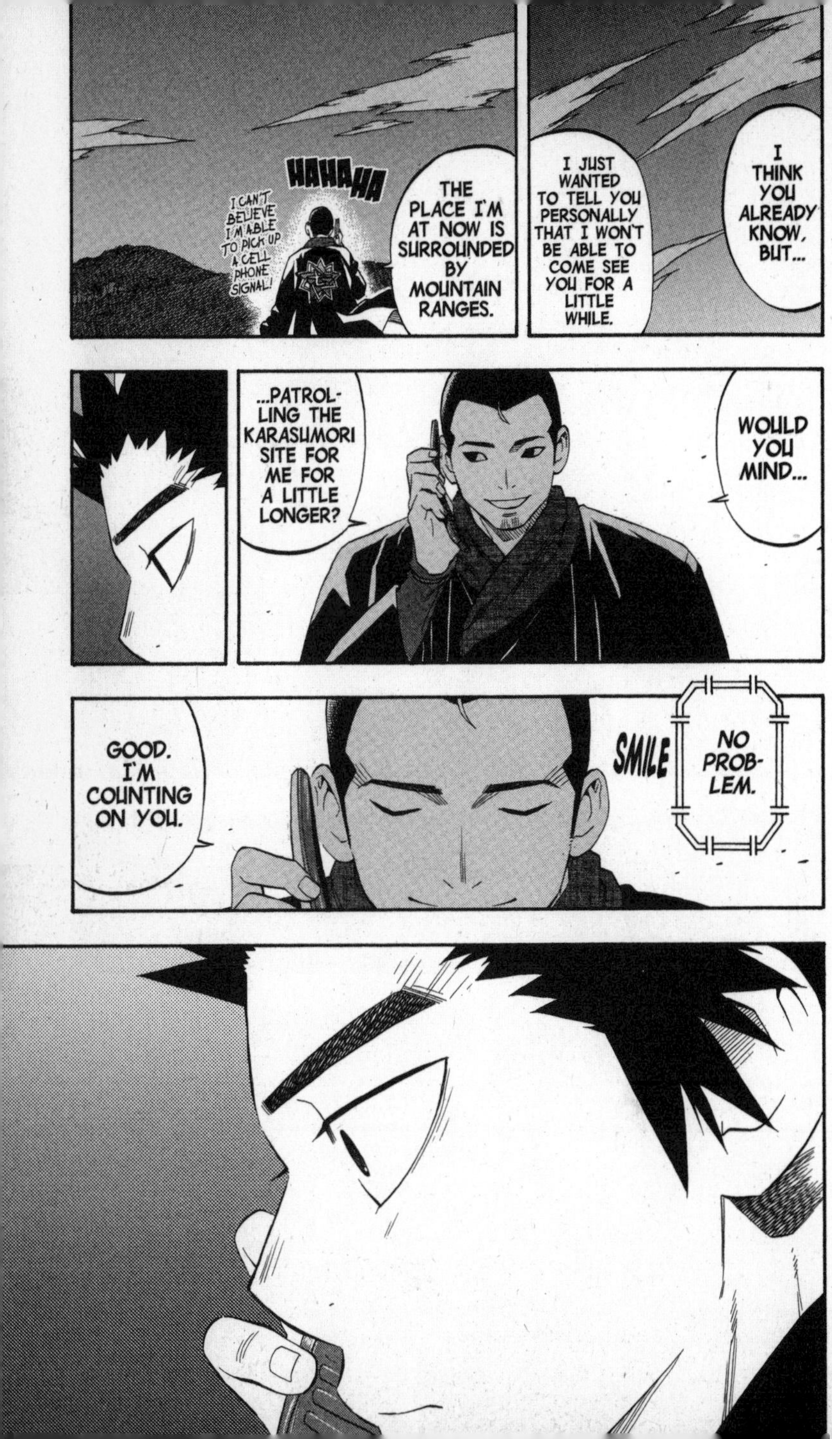
I THINK YOU ALREADY KNOW, BUT...
I JUST WANTED TO TELL YOU PERSONALLY THAT I WON'T BE ABLE TO COME SEE YOU FOR A LITTLE WHILE.
THE PLACE I'M AT NOW IS SURROUNDED BY MOUNTAIN RANGES.
HAHAHA
I CAN'T BELIEVE I'M ABLE TO PICK UP A CELL PHONE SIGNAL!
WOULD YOU MIND...
...PATROL-LING THE KARASUMORI SITE FOR ME FOR A LITTLE LONGER?
NO PROB-LEM.
SMILE
GOOD. I'M COUNTING ON YOU.

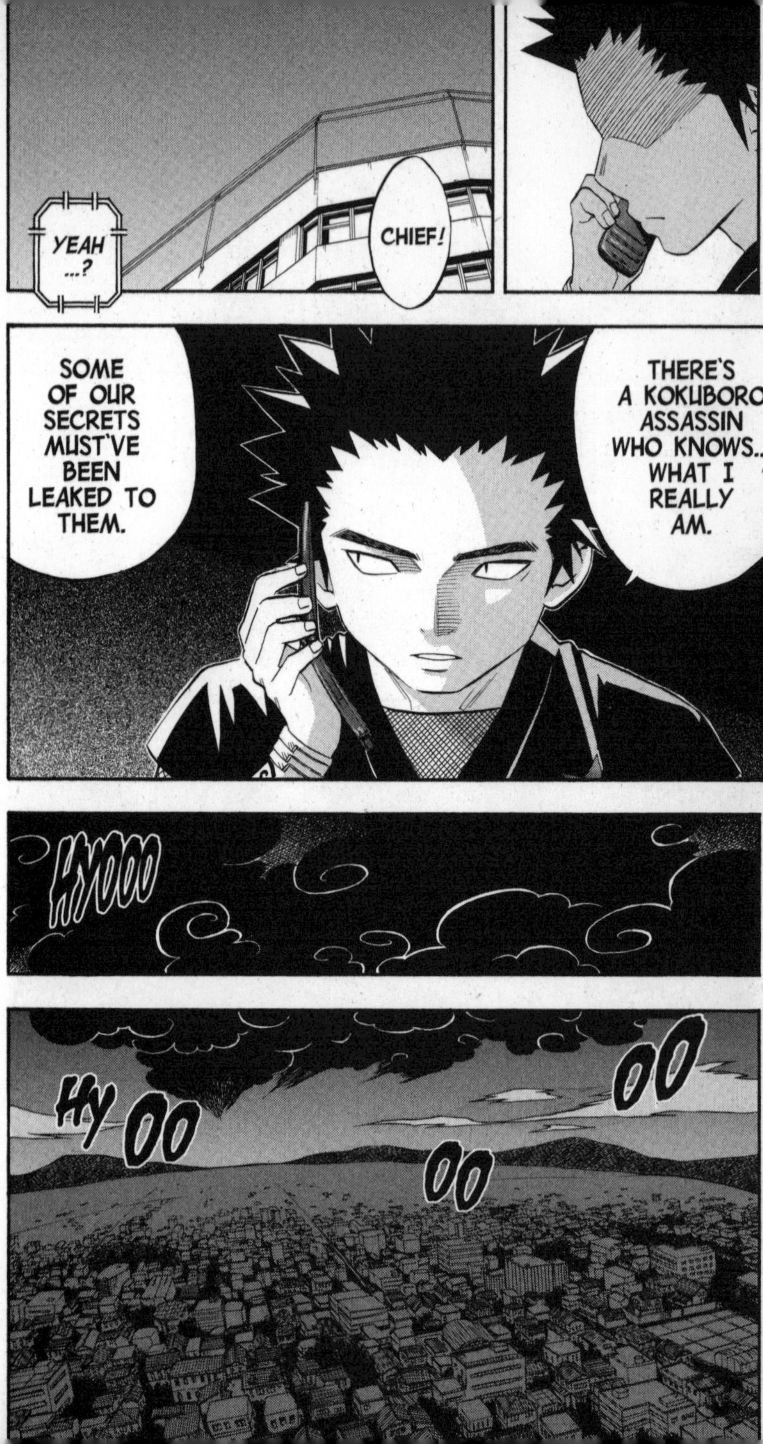
CHIEF!
YEAH ...?
THERE'S A KOKUBORO ASSASSIN WHO KNOWS... WHAT I REALLY AM.
SOME OF OUR SECRETS MUST'VE BEEN LEAKED TO THEM.
HYOOO
HY OO
OO
OO

WE'LL BE... THERE... SOON.

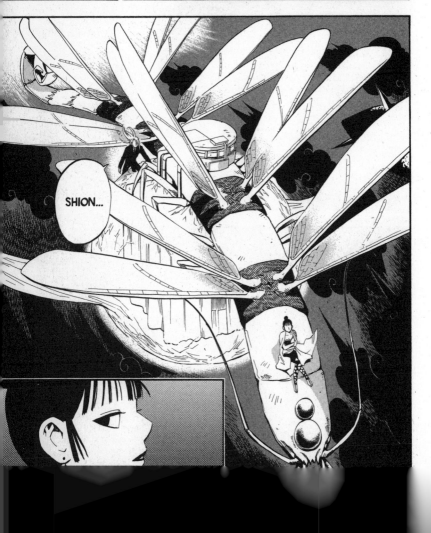

SHION...

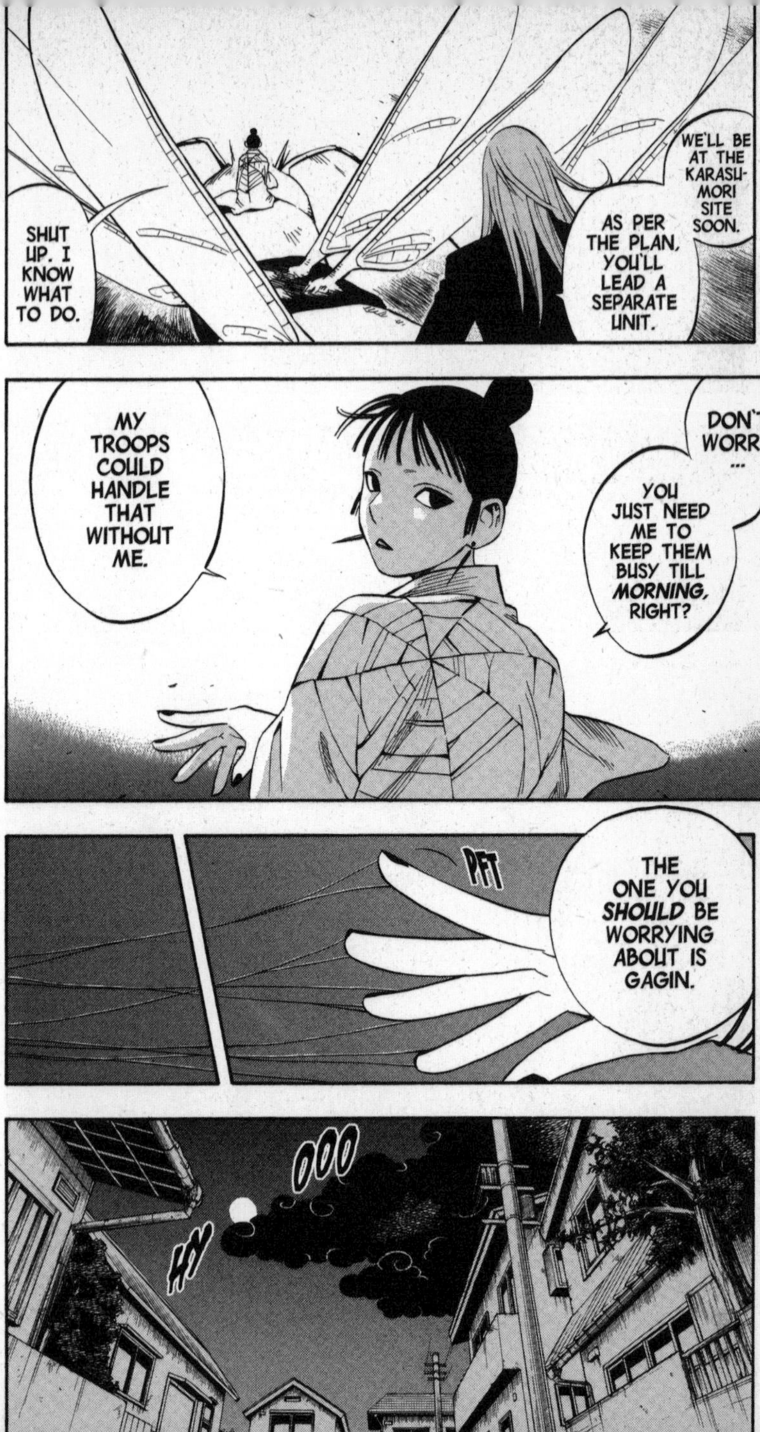
WE'LL BE AT THE KARASU-MORI SITE SOON.
AS PER THE PLAN, YOU'LL LEAD A SEPARATE UNIT.
SHUT UP. I KNOW WHAT TO DO.
DON'T WORRY ...
YOU JUST NEED ME TO KEEP THEM BUSY TILL *MORNING*, RIGHT?
MY TROOPS COULD HANDLE THAT WITHOUT ME.
THE ONE YOU *SHOULD* BE WORRYING ABOUT IS GAGIN.
PFT
OOO
HN

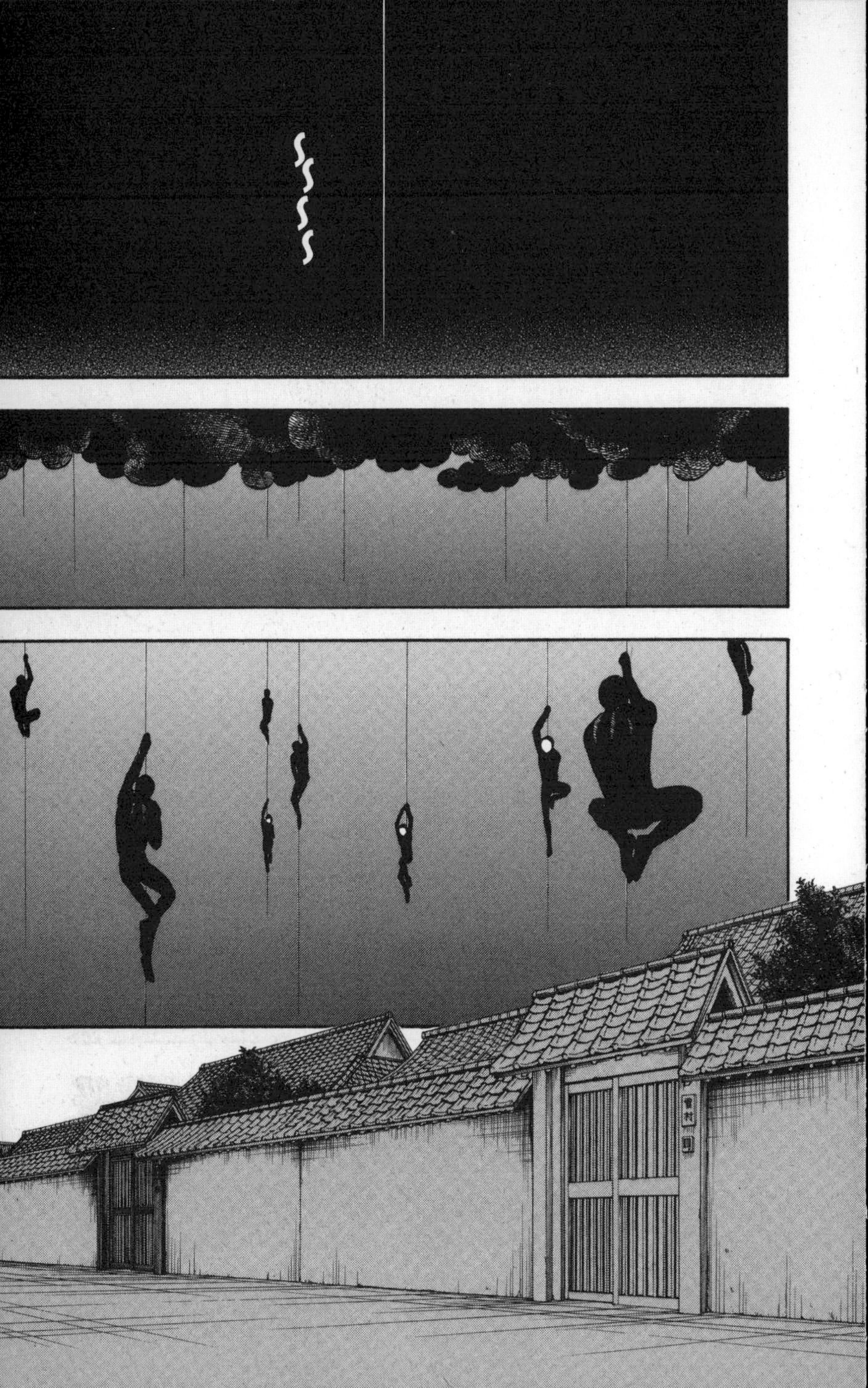

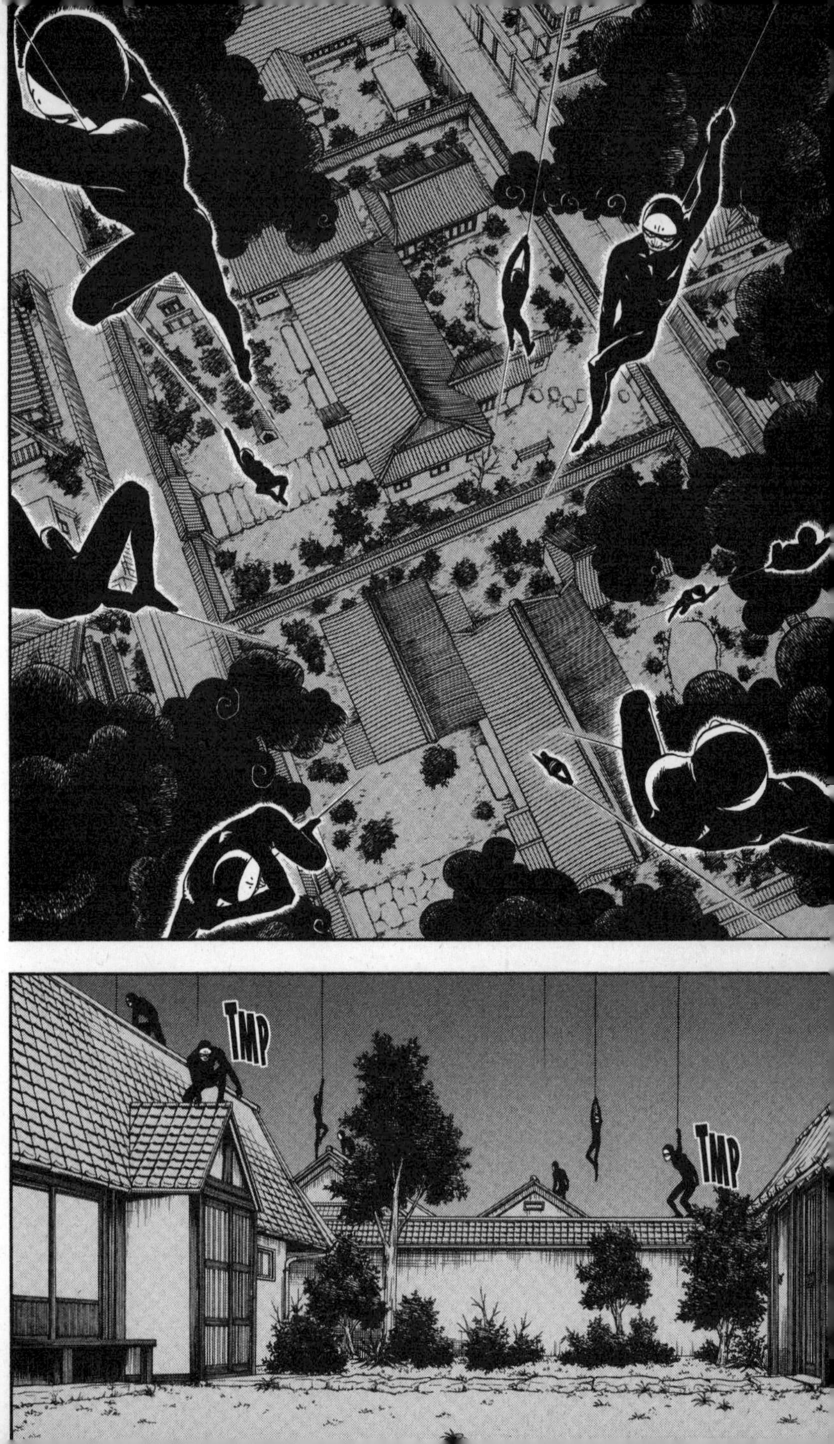
TMP
TMP

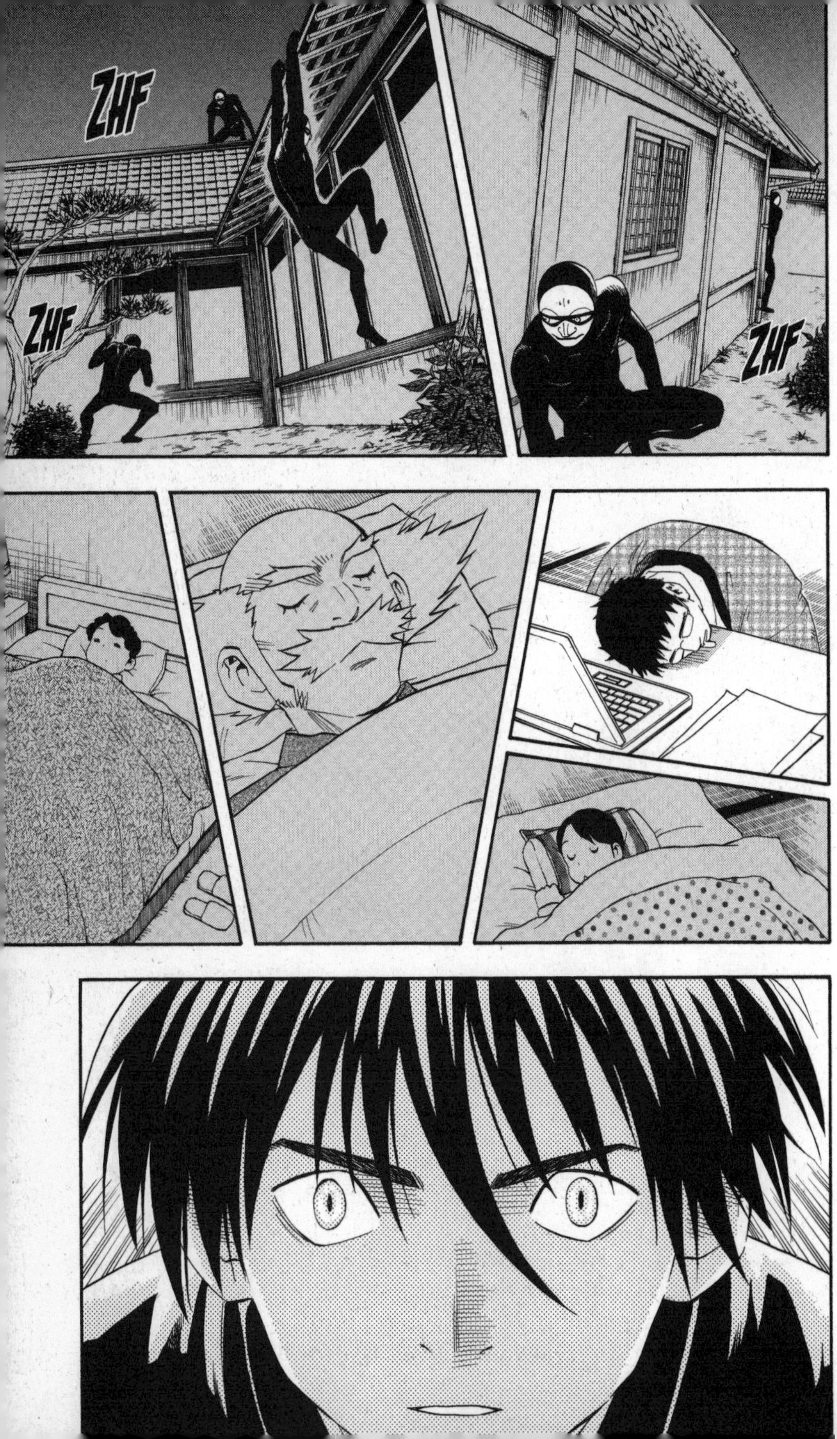
ZHF
ZHF
ZHF

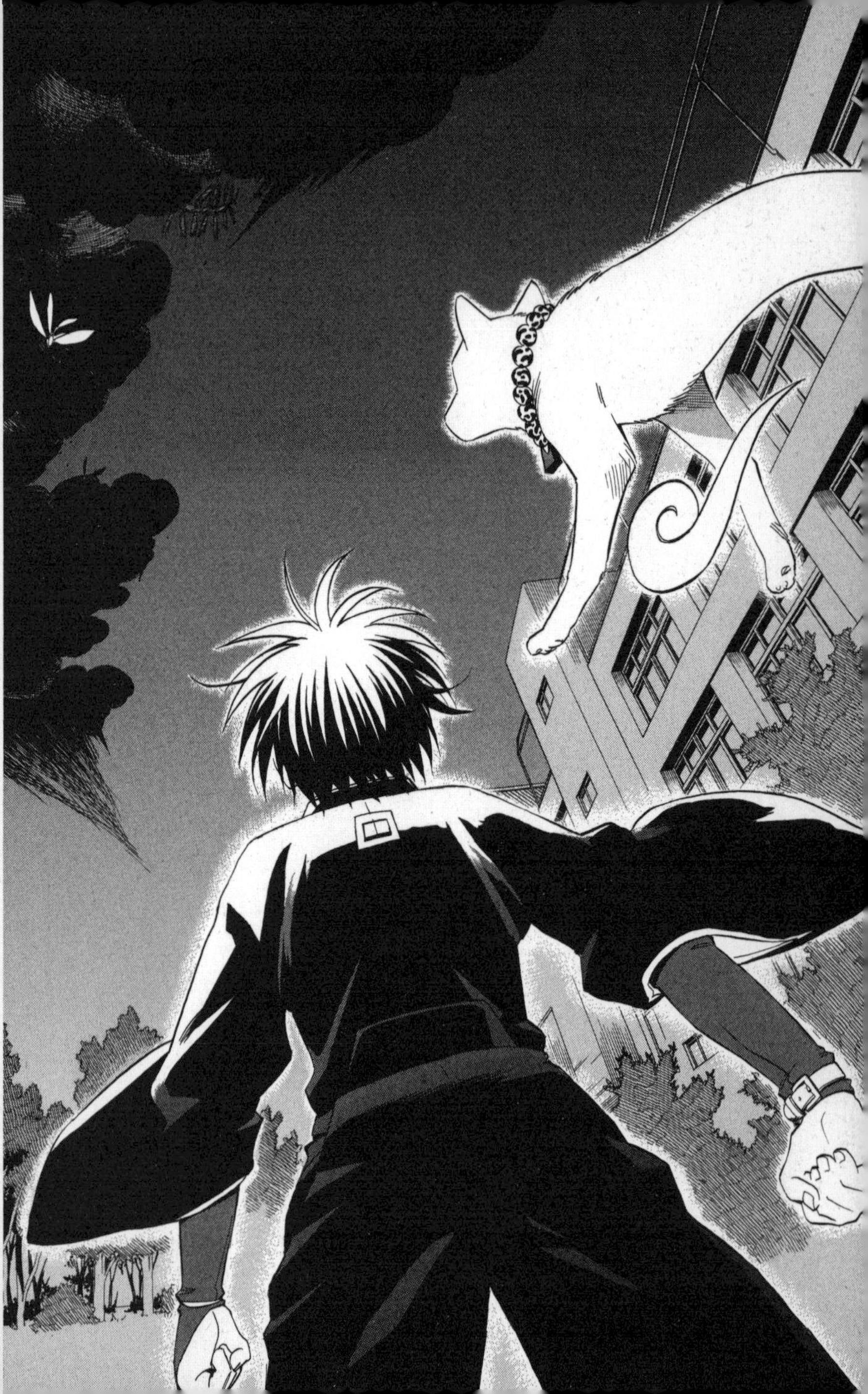

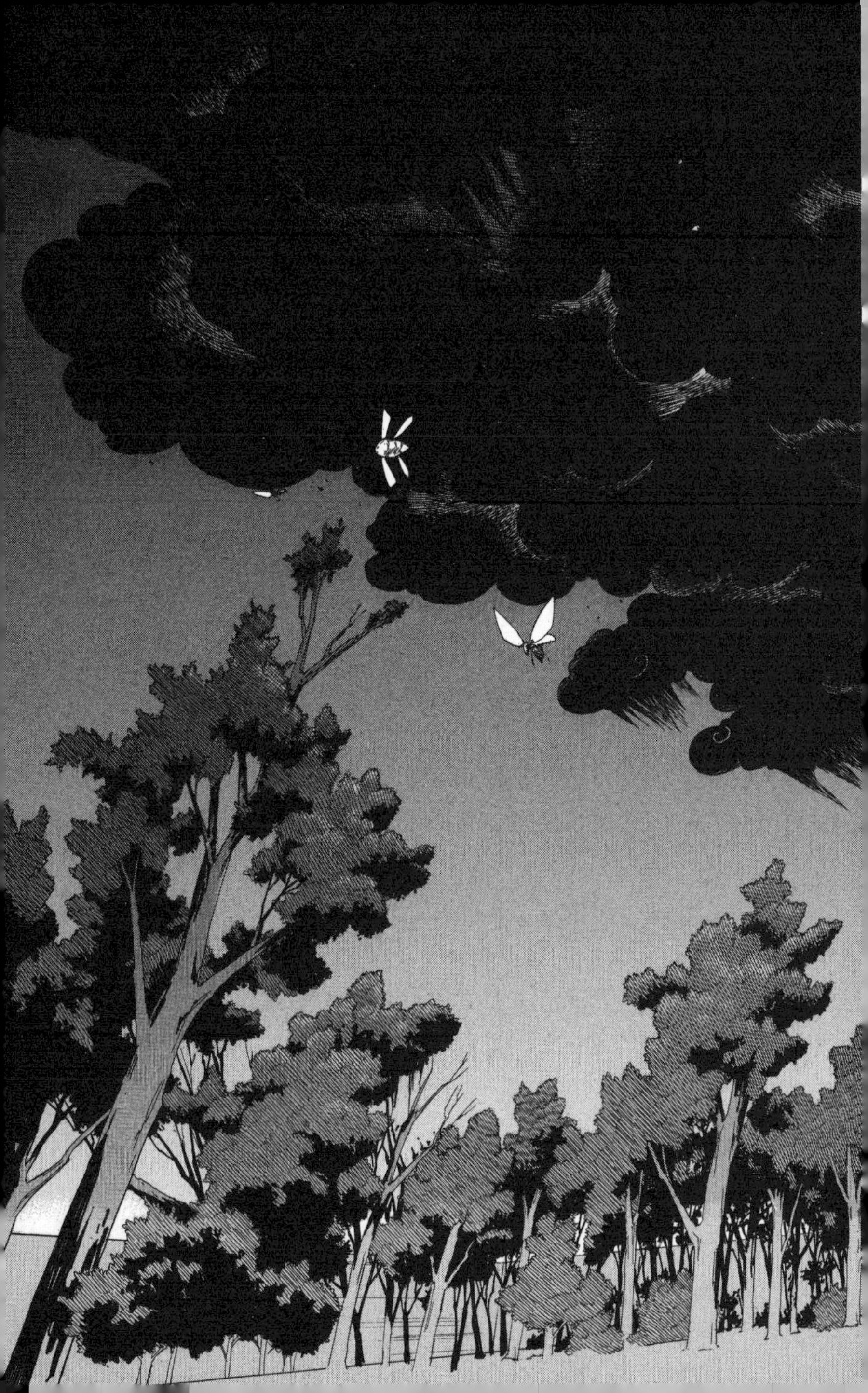

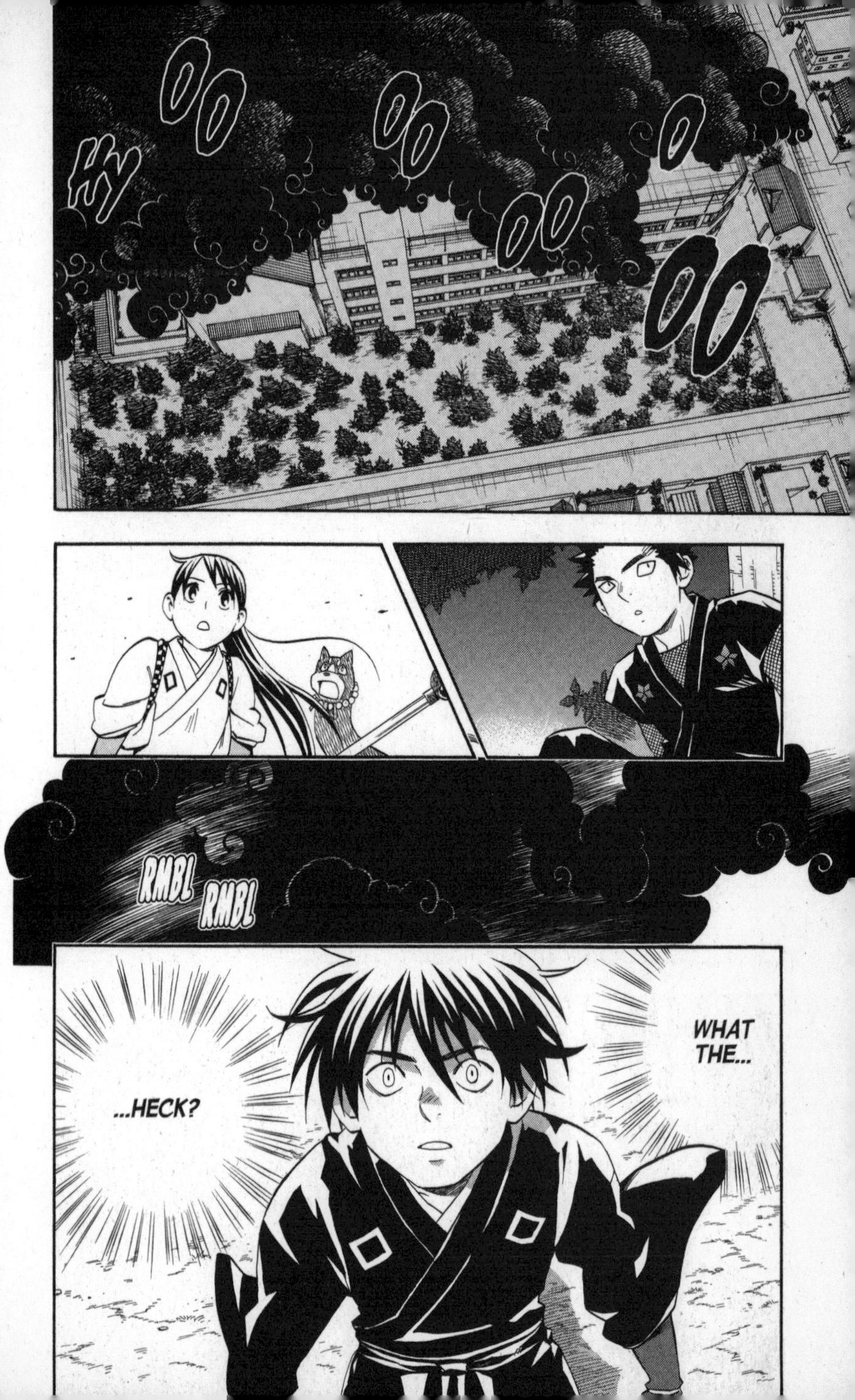
HYOOOOOOOOOOO
RMBL RMBL
WHAT THE...
...HECK?

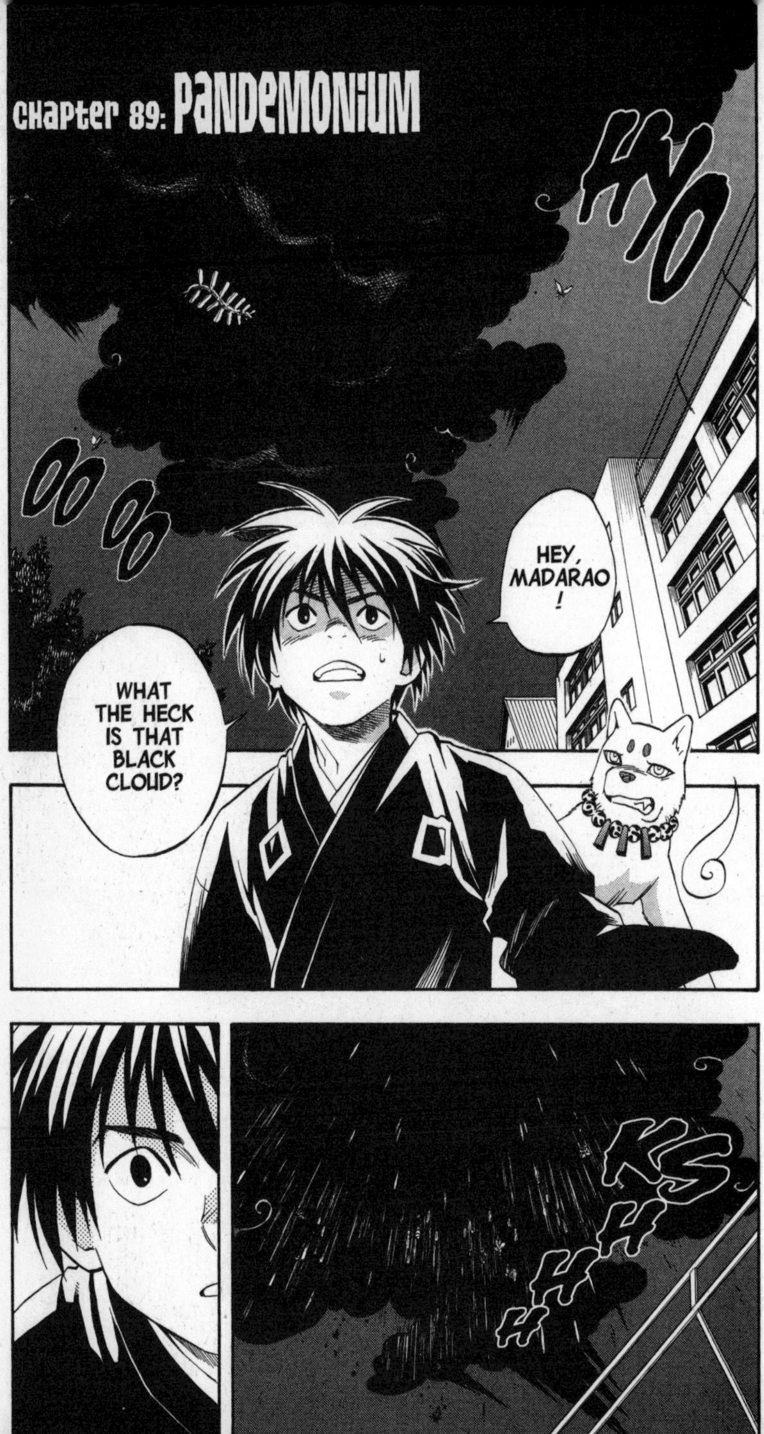
Chapter 89: Pandemonium
KYO
HEY, MADARAO!
OOOO
WHAT THE HECK IS THAT BLACK CLOUD?
KSHHHH

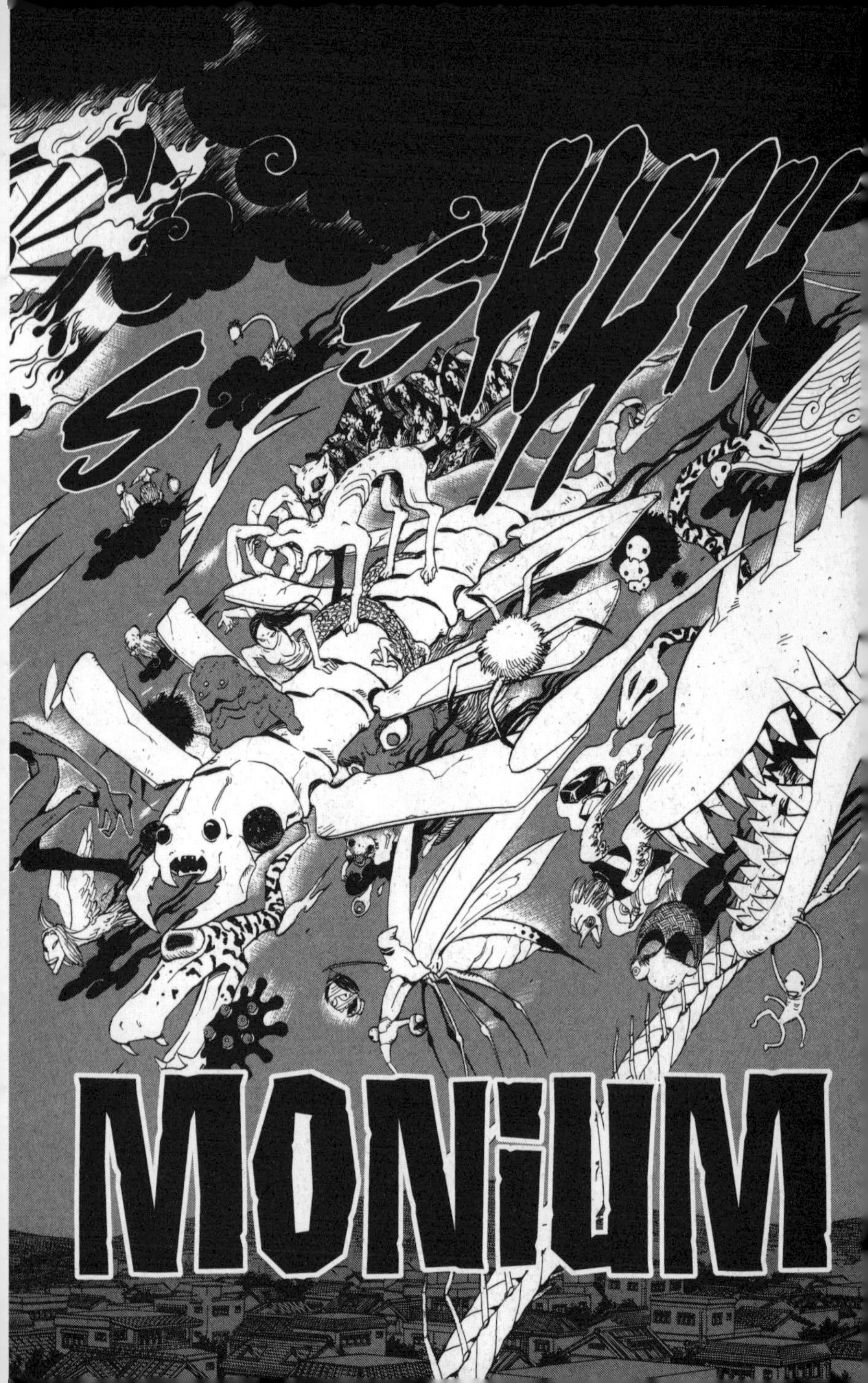
MONIUM

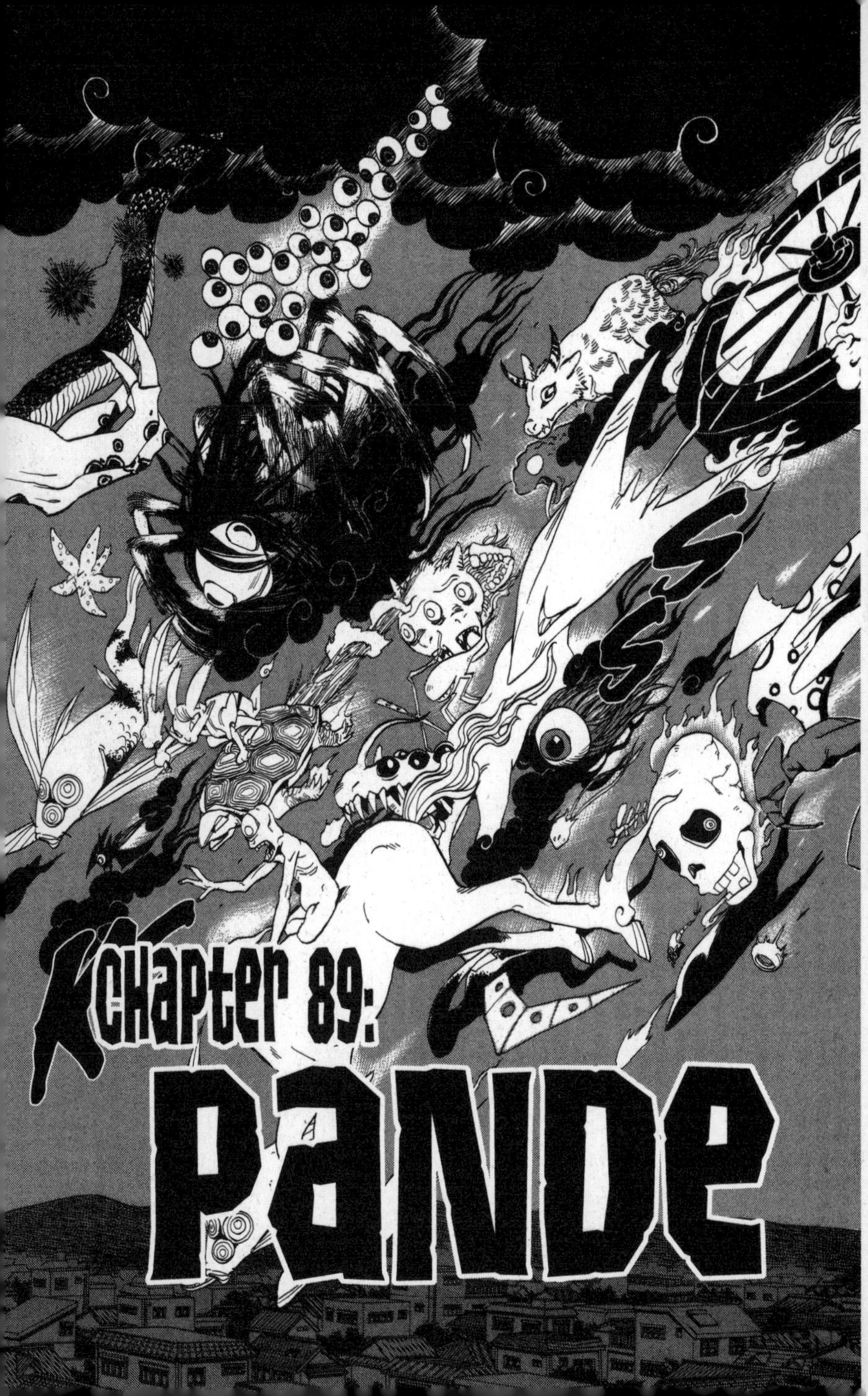

SSS
Chapter 89:
Pande

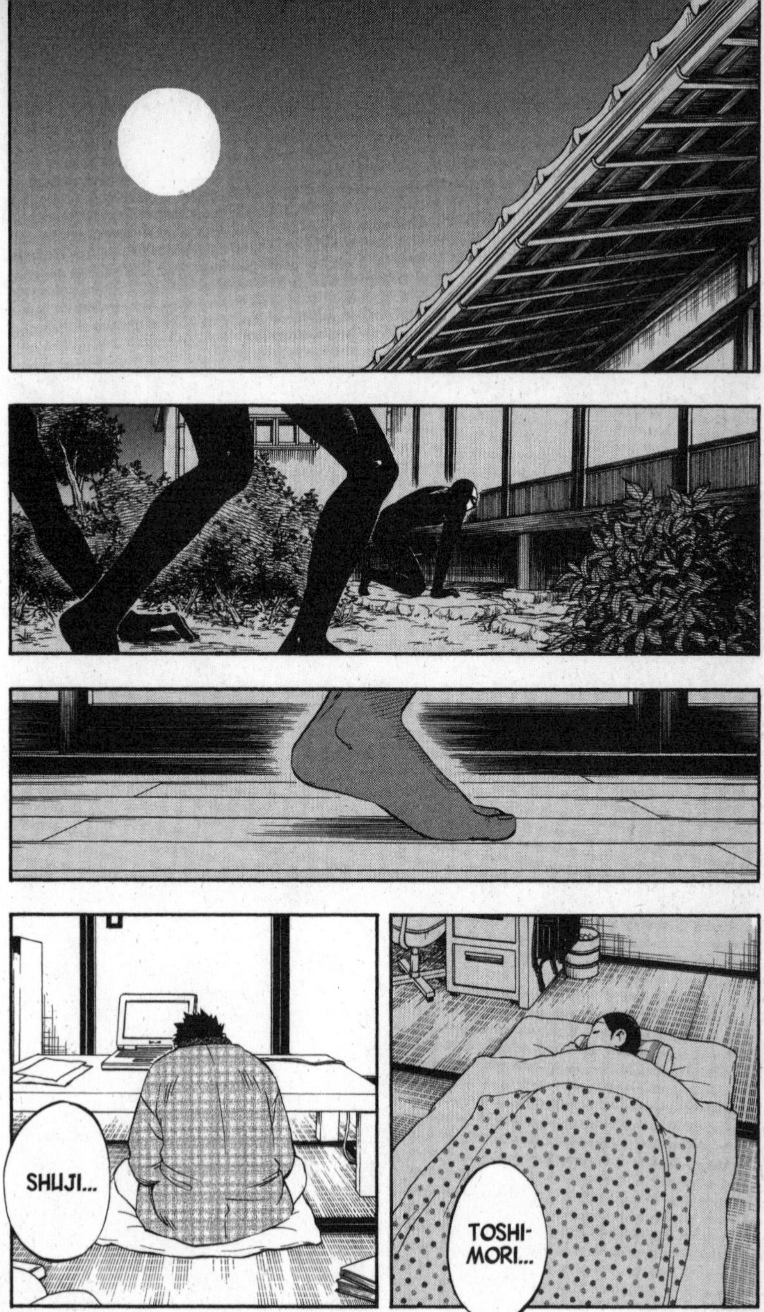
TOSHI-
MORI...
SHUJI...

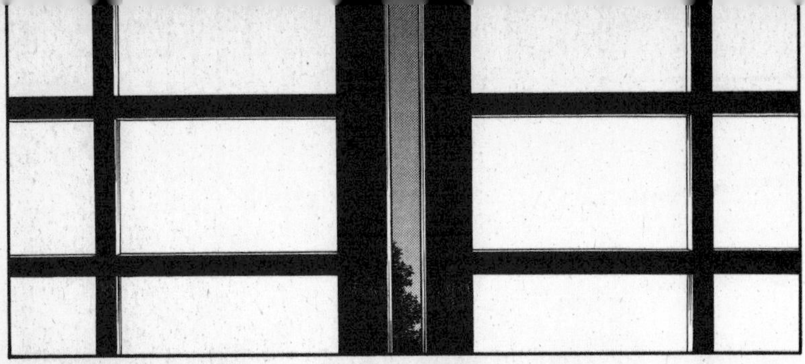
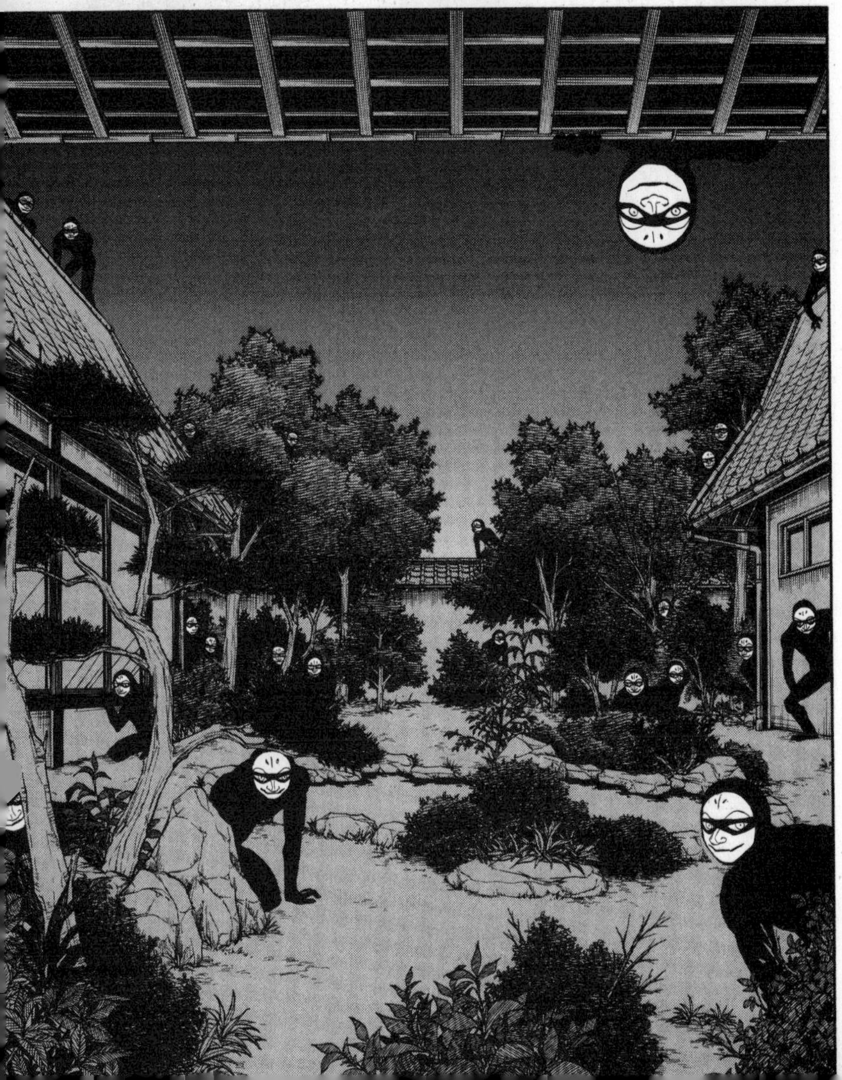

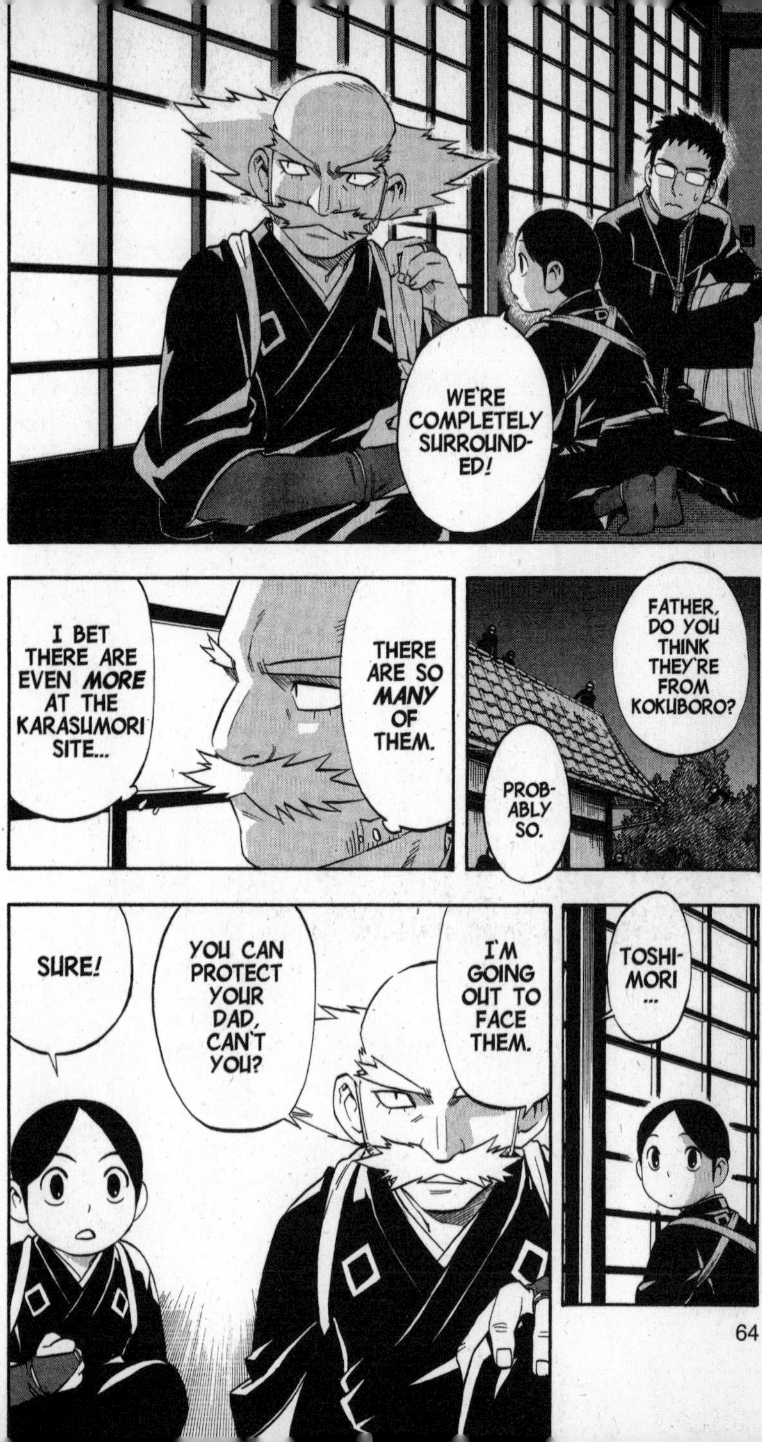
WE'RE COMPLETELY SURROUNDED!
FATHER, DO YOU THINK THEY'RE FROM KOKUBORO?
PROBABLY SO.
THERE ARE SO *MANY* OF THEM.
I BET THERE ARE EVEN *MORE* AT THE KARASUMORI SITE...
TOSHIMORI...
I'M GOING OUT TO FACE THEM.
YOU CAN PROTECT YOUR DAD, CAN'T YOU?
SURE!

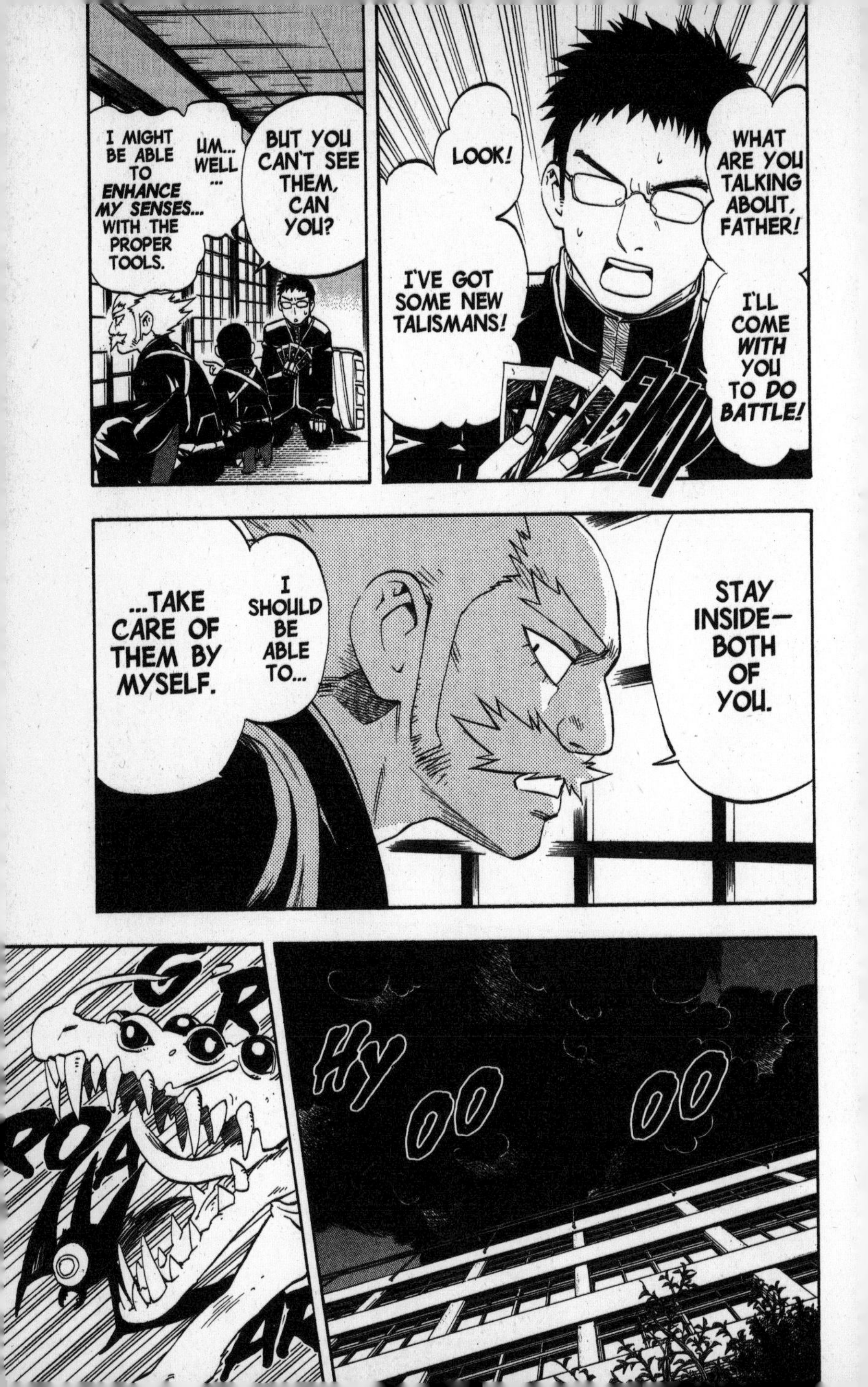
WHAT ARE YOU TALKING ABOUT, FATHER!
LOOK!
I'LL COME WITH YOU TO DO BATTLE!
I'VE GOT SOME NEW TALISMANS!
BUT YOU CAN'T SEE THEM, CAN YOU?
UM... WELL ...
I MIGHT BE ABLE TO ENHANCE MY SENSES... WITH THE PROPER TOOLS.
STAY INSIDE— BOTH OF YOU.
I SHOULD BE ABLE TO...
...TAKE CARE OF THEM BY MYSELF.
HYOOOO

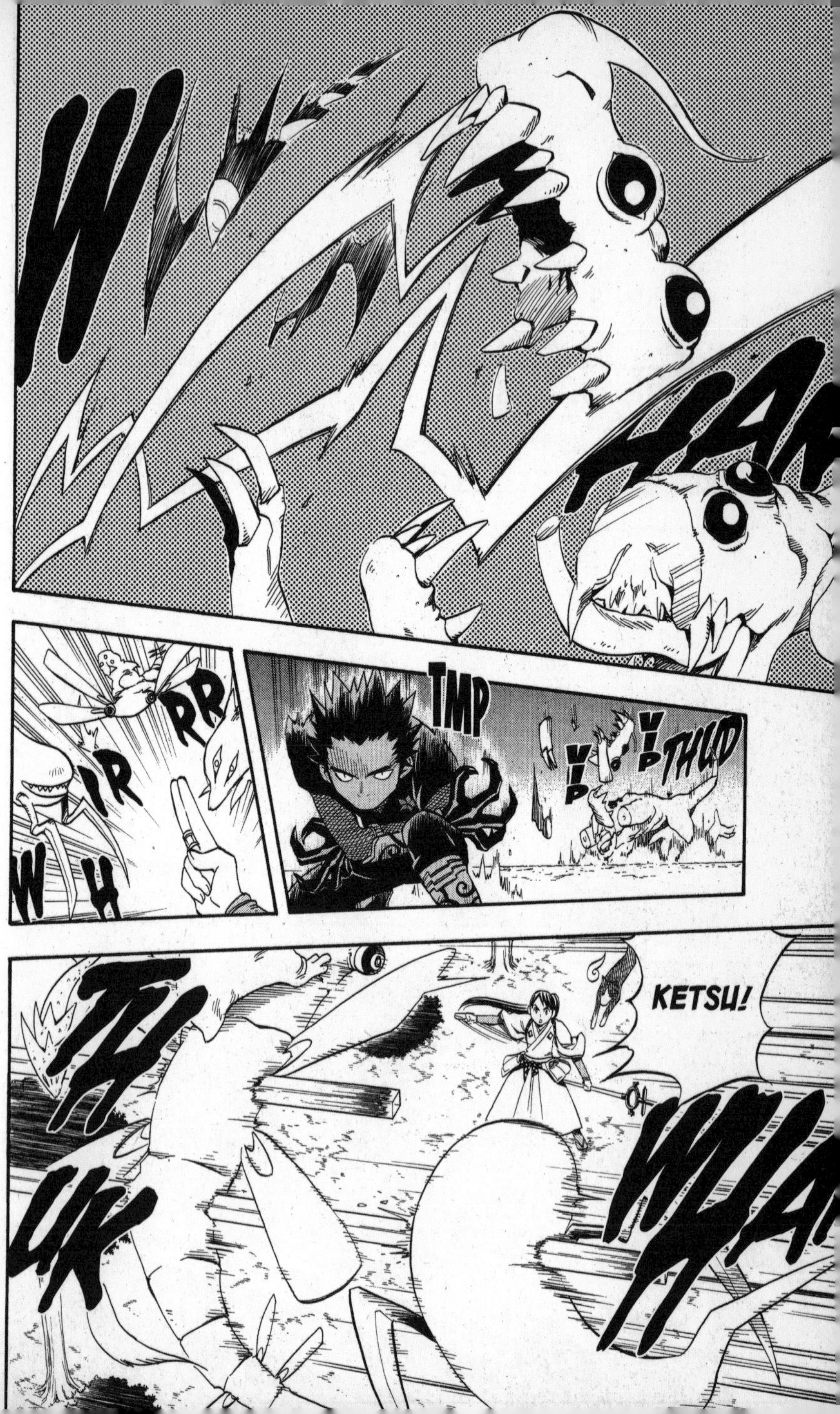
TMP
VIP
VIP
THUD
WHIRR
KETSU!

SO...
MANY...

CHA

DARN.

WH
A
R.

KETSU!

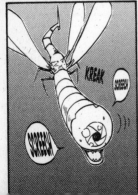

KREAK

SCREECH

SCREECH

KETSU!

BOO
OM

SCREECH

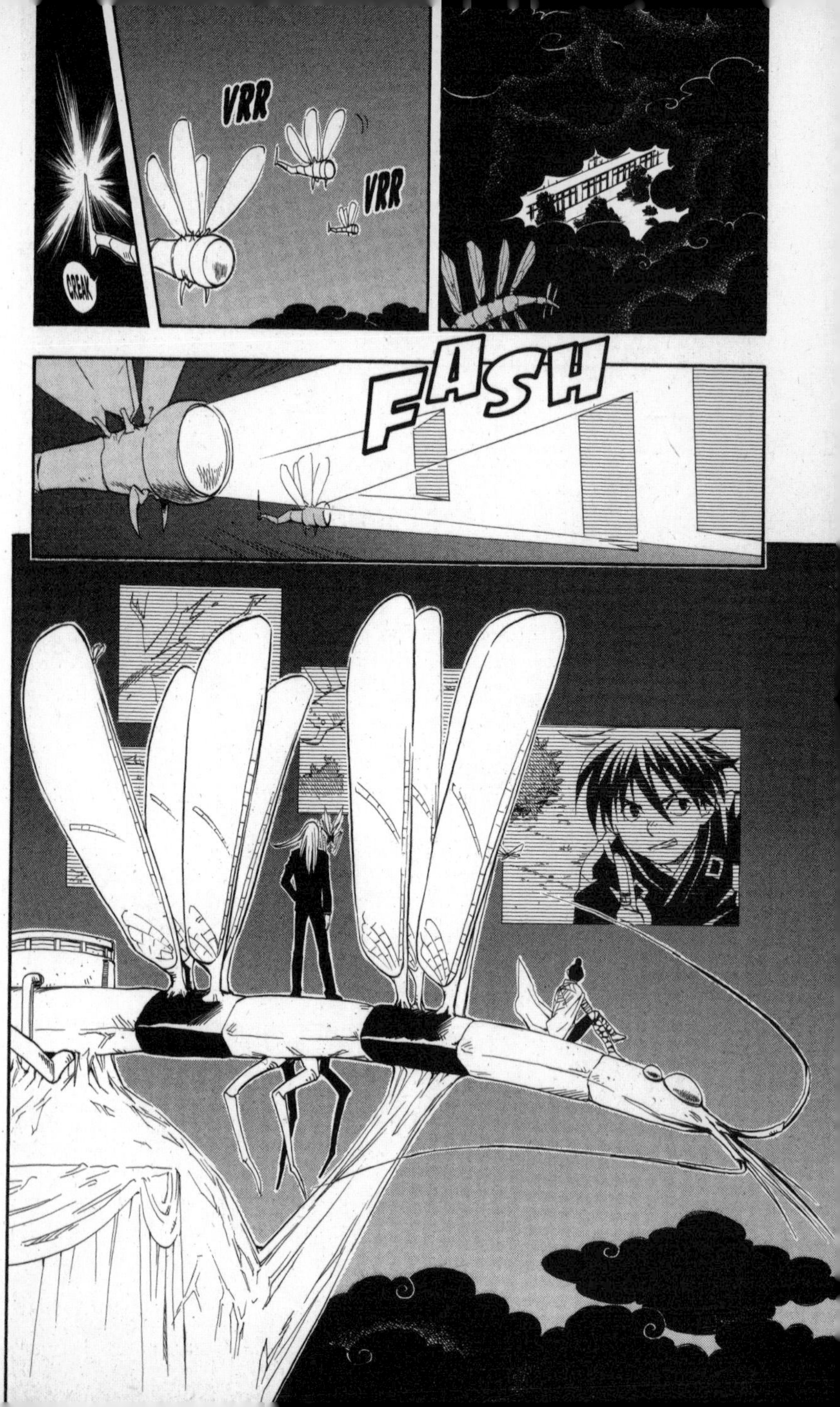
VRR
VRR
CREAK
FASH

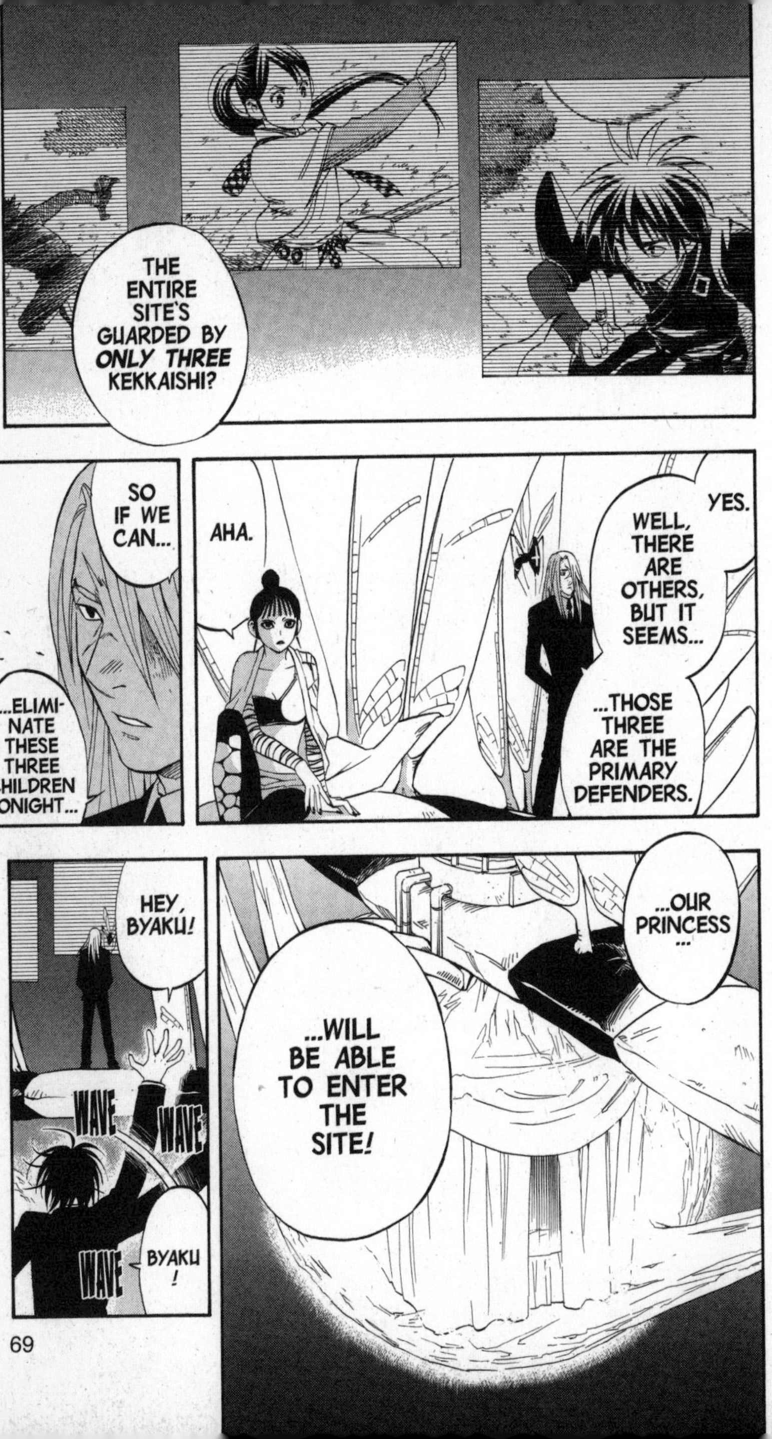
THE ENTIRE SITE'S GUARDED BY *ONLY THREE* KEKKAISHI?
YES.
WELL, THERE ARE OTHERS, BUT IT SEEMS...
...THOSE THREE ARE THE PRIMARY DEFENDERS.
AHA.
SO IF WE CAN...
...ELIMINATE THESE THREE CHILDREN TONIGHT...
...OUR PRINCESS ...
...WILL BE ABLE TO ENTER THE SITE!
HEY, BYAKU!
WAVE
WAVE
WAVE
BYAKU!

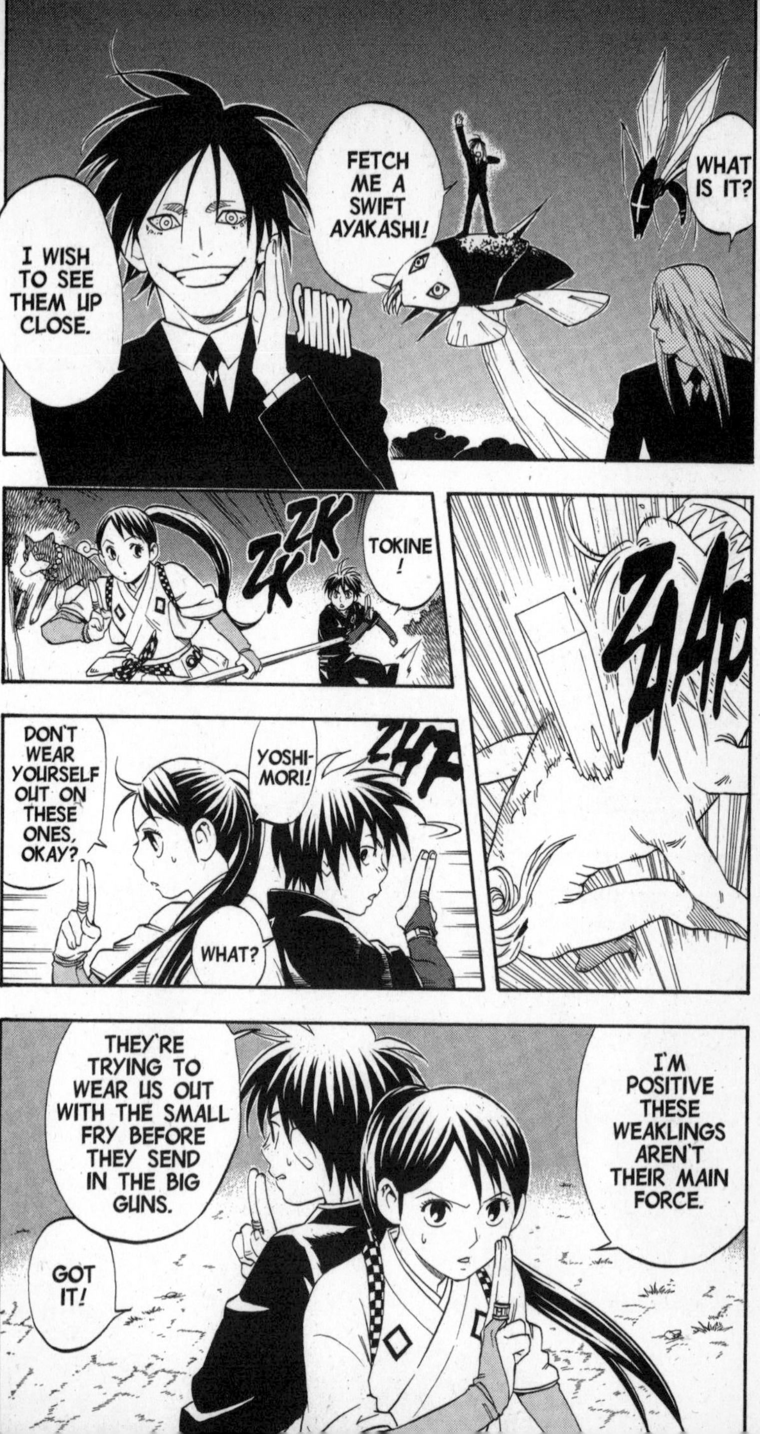
WHAT IS IT?
FETCH ME A SWIFT AYAKASHI!
SMIRK
I WISH TO SEE THEM UP CLOSE.
ZAP
TOKINE!
ZK ZK ZK
YOSHIMORI!
ZHP
DON'T WEAR YOURSELF OUT ON THESE ONES, OKAY?
WHAT?
I'M POSITIVE THESE WEAKLINGS AREN'T THEIR MAIN FORCE.
THEY'RE TRYING TO WEAR US OUT WITH THE SMALL FRY BEFORE THEY SEND IN THE BIG GUNS.
GOT IT!

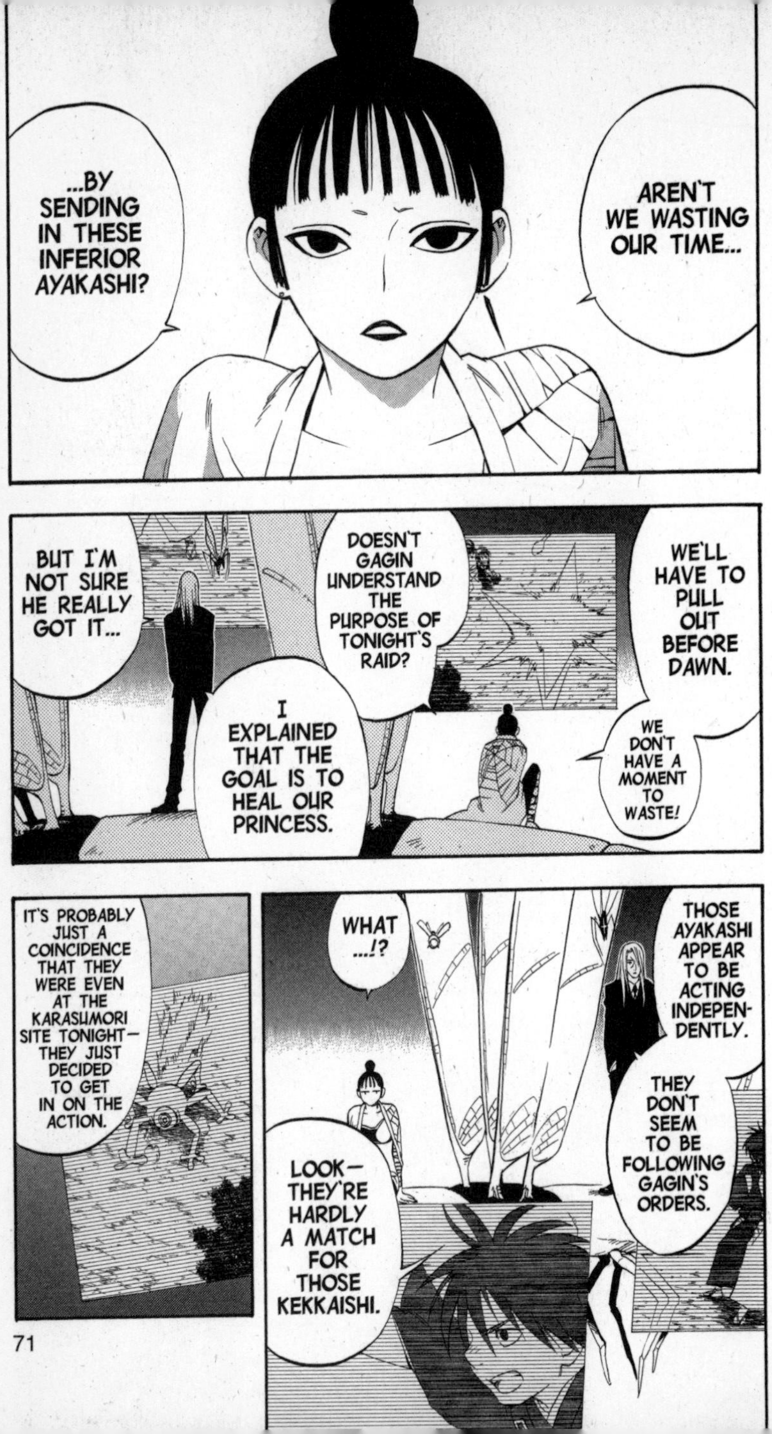

AREN'T WE WASTING OUR TIME...
...BY SENDING IN THESE INFERIOR AYAKASHI?
WE'LL HAVE TO PULL OUT BEFORE DAWN.
WE DON'T HAVE A MOMENT TO WASTE!
DOESN'T GAGIN UNDERSTAND THE PURPOSE OF TONIGHT'S RAID?
I EXPLAINED THAT THE GOAL IS TO HEAL OUR PRINCESS.
BUT I'M NOT SURE HE REALLY GOT IT...
THOSE AYAKASHI APPEAR TO BE ACTING INDEPENDENTLY.
WHAT ...!?
THEY DON'T SEEM TO BE FOLLOWING GAGIN'S ORDERS.
LOOK—THEY'RE HARDLY A MATCH FOR THOSE KEKKAISHI.
IT'S PROBABLY JUST A COINCIDENCE THAT THEY WERE EVEN AT THE KARASUMORI SITE TONIGHT—THEY JUST DECIDED TO GET IN ON THE ACTION.

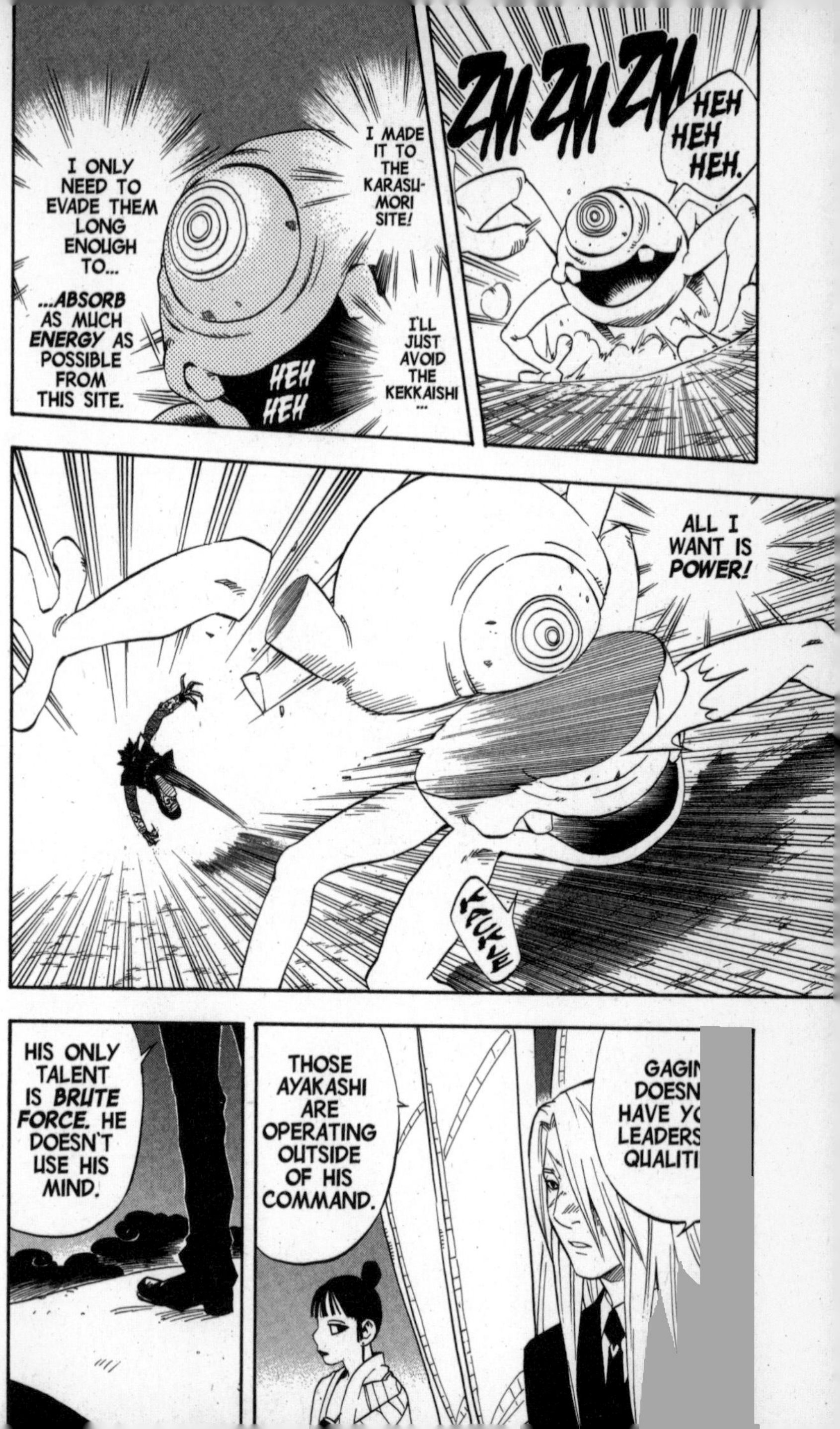
ZM ZM ZM
HEH HEH HEH.
I MADE IT TO THE KARASU-MORI SITE!
I'LL JUST AVOID THE KEKKAISHI...
I ONLY NEED TO EVADE THEM LONG ENOUGH TO...
...*ABSORB* AS MUCH *ENERGY* AS POSSIBLE FROM THIS SITE.
HEH HEH
ALL I WANT IS *POWER!*
GAGIN
DOESN
HAVE YO
LEADERS
QUALITI
THOSE AYAKASHI ARE OPERATING OUTSIDE OF HIS COMMAND.
HIS ONLY TALENT IS *BRUTE FORCE.* HE DOESN'T USE HIS MIND.

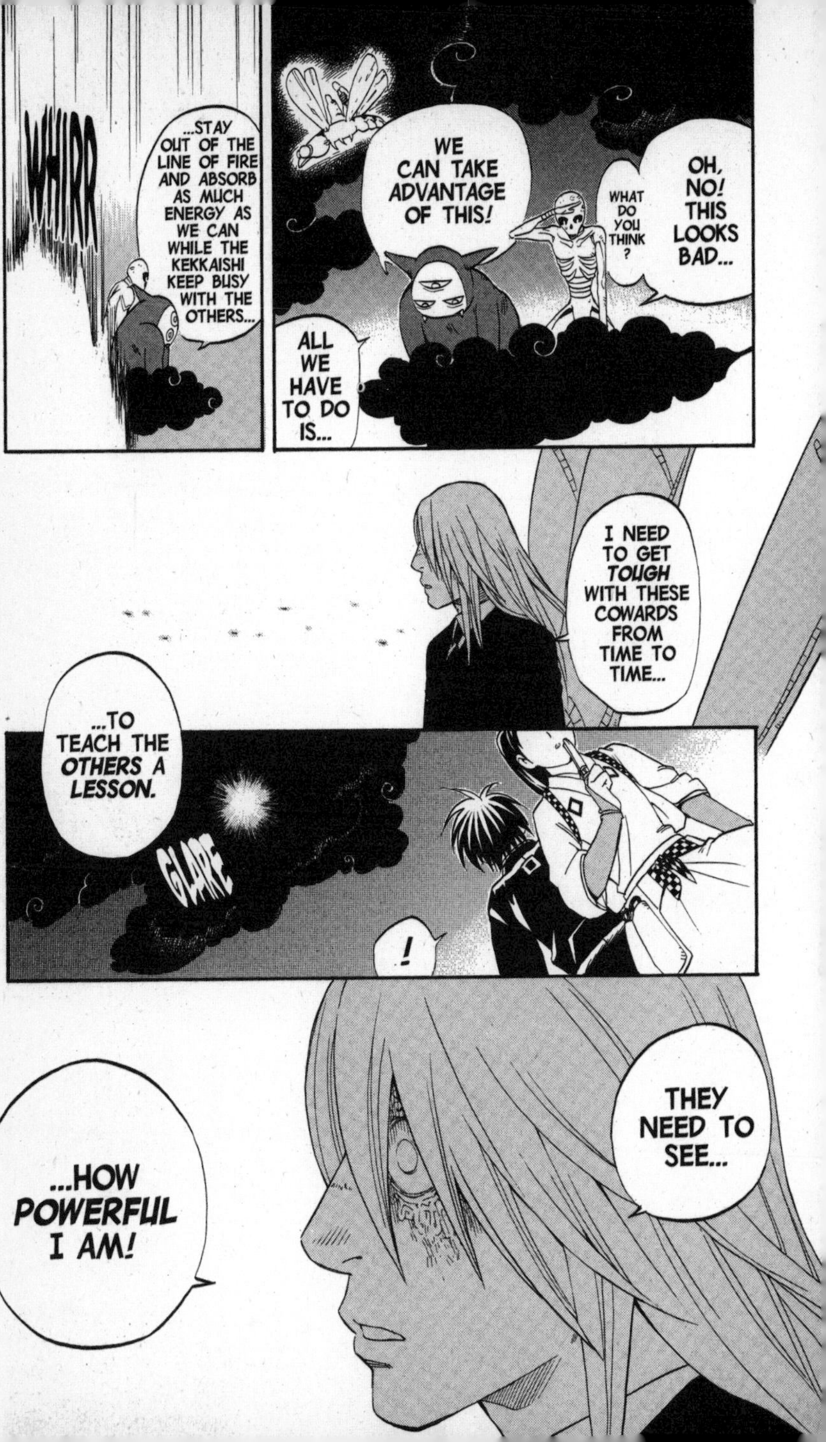

OH, NO! THIS LOOKS BAD...
WHAT DO YOU THINK?
WE CAN TAKE ADVANTAGE OF THIS!
ALL WE HAVE TO DO IS...
WHIRR
...STAY OUT OF THE LINE OF FIRE AND ABSORB AS MUCH ENERGY AS WE CAN WHILE THE KEKKAISHI KEEP BUSY WITH THE OTHERS...
I NEED TO GET TOUGH WITH THESE COWARDS FROM TIME TO TIME...
...TO TEACH THE OTHERS A LESSON.
!
GLARE
THEY NEED TO SEE...
...HOW POWERFUL I AM!

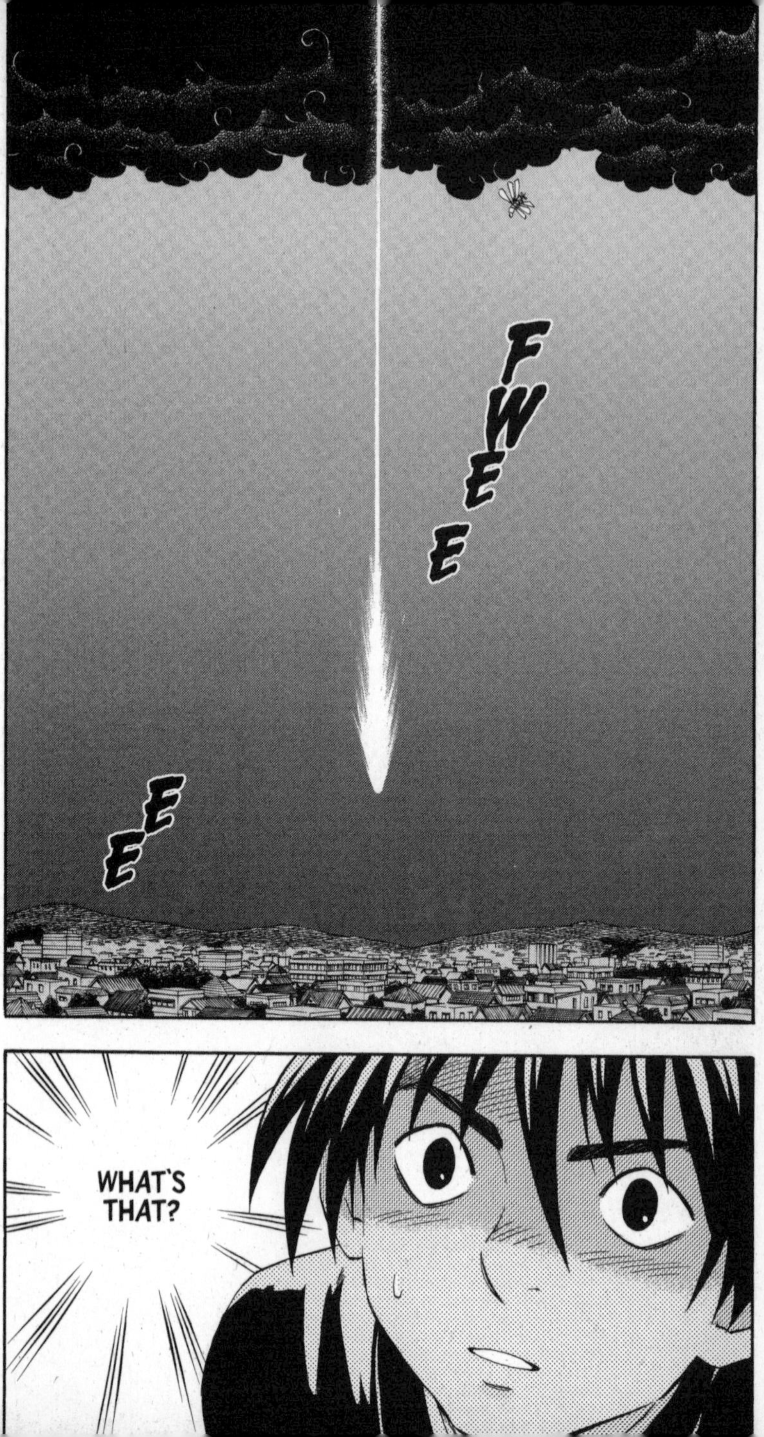
FWEEEE
WHAT'S THAT?

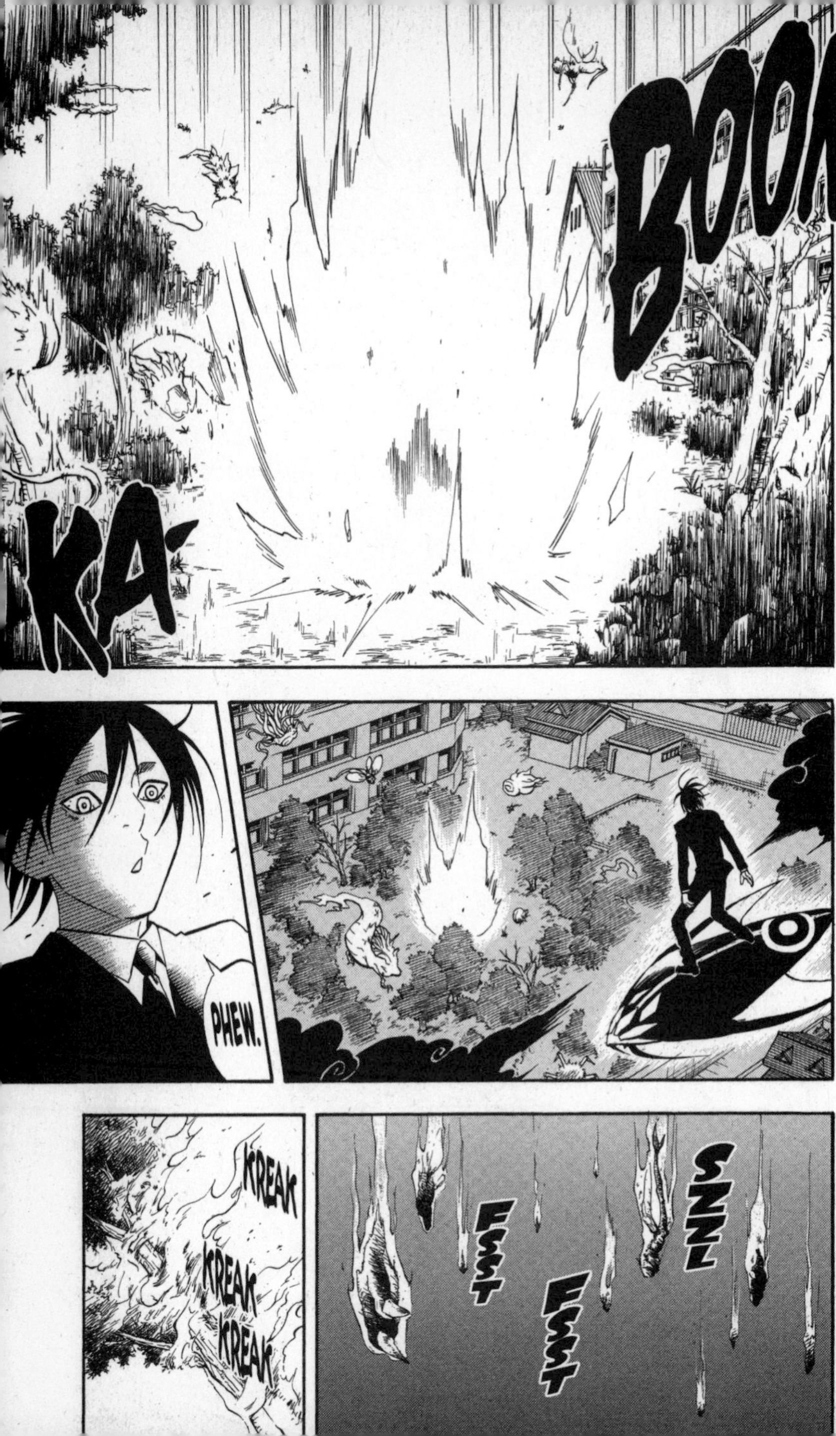
BOOM
KA
PHEW.
SZZL
FSST
FSST
KREAK
KREAK
KREAK

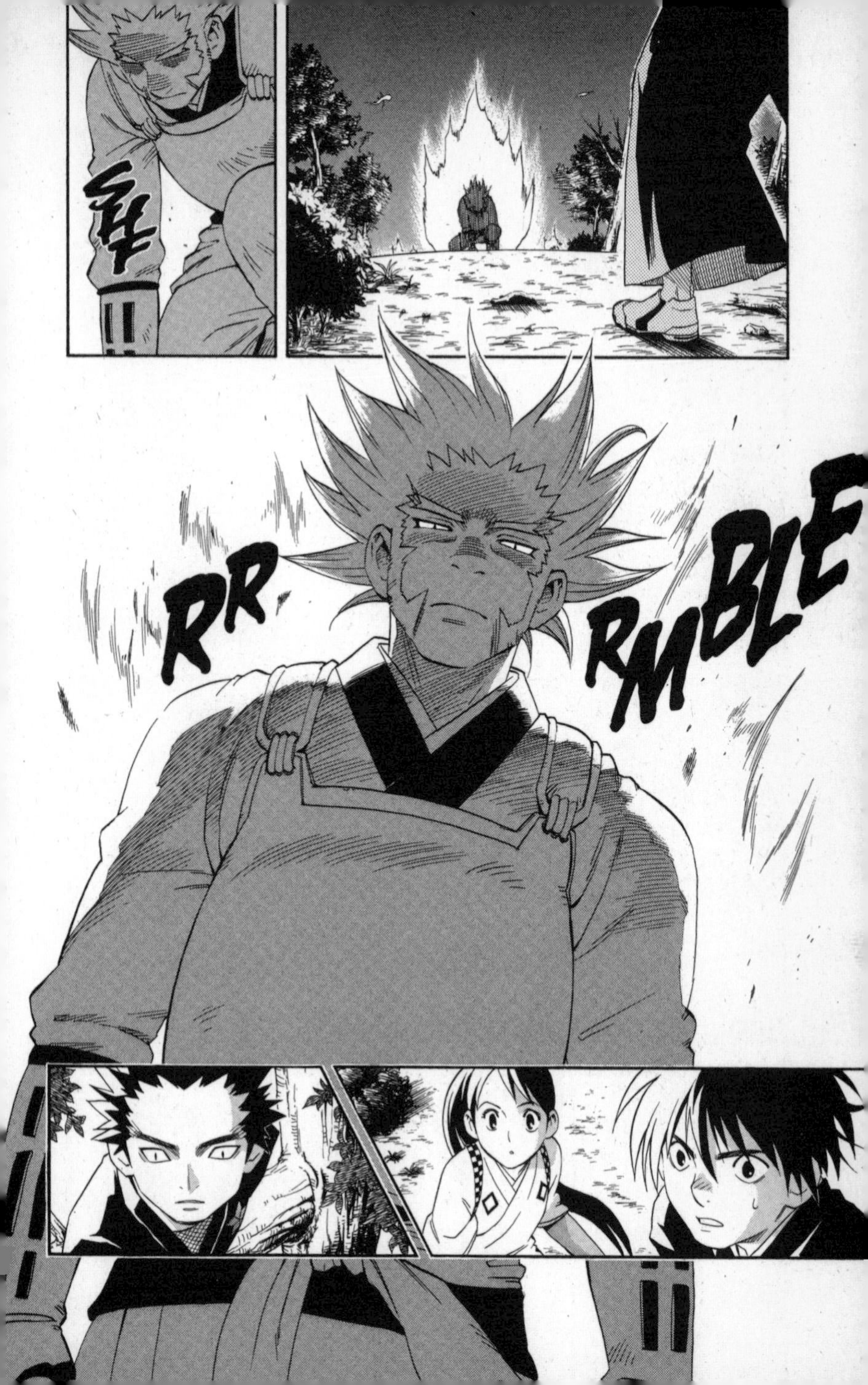
RR
RMBLE

Chapter 90:
Alliance

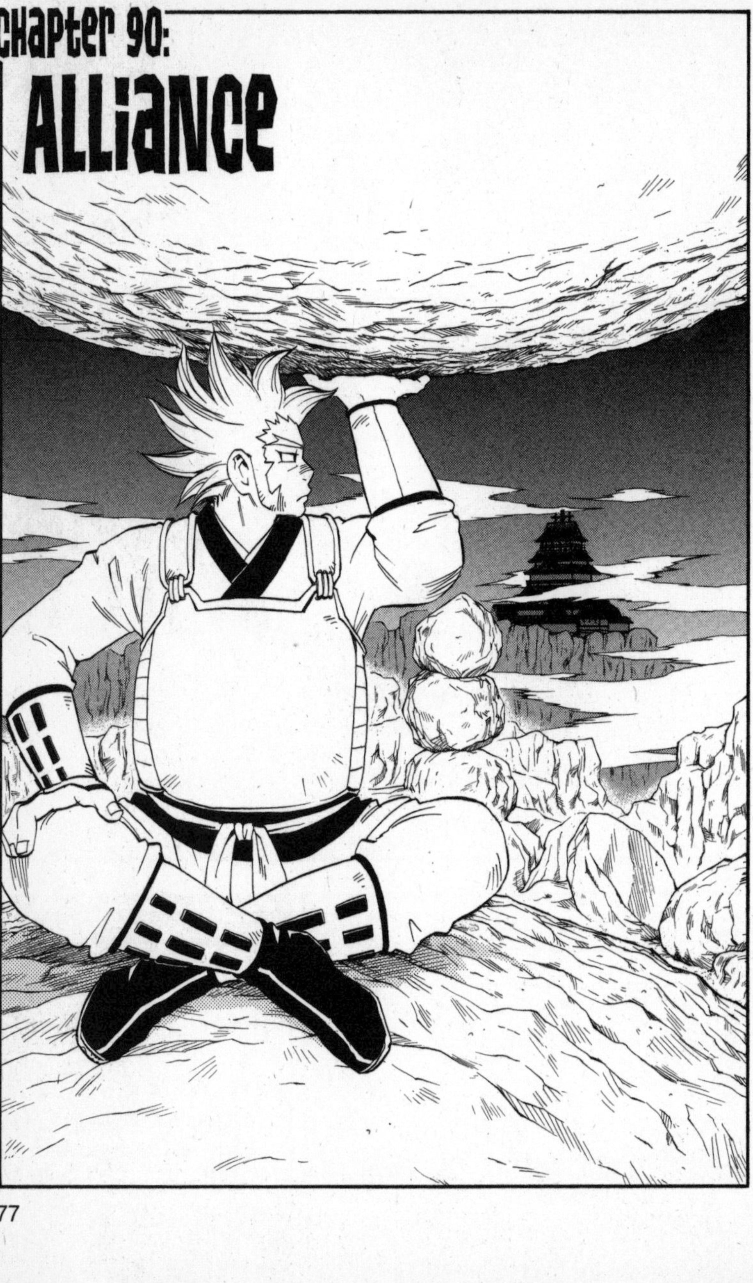

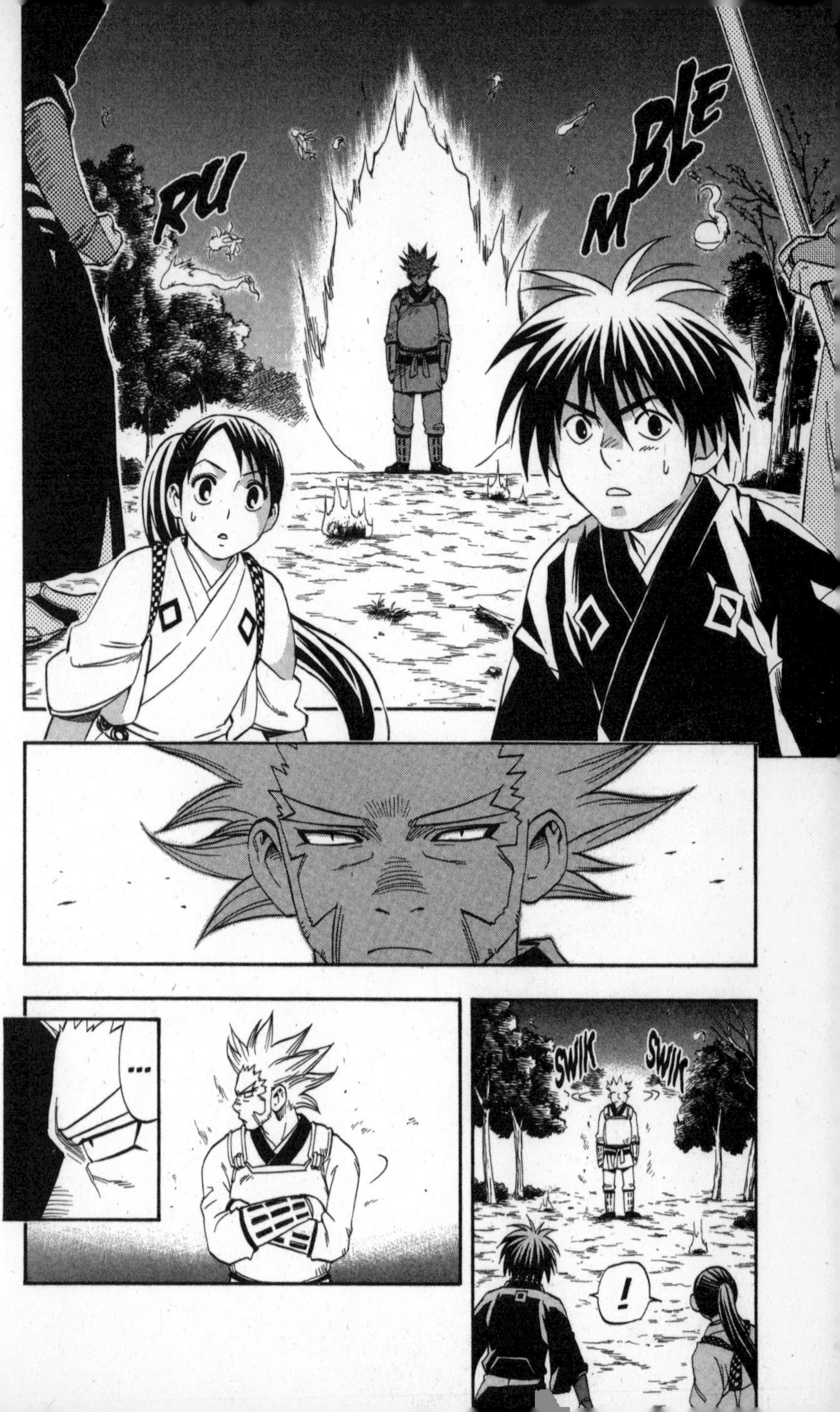
RUMBLE
SWIK SWIK
!
...

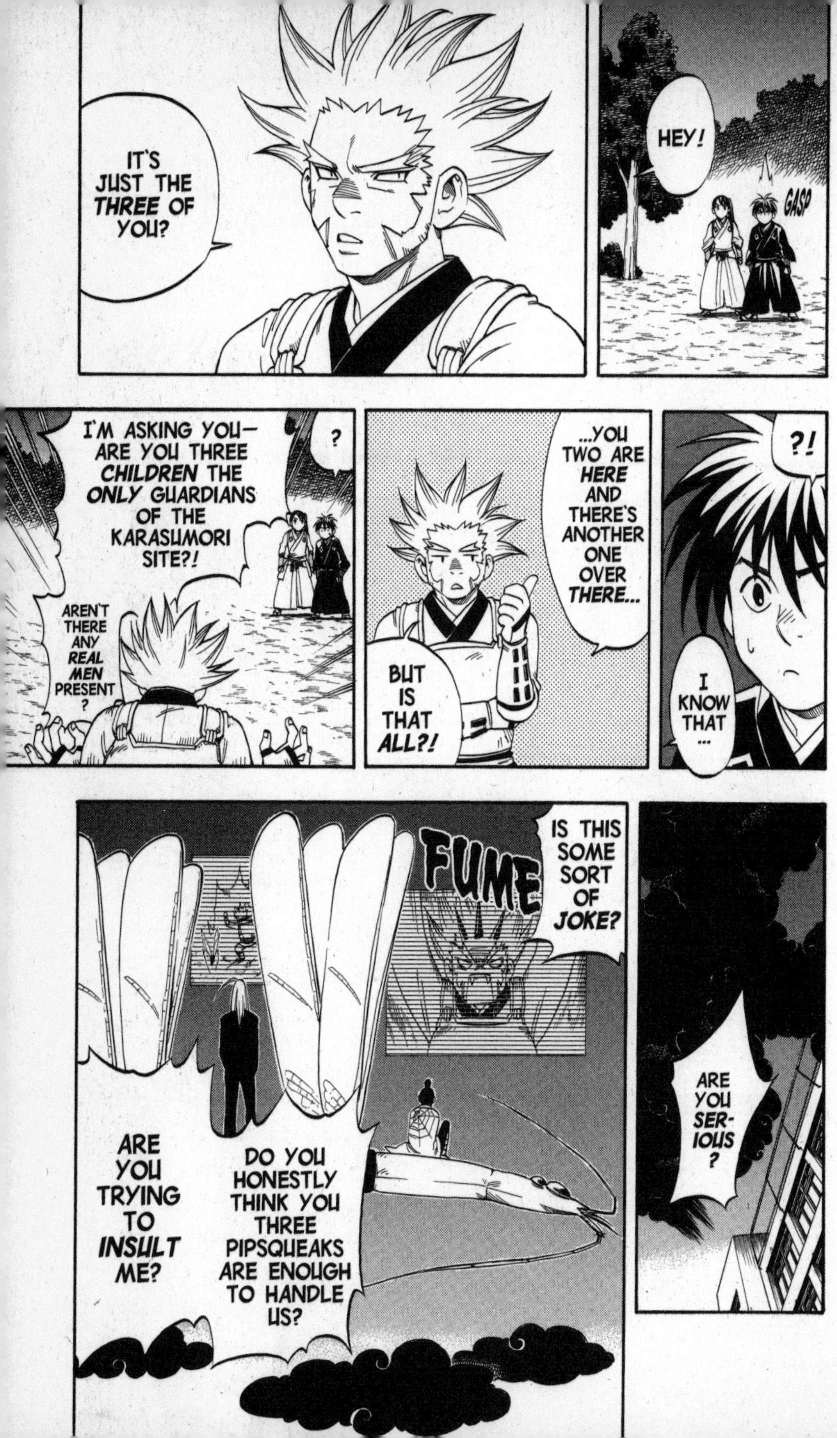
HEY!
GASP
IT'S JUST THE THREE OF YOU?
?!
I KNOW THAT ...
...YOU TWO ARE HERE AND THERE'S ANOTHER ONE OVER THERE...
BUT IS THAT ALL?!
?
I'M ASKING YOU— ARE YOU THREE CHILDREN THE ONLY GUARDIANS OF THE KARASUMORI SITE?!
AREN'T THERE ANY REAL MEN PRESENT?
ARE YOU SER-IOUS?
FUME
IS THIS SOME SORT OF JOKE?
DO YOU HONESTLY THINK YOU THREE PIPSQUEAKS ARE ENOUGH TO HANDLE US?
ARE YOU TRYING TO INSULT ME?

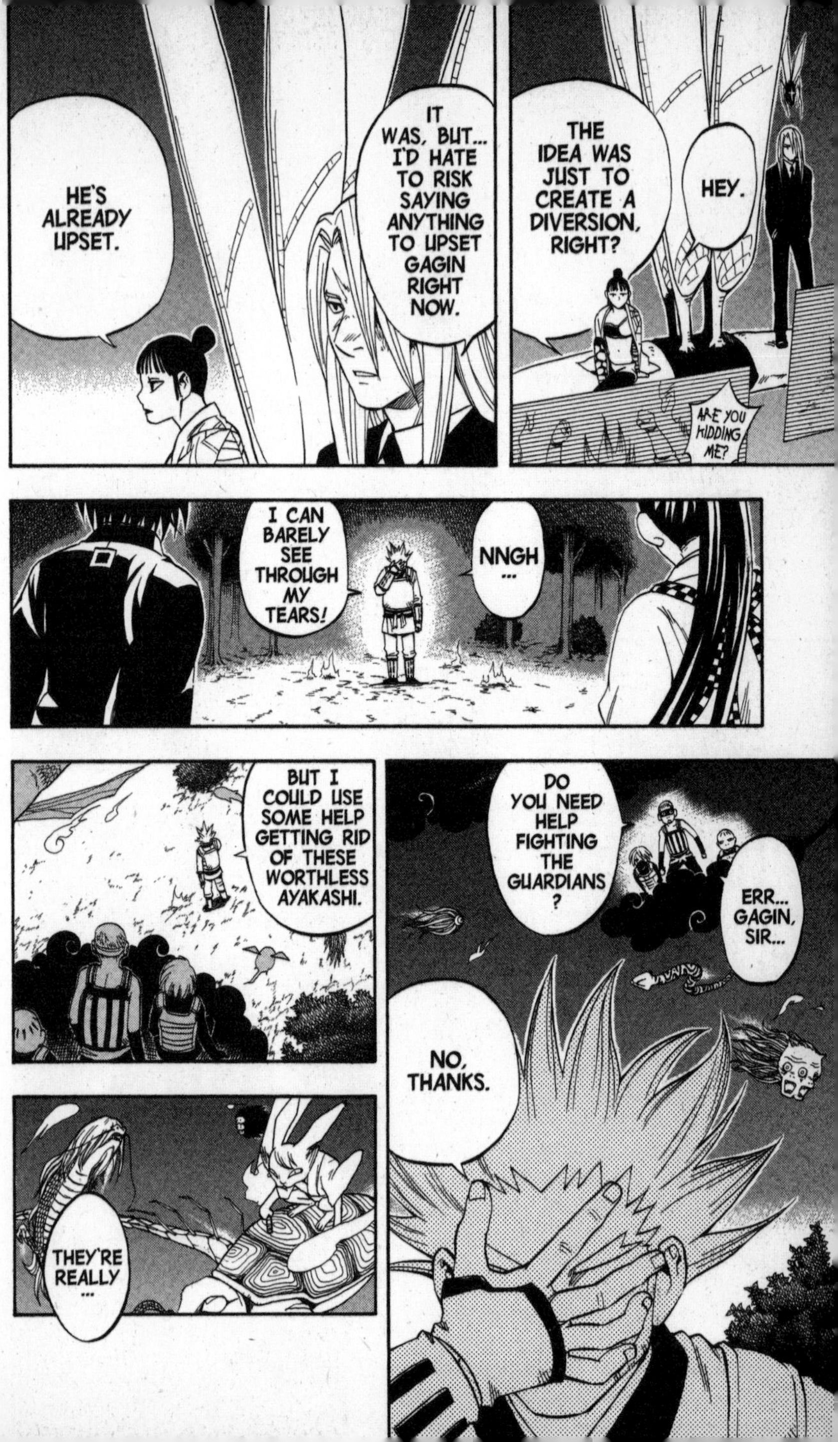
HEY.
THE IDEA WAS JUST TO CREATE A DIVERSION, RIGHT?
ARE YOU KIDDING ME?
IT WAS, BUT... I'D HATE TO RISK SAYING ANYTHING TO UPSET GAGIN RIGHT NOW.
HE'S ALREADY UPSET.
NNGH ...
I CAN BARELY SEE THROUGH MY TEARS!
ERR... GAGIN, SIR...
DO YOU NEED HELP FIGHTING THE GUARDIANS ?
NO, THANKS.
BUT I COULD USE SOME HELP GETTING RID OF THESE WORTHLESS AYAKASHI.
THEY'RE REALLY ...

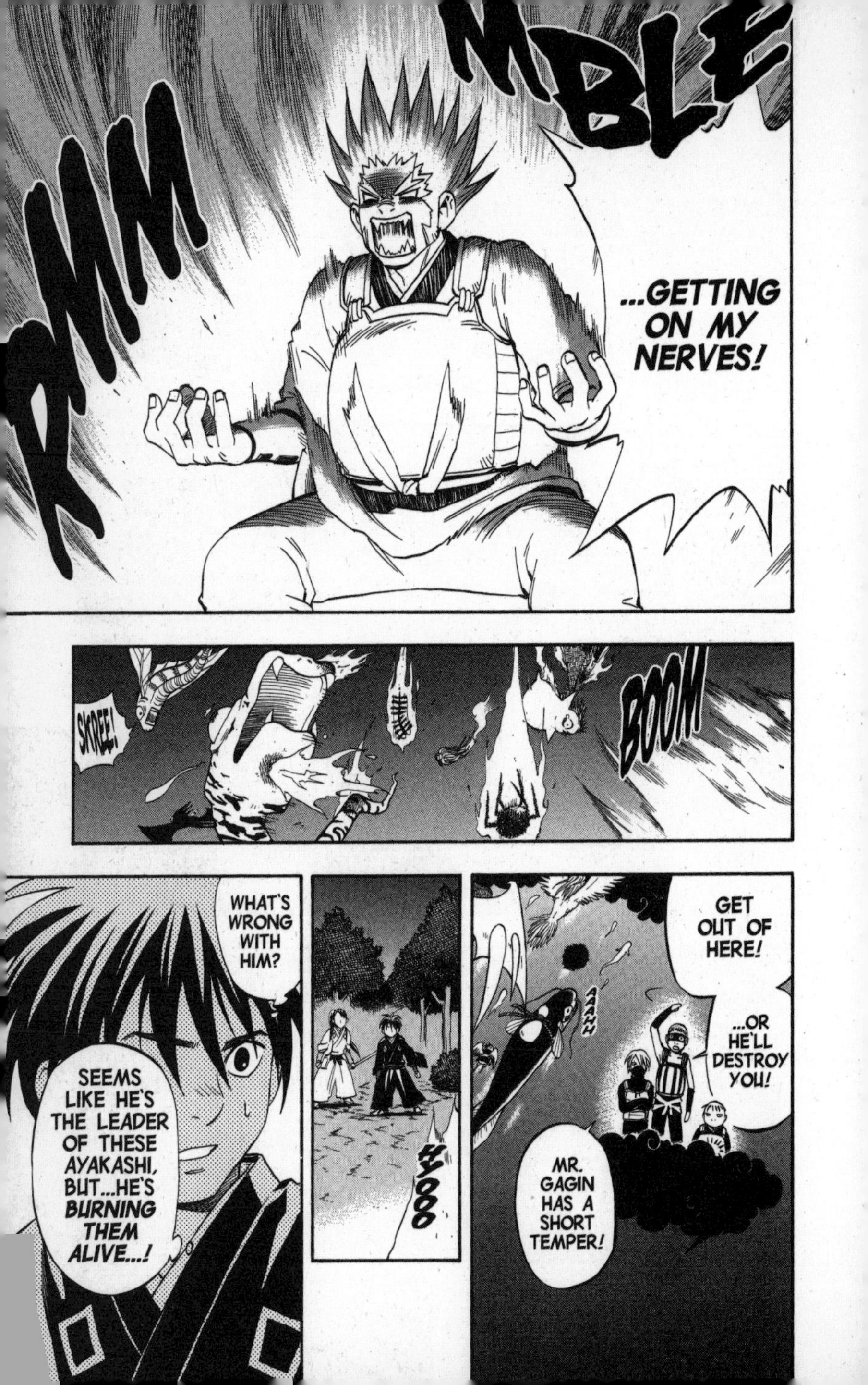
MBLE
...GETTING ON MY NERVES!
RMM
BOOM
SKREE!
GET OUT OF HERE!
...OR HE'LL DESTROY YOU!
AAAHH
MR. GAGIN HAS A SHORT TEMPER!
HYOOO
WHAT'S WRONG WITH HIM?
SEEMS LIKE HE'S THE LEADER OF THESE AYAKASHI, BUT...HE'S BURNING THEM ALIVE...!

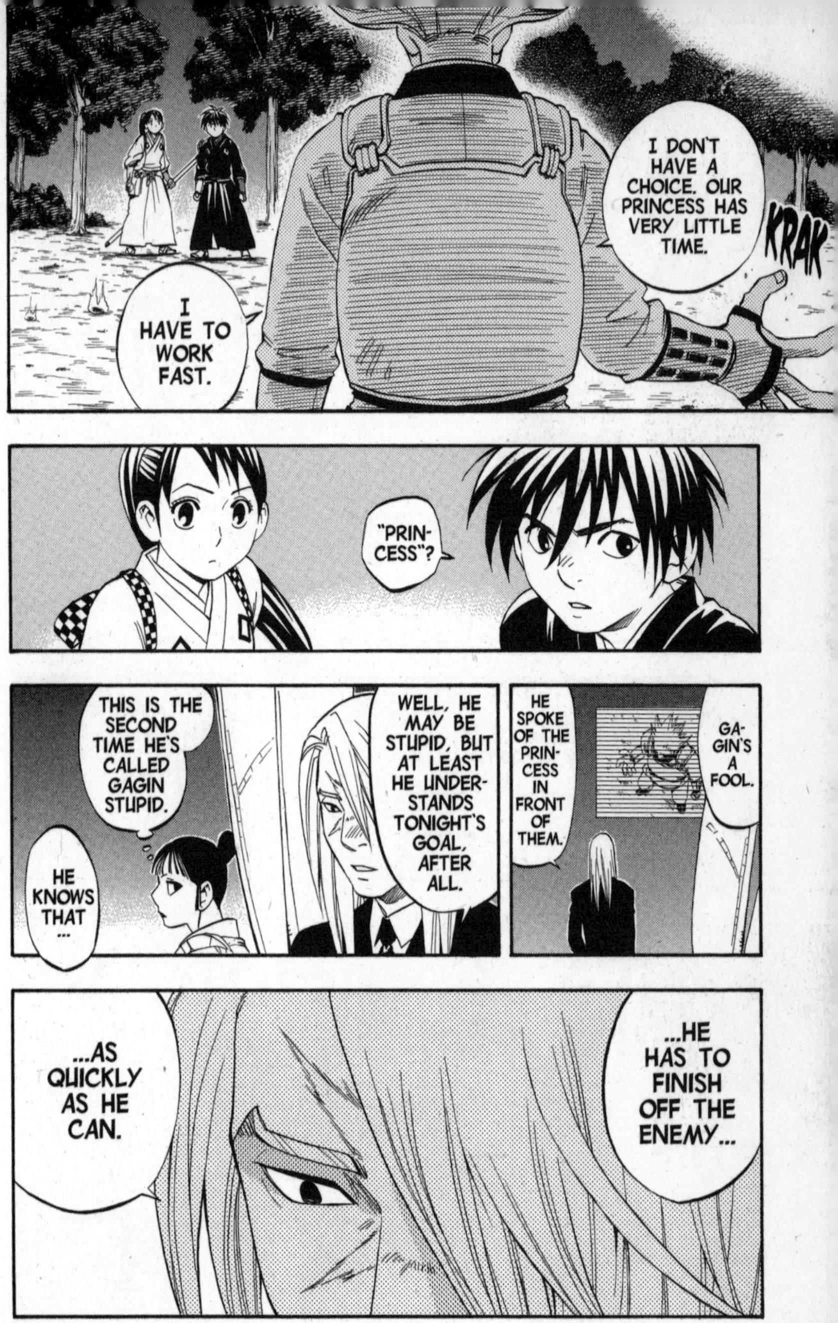
I DON'T HAVE A CHOICE. OUR PRINCESS HAS VERY LITTLE TIME.
KRAK
I HAVE TO WORK FAST.
"PRIN-CESS"?
GA-GIN'S A FOOL.
HE SPOKE OF THE PRIN-CESS IN FRONT OF THEM.
WELL, HE MAY BE STUPID, BUT AT LEAST HE UNDER-STANDS TONIGHT'S GOAL, AFTER ALL.
THIS IS THE SECOND TIME HE'S CALLED GAGIN STUPID.
HE KNOWS THAT ...
...HE HAS TO FINISH OFF THE ENEMY...
...AS QUICKLY AS HE CAN.

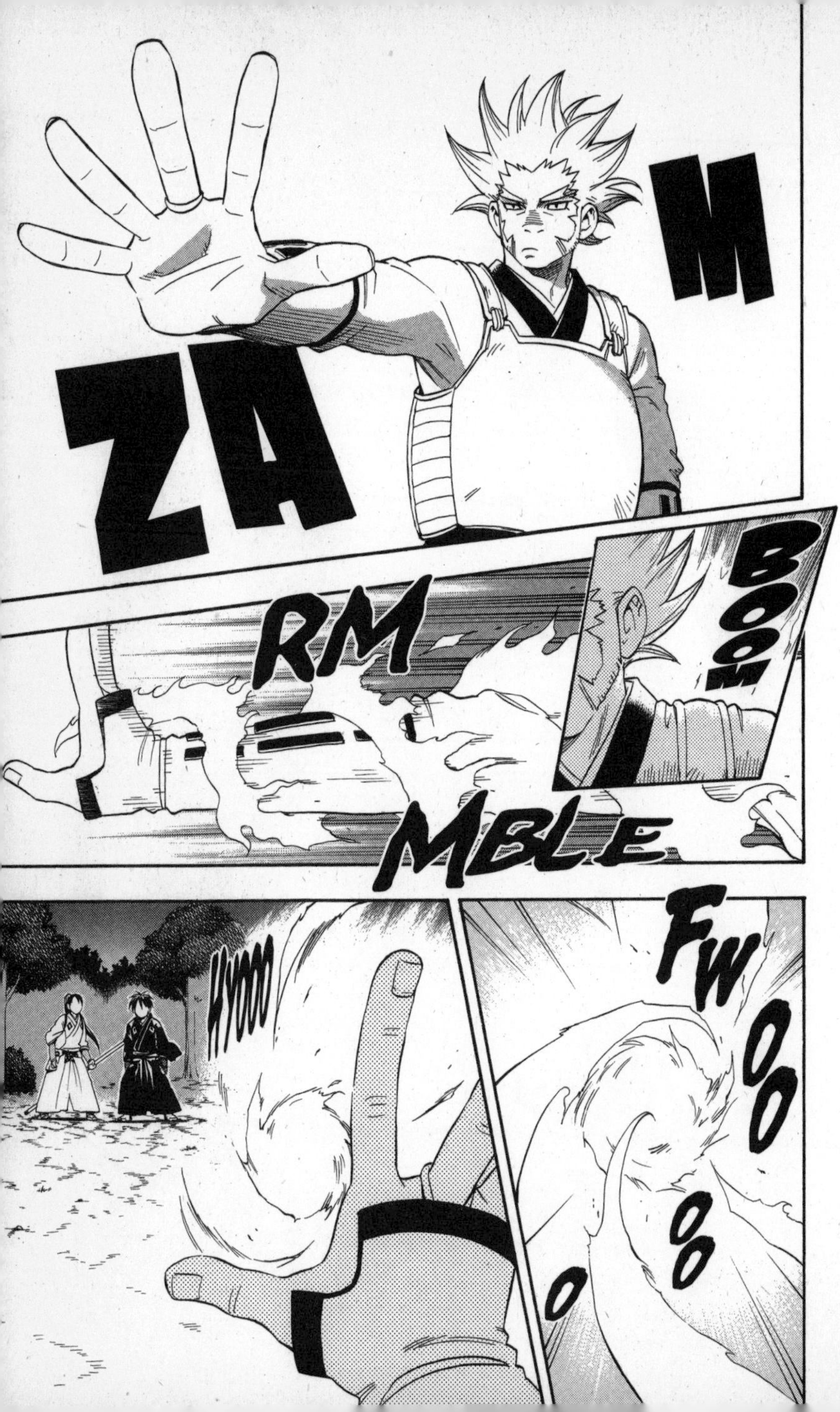
ZA
M
BOOOM
RM
MBLE
FWOOOOOO
HYOOO

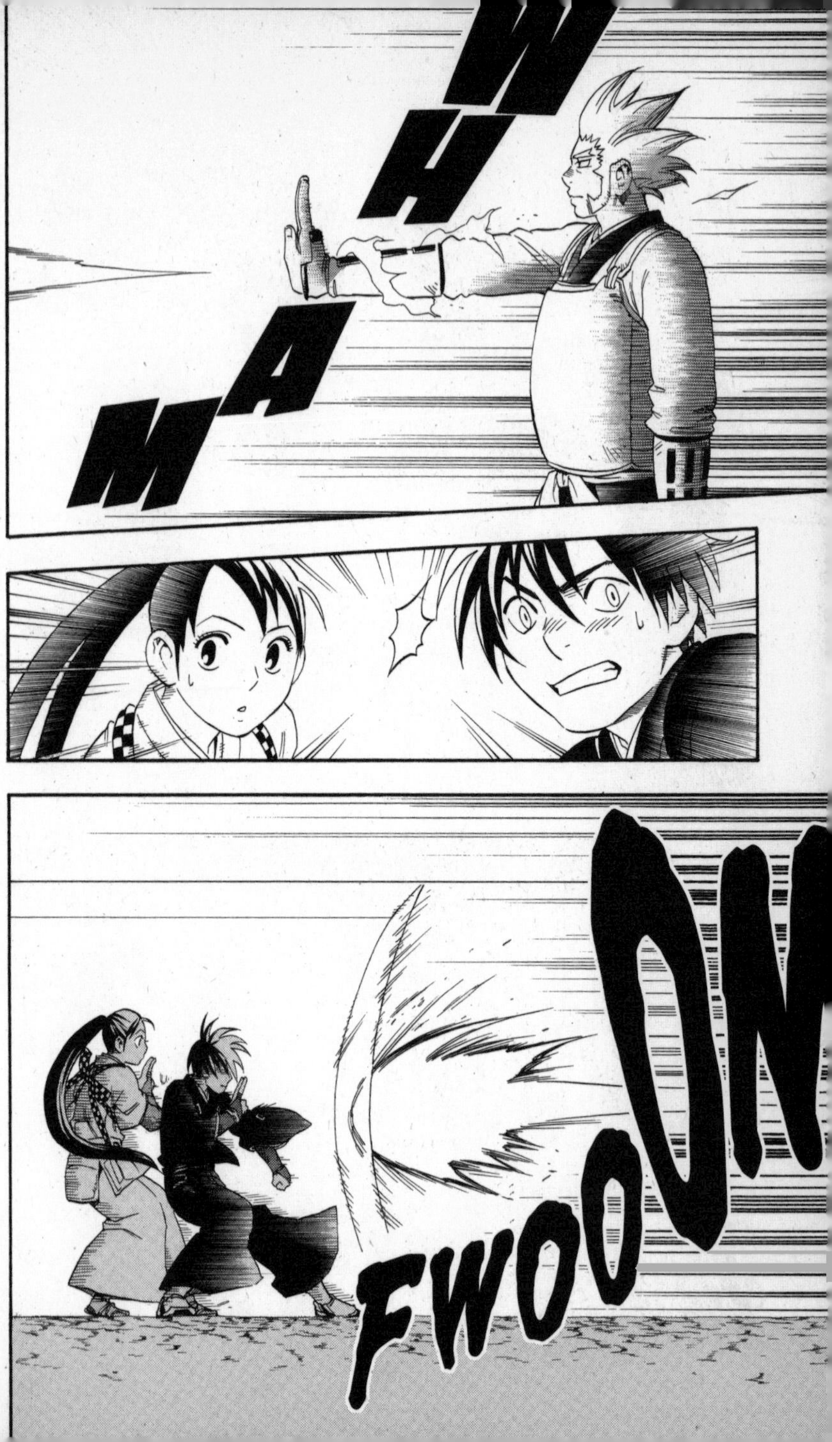
WHAM
FWOOON

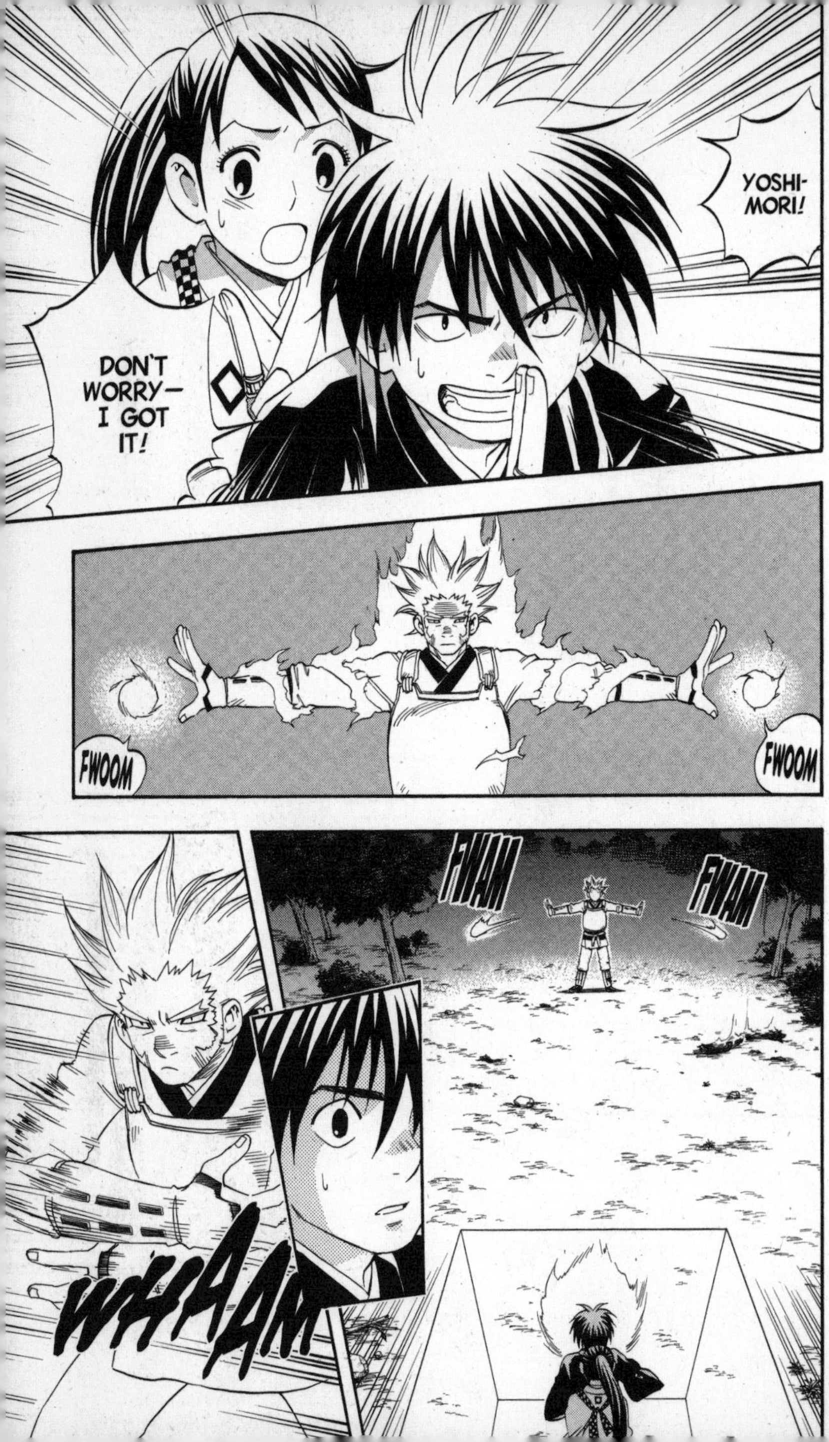
YOSHI-MORI!
DON'T WORRY— I GOT IT!
FWOOM
FWOOM
FWAM
FWAM
WHAAM

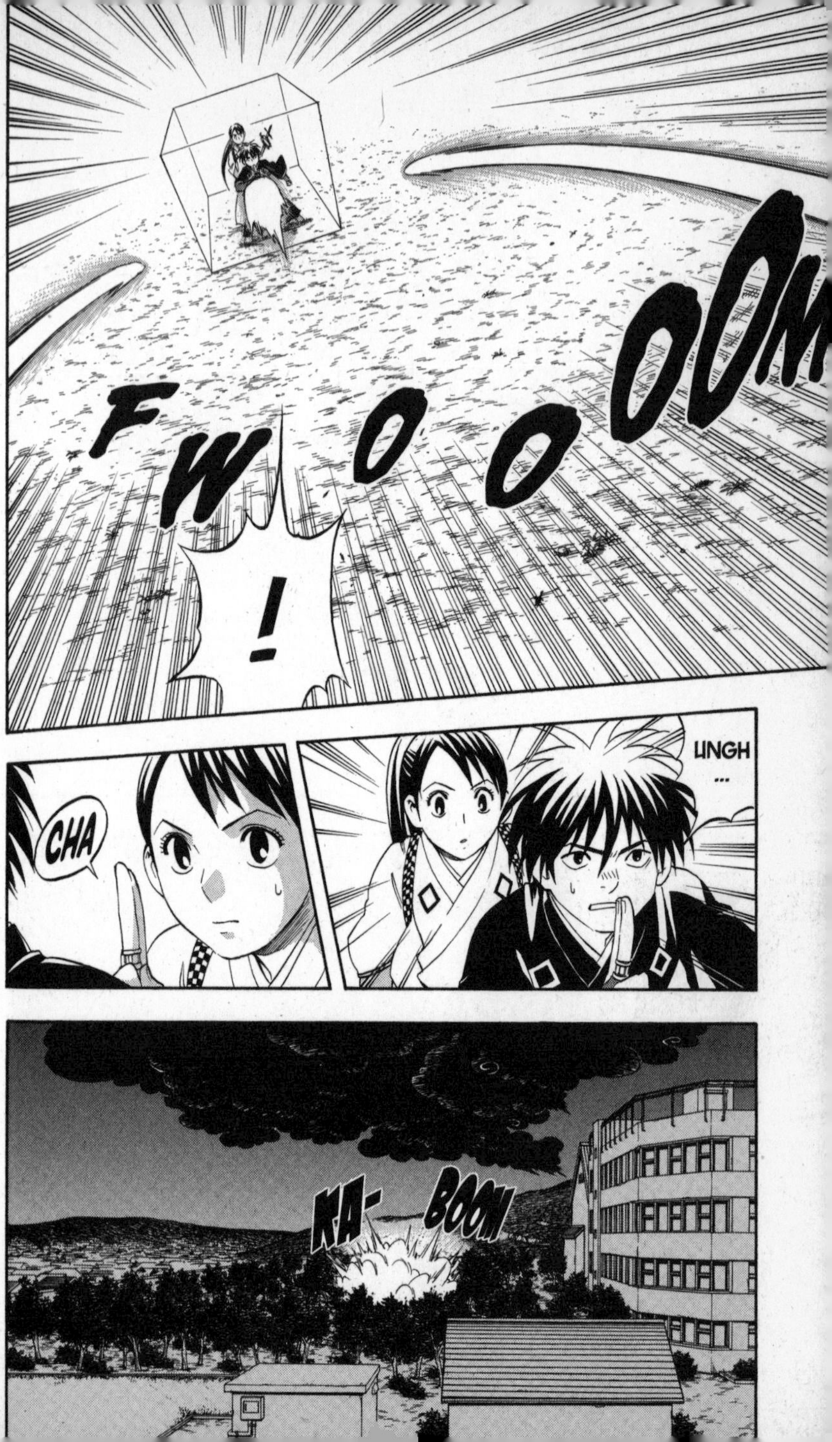
FWOOOOM
!
UNGH ...
CHA
KA-BOOM

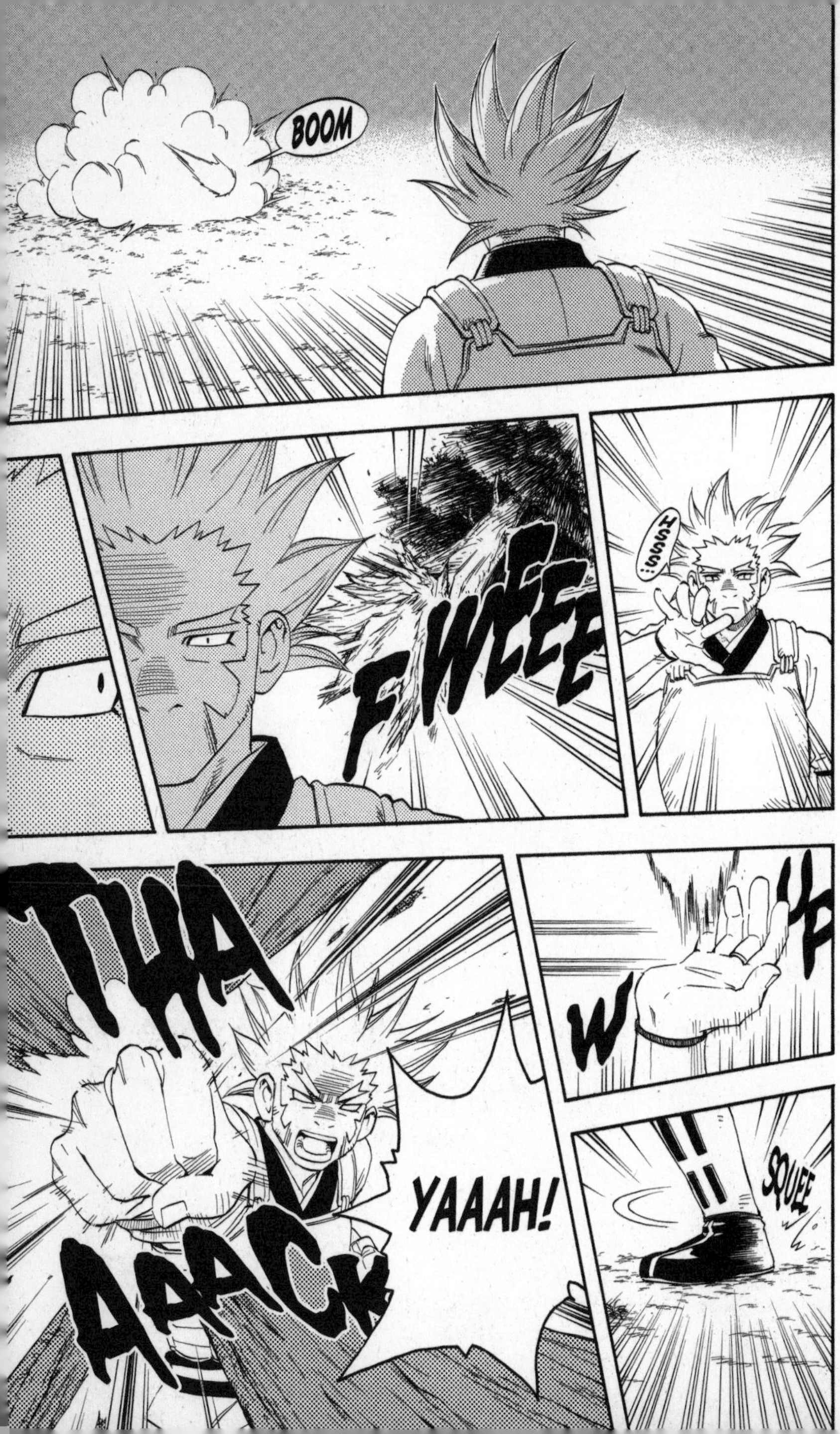
BOOM
HSSS!!
FWEE
WUP
SQUEE
THA AAACK
YAAAH!

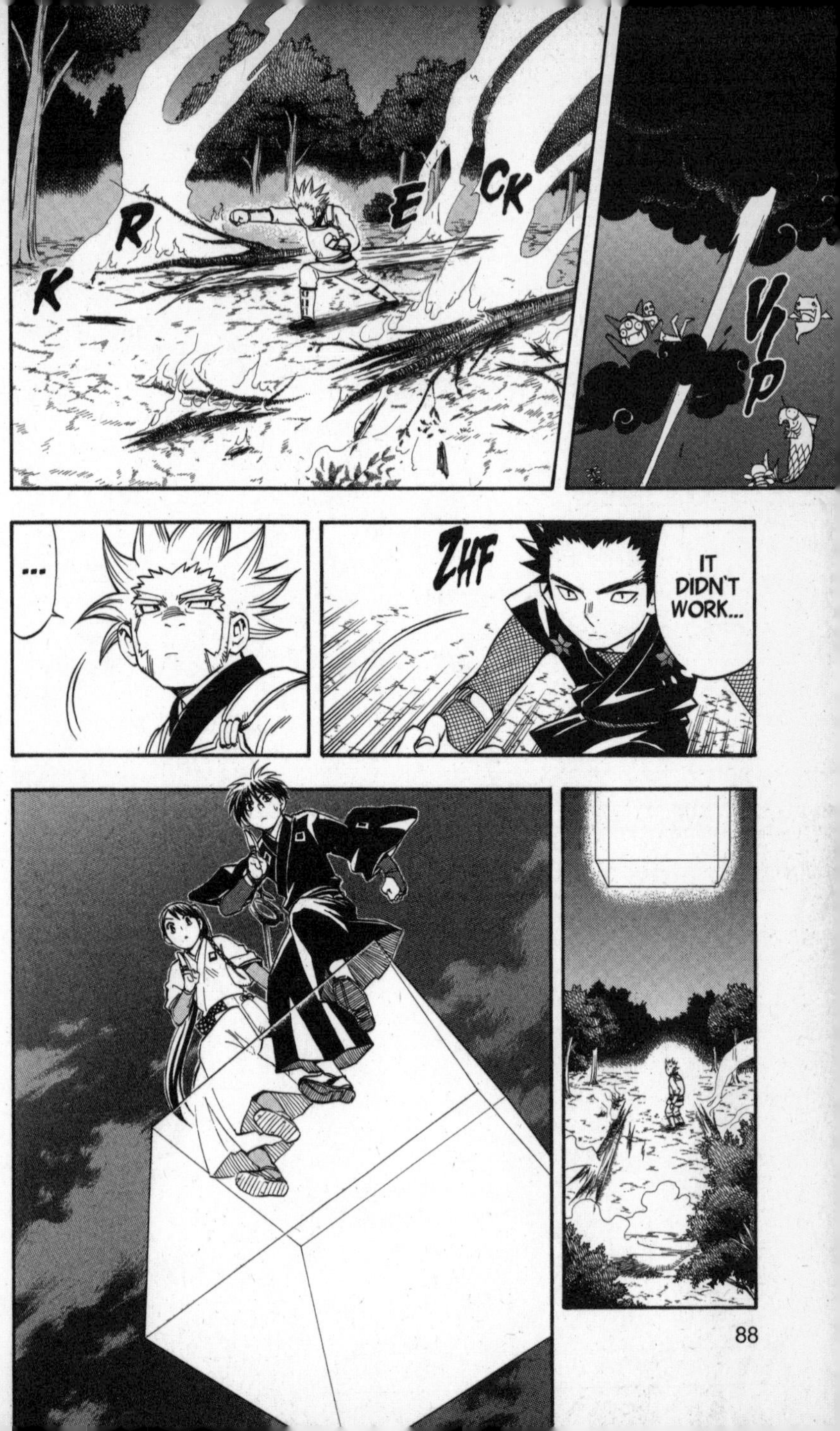
VIP
KRECK
ZHF
IT DIDN'T WORK...
...

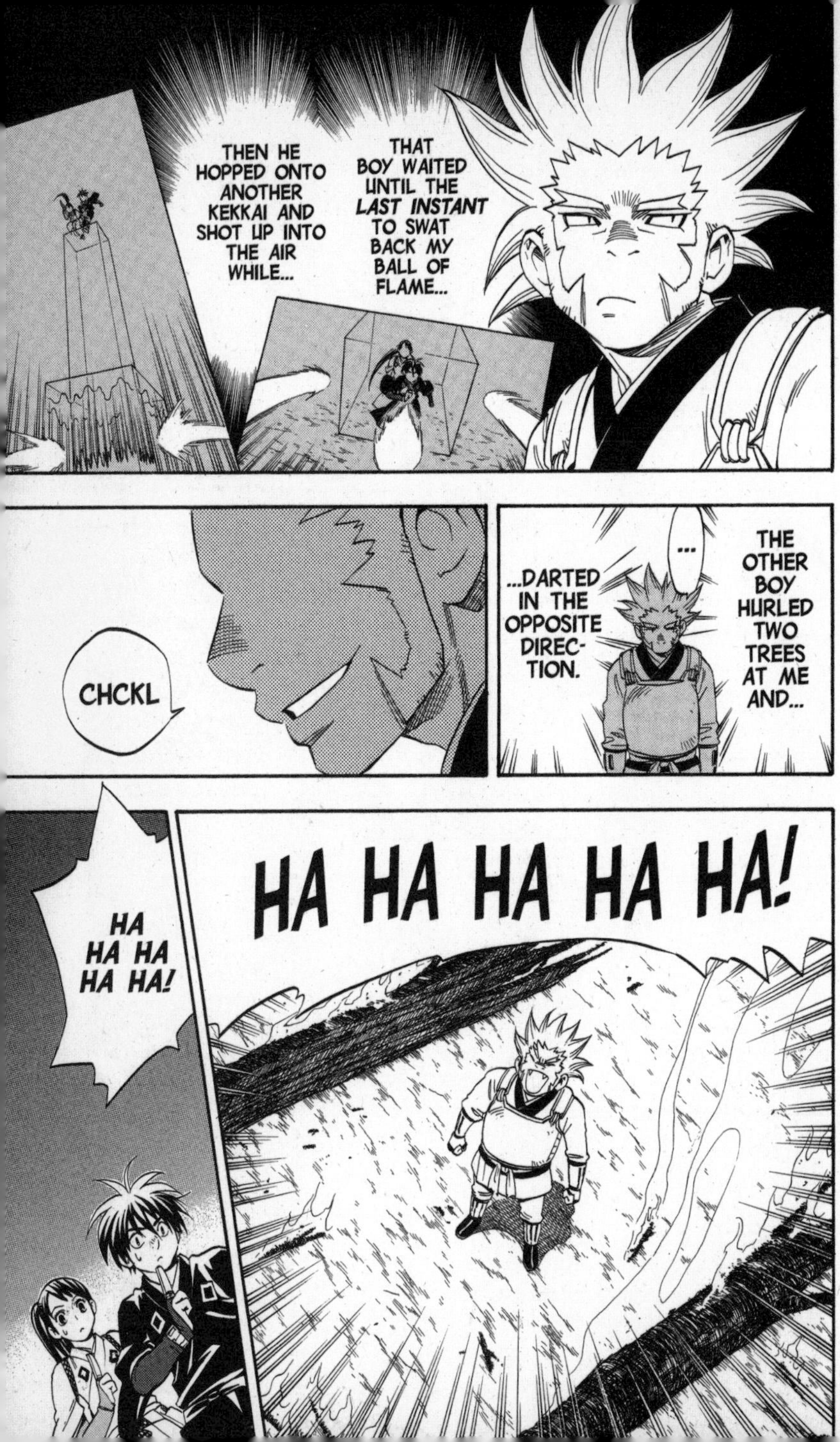
THAT BOY WAITED UNTIL THE *LAST INSTANT* TO SWAT BACK MY BALL OF FLAME...
THEN HE HOPPED ONTO ANOTHER KEKKAI AND SHOT UP INTO THE AIR WHILE...
THE OTHER BOY HURLED TWO TREES AT ME AND...
...
...DARTED IN THE OPPOSITE DIRECTION.
CHCKL
HA HA HA HA HA HA!
HA HA HA HA HA!

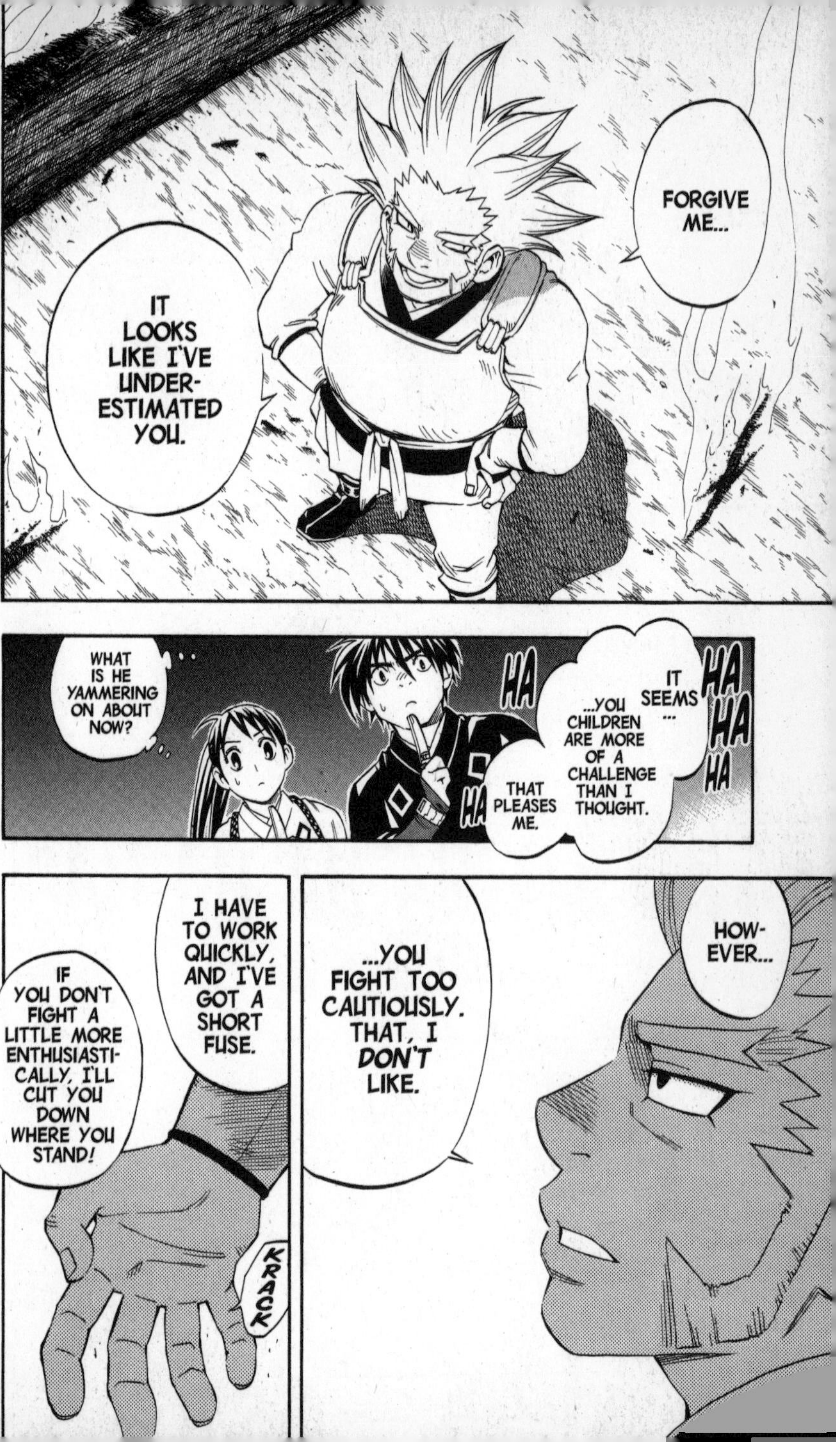
FORGIVE ME...
IT LOOKS LIKE I'VE UNDER-ESTIMATED YOU.
HA HA HA HA
IT SEEMS... ...YOU CHILDREN ARE MORE OF A CHALLENGE THAN I THOUGHT.
THAT PLEASES ME.
HA HA
WHAT IS HE YAMMERING ON ABOUT NOW?
HOW-EVER...
...YOU FIGHT TOO CAUTIOUSLY. THAT, I *DON'T* LIKE.
I HAVE TO WORK QUICKLY, AND I'VE GOT A SHORT FUSE.
IF YOU DON'T FIGHT A LITTLE MORE ENTHUSIASTI-CALLY, I'LL CUT YOU DOWN WHERE YOU STAND!
KRACK

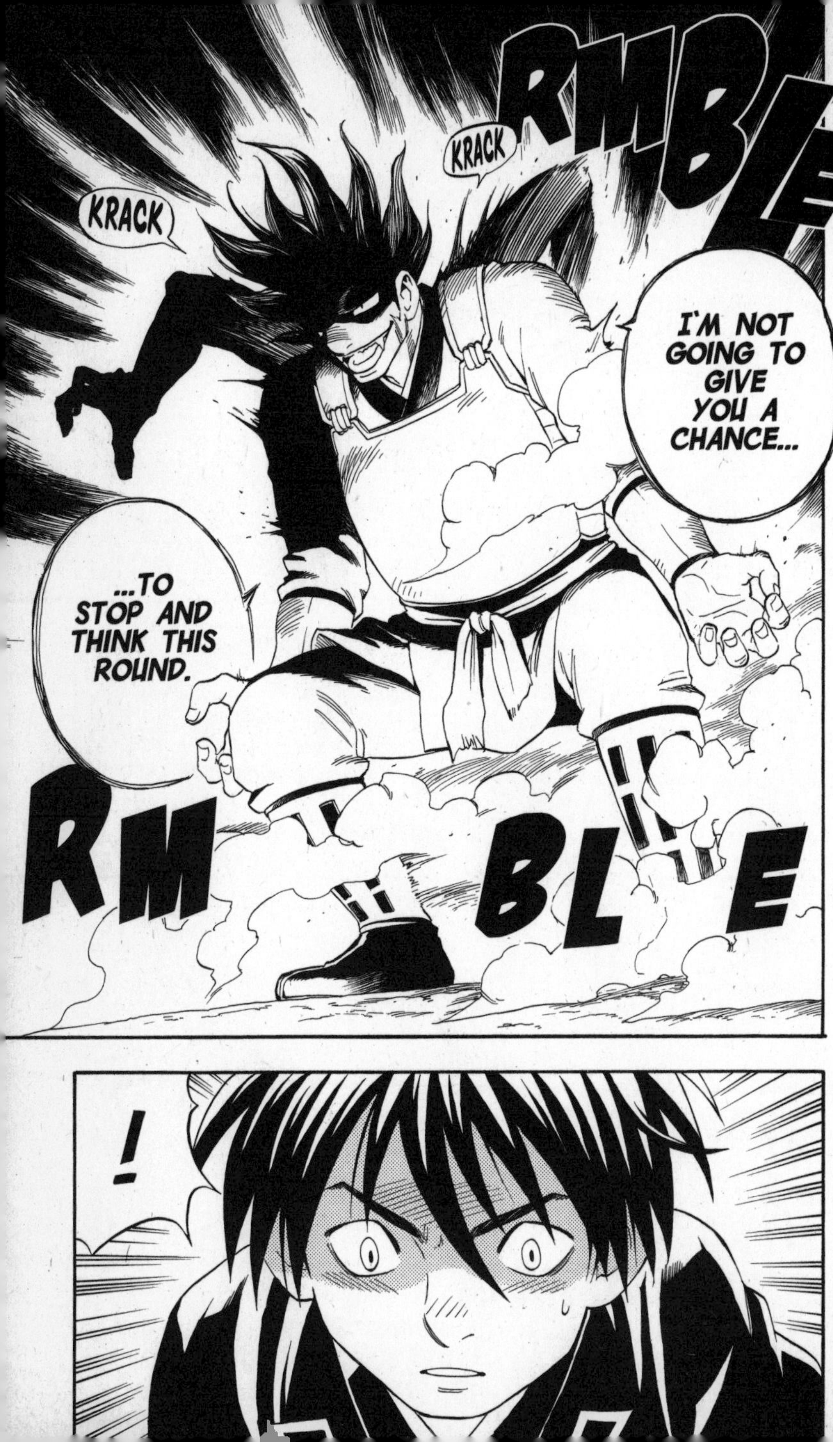
RMBLE
KRACK
KRACK
I'M NOT GOING TO GIVE YOU A CHANCE...
...TO STOP AND THINK THIS ROUND.
RMBLE
!

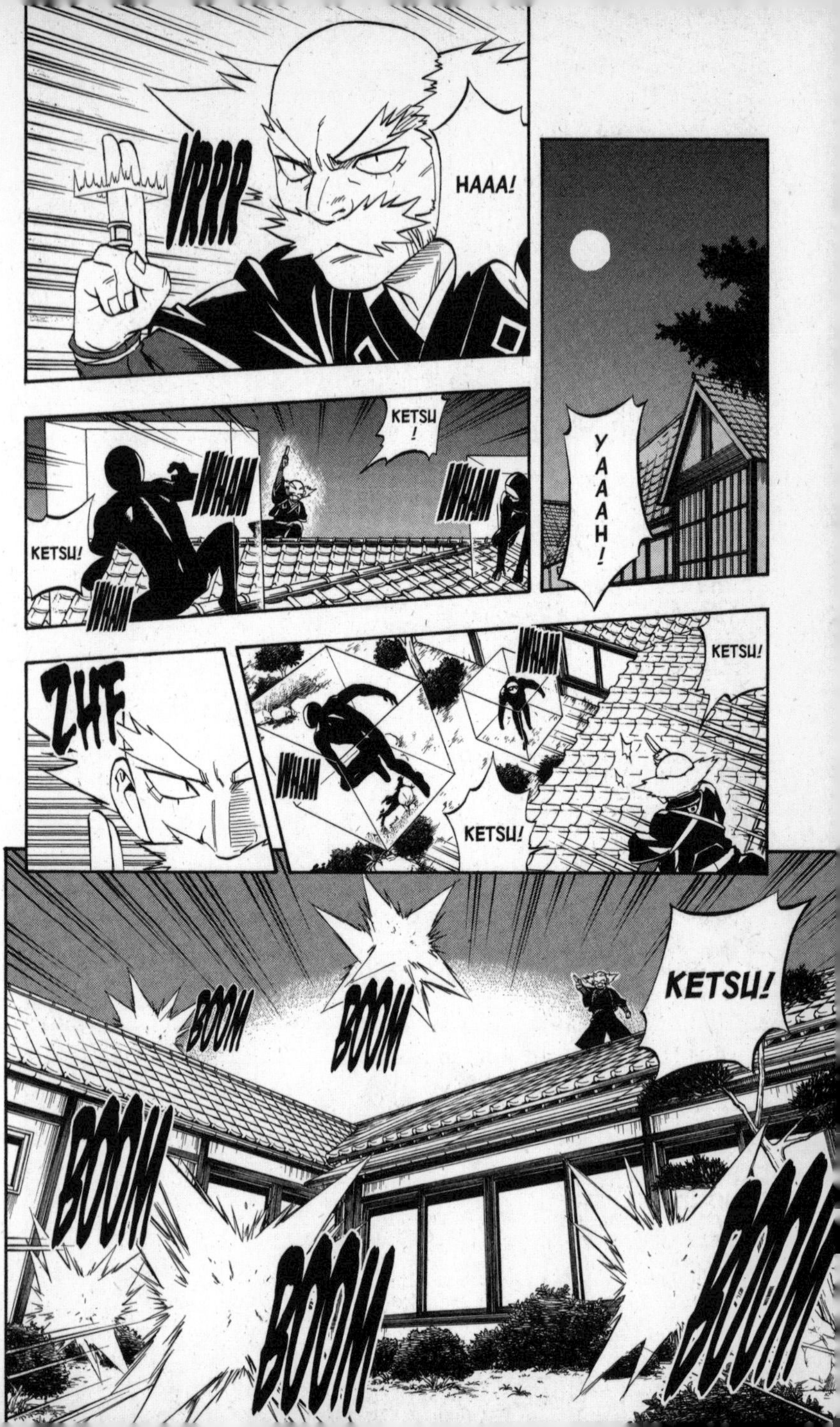
YAAAAH!
HAAA!
VRRR
KETSU!
WHAM
WHAM
KETSU!
WHAM
KETSU!
WHAM
KETSU!
WHAM
ZHF
KETSU!
BOOM
BOOM
BOOM
BOOM
BOOM

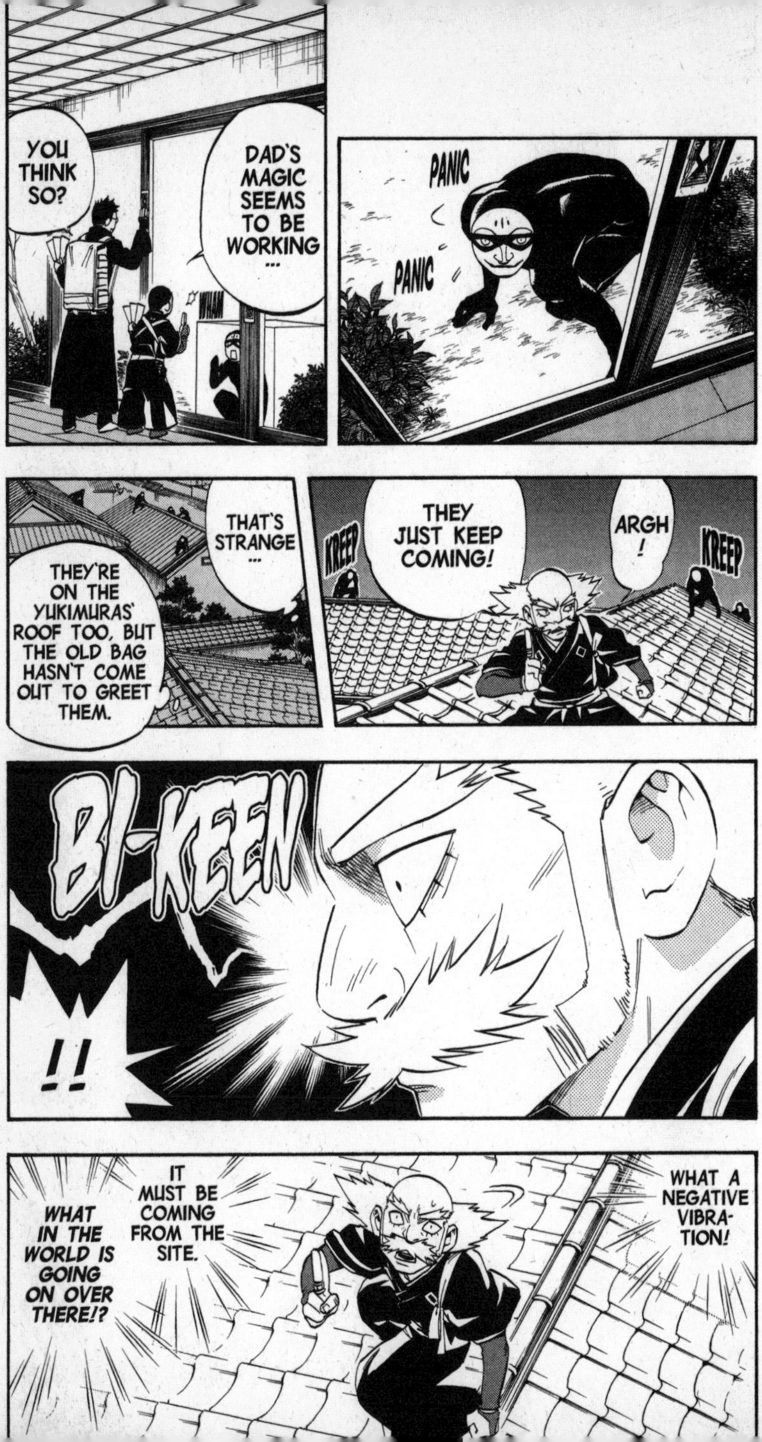
PANIC
PANIC
DAD'S MAGIC SEEMS TO BE WORKING...
WHAM
YOU THINK SO?
ARGH!
KREEP
THEY JUST KEEP COMING!
KREEP
THAT'S STRANGE...
THEY'RE ON THE YUKIMURAS' ROOF TOO, BUT THE OLD BAG HASN'T COME OUT TO GREET THEM.
BI-KEEN
!!
WHAT A NEGATIVE VIBRATION!
IT MUST BE COMING FROM THE SITE.
WHAT IN THE WORLD IS GOING ON OVER THERE!?

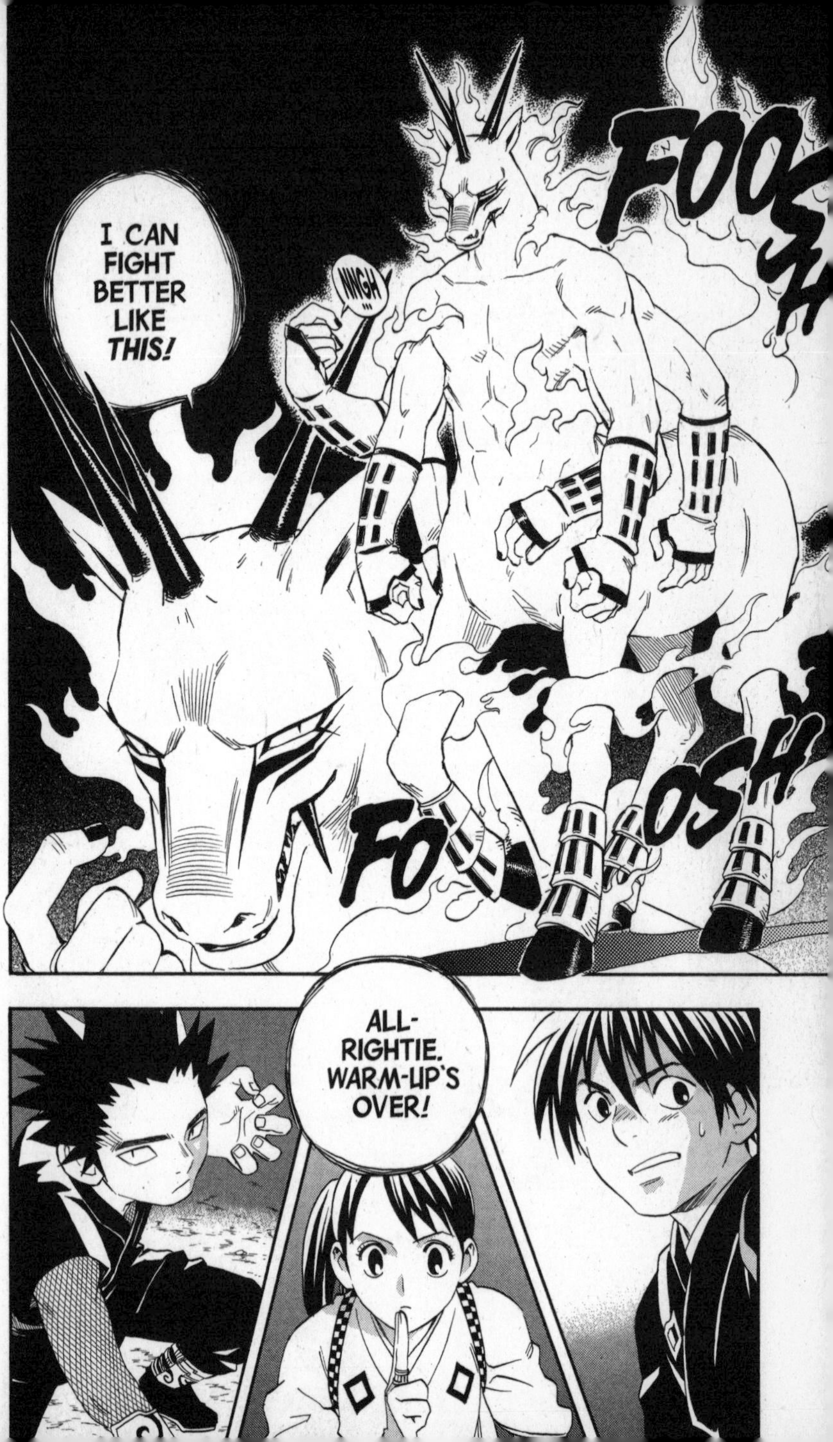
FOOSH
NNGH
I CAN FIGHT BETTER LIKE THIS!
FOOSH
ALL-RIGHTIE. WARM-UP'S OVER!

Chapter 91: Flame Monster

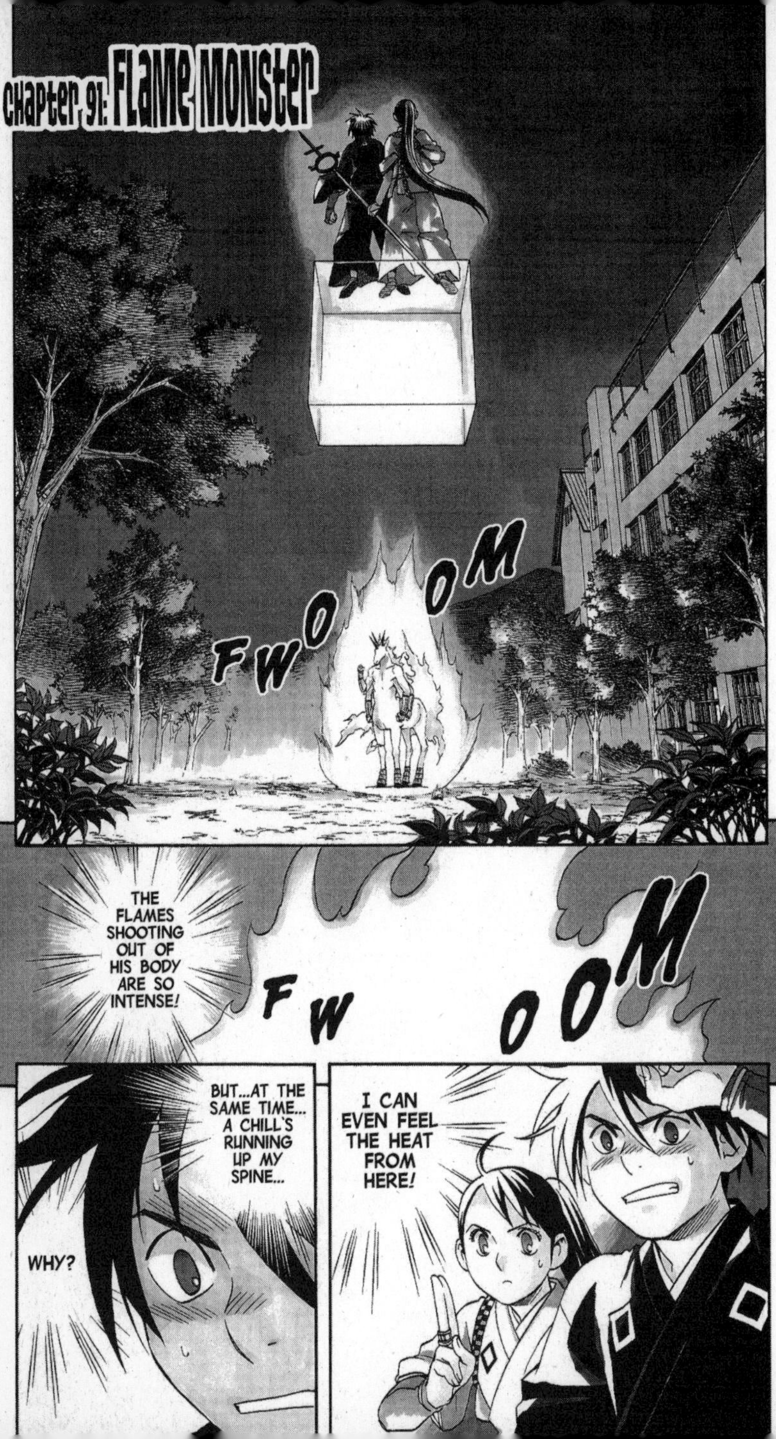
Chapter 91: Flame Monster
FWOOOM
THE FLAMES SHOOTING OUT OF HIS BODY ARE SO INTENSE!
FWOOOM
I CAN EVEN FEEL THE HEAT FROM HERE!
BUT...AT THE SAME TIME... A CHILL'S RUNNING UP MY SPINE...
WHY?

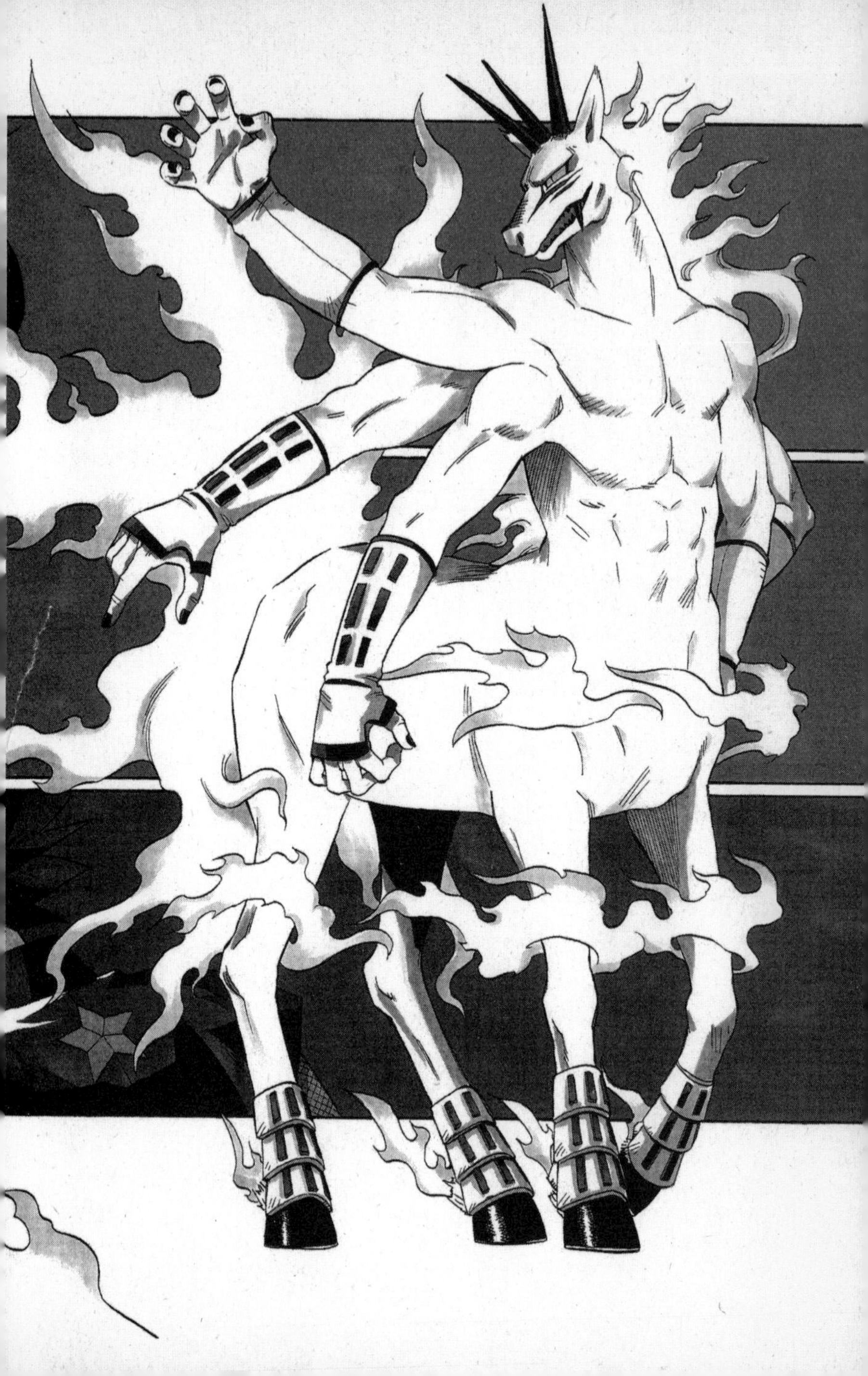

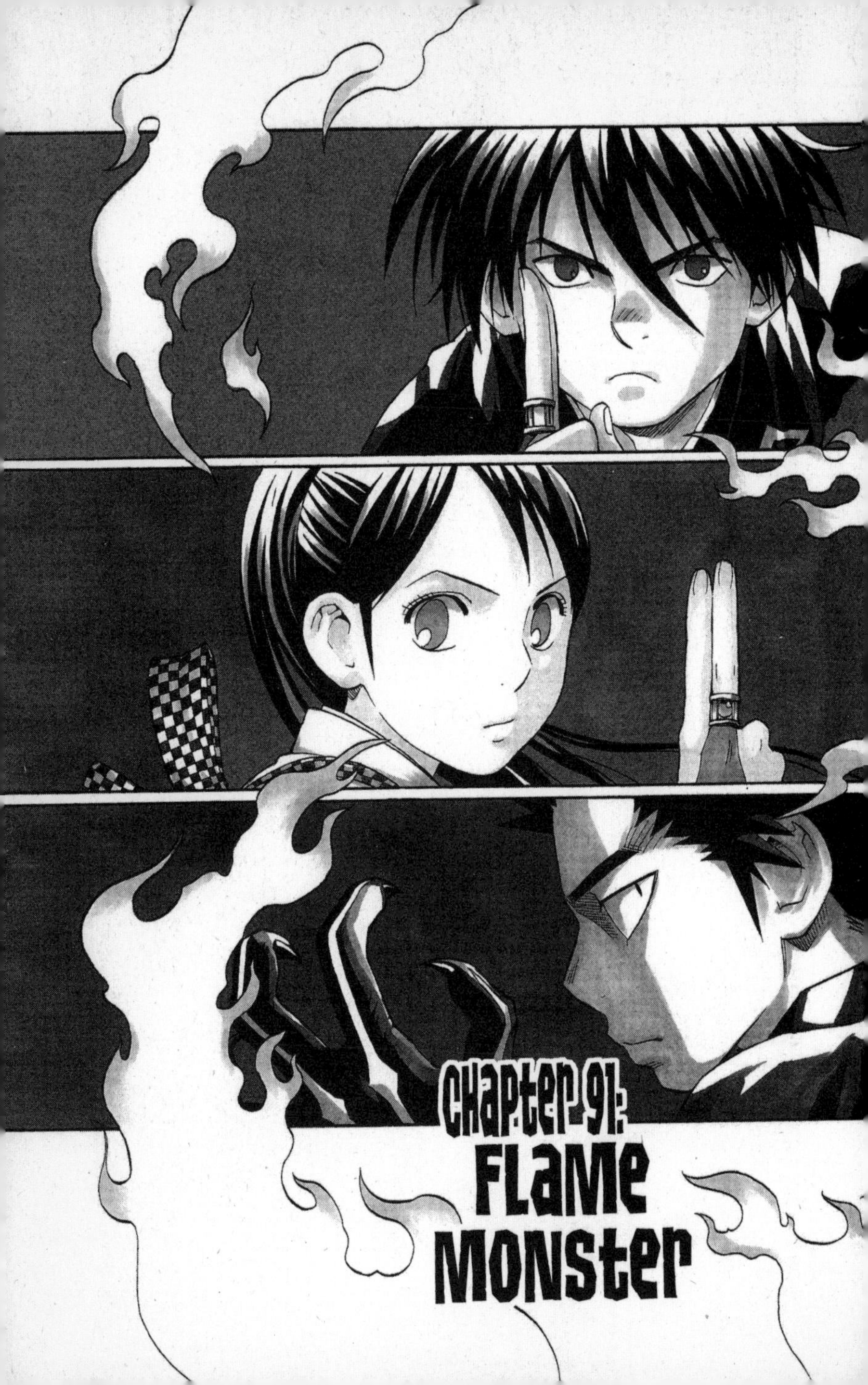
Chapter 91:
Flame Monster

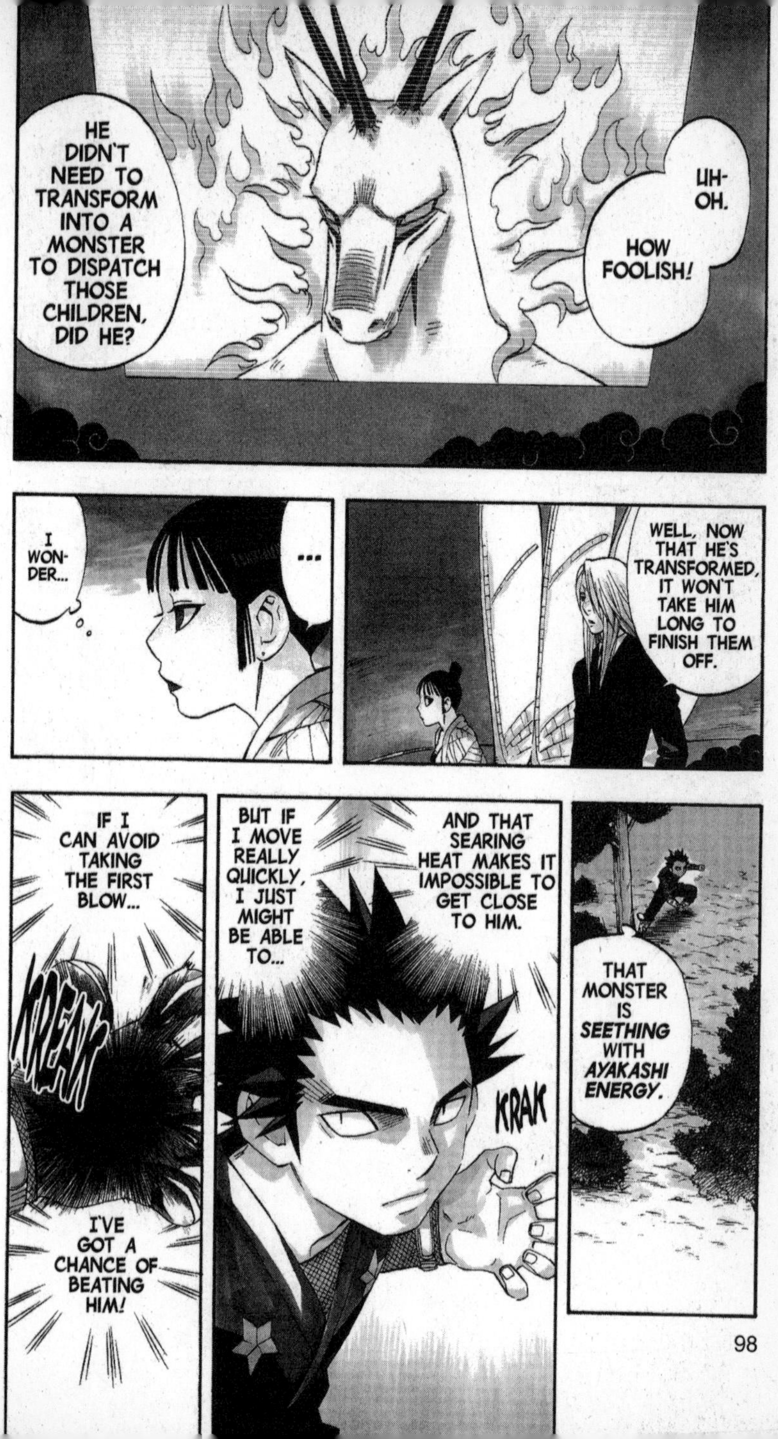
UH-OH.
HOW FOOLISH!
HE DIDN'T NEED TO TRANSFORM INTO A MONSTER TO DISPATCH THOSE CHILDREN, DID HE?
WELL, NOW THAT HE'S TRANSFORMED, IT WON'T TAKE HIM LONG TO FINISH THEM OFF.
...
I WONDER...
THAT MONSTER IS SEETHING WITH AYAKASHI ENERGY.
AND THAT SEARING HEAT MAKES IT IMPOSSIBLE TO GET CLOSE TO HIM.
BUT IF I MOVE REALLY QUICKLY, I JUST MIGHT BE ABLE TO...
KRAK
IF I CAN AVOID TAKING THE FIRST BLOW...
KREAK
I'VE GOT A CHANCE OF BEATING HIM!

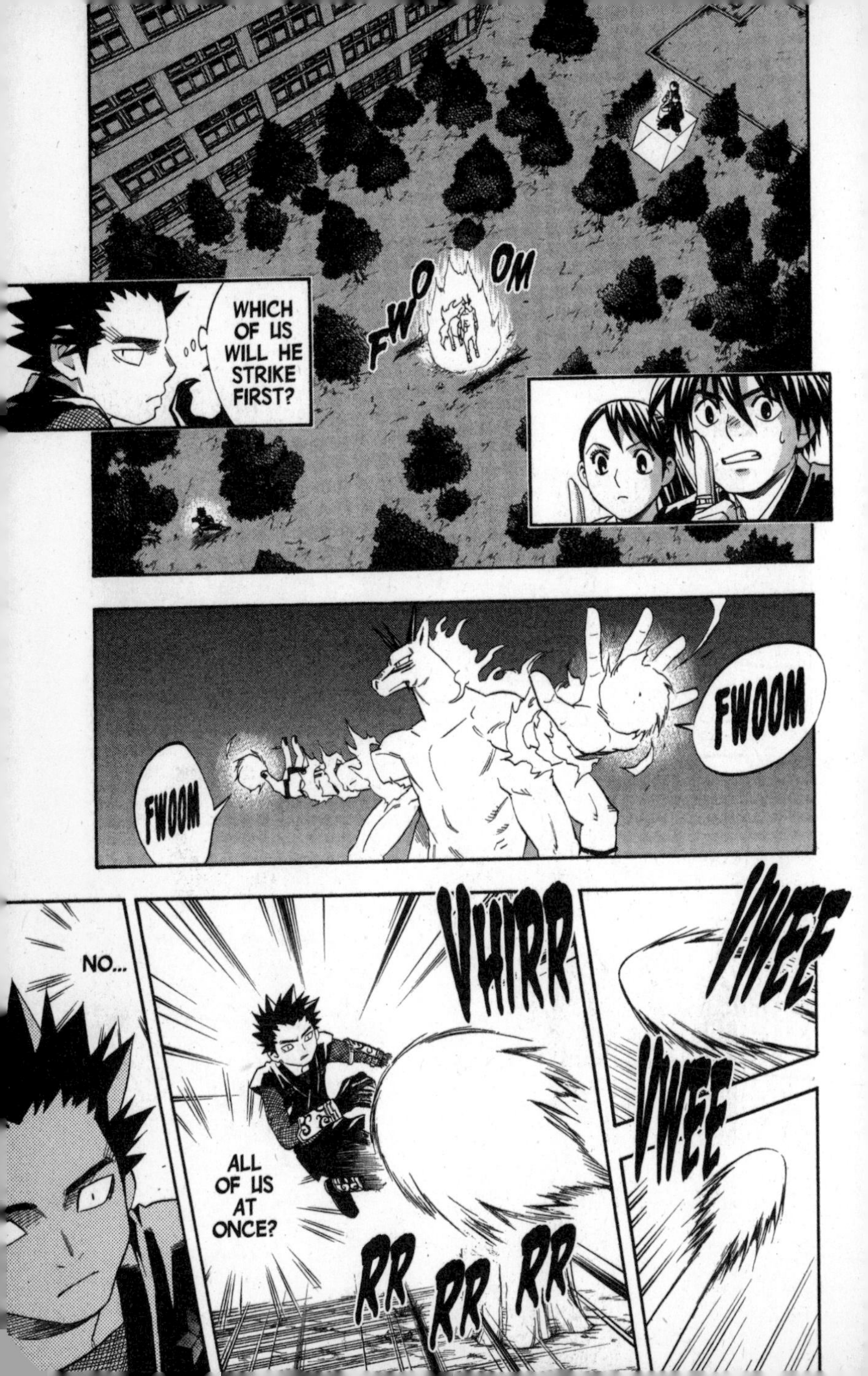
FWOOOM
WHICH OF US WILL HE STRIKE FIRST?
FWOOM
FWOOM
VWEE
VWEE
VHIRR
ALL OF US AT ONCE?
RR RR RR
NO...

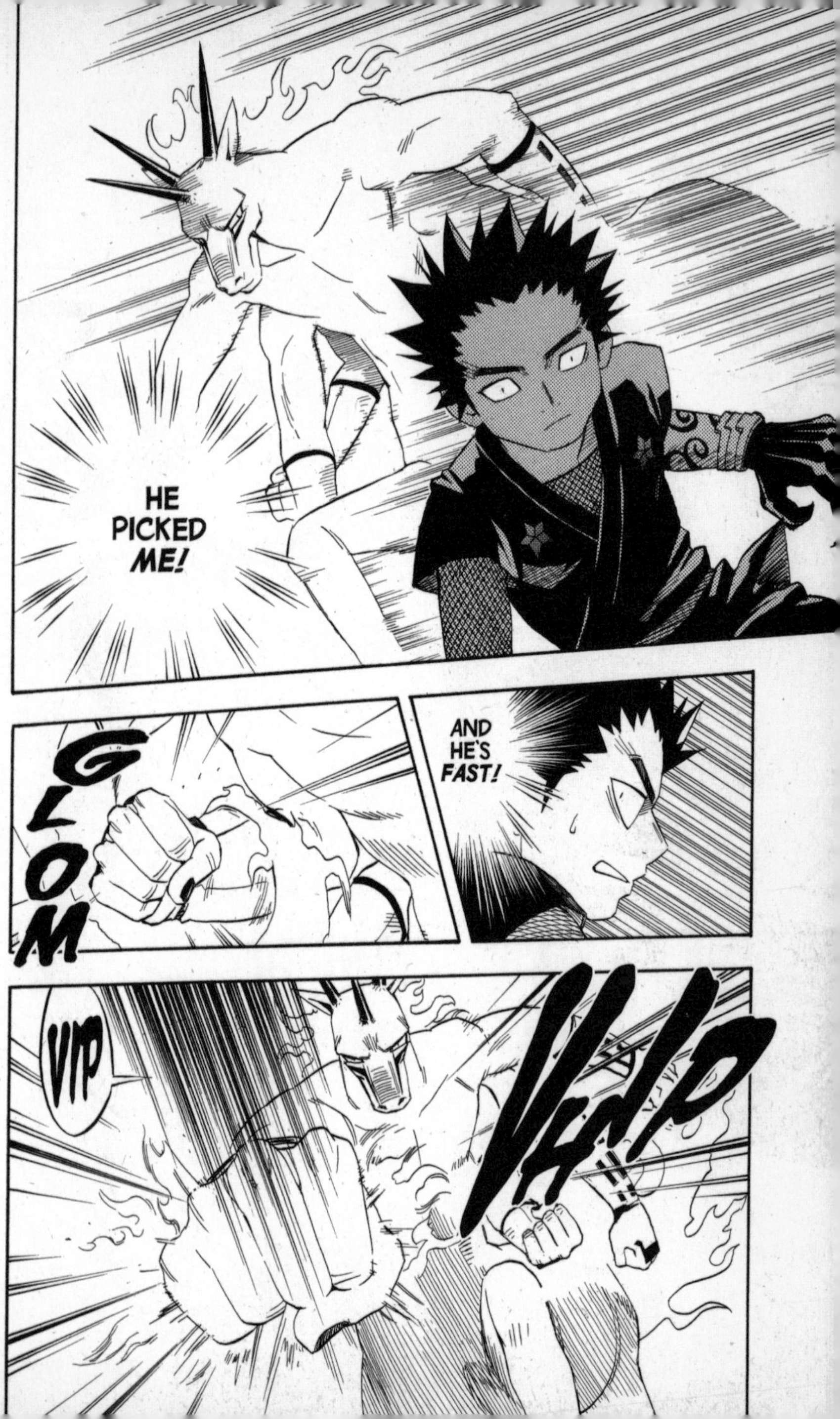
HE PICKED *ME!*
AND HE'S *FAST!*
GLOM
VIP

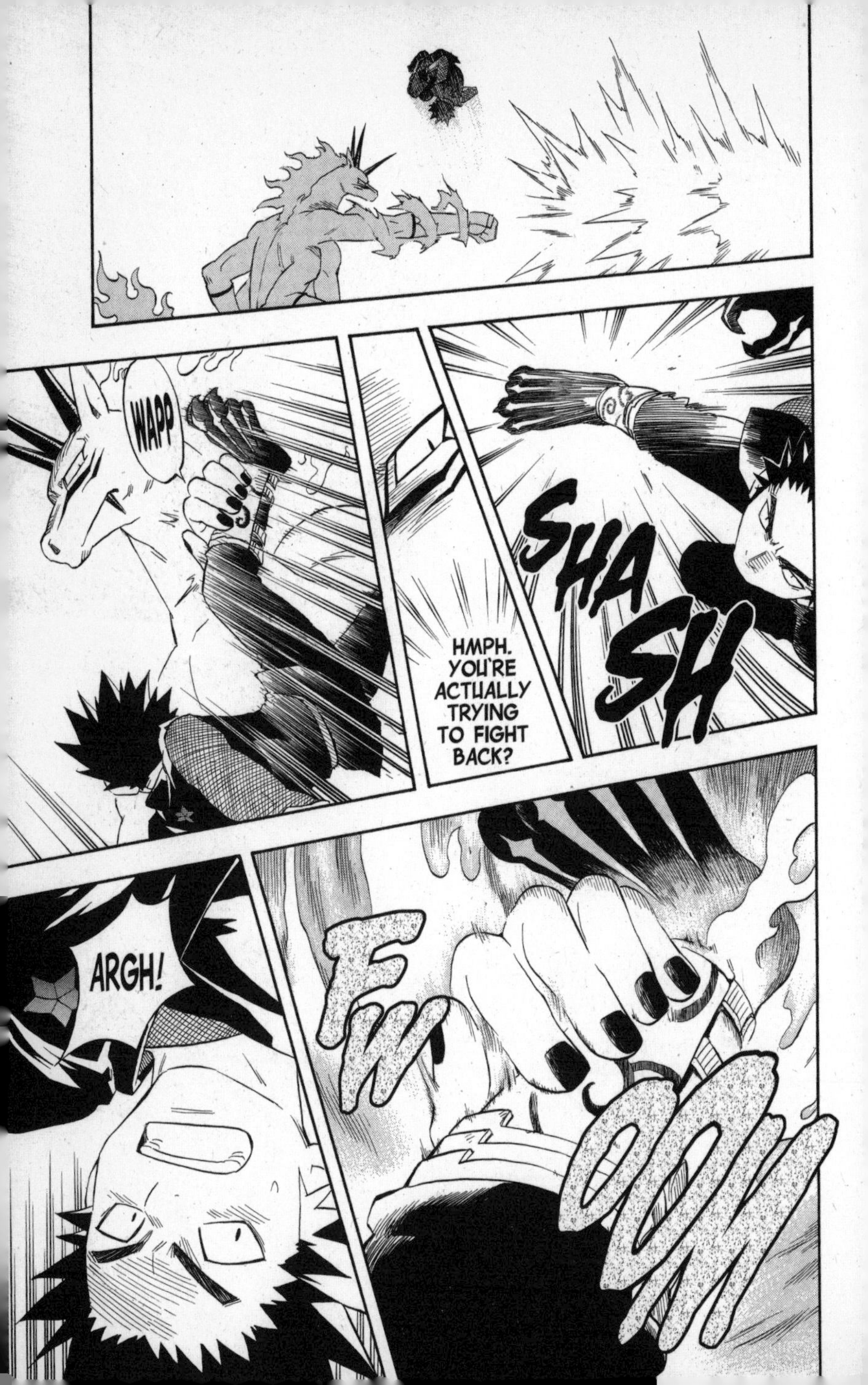
SHASHSH
HMPH. YOU'RE ACTUALLY TRYING TO FIGHT BACK?
WAPP
FWOOM
ARGH!

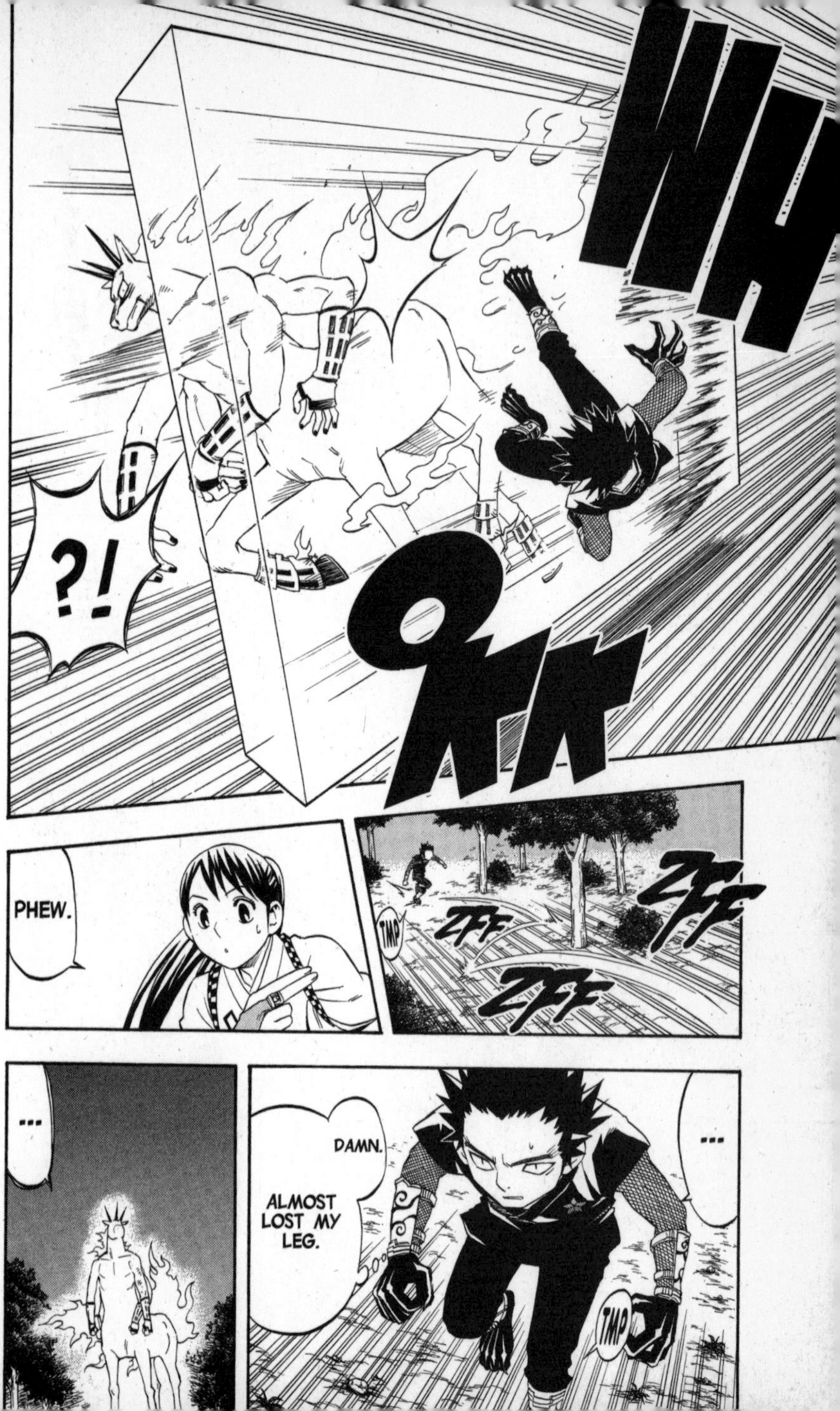
?!
TMP
ZFF
ZFF
ZFF
PHEW.
...
DAMN.
ALMOST LOST MY LEG.
TMP
...

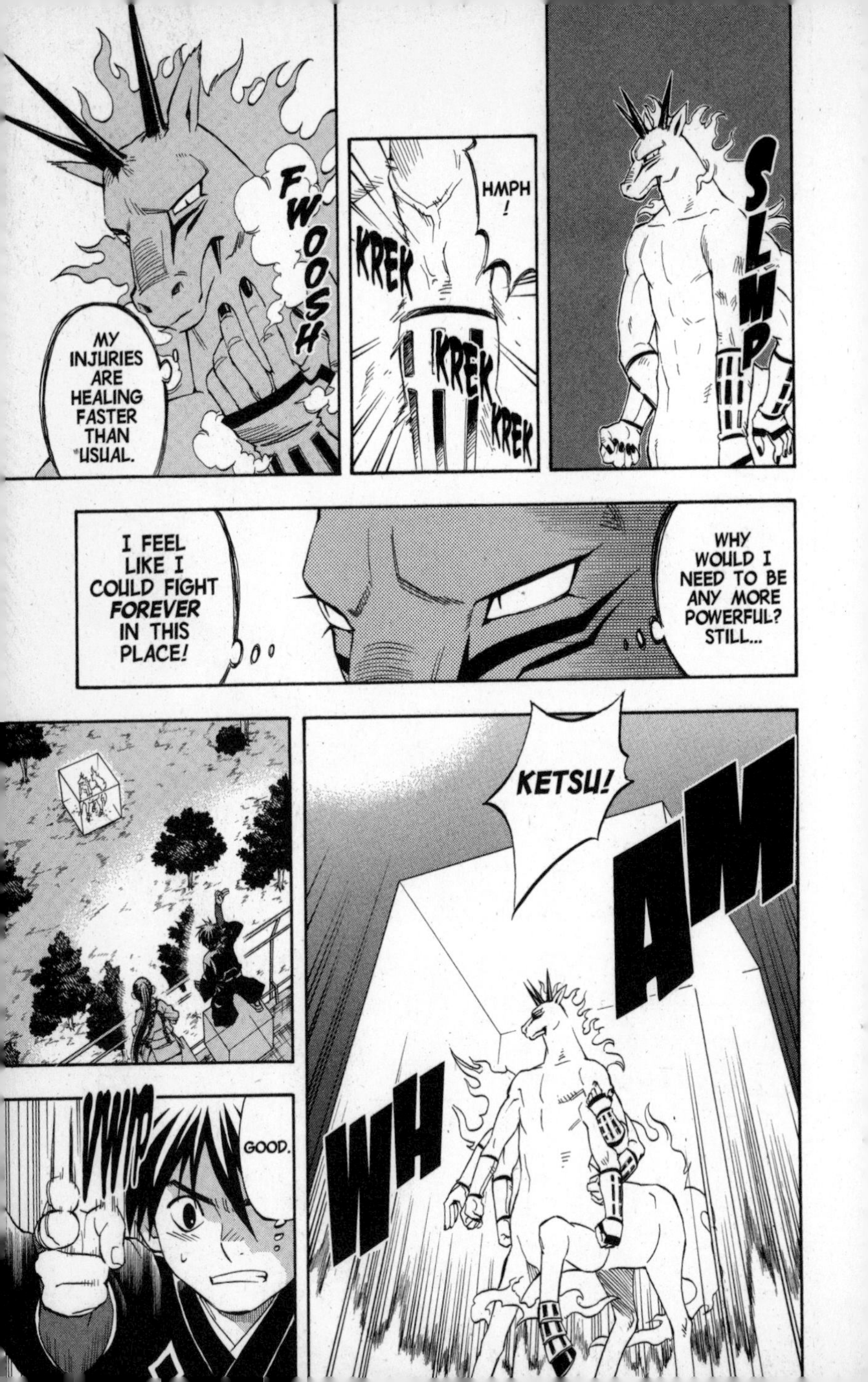
SLMP
HMPH!
KREK
KREK
KREK
FWOOSH
MY INJURIES ARE HEALING FASTER THAN USUAL.
WHY WOULD I NEED TO BE ANY MORE POWERFUL? STILL...
I FEEL LIKE I COULD FIGHT *FOREVER* IN THIS PLACE!
KETSU!
WHAM
VWIP
GOOD.

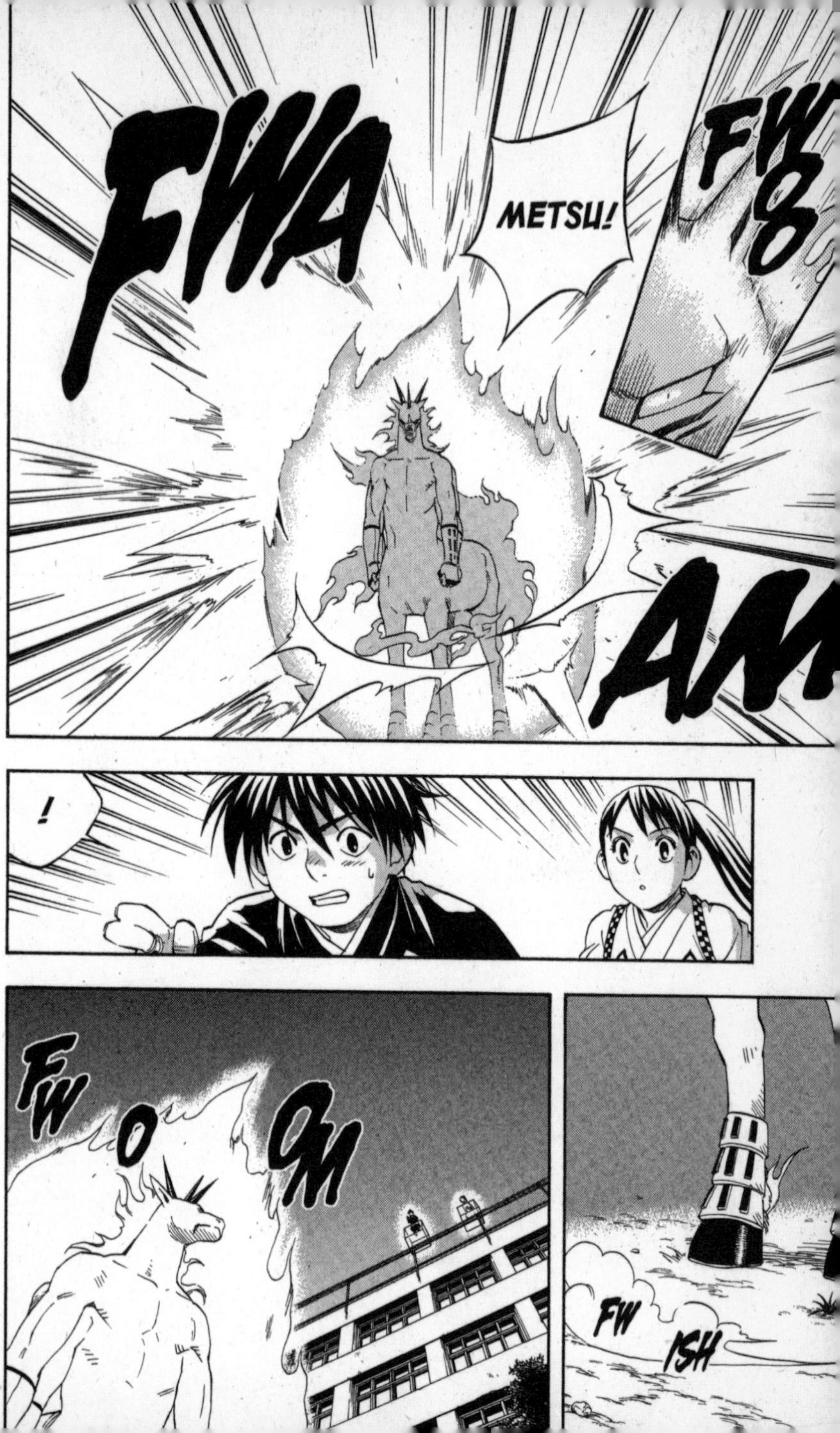
FWO
METSU!
FWA
AM
!
FW
ISH
FW
O
OM

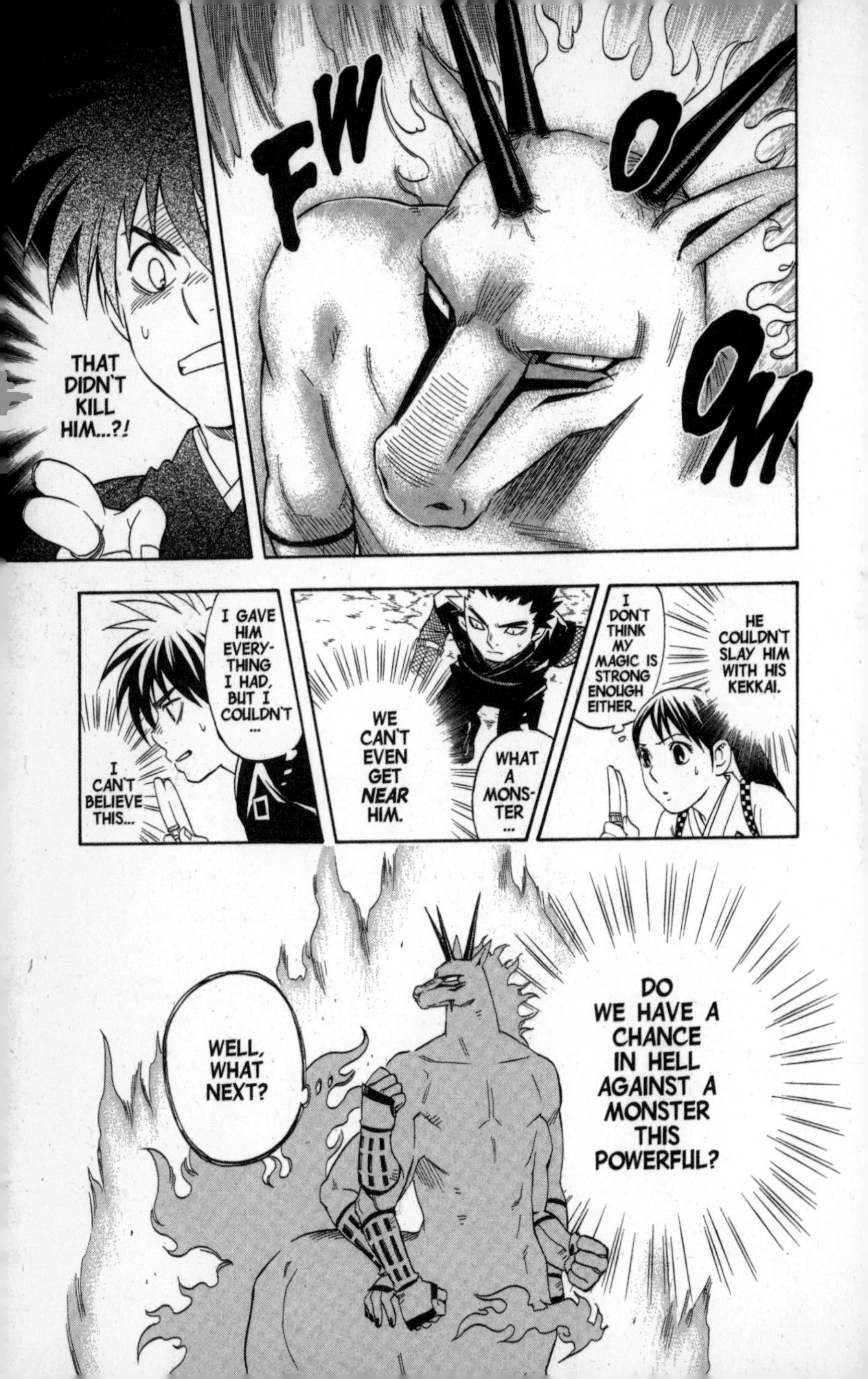
FWOOM
THAT DIDN'T KILL HIM...?!
HE COULDN'T SLAY HIM WITH HIS KEKKAI.
I DON'T THINK MY MAGIC IS STRONG ENOUGH EITHER.
WHAT A MONSTER...
WE CAN'T EVEN GET *NEAR* HIM.
I GAVE HIM EVERYTHING I HAD, BUT I COULDN'T...
I CAN'T BELIEVE THIS...
DO WE HAVE A CHANCE IN HELL AGAINST A MONSTER THIS POWERFUL?
WELL, WHAT NEXT?

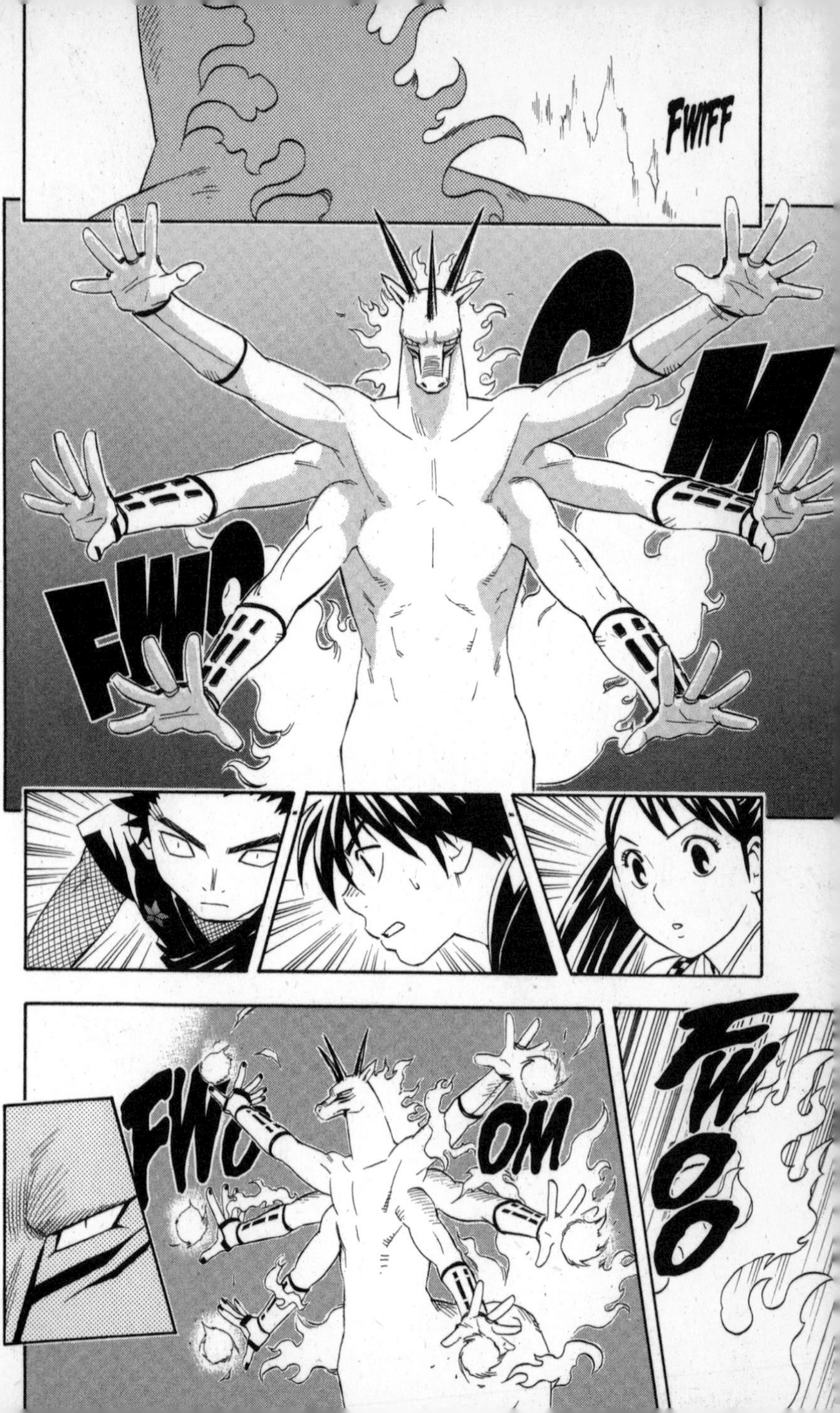
FWIFF
FWO
OM
FWOO
FWO
OM

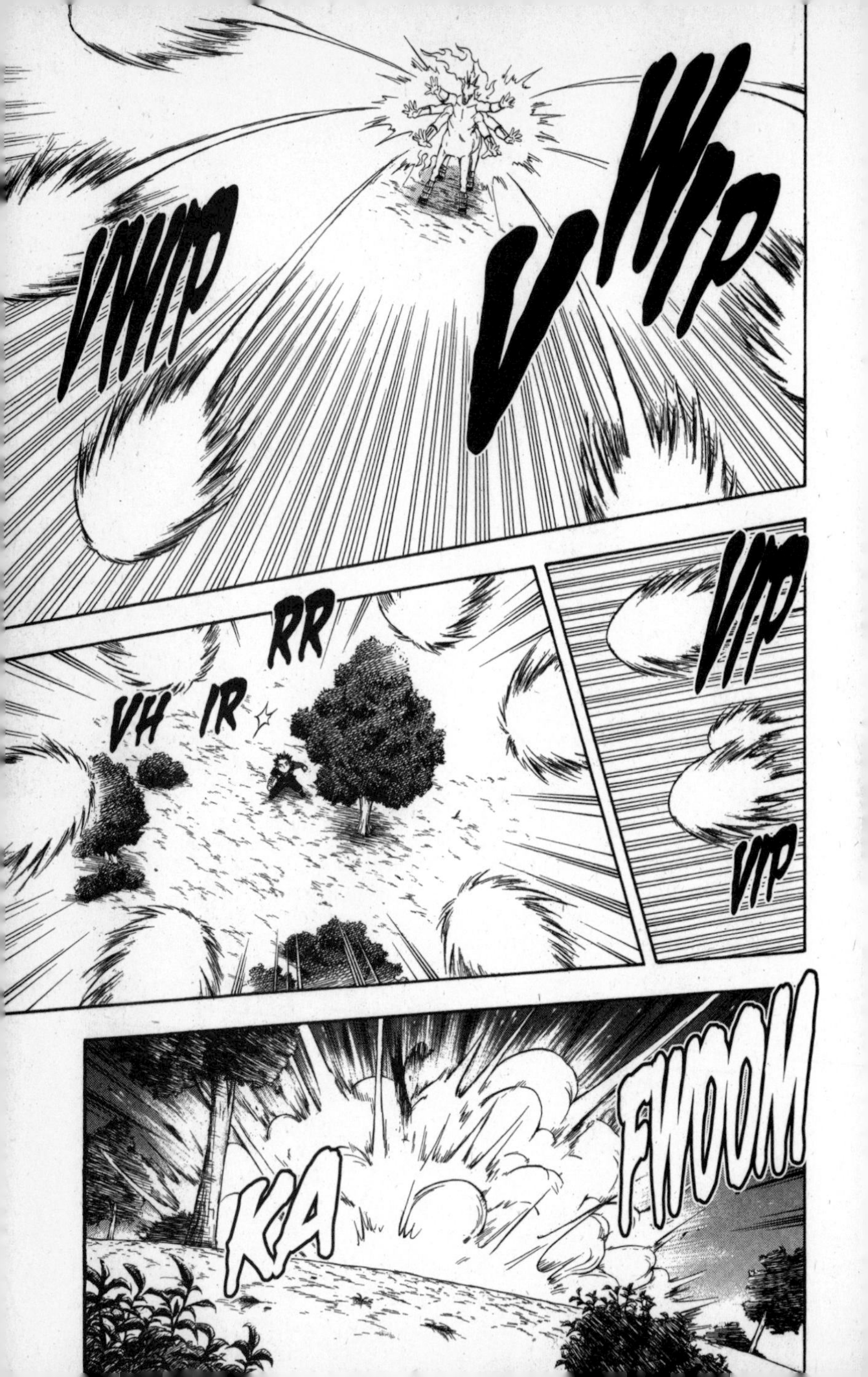
VWIP
VWIP
VIP
VIP
VHIRRR
KA
FWOOM

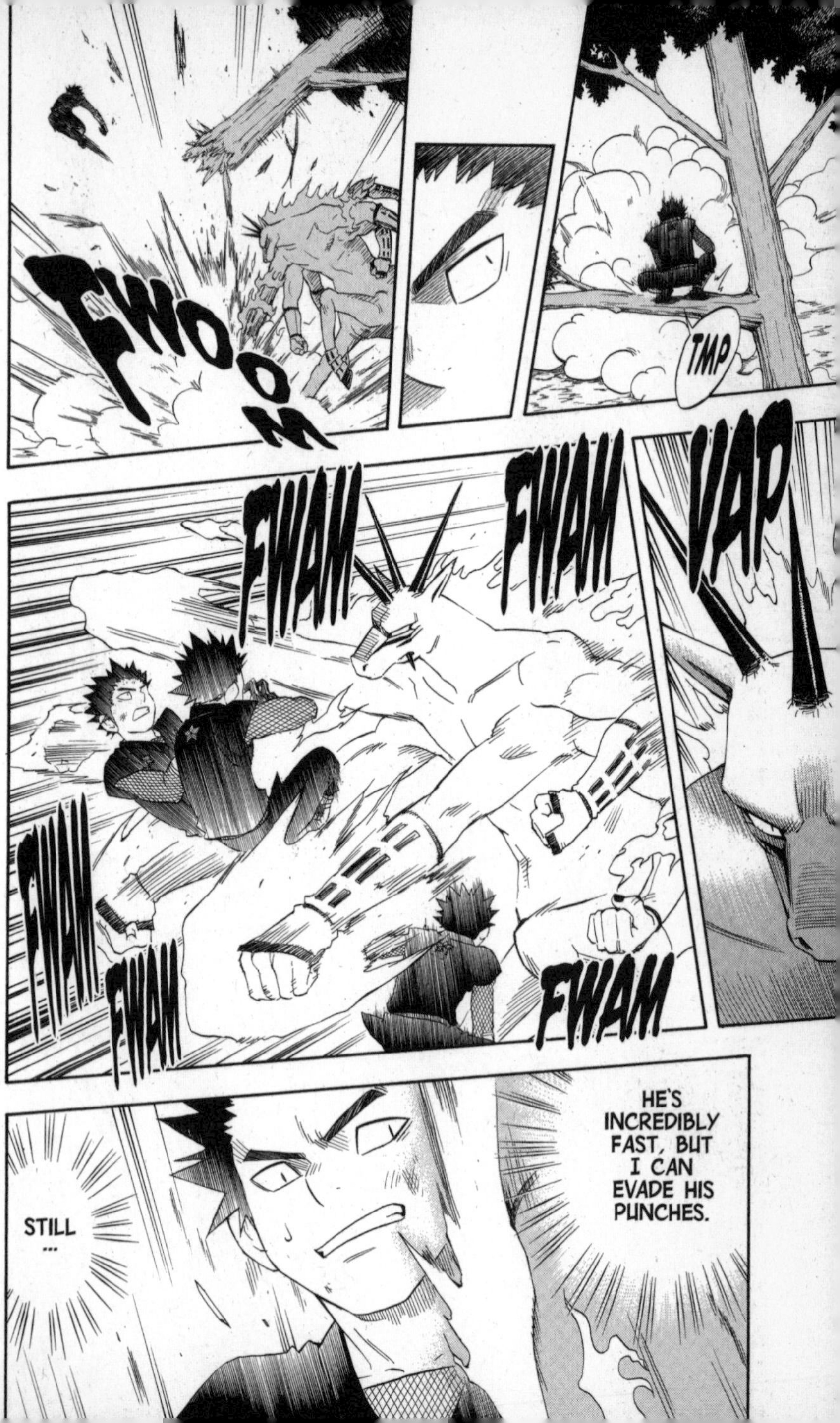
TMP
FWOOM
VAP
FWAM
FWAM
FWAM
FWAM
FWAM
HE'S INCREDIBLY FAST, BUT I CAN EVADE HIS PUNCHES.
STILL ...

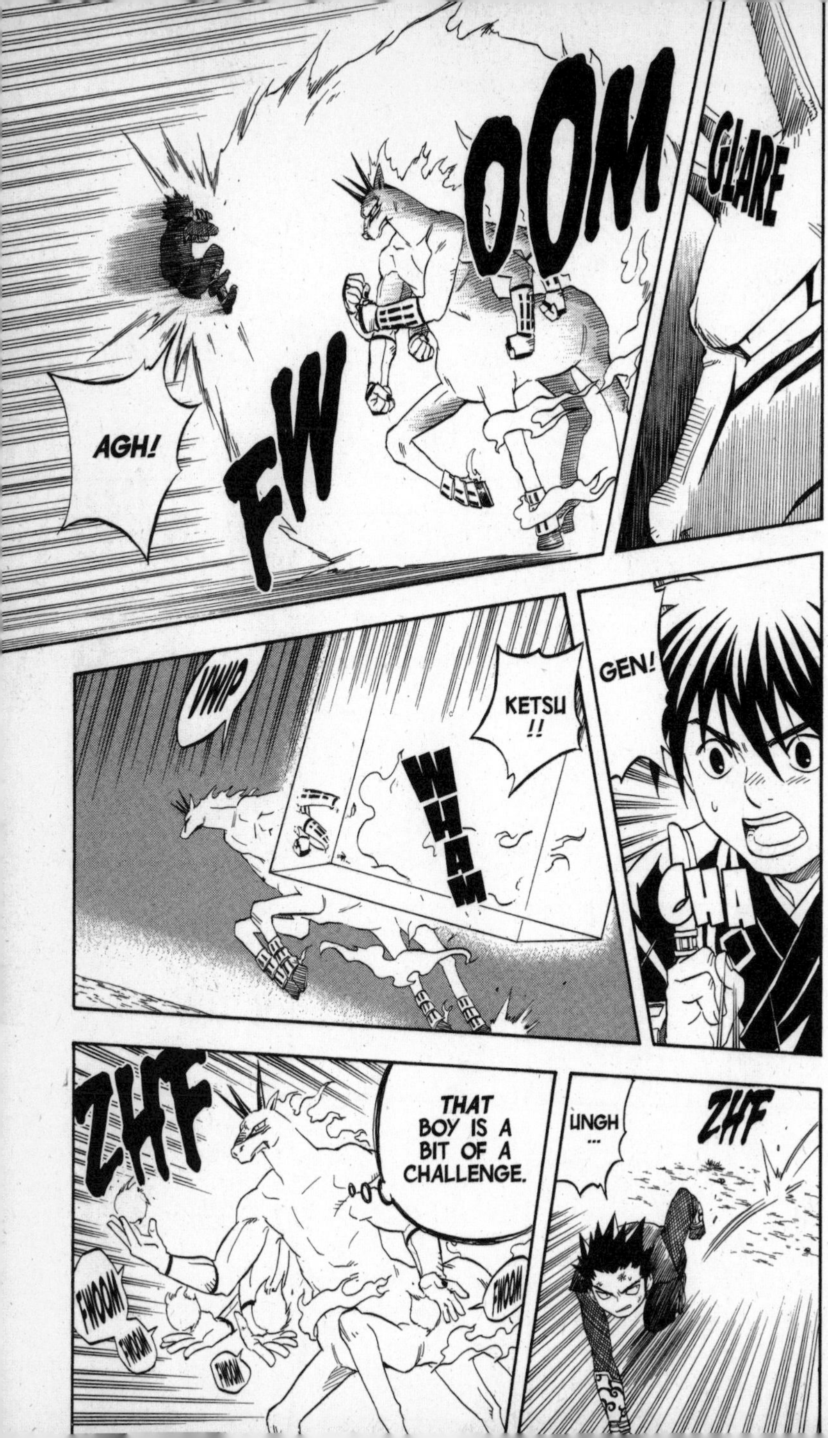
GLARE
FW
OOM
AGH!
GEN!
CHA
KETSU !!
WHAM
VWIP
ZHF
UNGH ...
THAT BOY IS A BIT OF A CHALLENGE.
ZHF
FWOOM
FWOOM
FWOOM
FWOOM

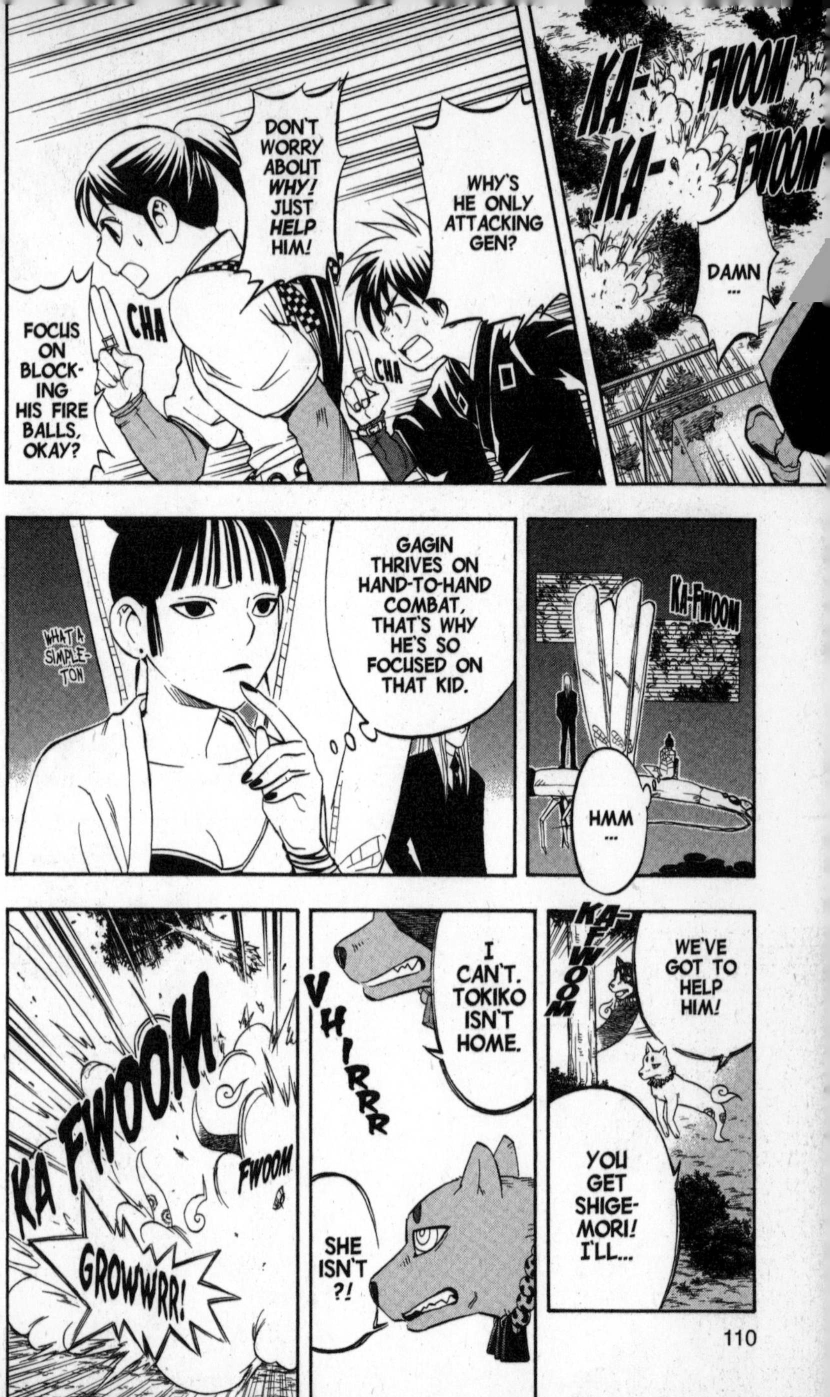
KA-FWOOM
KA-FWOOM
DAMN...
WHY'S HE ONLY ATTACKING GEN?
DON'T WORRY ABOUT WHY! JUST HELP HIM!
CHA
CHA
FOCUS ON BLOCKING HIS FIRE BALLS, OKAY?
KA-FWOOM
HMM...
GAGIN THRIVES ON HAND-TO-HAND COMBAT, THAT'S WHY HE'S SO FOCUSED ON THAT KID.
WHAT A SIMPLETON
KA-FWOOM
WE'VE GOT TO HELP HIM!
YOU GET SHIGEMORI! I'LL...
I CAN'T. TOKIKO ISN'T HOME.
VHIRRR
SHE ISN'T?!
KA FWOOM
FWOOM
GROWWRR!

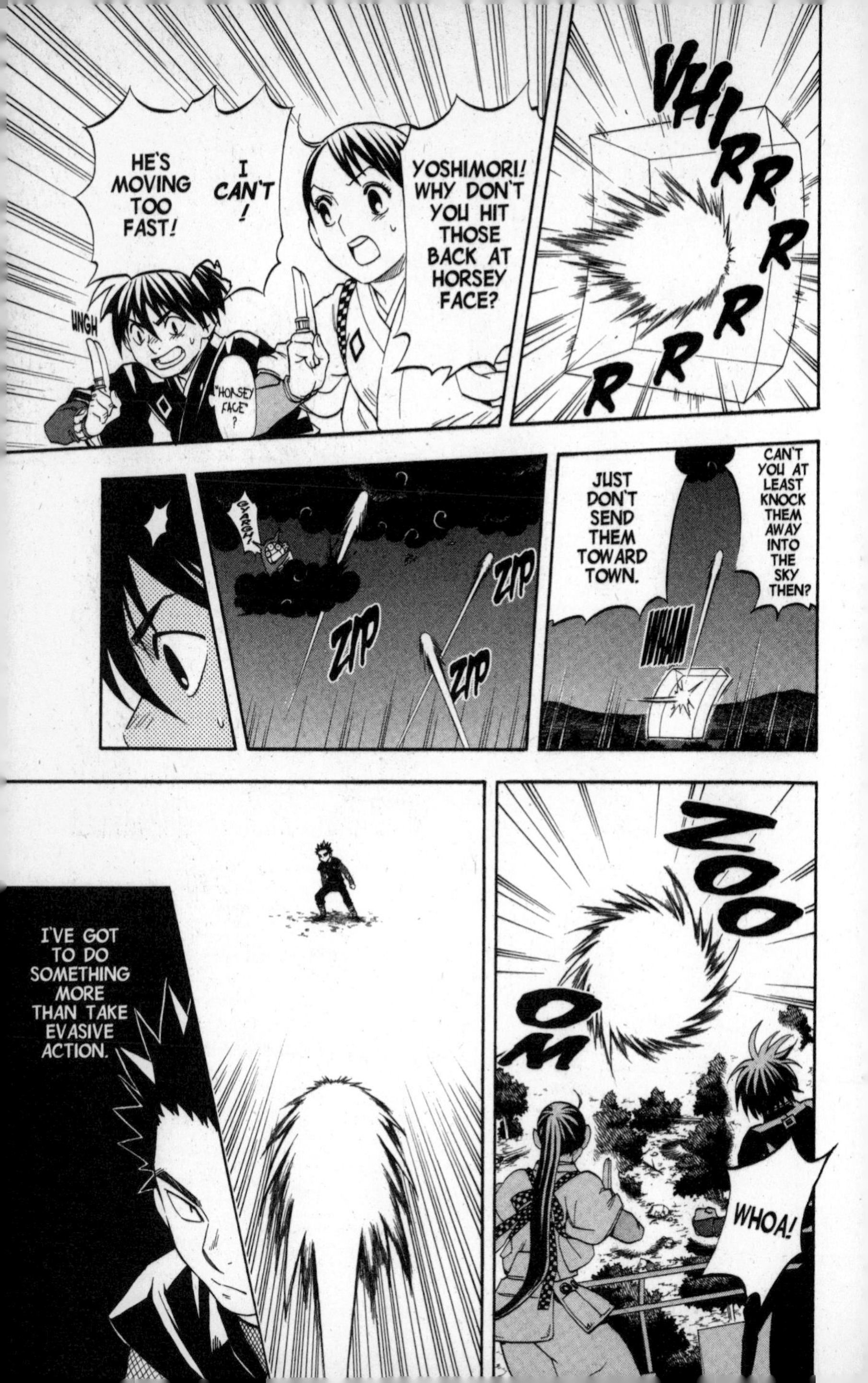
VHIRRRRRRR
YOSHIMORI! WHY DON'T YOU HIT THOSE BACK AT HORSEY FACE?
I CAN'T!
HE'S MOVING TOO FAST!
UNGH
"HORSEY FACE"?
CAN'T YOU AT LEAST KNOCK THEM AWAY INTO THE SKY THEN?
JUST DON'T SEND THEM TOWARD TOWN.
WHAM
ZIP
GYARGH!
ZIP
ZIP
ZOOOM
WHOA!
I'VE GOT TO DO SOMETHING MORE THAN TAKE EVASIVE ACTION.

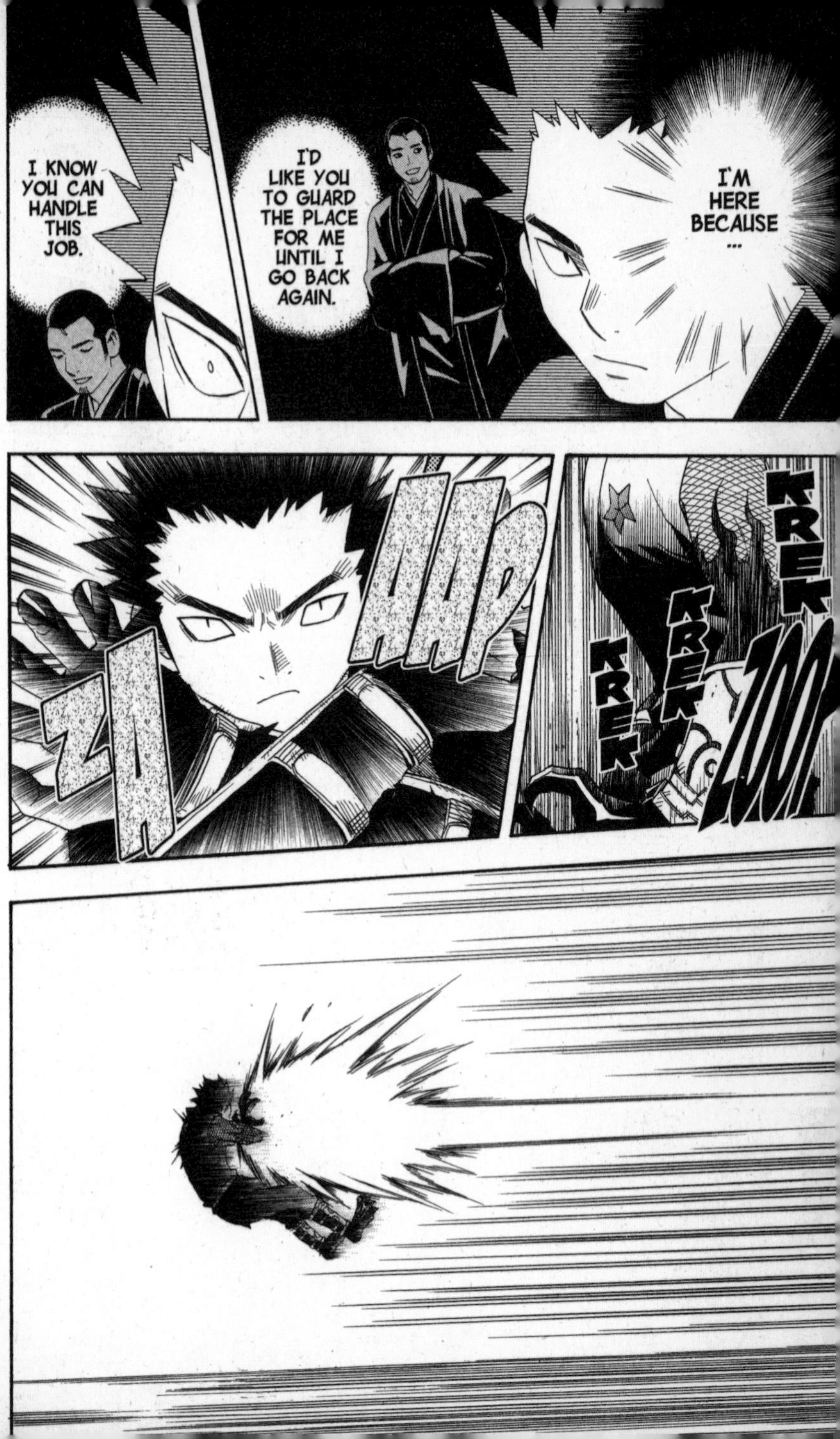
I'M HERE BECAUSE ...
I'D LIKE YOU TO GUARD THE PLACE FOR ME UNTIL I GO BACK AGAIN.
I KNOW YOU CAN HANDLE THIS JOB.
KREK
KREK
KREK
ZOO
AAP
ZA

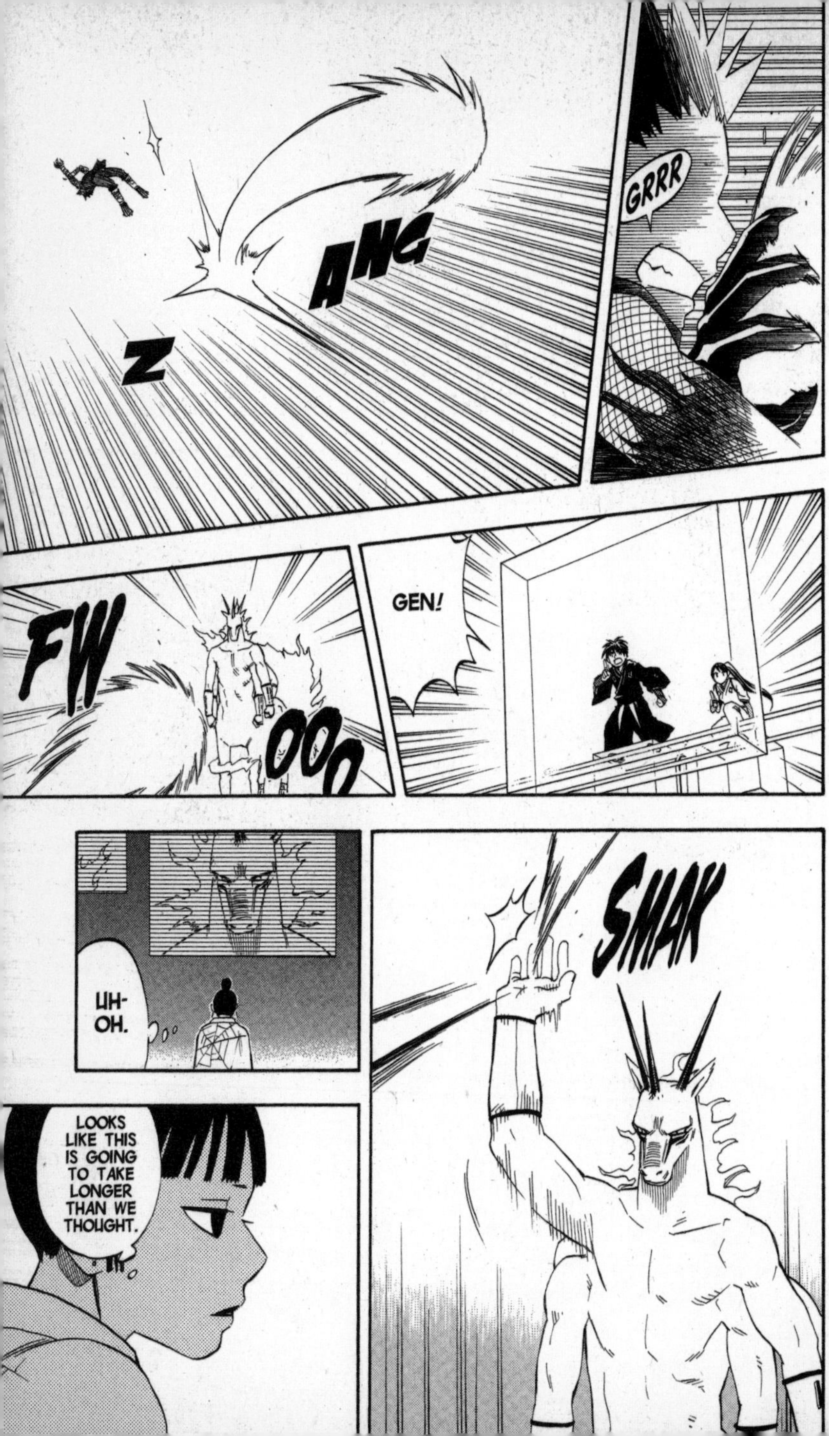
GRRR
ANG
Z
GEN!
FW
OOO
SMAK
UH-OH.
LOOKS LIKE THIS IS GOING TO TAKE LONGER THAN WE THOUGHT.

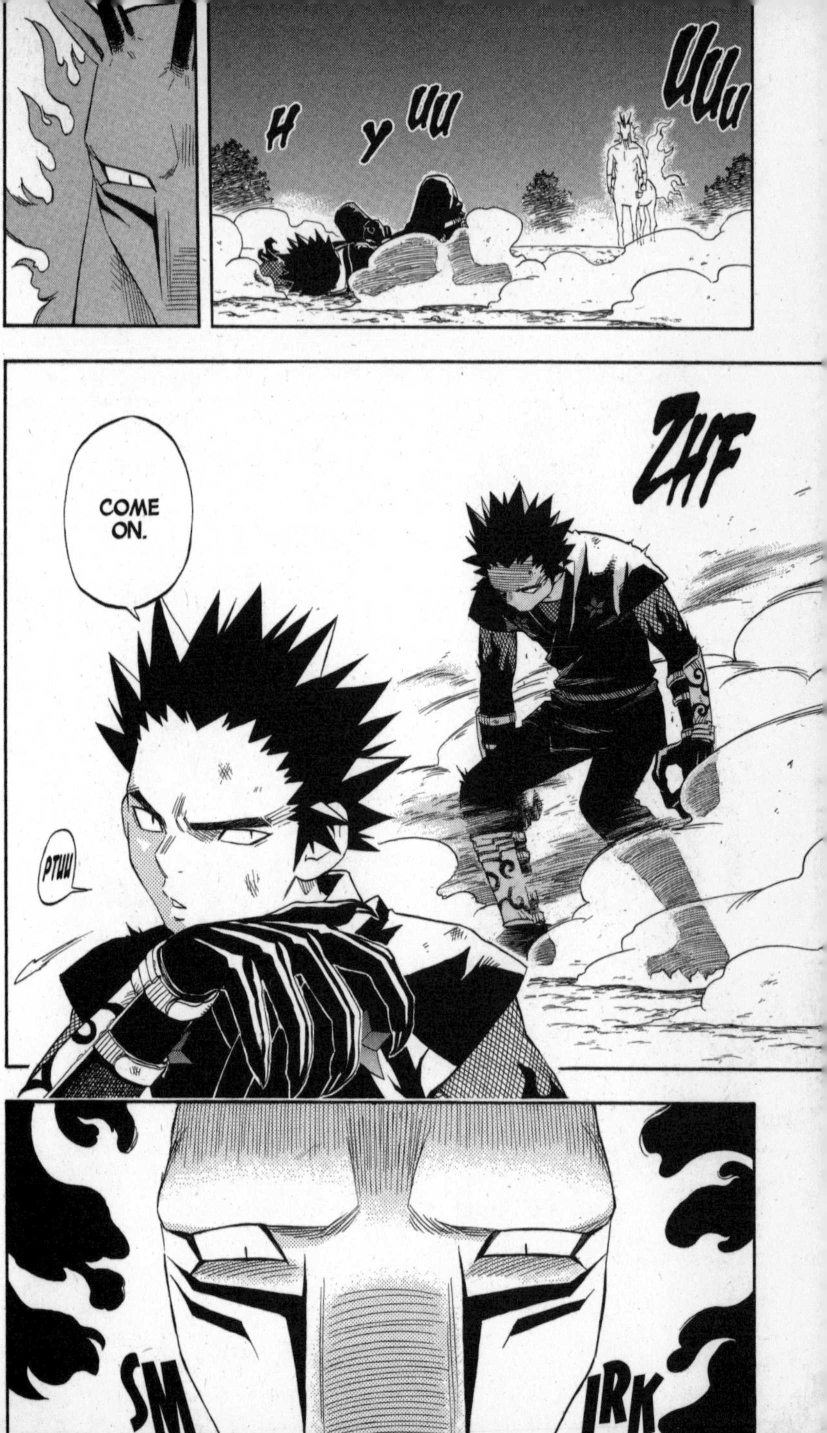

HyUU
UUu
ZHF
COME ON.
PTUU
SM
IRK

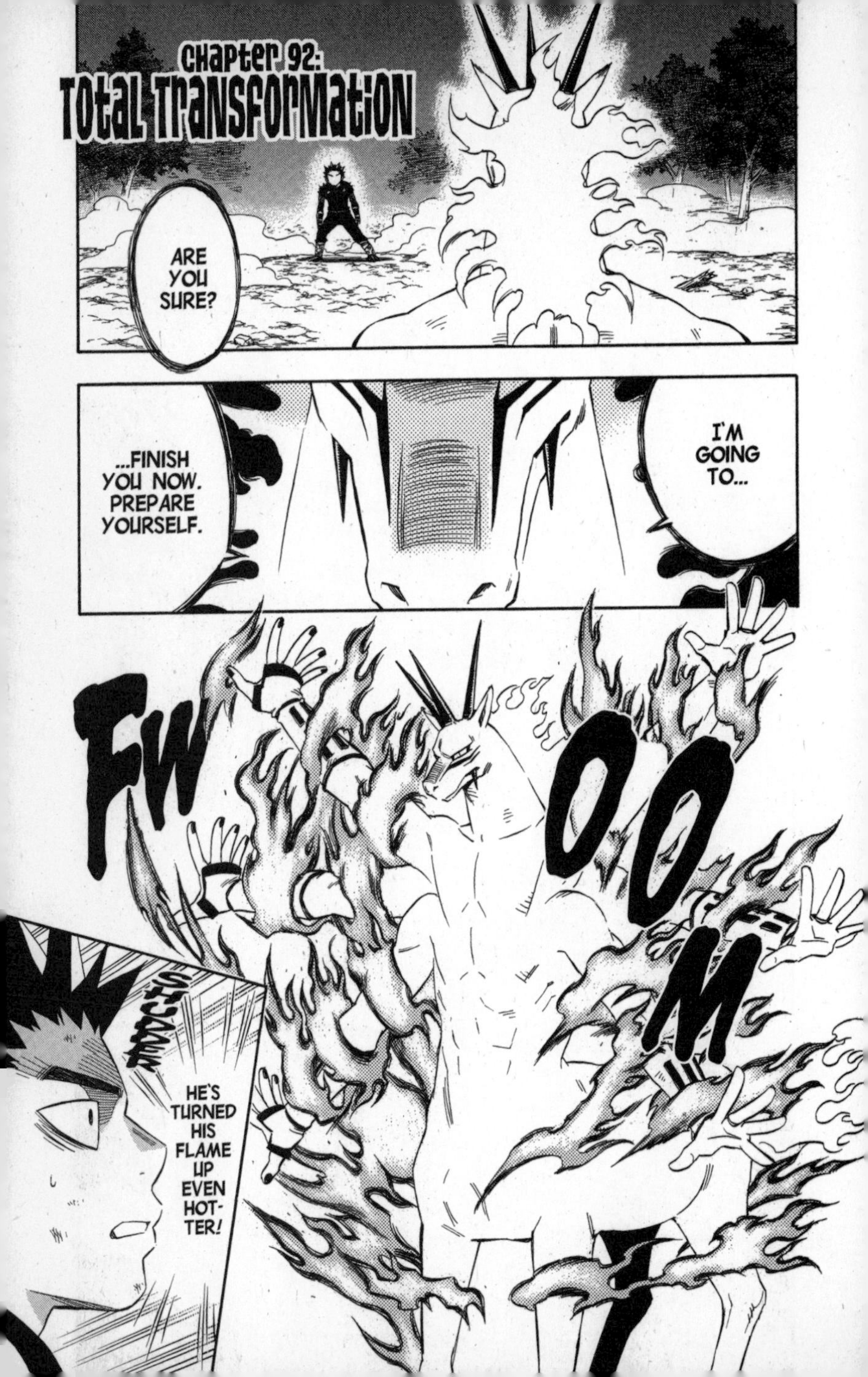
Chapter 92:
Total Transformation
ARE YOU SURE?
I'M GOING TO...
...FINISH YOU NOW. PREPARE YOURSELF.
FWOOM
HE'S TURNED HIS FLAME UP EVEN HOT-TER!

Chapter 92: Total Transformation

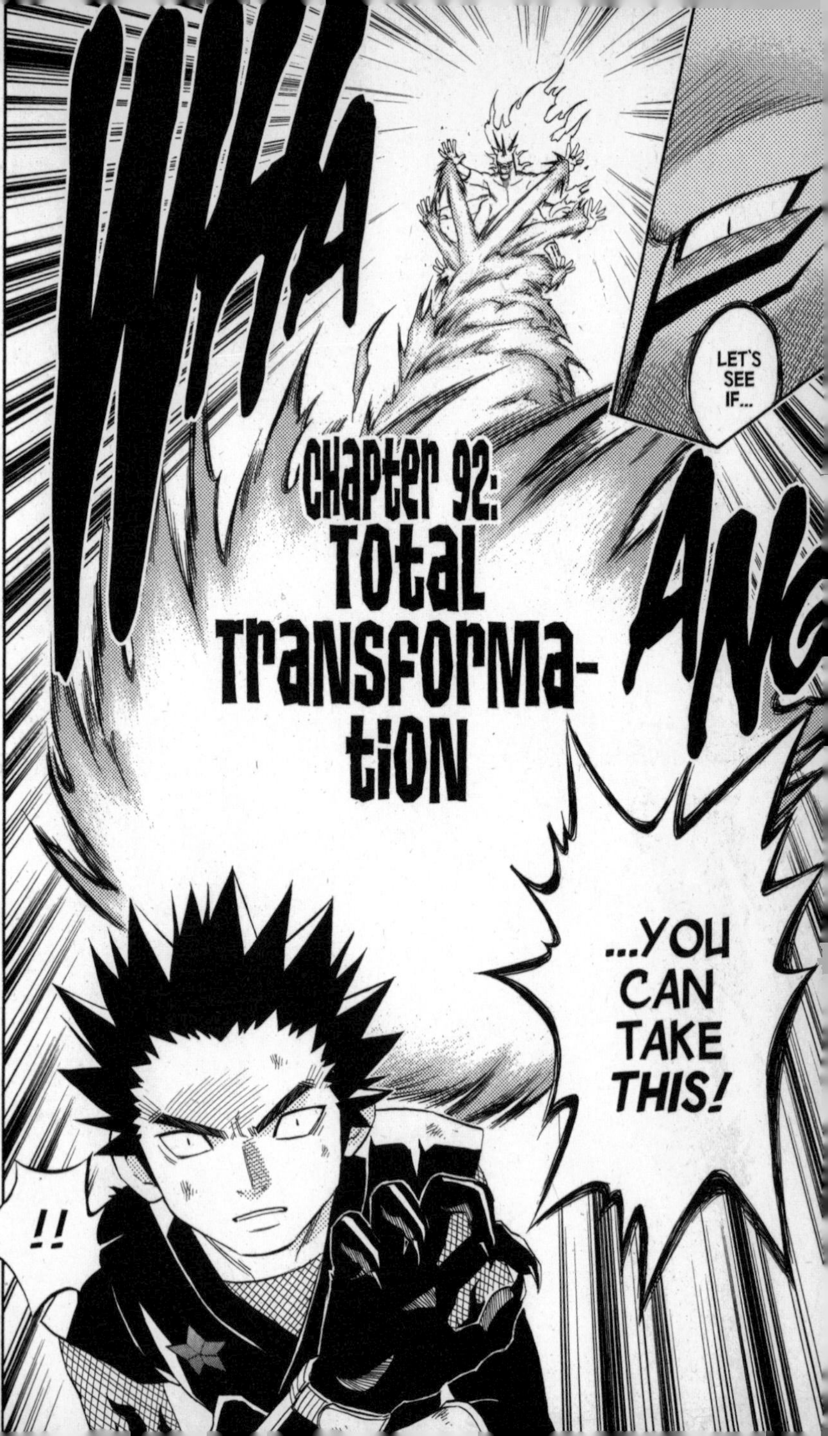
LET'S SEE IF...
...YOU CAN TAKE THIS!
!!

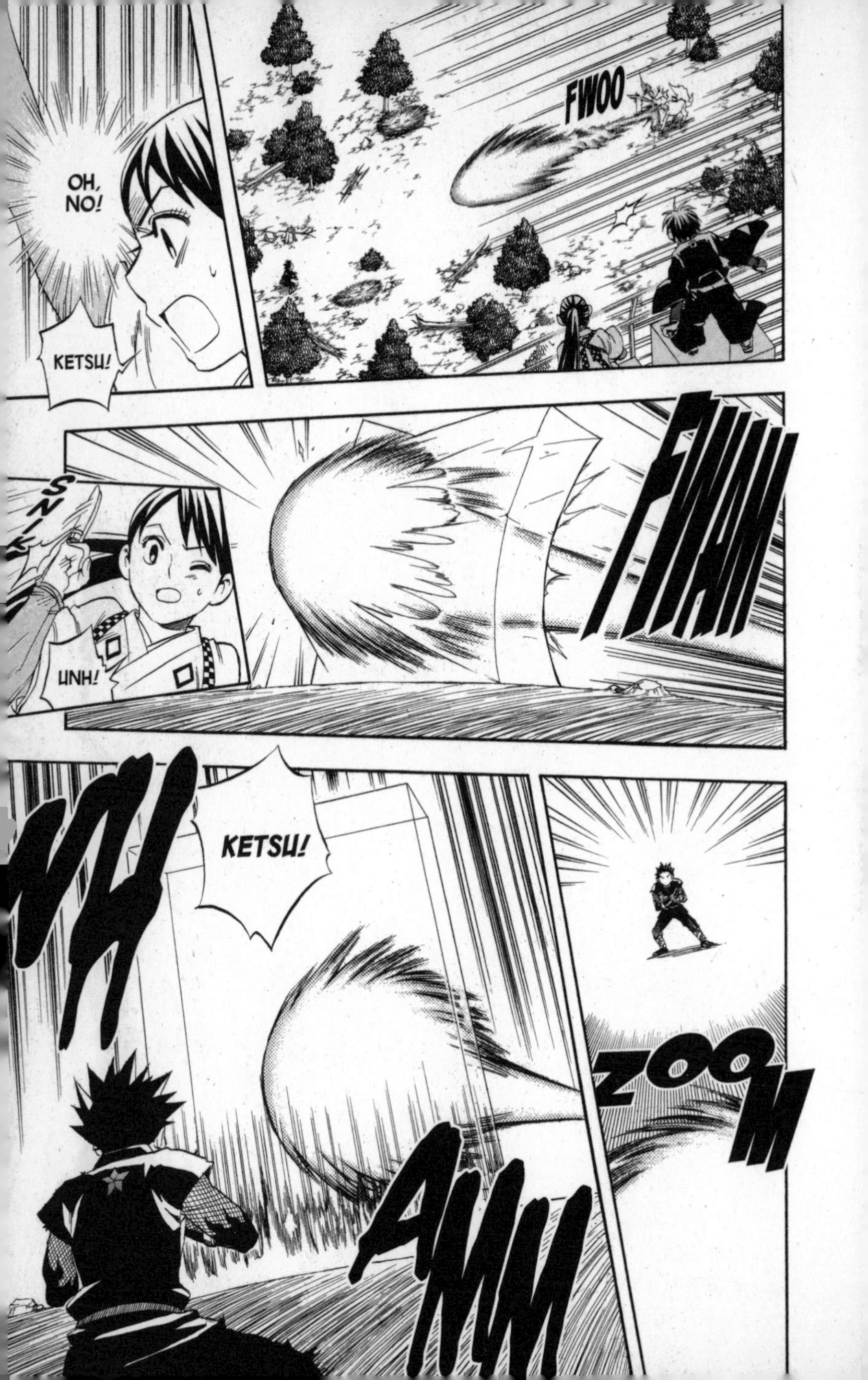
FWOO
OH, NO!
KETSU!
FWAM
SNIK
UNH!
ZOOM
KETSU!
WH
AMM

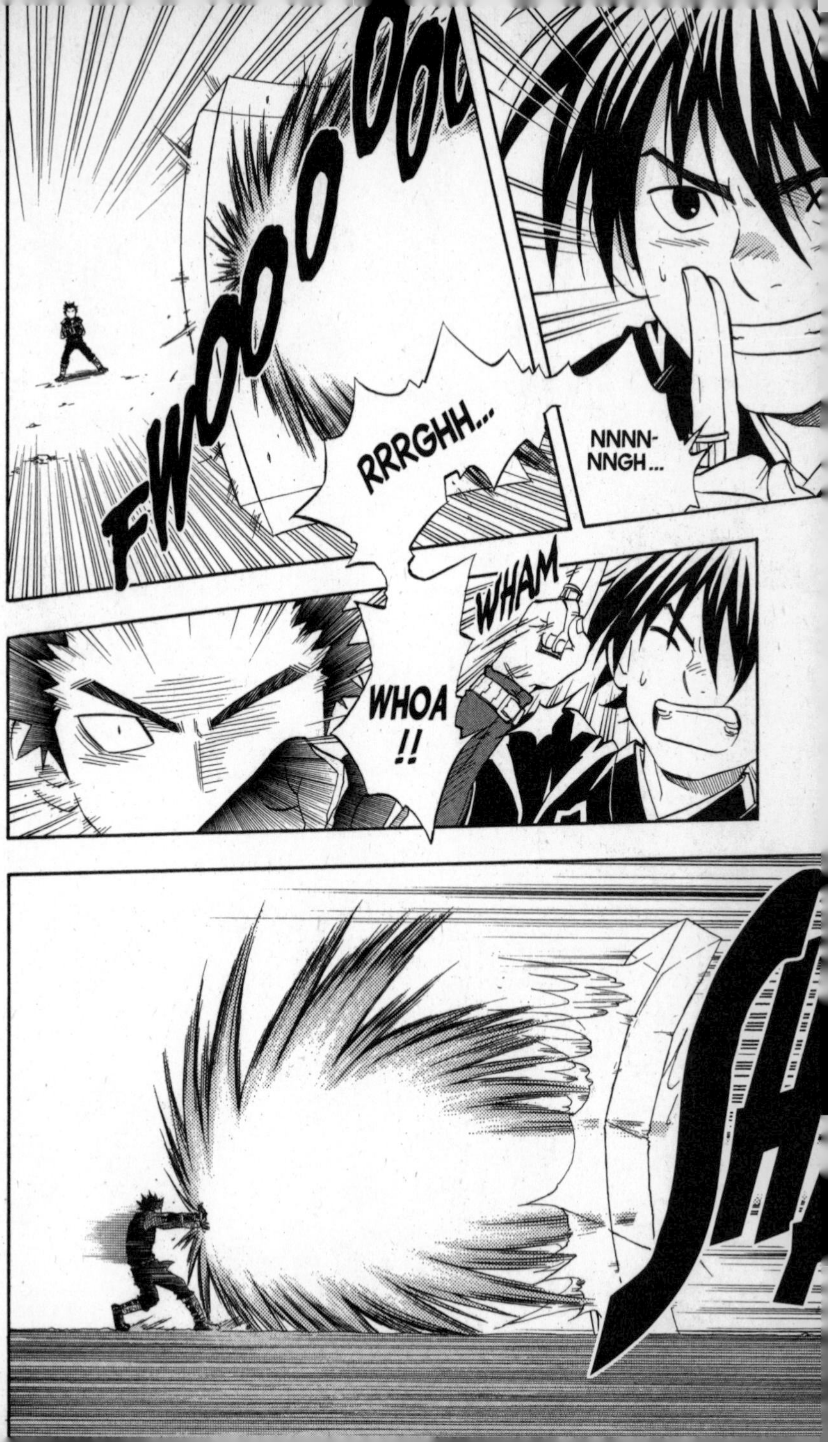
NNNN-
NNGH...
FWOOOOOOOO
RRRGHH...
WHAM
WHOA
!!

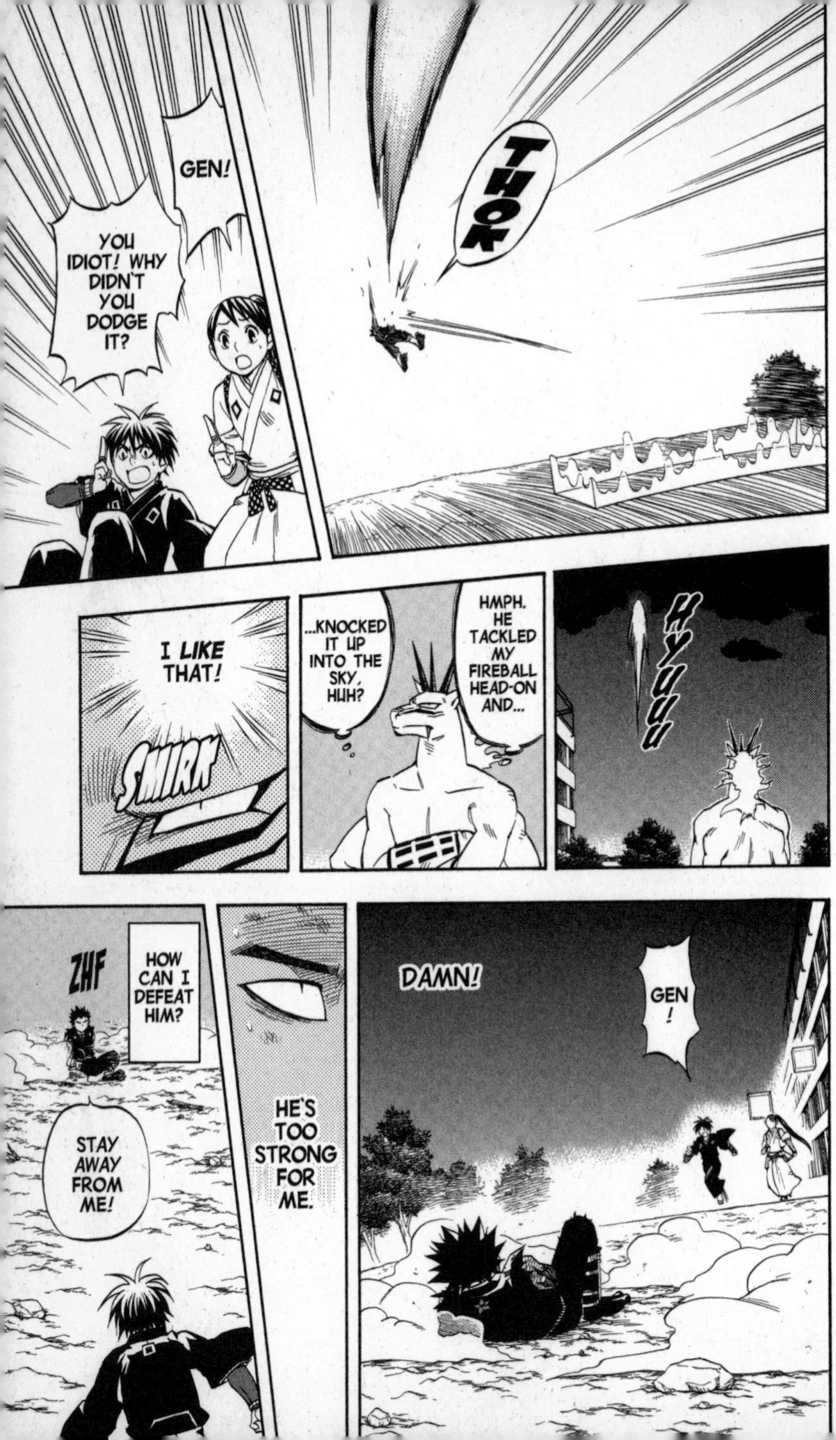
THOK
GEN!
YOU IDIOT! WHY DIDN'T YOU DODGE IT?
HYUUUU
HMPH. HE TACKLED MY FIREBALL HEAD-ON AND...
...KNOCKED IT UP INTO THE SKY, HUH?
I LIKE THAT!
SMIRK
GEN!
DAMN!
HE'S TOO STRONG FOR ME.
HOW CAN I DEFEAT HIM?
ZHF
STAY AWAY FROM ME!

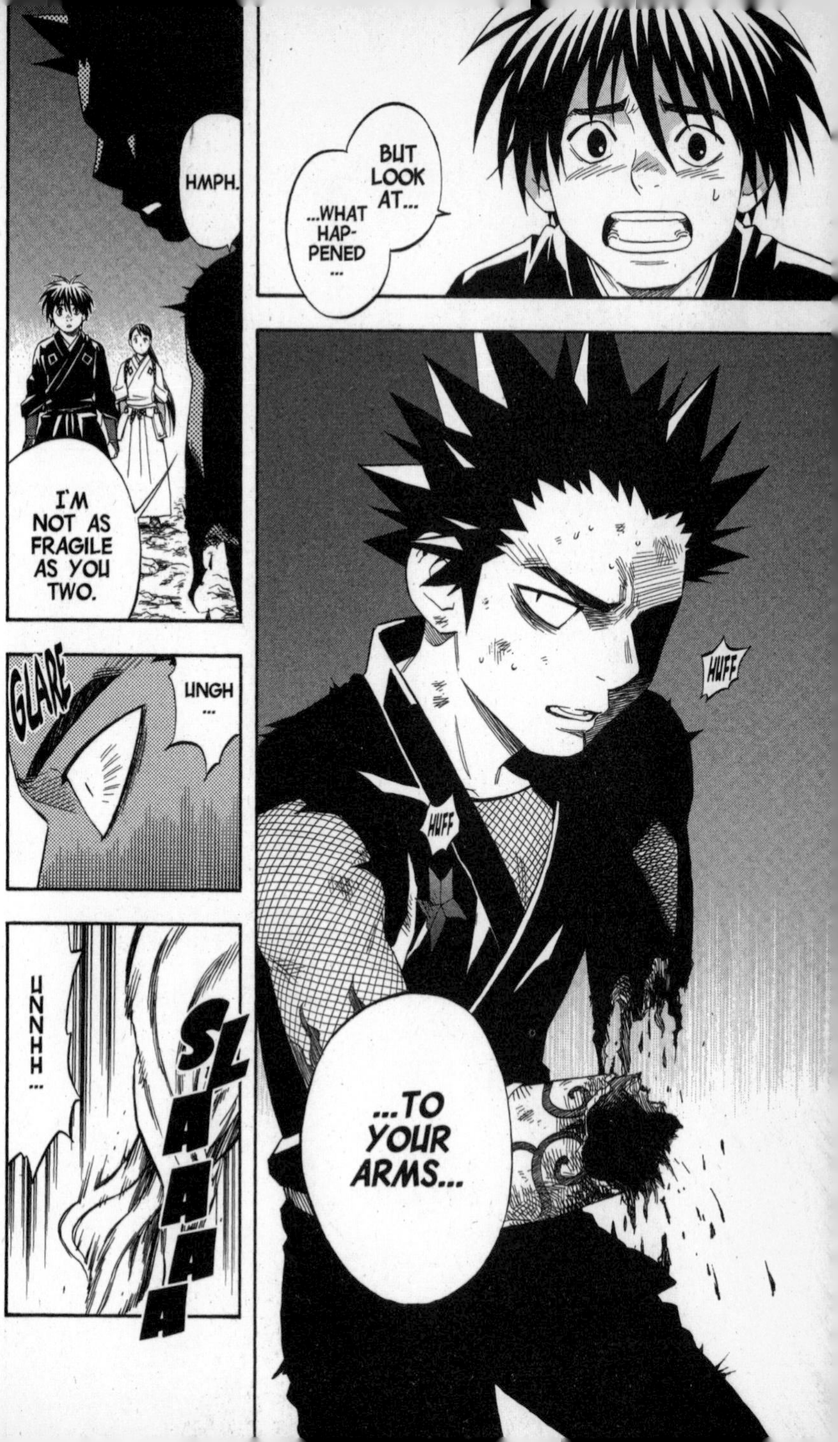
BUT LOOK AT...
...WHAT HAP-PENED...
HUFF
HUFF
...TO YOUR ARMS...
HMPH.
I'M NOT AS FRAGILE AS YOU TWO.
GLARE
UNGH...
UNNHH...
SLAAAAAA

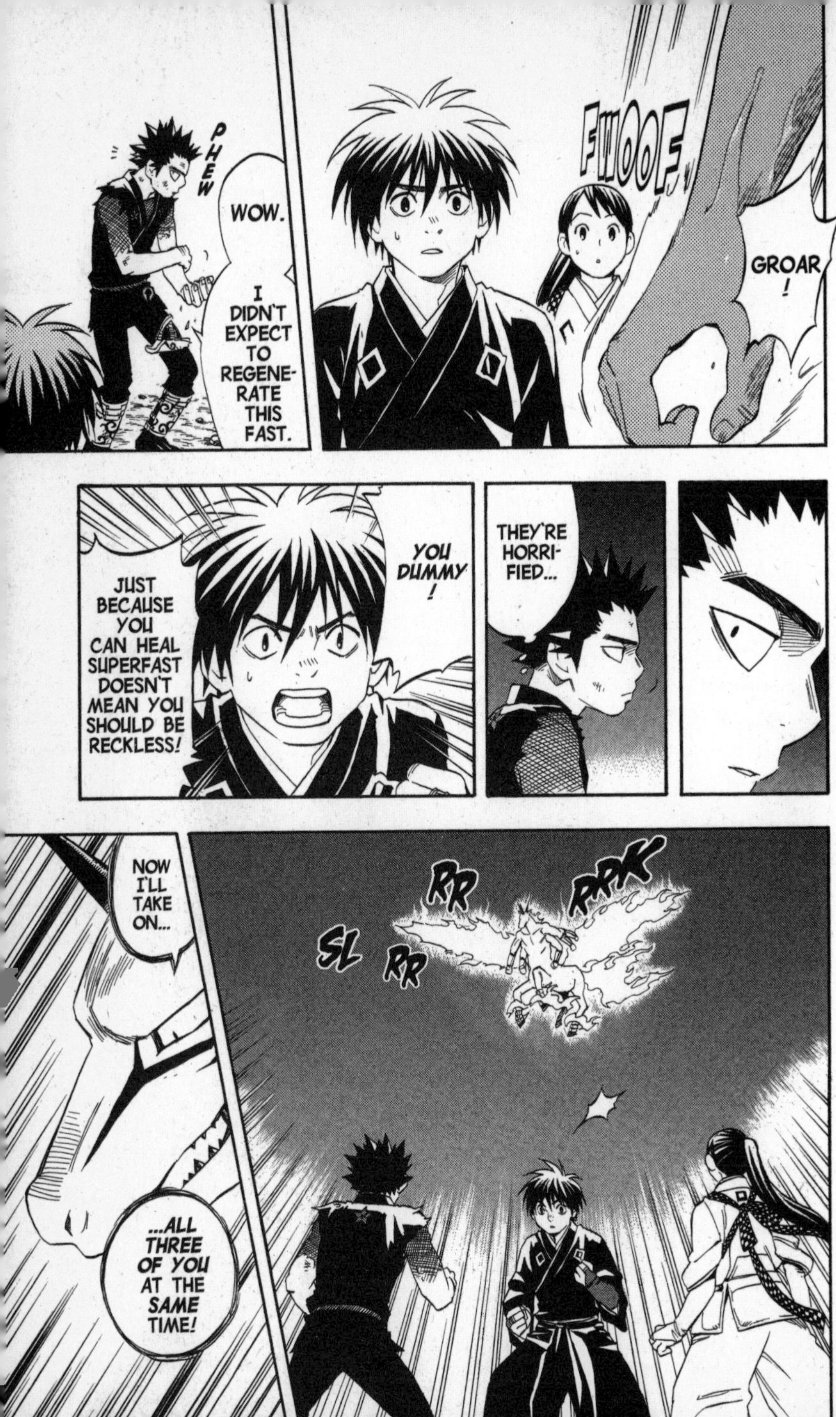
FWOOF
GROAR!
PHEW
WOW.
I DIDN'T EXPECT TO REGENERATE THIS FAST.
THEY'RE HORRIFIED...
YOU DUMMY!
JUST BECAUSE YOU CAN HEAL SUPERFAST DOESN'T MEAN YOU SHOULD BE RECKLESS!
RR
RPK
SL
RR
NOW I'LL TAKE ON...
...ALL THREE OF YOU AT THE SAME TIME!

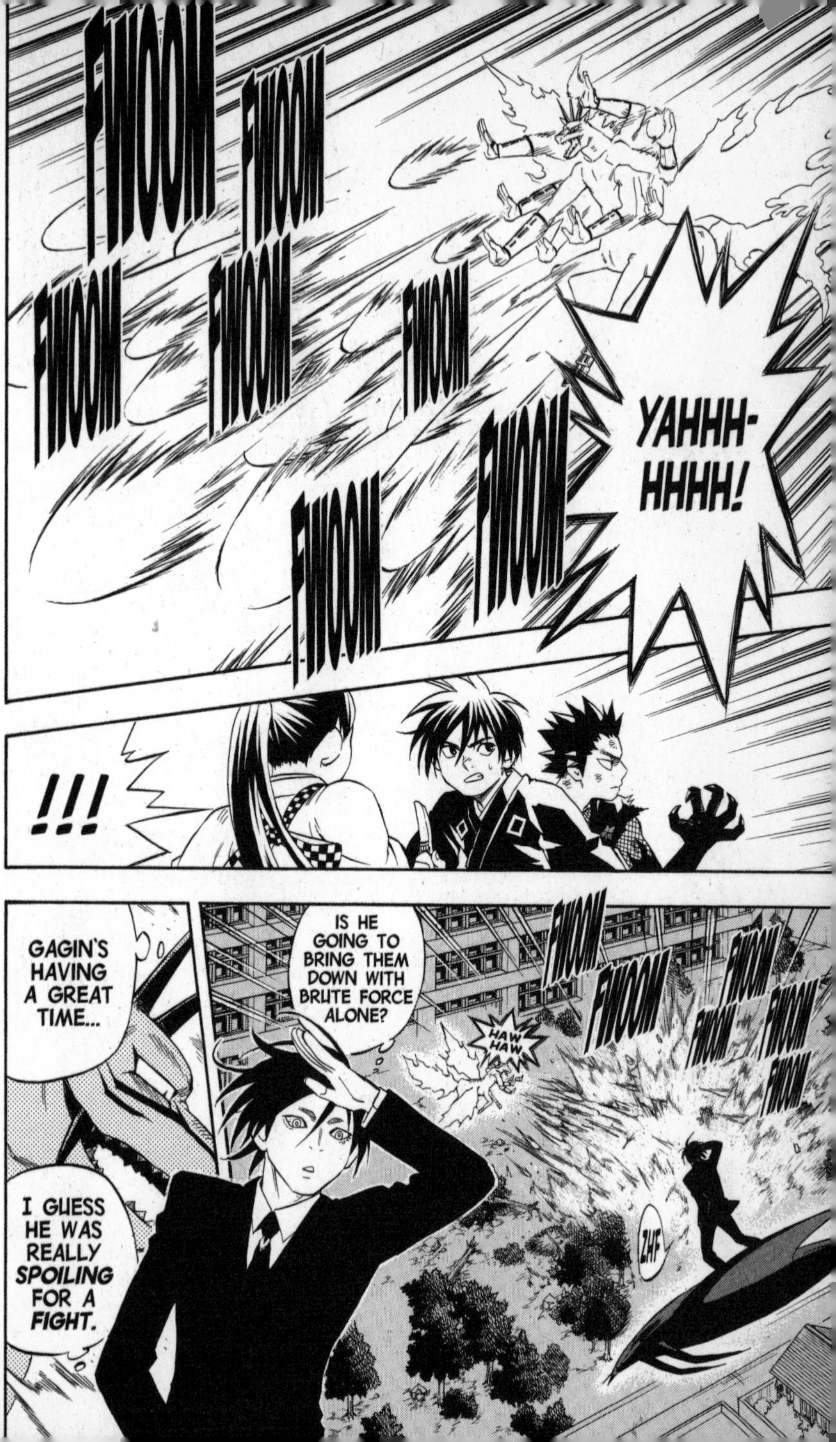
YAHHH-HHHH!
FWOOM
FWOOM
FWOOM
FWOOM
FWOOM
FWOOM
FWOOM
!!!
FWOOM
FWOOM
FWOOM
FWOOM
FWOOM
FWOOM
HAW HAW
IS HE GOING TO BRING THEM DOWN WITH BRUTE FORCE ALONE?
ZHF
GAGIN'S HAVING A GREAT TIME...
I GUESS HE WAS REALLY SPOILING FOR A FIGHT.

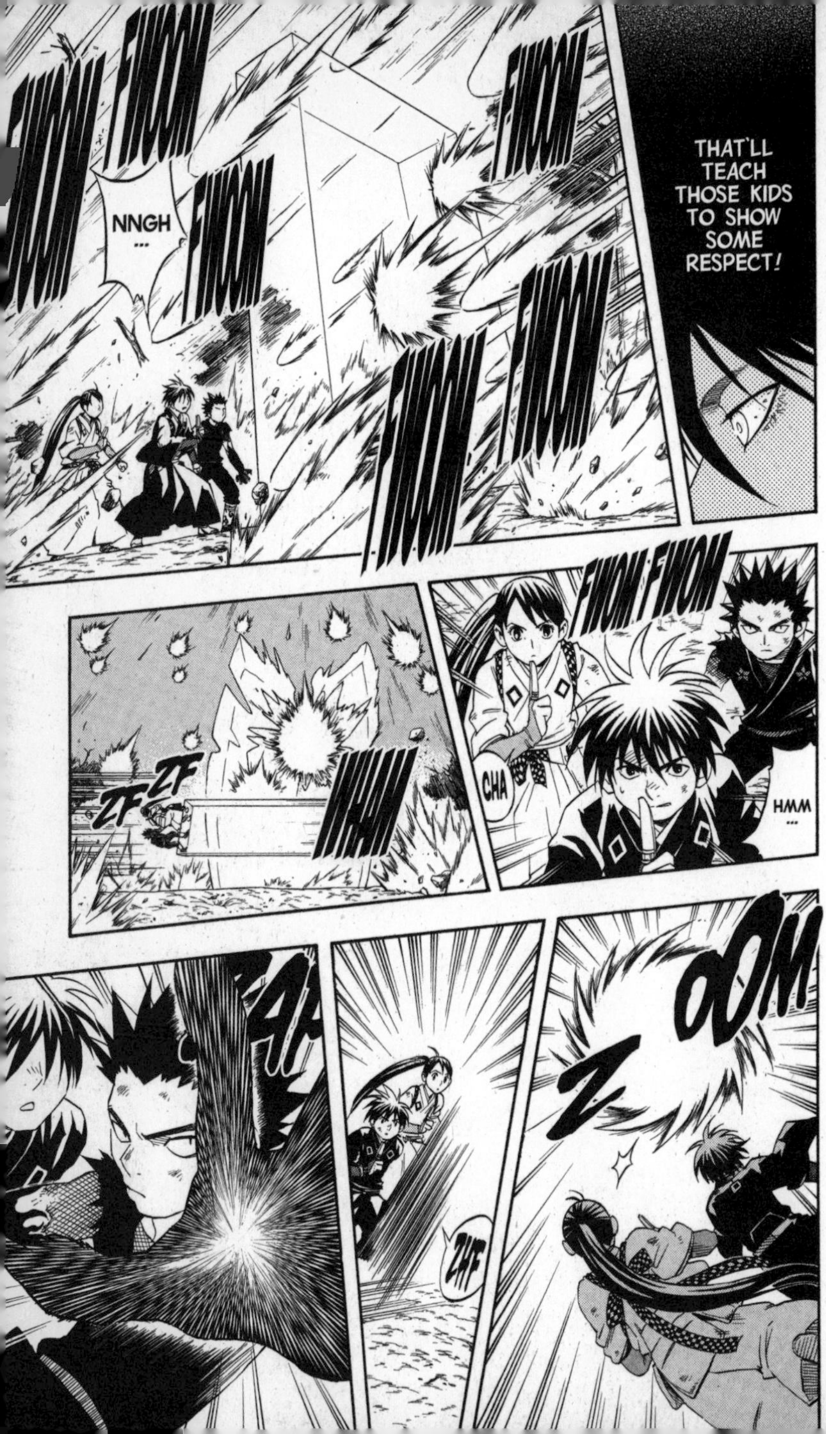
THAT'LL TEACH THOSE KIDS TO SHOW SOME RESPECT!
NNGH ...
FWOM FWOM
CHA
HMM ...
ZF ZF
ZHF

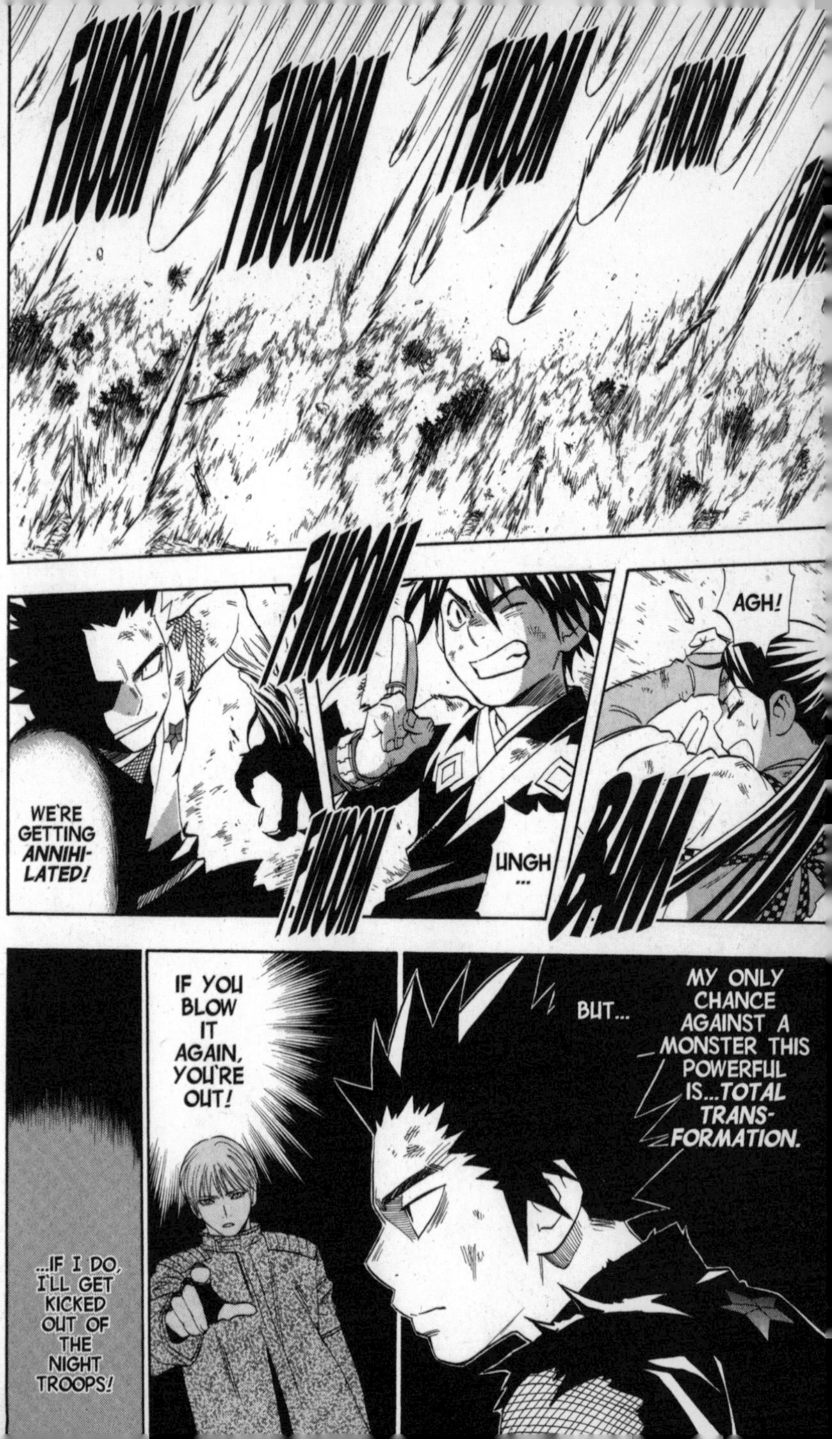
FWOOM
FWOOM
FWOOM
FWOOM
AGH!
BAM
FWOOM
FWOOM
UNGH...
WE'RE GETTING ANNIHILATED!
MY ONLY CHANCE AGAINST A MONSTER THIS POWERFUL IS...TOTAL TRANSFORMATION.
BUT...
IF YOU BLOW IT AGAIN, YOU'RE OUT!
...IF I DO, I'LL GET KICKED OUT OF THE NIGHT TROOPS!

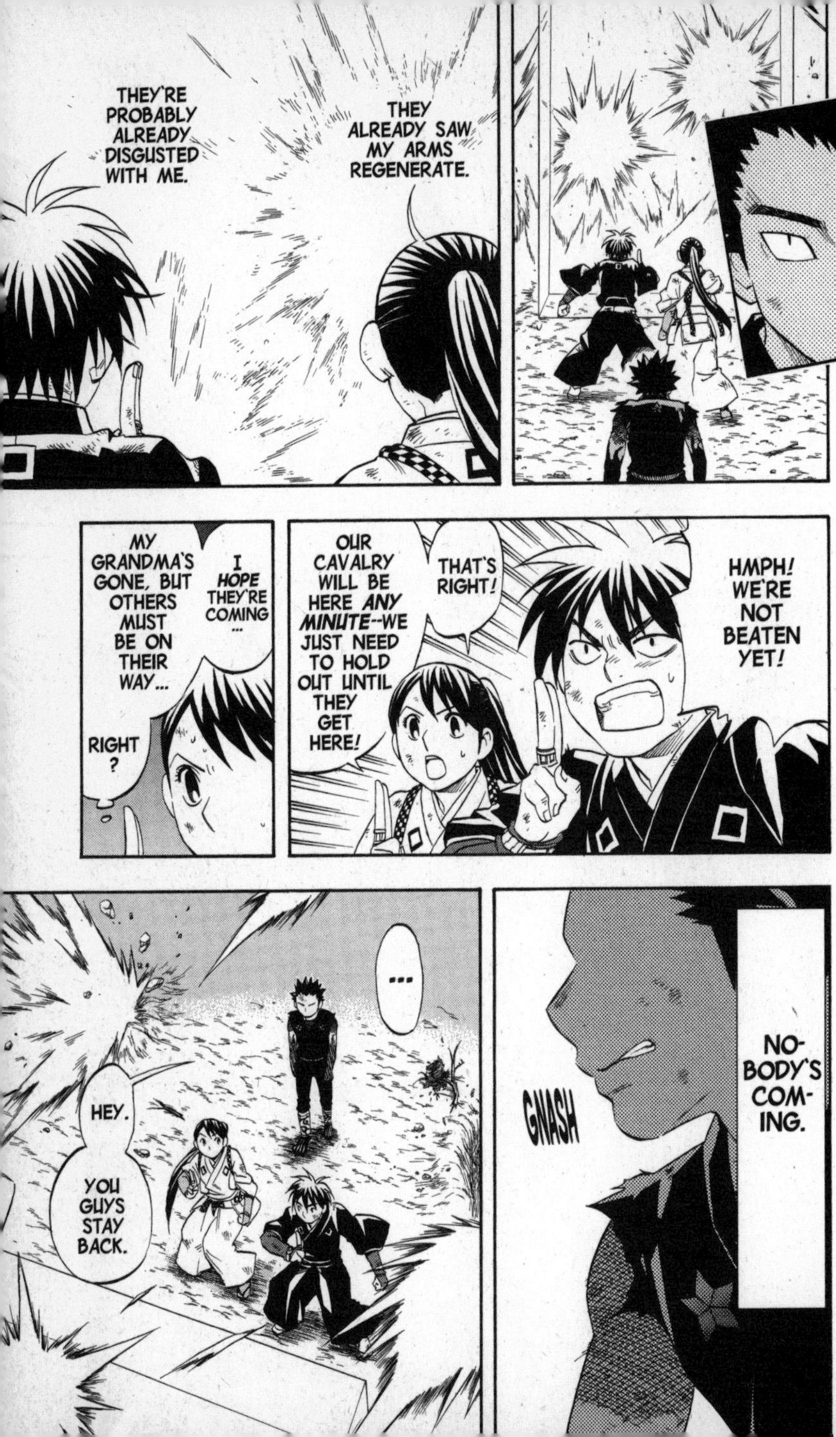
THEY ALREADY SAW MY ARMS REGENERATE.
THEY'RE PROBABLY ALREADY DISGUSTED WITH ME.
HMPH! WE'RE NOT BEATEN YET!
THAT'S RIGHT!
OUR CAVALRY WILL BE HERE *ANY MINUTE*--WE JUST NEED TO HOLD OUT UNTIL THEY GET HERE!
I *HOPE* THEY'RE COMING ...
MY GRANDMA'S GONE, BUT OTHERS MUST BE ON THEIR WAY...
RIGHT?
NO-BODY'S COM-ING.
GNASH
...
HEY.
YOU GUYS STAY BACK.

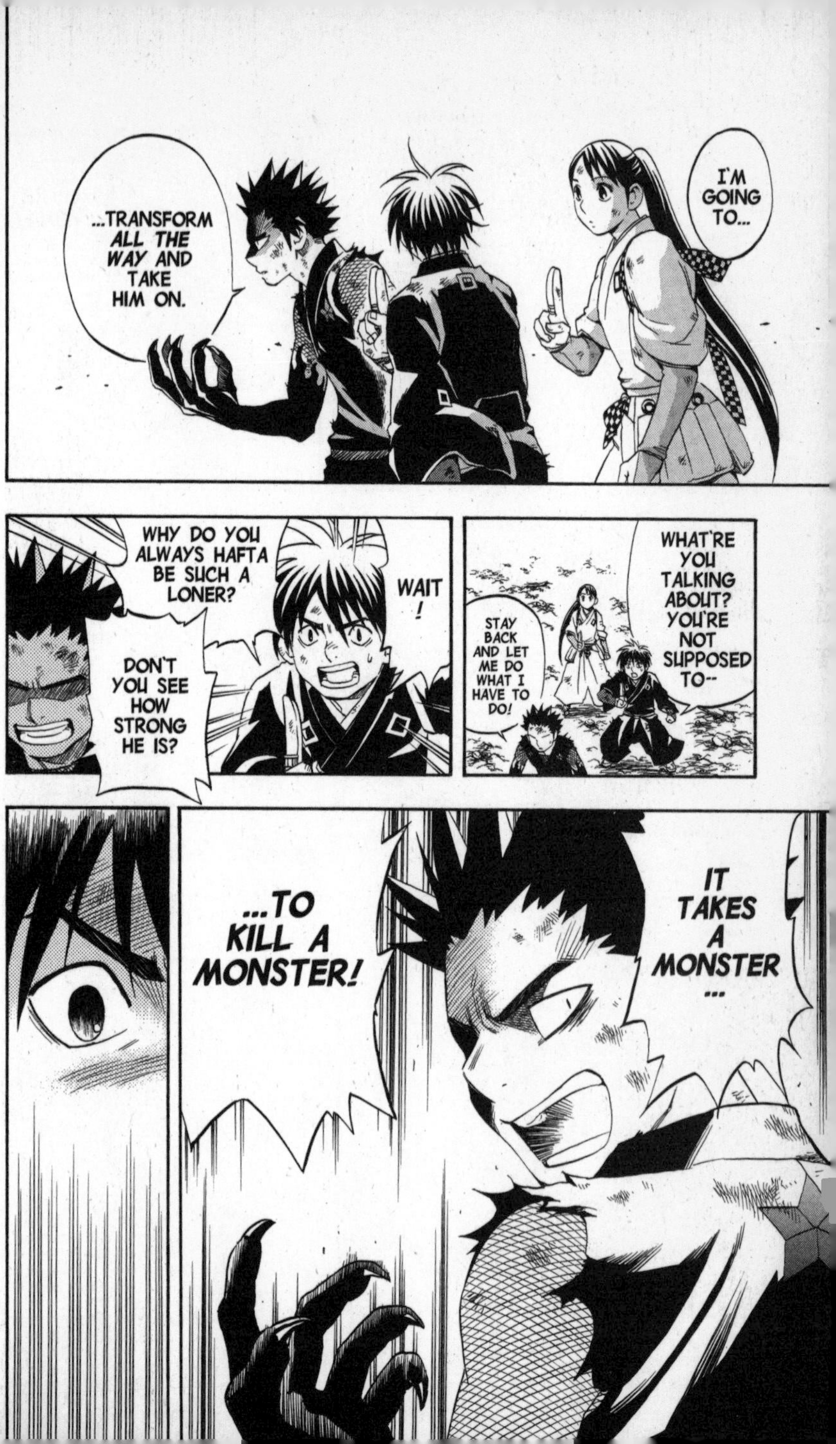
I'M GOING TO...
...TRANSFORM ALL THE WAY AND TAKE HIM ON.
WHAT'RE YOU TALKING ABOUT? YOU'RE NOT SUPPOSED TO--
STAY BACK AND LET ME DO WHAT I HAVE TO DO!
WAIT!
WHY DO YOU ALWAYS HAFTA BE SUCH A LONER?
DON'T YOU SEE HOW STRONG HE IS?
IT TAKES A MONSTER...
...TO KILL A MONSTER!

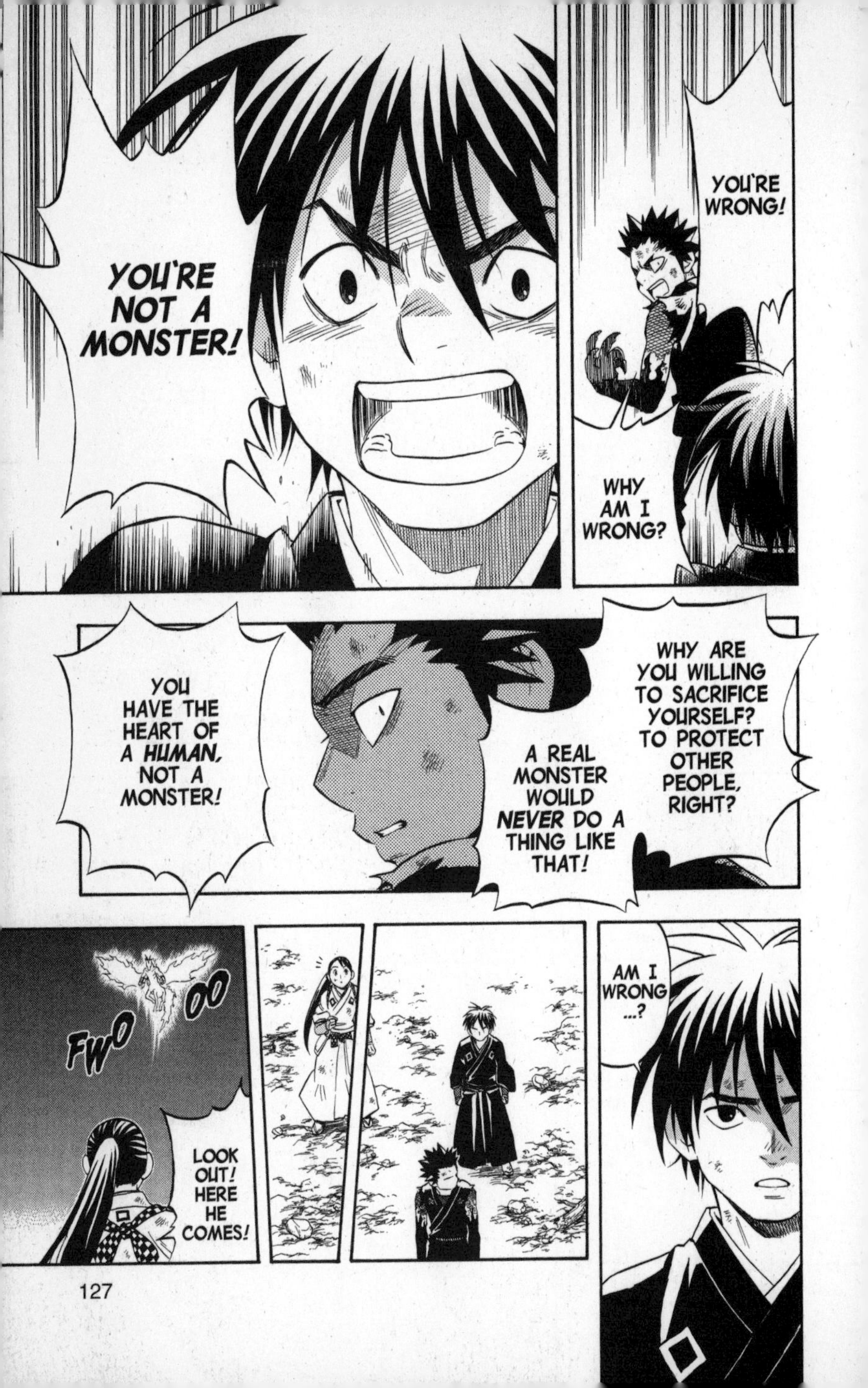
YOU'RE WRONG!
WHY AM I WRONG?
YOU'RE NOT A MONSTER!
WHY ARE YOU WILLING TO SACRIFICE YOURSELF? TO PROTECT OTHER PEOPLE, RIGHT?
A REAL MONSTER WOULD NEVER DO A THING LIKE THAT!
YOU HAVE THE HEART OF A HUMAN, NOT A MONSTER!
AM I WRONG ...?
FWOOO
LOOK OUT! HERE HE COMES!

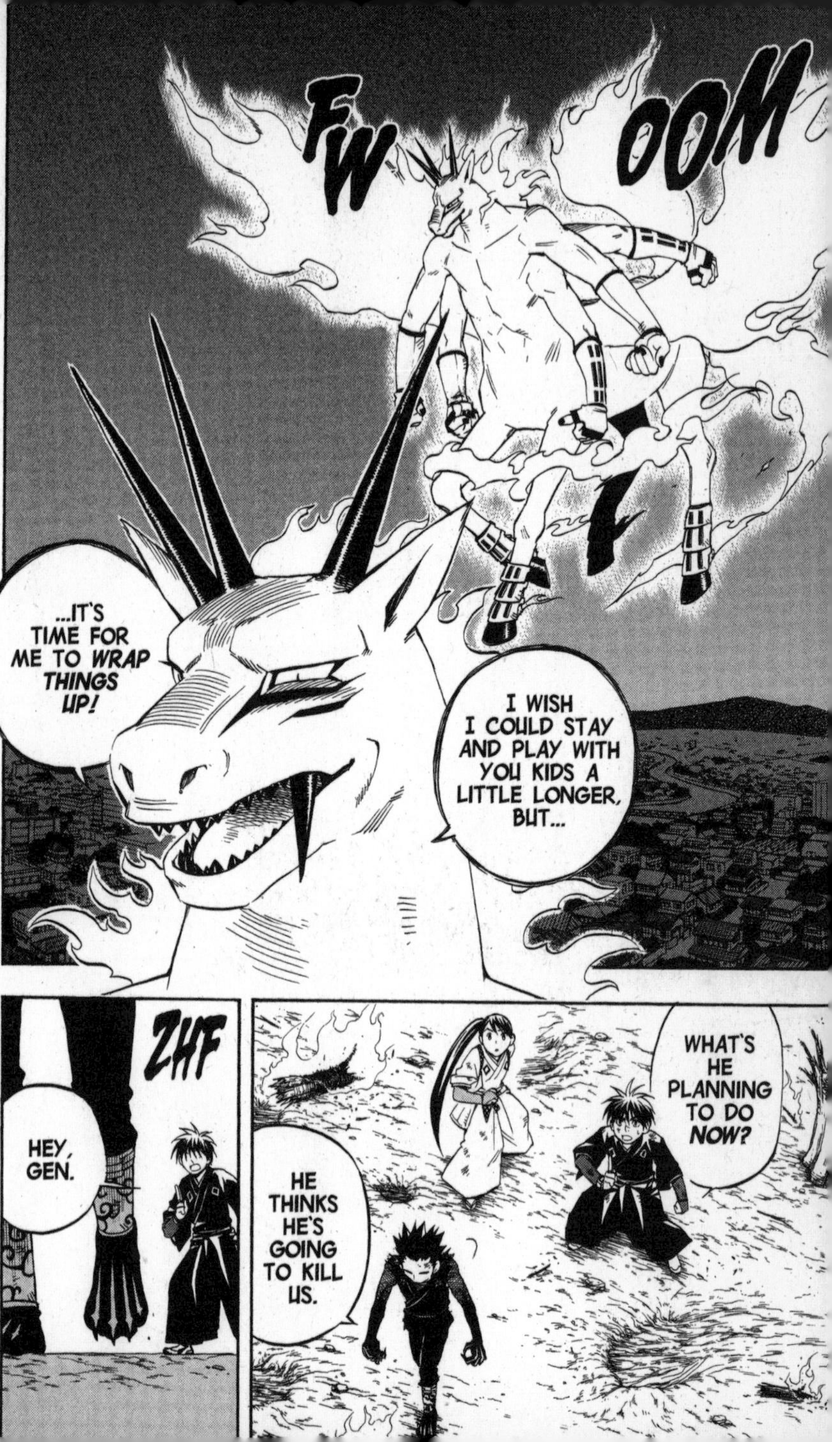
FWOOOM
I WISH I COULD STAY AND PLAY WITH YOU KIDS A LITTLE LONGER, BUT...
...IT'S TIME FOR ME TO *WRAP THINGS UP!*
WHAT'S HE PLANNING TO DO *NOW?*
HE THINKS HE'S GOING TO KILL US.
ZHF
HEY, GEN.

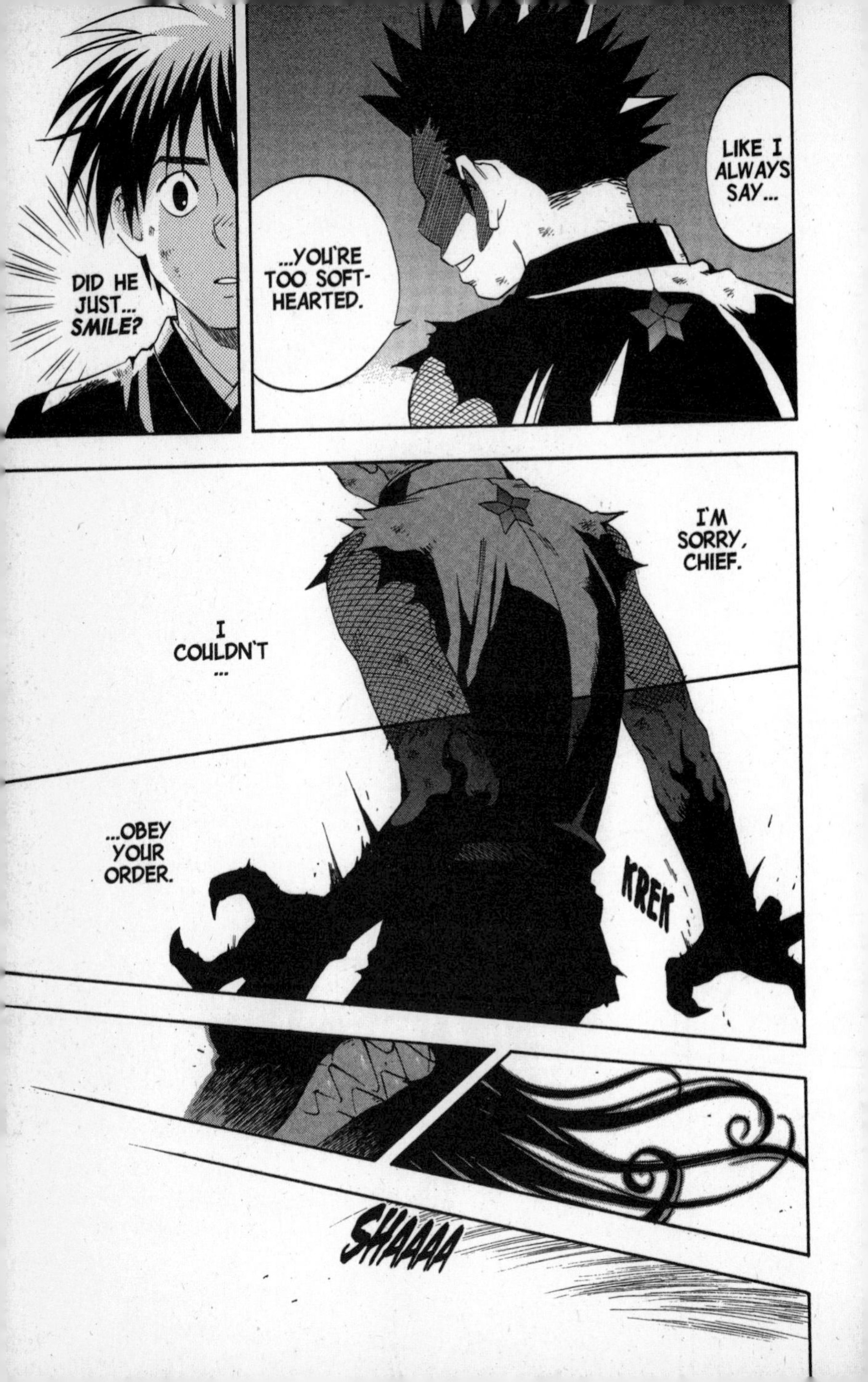
LIKE I ALWAYS SAY...
...YOU'RE TOO SOFT-HEARTED.
DID HE JUST... SMILE?
I'M SORRY, CHIEF.
I COULDN'T ...
...OBEY YOUR ORDER.
KREK
SHAAAA

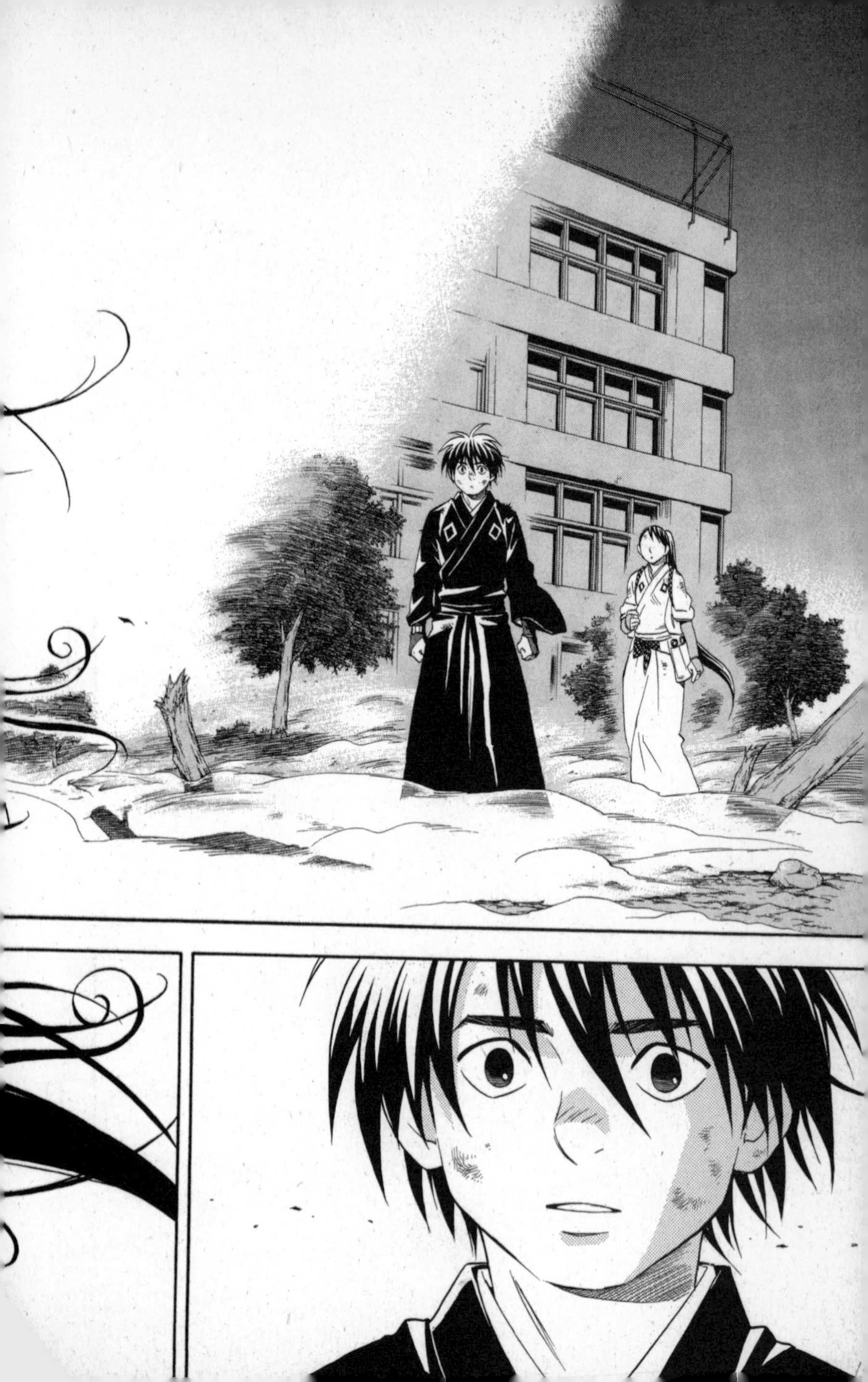

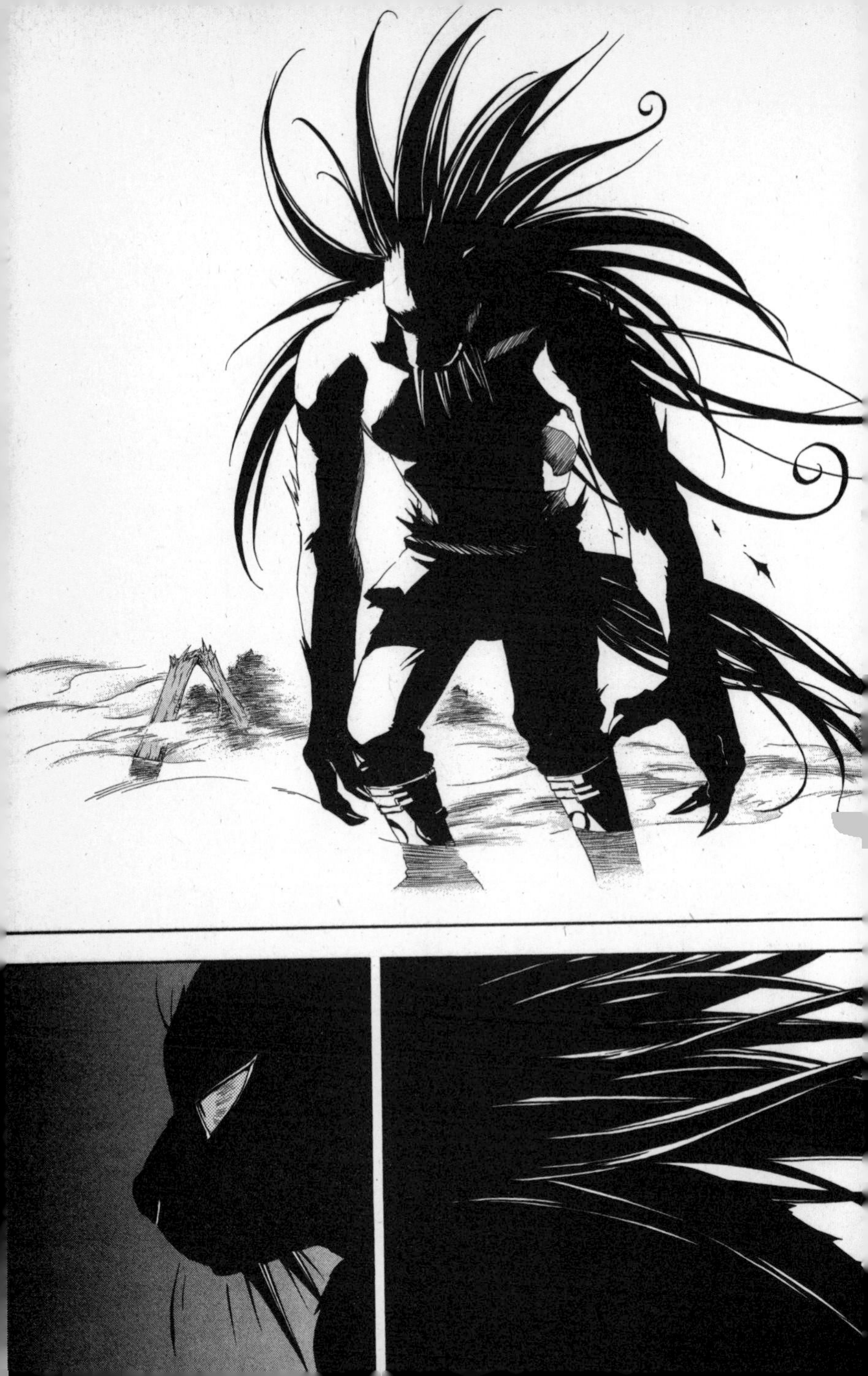

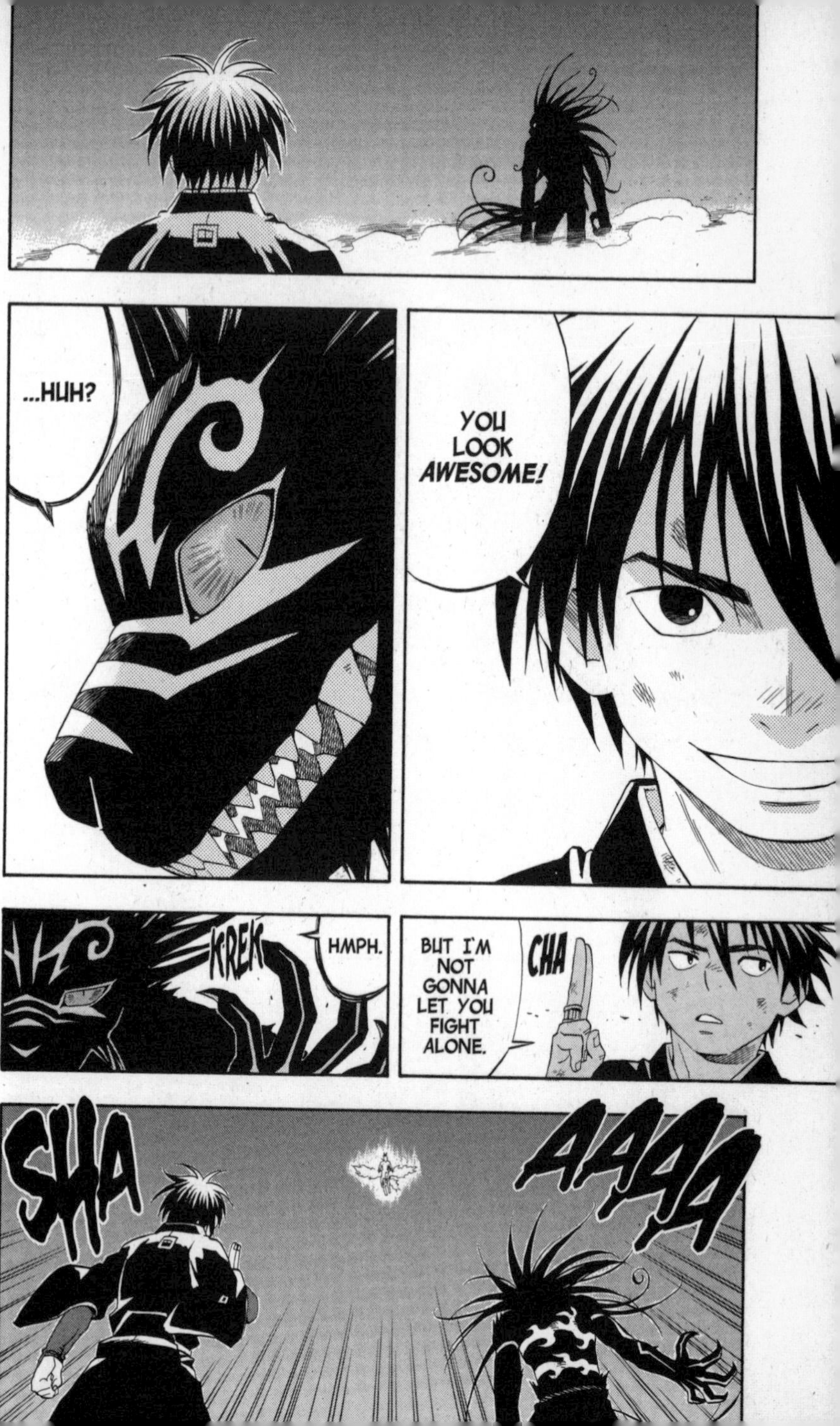
YOU LOOK AWESOME!
...HUH?
CHA
BUT I'M NOT GONNA LET YOU FIGHT ALONE.
HMPH.
KREK
AAAA
SHA

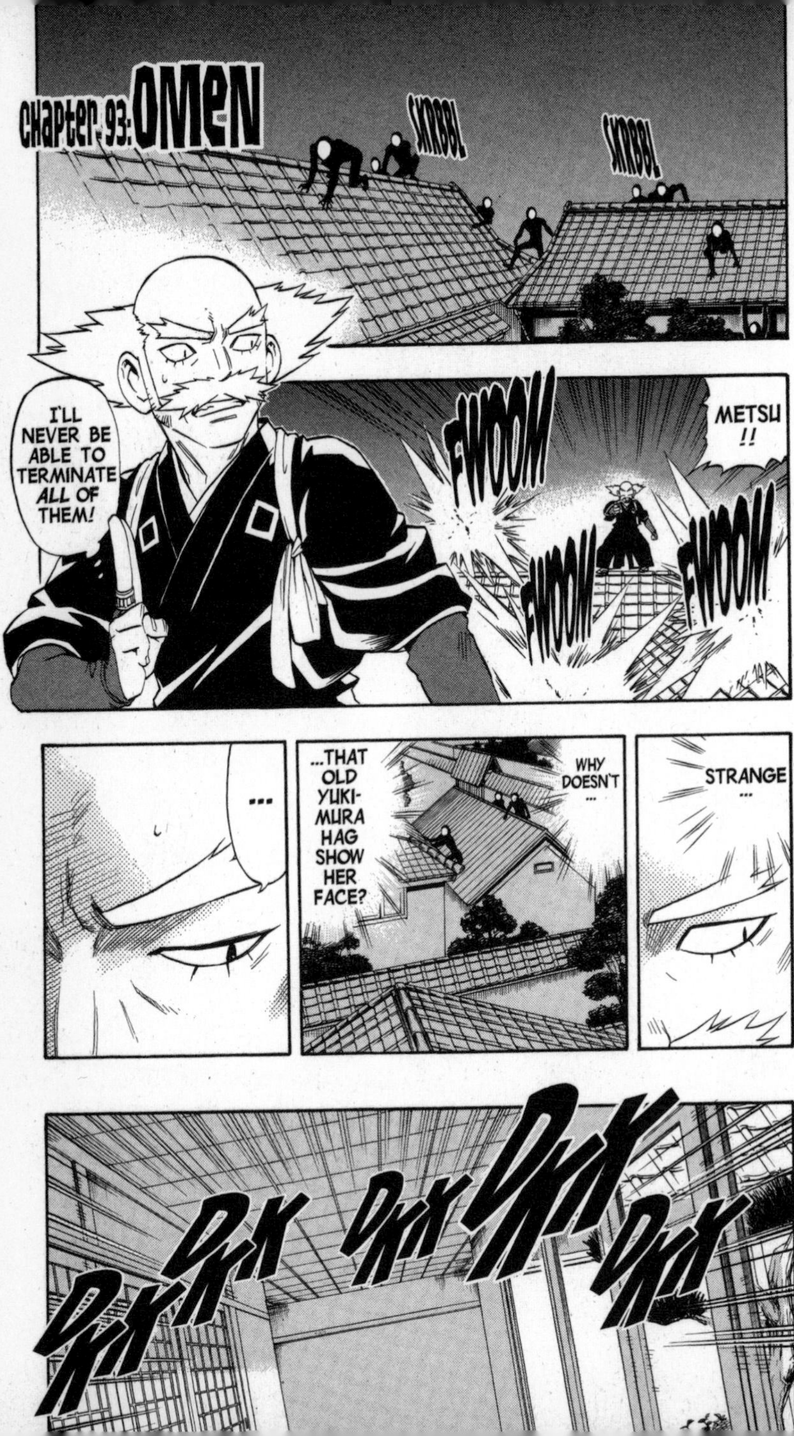
Chapter 93: Omen
SKRBBL
SKRBBL
METSU!!
FWOOM
FWOOM
FWOOM
I'LL NEVER BE ABLE TO TERMINATE ALL OF THEM!
STRANGE...
WHY DOESN'T...
...THAT OLD YUKIMURA HAG SHOW HER FACE?
...
DKK
DKK
DKK
DKK
DKK

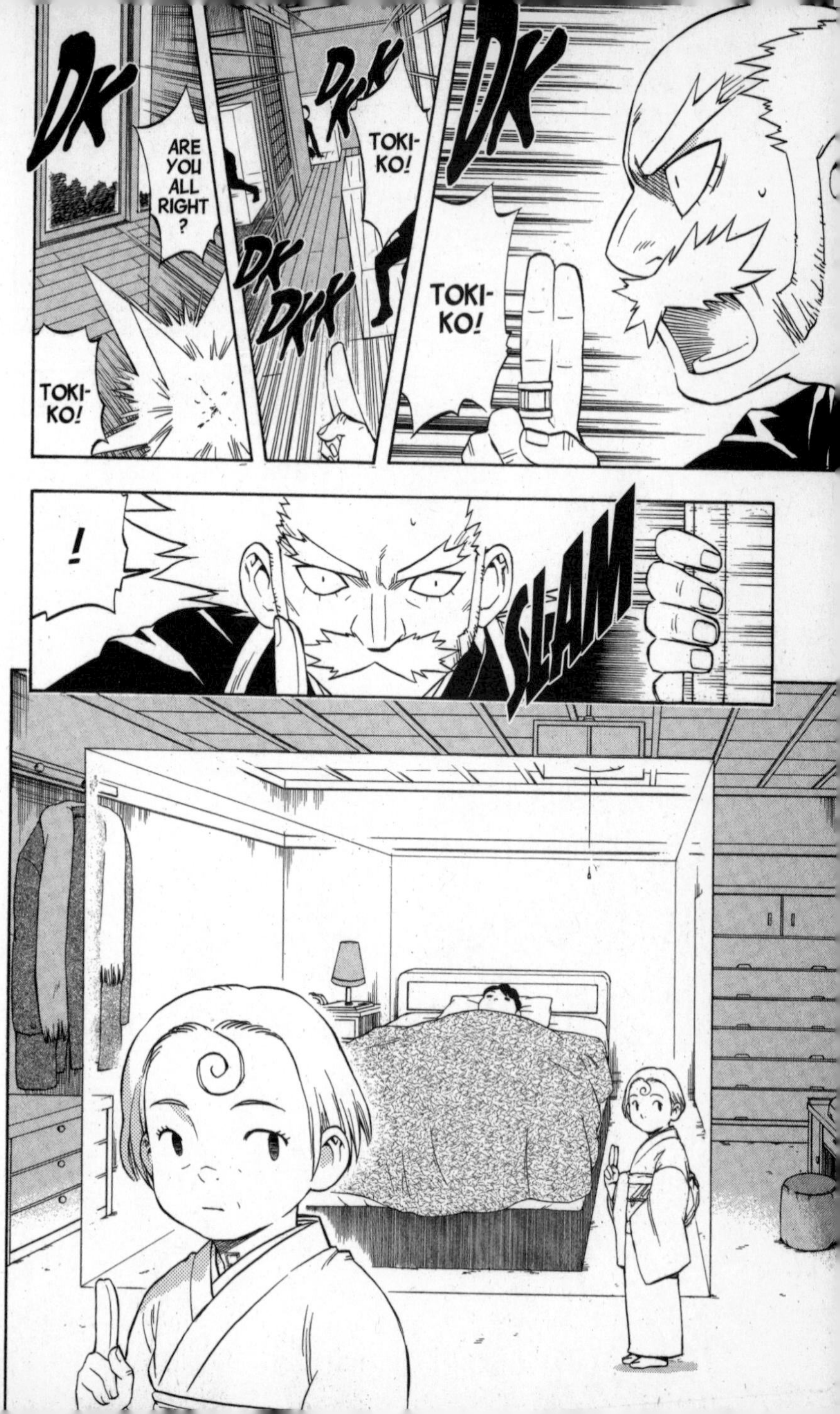
DK
TOKI-KO!
DKK
TOKI-KO!
DK DKK
DK
ARE YOU ALL RIGHT?
TOKI-KO!
SLAM
!

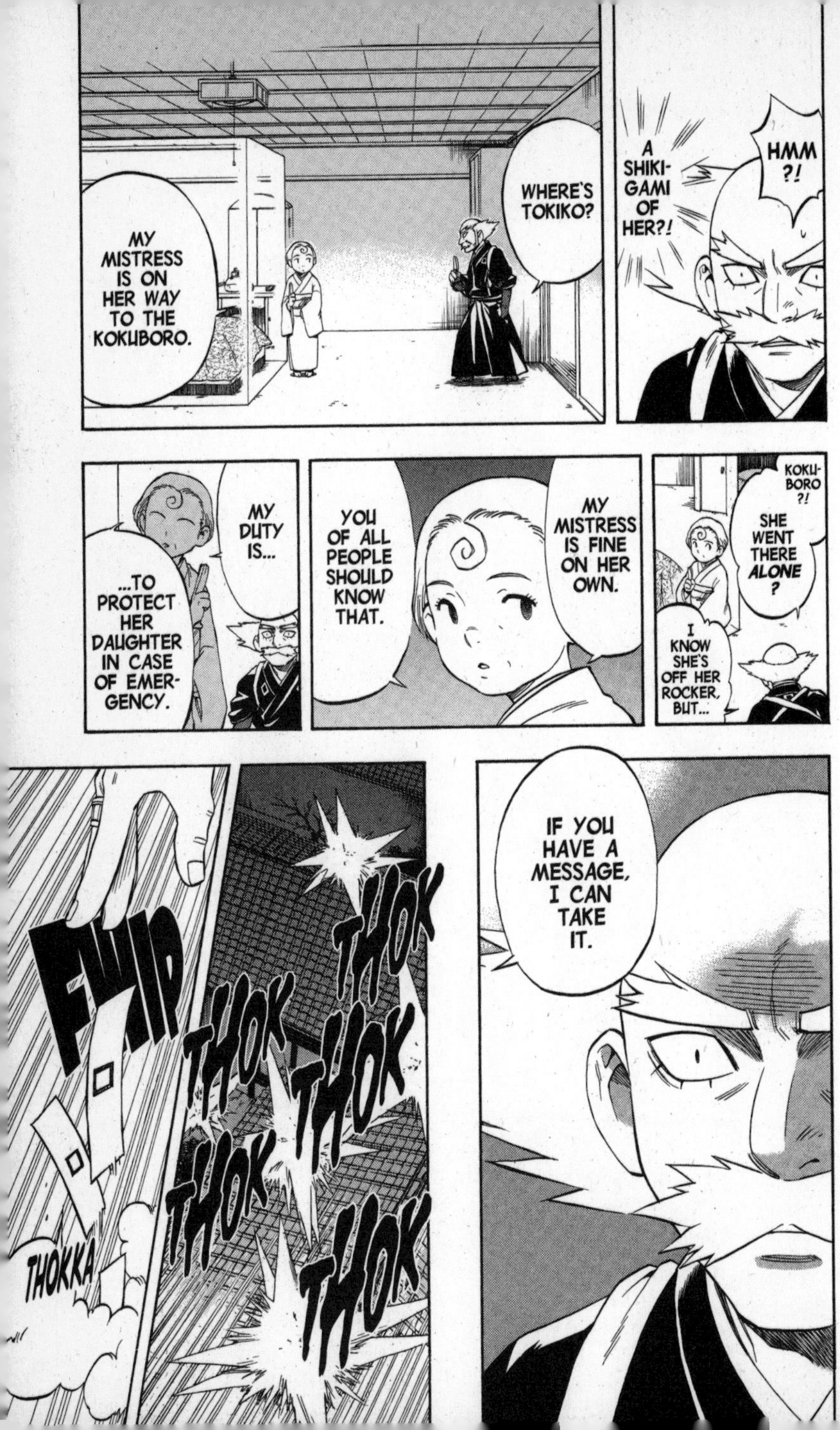
HMM?!
A SHIKIGAMI OF HER?!
WHERE'S TOKIKO?
MY MISTRESS IS ON HER WAY TO THE KOKUBORO.
KOKUBORO?!
SHE WENT THERE ALONE?
I KNOW SHE'S OFF HER ROCKER, BUT...
MY MISTRESS IS FINE ON HER OWN.
YOU OF ALL PEOPLE SHOULD KNOW THAT.
MY DUTY IS...
...TO PROTECT HER DAUGHTER IN CASE OF EMERGENCY.
IF YOU HAVE A MESSAGE, I CAN TAKE IT.
FWIP
THOK THOK THOK THOK THOK THOK
THOKKA

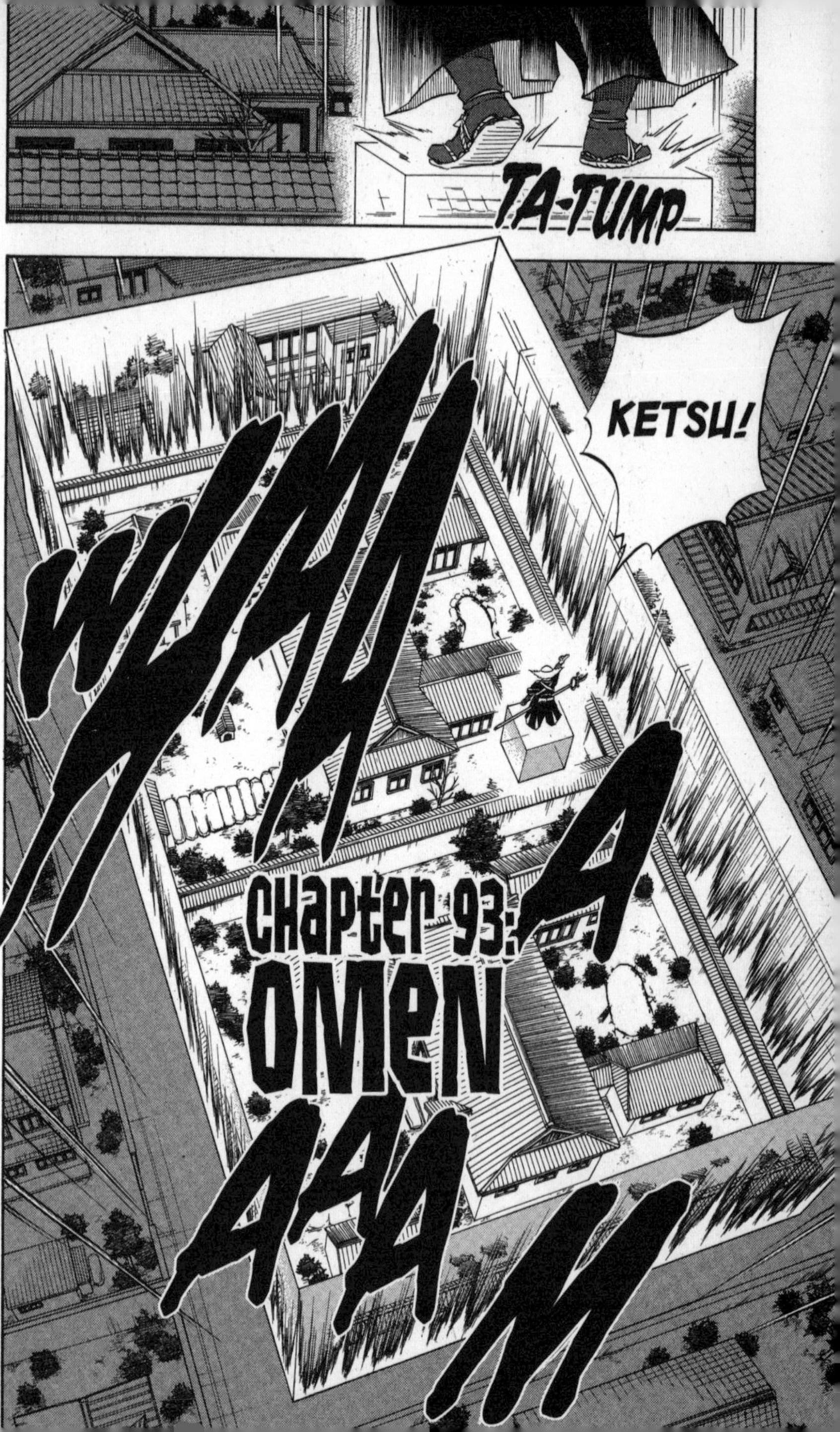
TA-TUMP
KETSU!
Chapter 93:
Omen

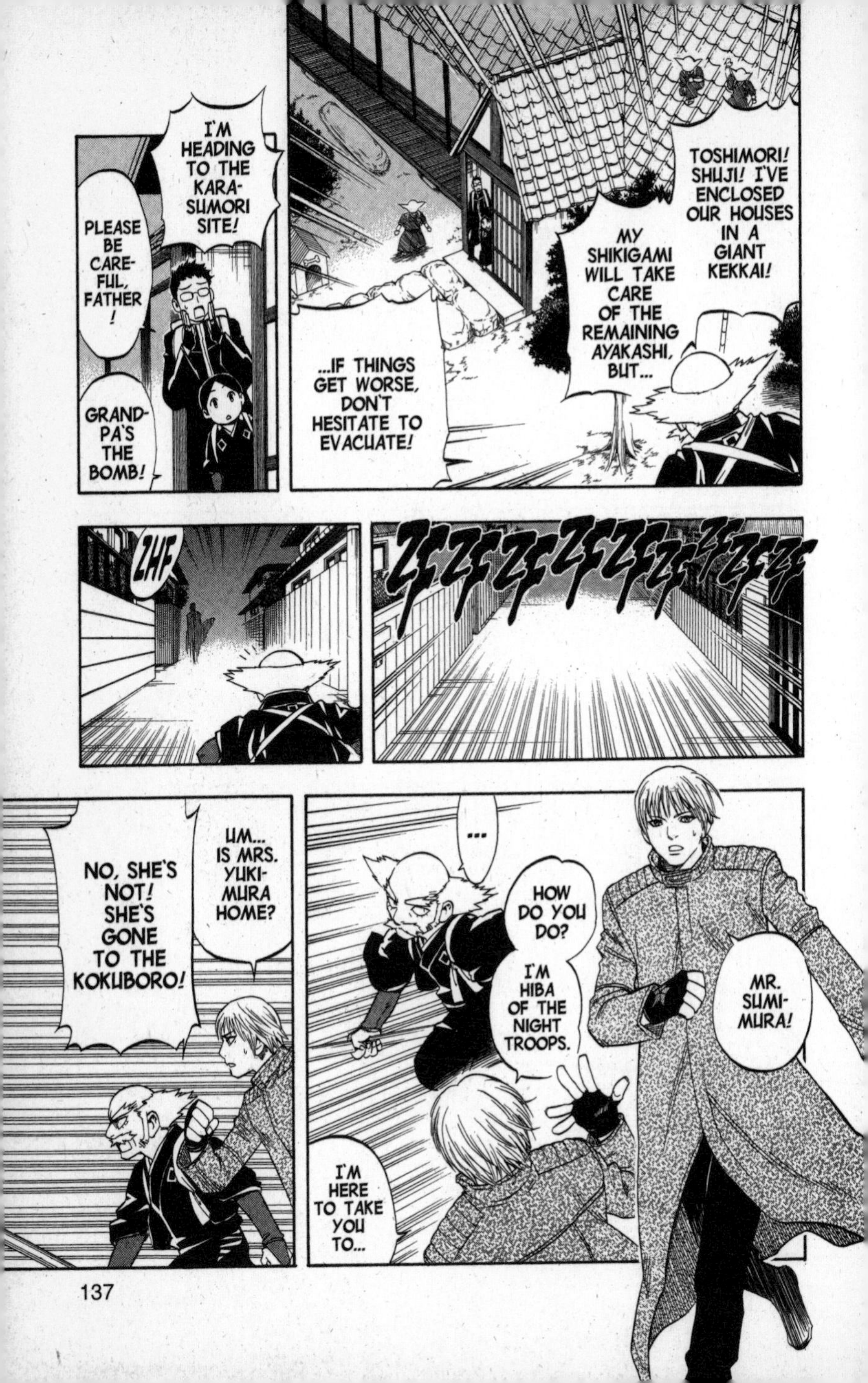
TOSHIMORI! SHUJI! I'VE ENCLOSED OUR HOUSES IN A GIANT KEKKAI!
MY SHIKIGAMI WILL TAKE CARE OF THE REMAINING AYAKASHI, BUT...
...IF THINGS GET WORSE, DON'T HESITATE TO EVACUATE!
I'M HEADING TO THE KARA-SUMORI SITE!
PLEASE BE CARE-FUL, FATHER!
GRAND-PA'S THE BOMB!
ZHF
MR. SUMI-MURA!
...
HOW DO YOU DO?
I'M HIBA OF THE NIGHT TROOPS.
I'M HERE TO TAKE YOU TO...
UM... IS MRS. YUKI-MURA HOME?
NO, SHE'S NOT! SHE'S GONE TO THE KOKUBORO!

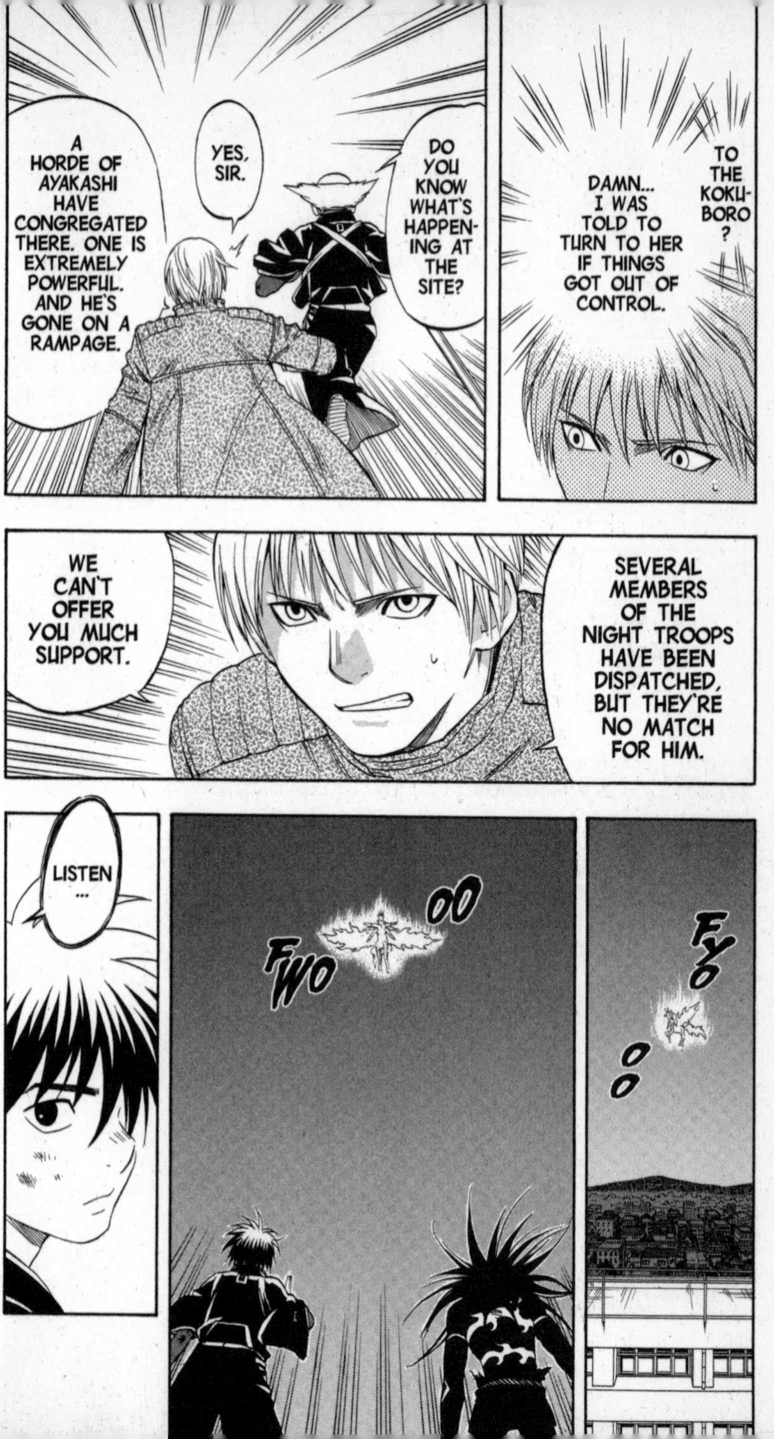
TO THE KOKU-BORO?
DAMN... I WAS TOLD TO TURN TO HER IF THINGS GOT OUT OF CONTROL.
DO YOU KNOW WHAT'S HAPPEN-ING AT THE SITE?
YES, SIR.
A HORDE OF AYAKASHI HAVE CONGREGATED THERE. ONE IS EXTREMELY POWERFUL. AND HE'S GONE ON A RAMPAGE.
SEVERAL MEMBERS OF THE NIGHT TROOPS HAVE BEEN DISPATCHED, BUT THEY'RE NO MATCH FOR HIM.
WE CAN'T OFFER YOU MUCH SUPPORT.
FYOOO
FWOOO
LISTEN...

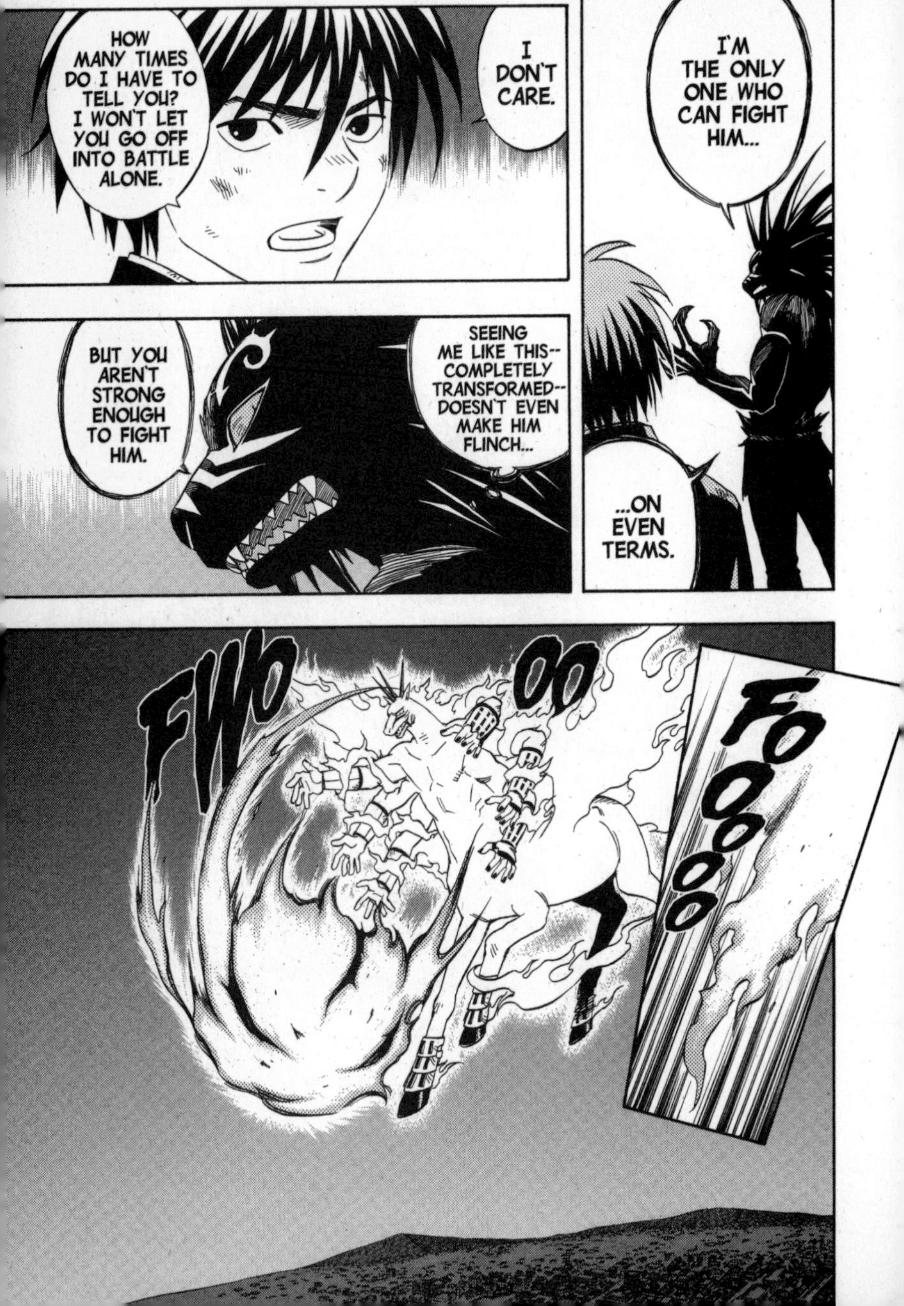
I'M THE ONLY ONE WHO CAN FIGHT HIM...
...ON EVEN TERMS.
I DON'T CARE.
HOW MANY TIMES DO I HAVE TO TELL YOU? I WON'T LET YOU GO OFF INTO BATTLE ALONE.
SEEING ME LIKE THIS--COMPLETELY TRANSFORMED--DOESN'T EVEN MAKE HIM FLINCH...
BUT YOU AREN'T STRONG ENOUGH TO FIGHT HIM.
FOOOOOO
FWOOO

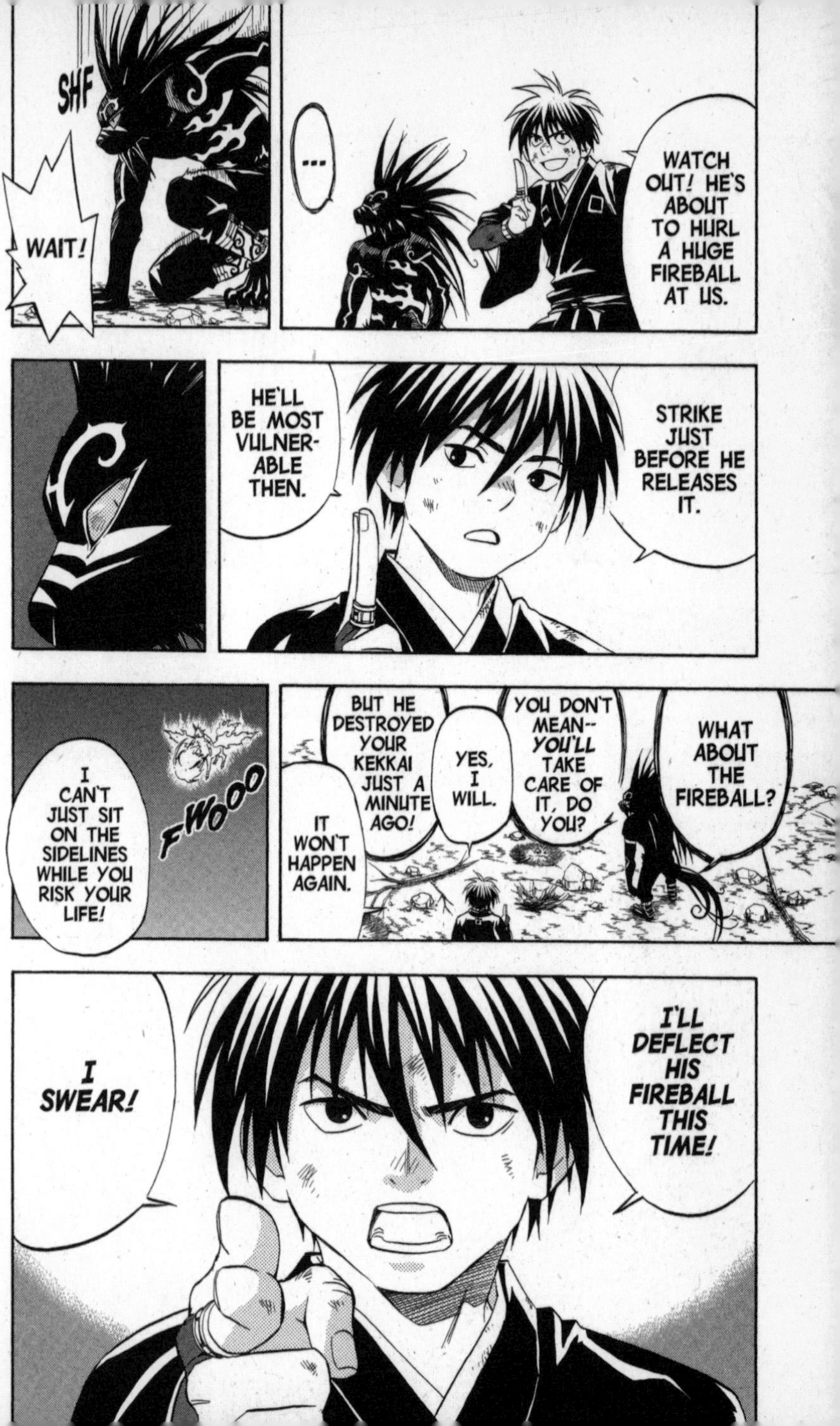
WATCH OUT! HE'S ABOUT TO HURL A HUGE FIREBALL AT US.
...
SHF
WAIT!
STRIKE JUST BEFORE HE RELEASES IT.
HE'LL BE MOST VULNER-ABLE THEN.
WHAT ABOUT THE FIREBALL?
YOU DON'T MEAN-- *YOU'LL* TAKE CARE OF IT, DO YOU?
YES, I WILL.
BUT HE DESTROYED YOUR KEKKAI JUST A MINUTE AGO!
IT WON'T HAPPEN AGAIN.
F-WOOO
I CAN'T JUST SIT ON THE SIDELINES WHILE YOU RISK YOUR LIFE!
I'LL DEFLECT HIS FIREBALL THIS TIME!
I SWEAR!

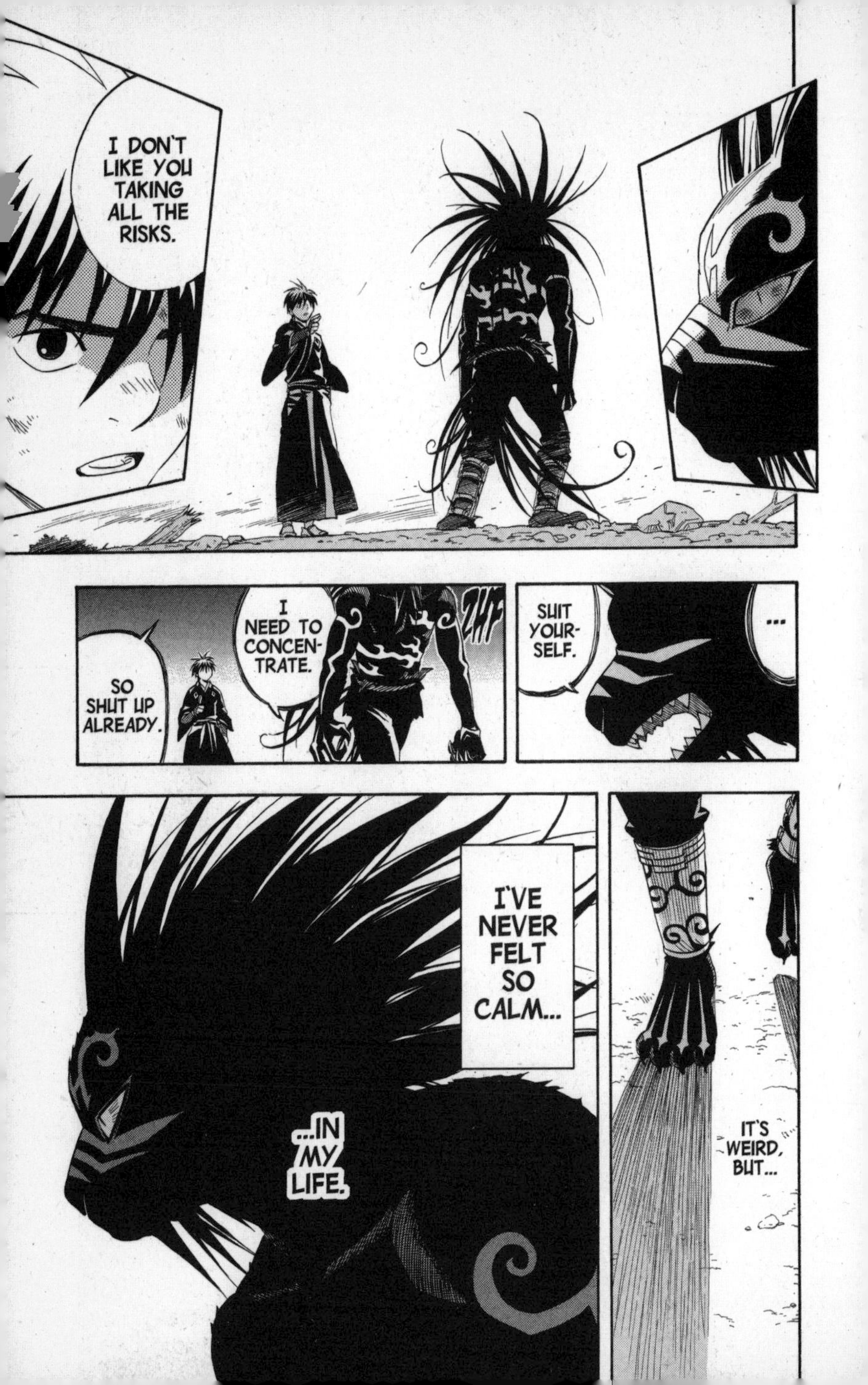
I DON'T LIKE YOU TAKING ALL THE RISKS.
...
SUIT YOURSELF.
ZHF
I NEED TO CONCENTRATE.
SO SHUT UP ALREADY.
IT'S WEIRD, BUT...
I'VE NEVER FELT SO CALM...
...IN MY LIFE.

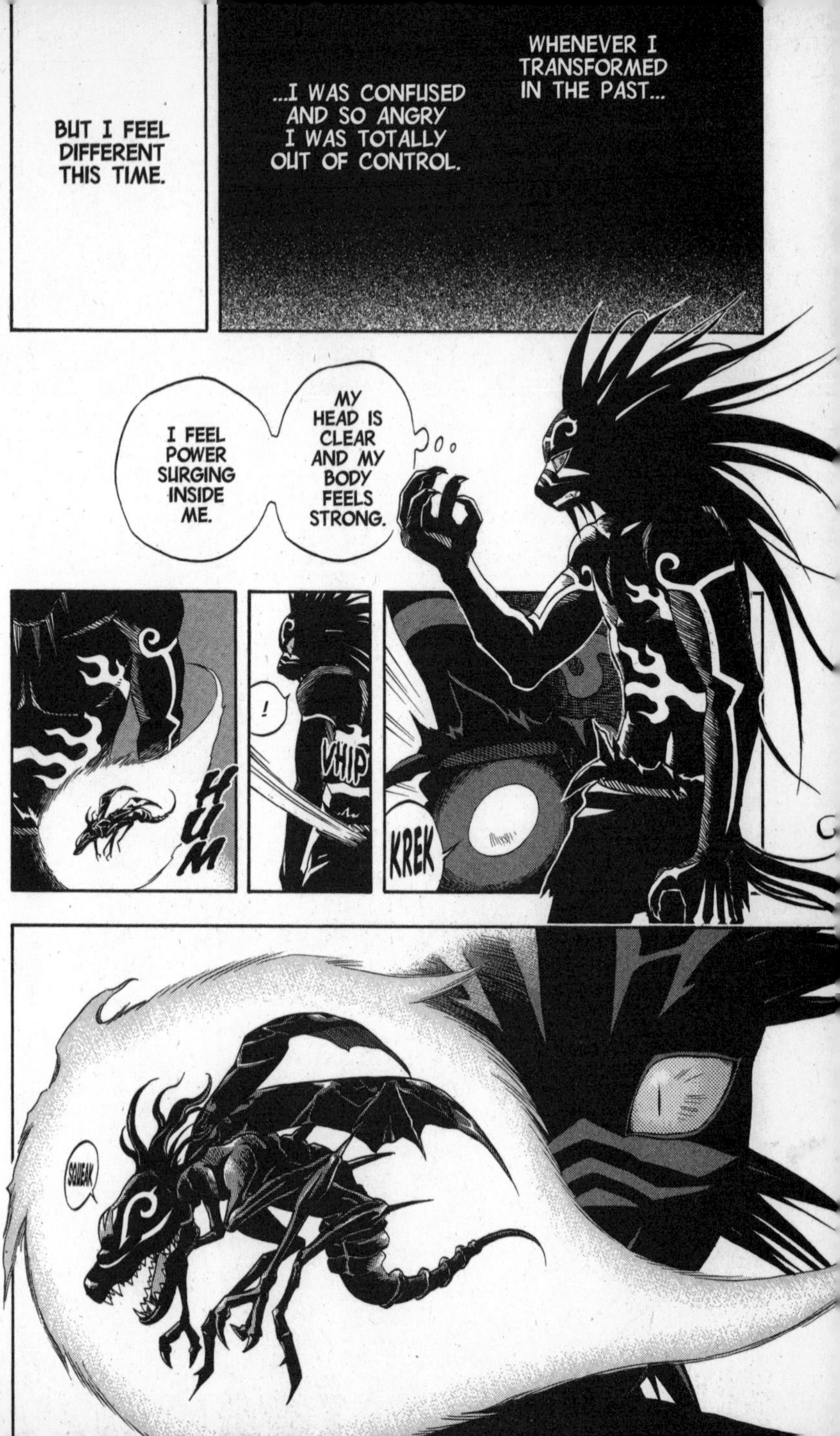
WHENEVER I TRANSFORMED IN THE PAST...
...I WAS CONFUSED AND SO ANGRY I WAS TOTALLY OUT OF CONTROL.
BUT I FEEL DIFFERENT THIS TIME.
MY HEAD IS CLEAR AND MY BODY FEELS STRONG.
I FEEL POWER SURGING INSIDE ME.
KREK
!
VHIP
HUM
SQUEAK

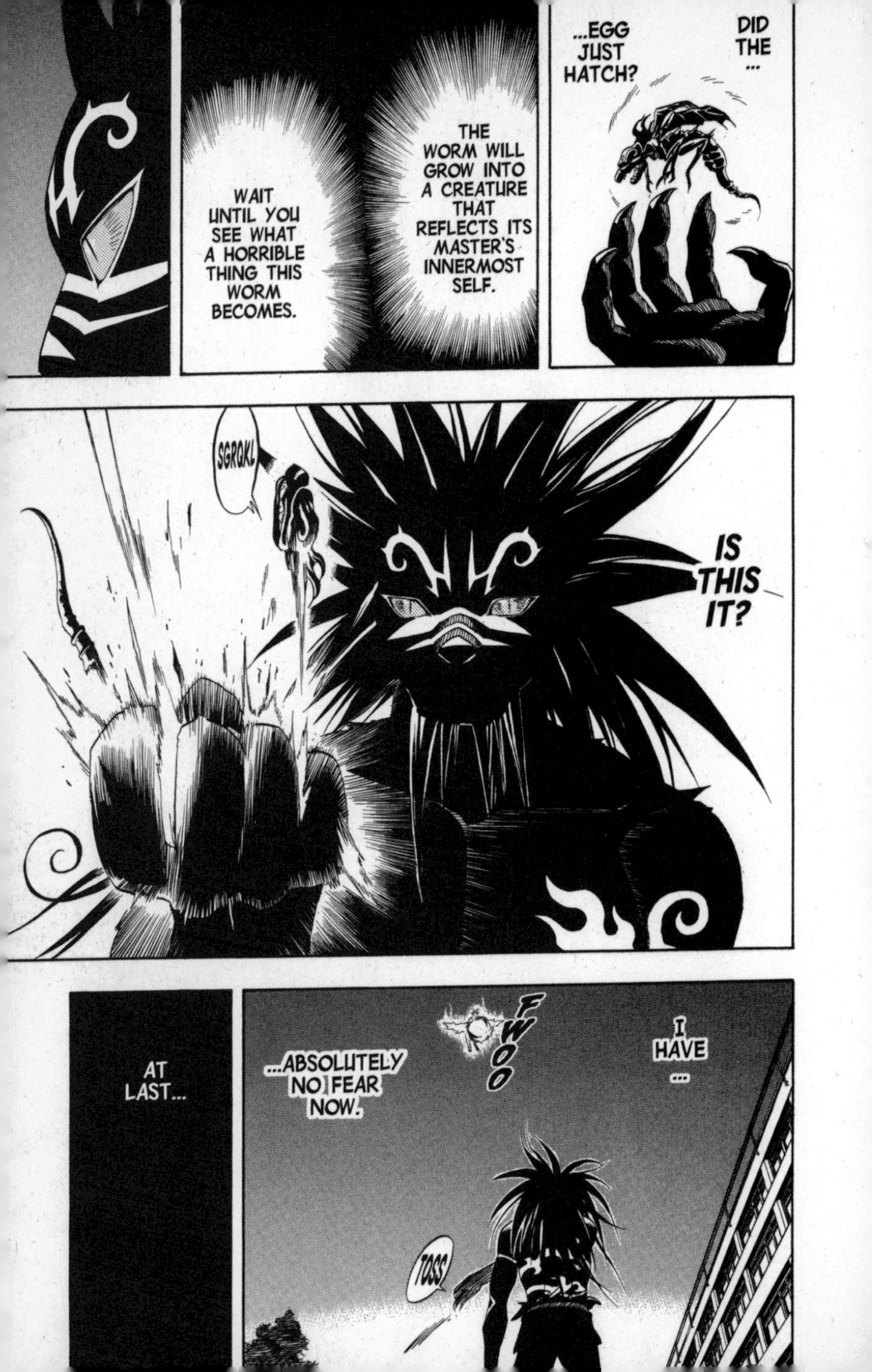
DID THE ...
...EGG JUST HATCH?
THE WORM WILL GROW INTO A CREATURE THAT REFLECTS ITS MASTER'S INNERMOST SELF.
WAIT UNTIL YOU SEE WHAT A HORRIBLE THING THIS WORM BECOMES.
IS THIS IT?
SGRQKL
I HAVE ...
FWOO
...ABSOLUTELY NO FEAR NOW.
TOSS
AT LAST...

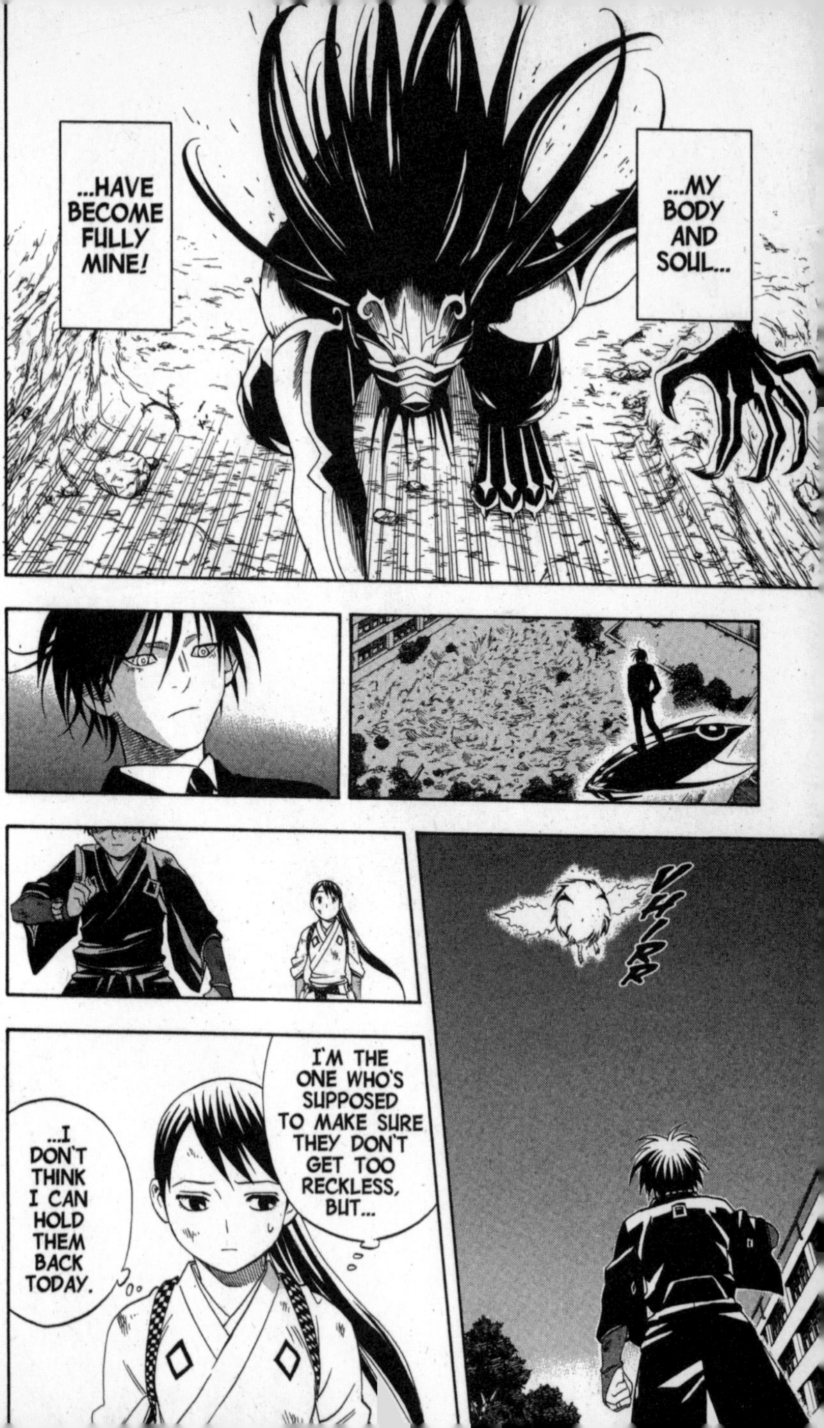
...MY BODY AND SOUL...
...HAVE BECOME FULLY MINE!
VHIRR
I'M THE ONE WHO'S SUPPOSED TO MAKE SURE THEY DON'T GET TOO RECKLESS, BUT...
...I DON'T THINK I CAN HOLD THEM BACK TODAY.

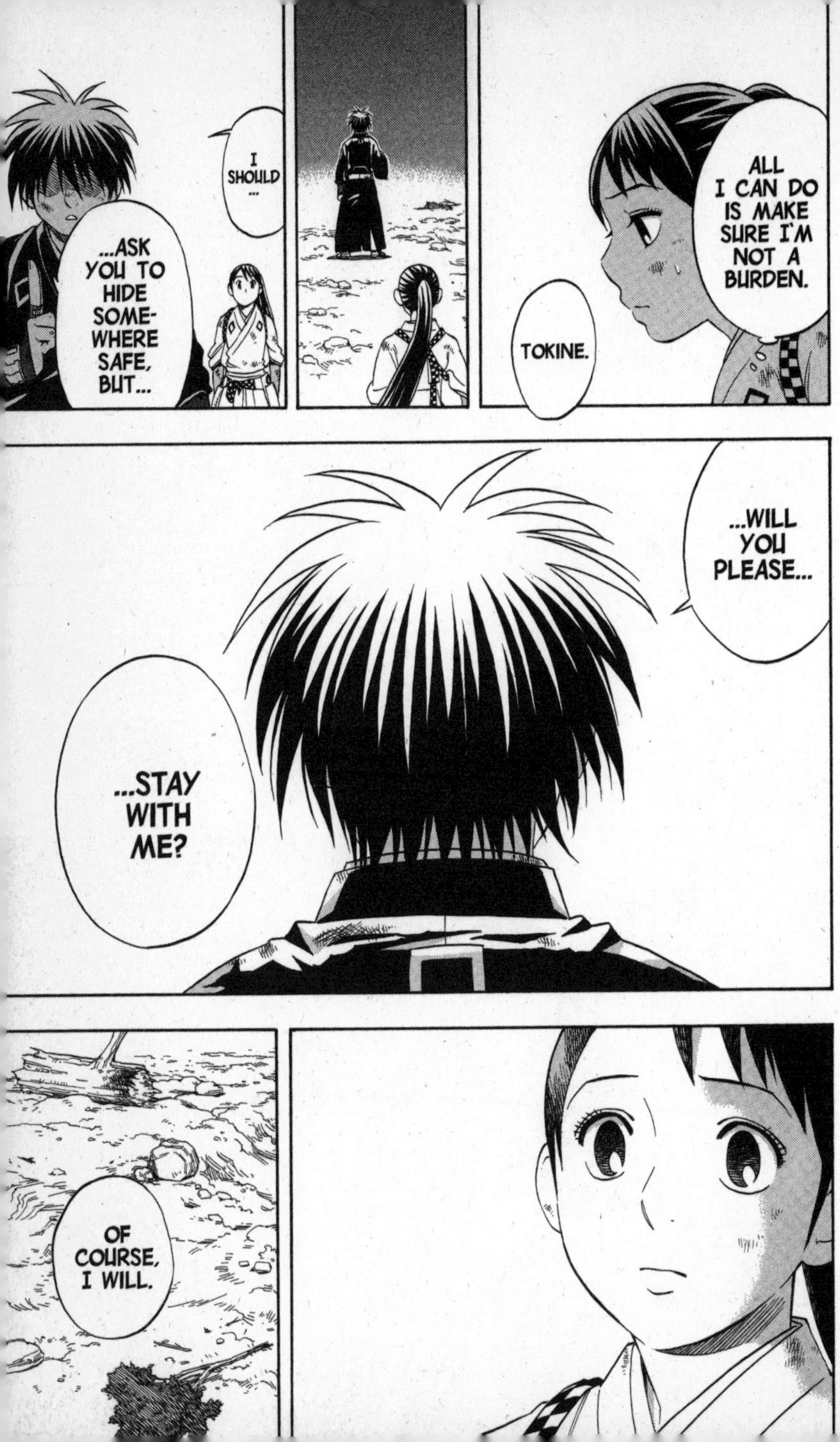
ALL I CAN DO IS MAKE SURE I'M NOT A BURDEN.
TOKINE.
I SHOULD...
...ASK YOU TO HIDE SOME-WHERE SAFE, BUT...
...WILL YOU PLEASE...
...STAY WITH ME?
OF COURSE, I WILL.

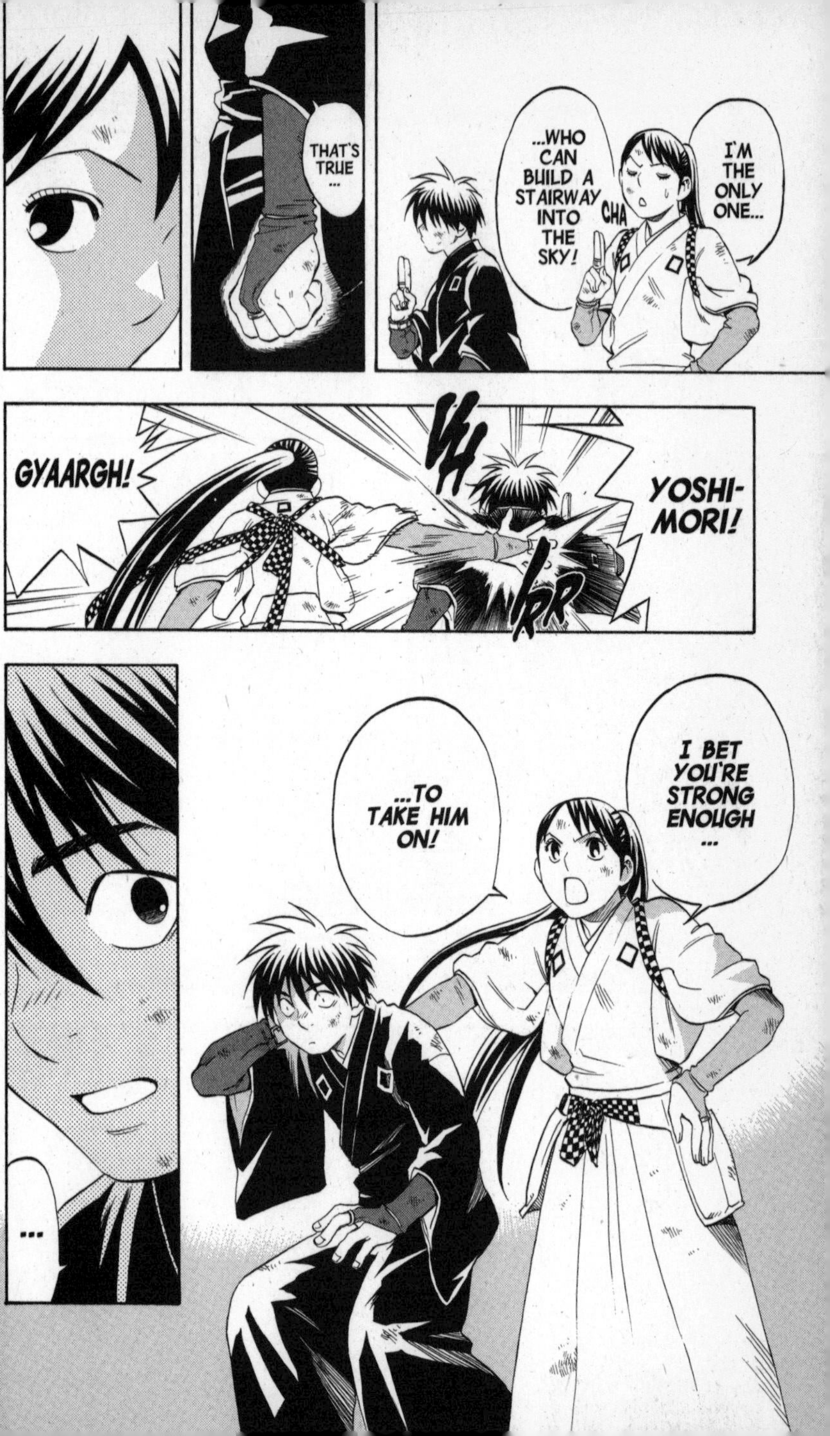
I'M THE ONLY ONE...
...WHO CAN BUILD A STAIRWAY INTO THE SKY!
CHA
THAT'S TRUE ...
YOSHI-MORI!
GYAARGH!
I BET YOU'RE STRONG ENOUGH ...
...TO TAKE HIM ON!
...

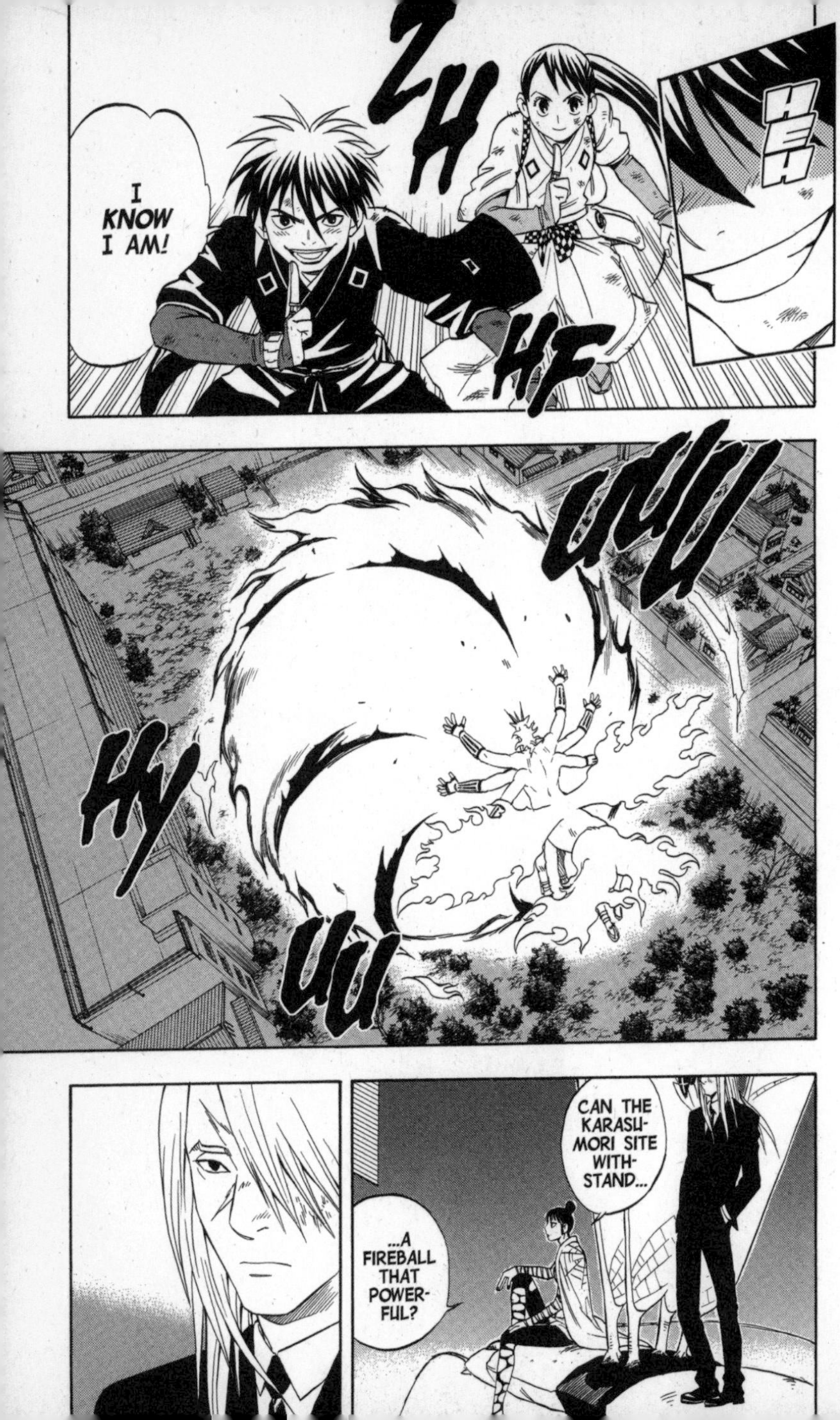
HEH
ZH
HF
I KNOW I AM!
CAN THE KARASUMORI SITE WITHSTAND...
...A FIREBALL THAT POWERFUL?

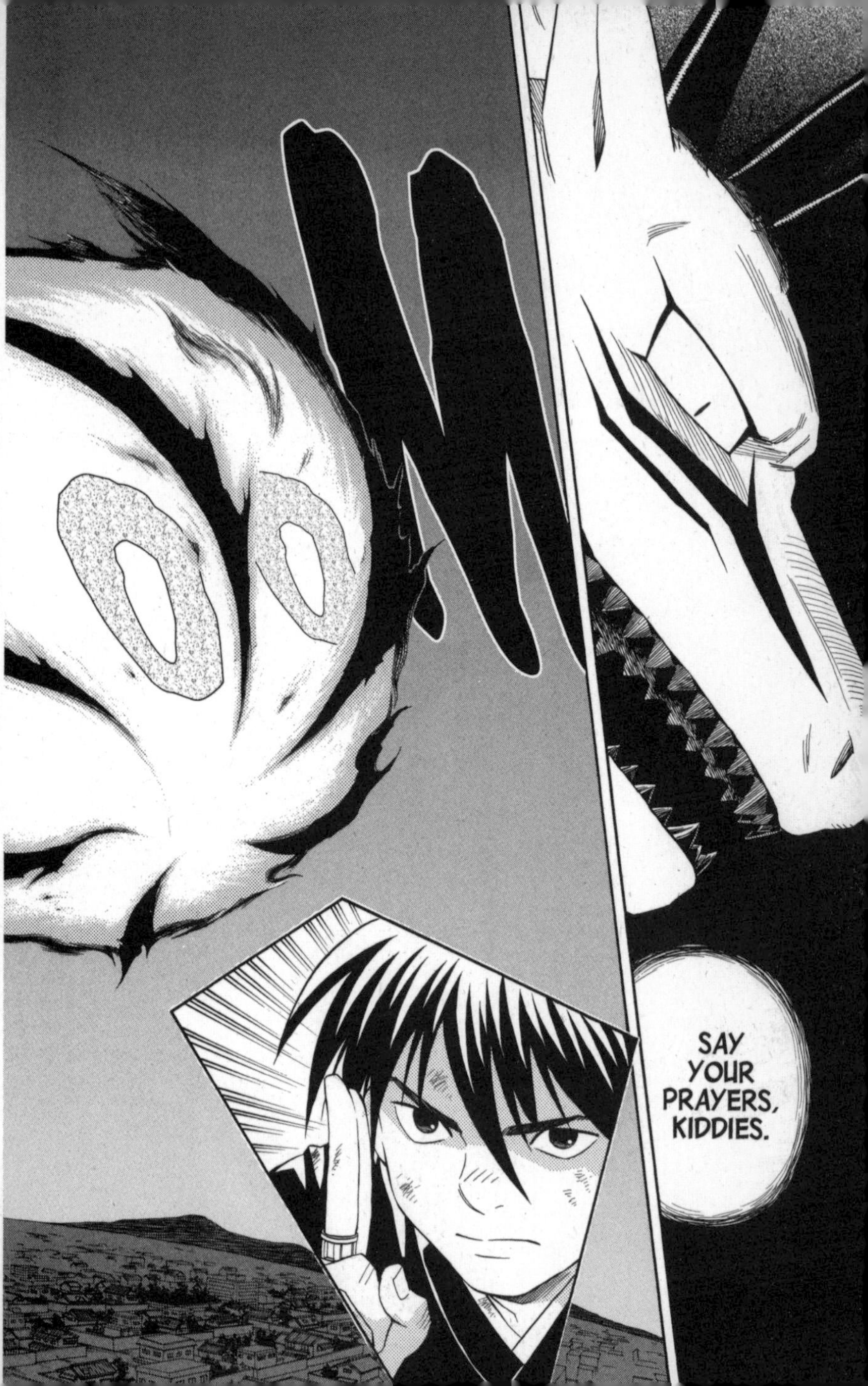
SAY YOUR PRAYERS, KIDDIES.

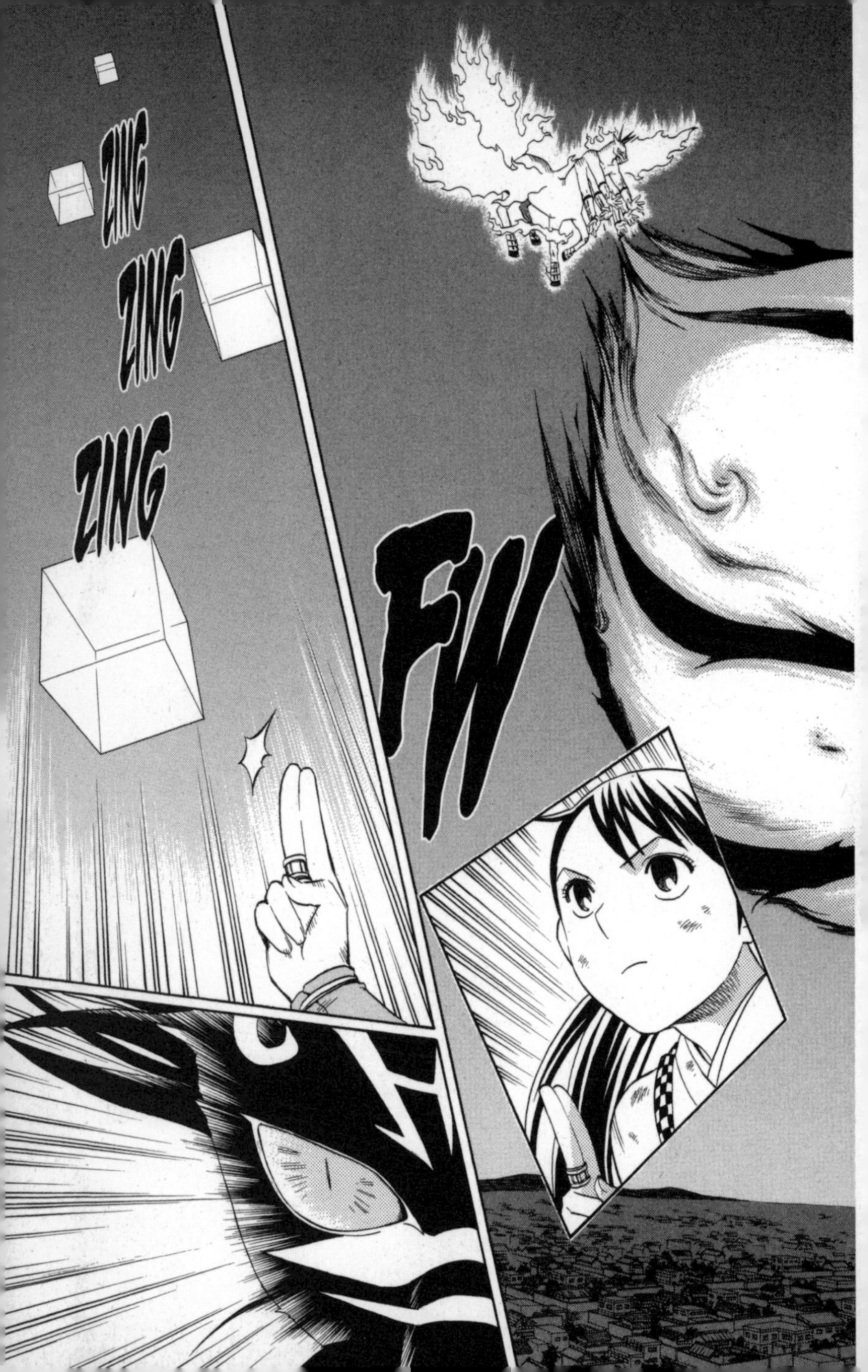
FW
ZING
ZING
ZING

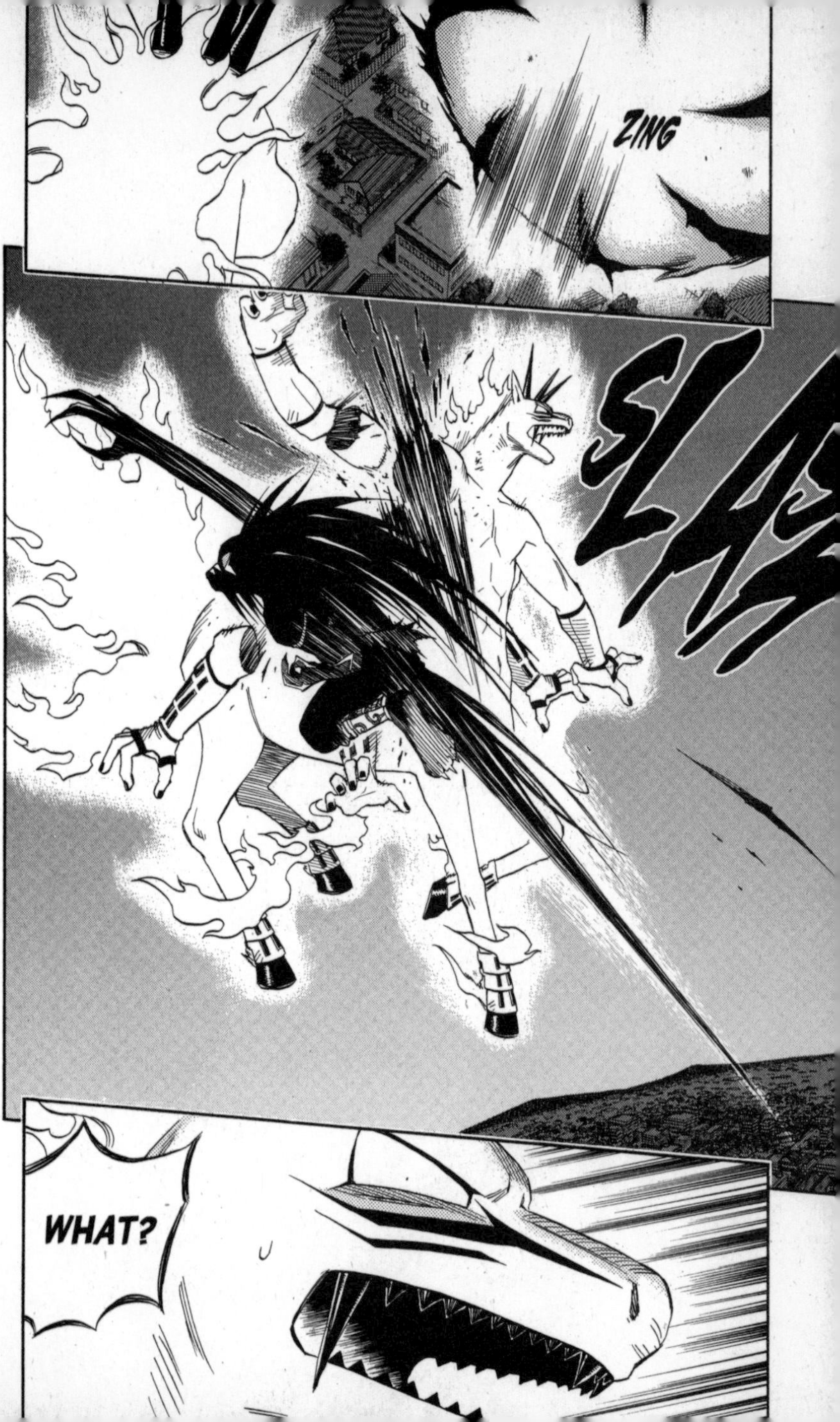
ZING
WHAT?

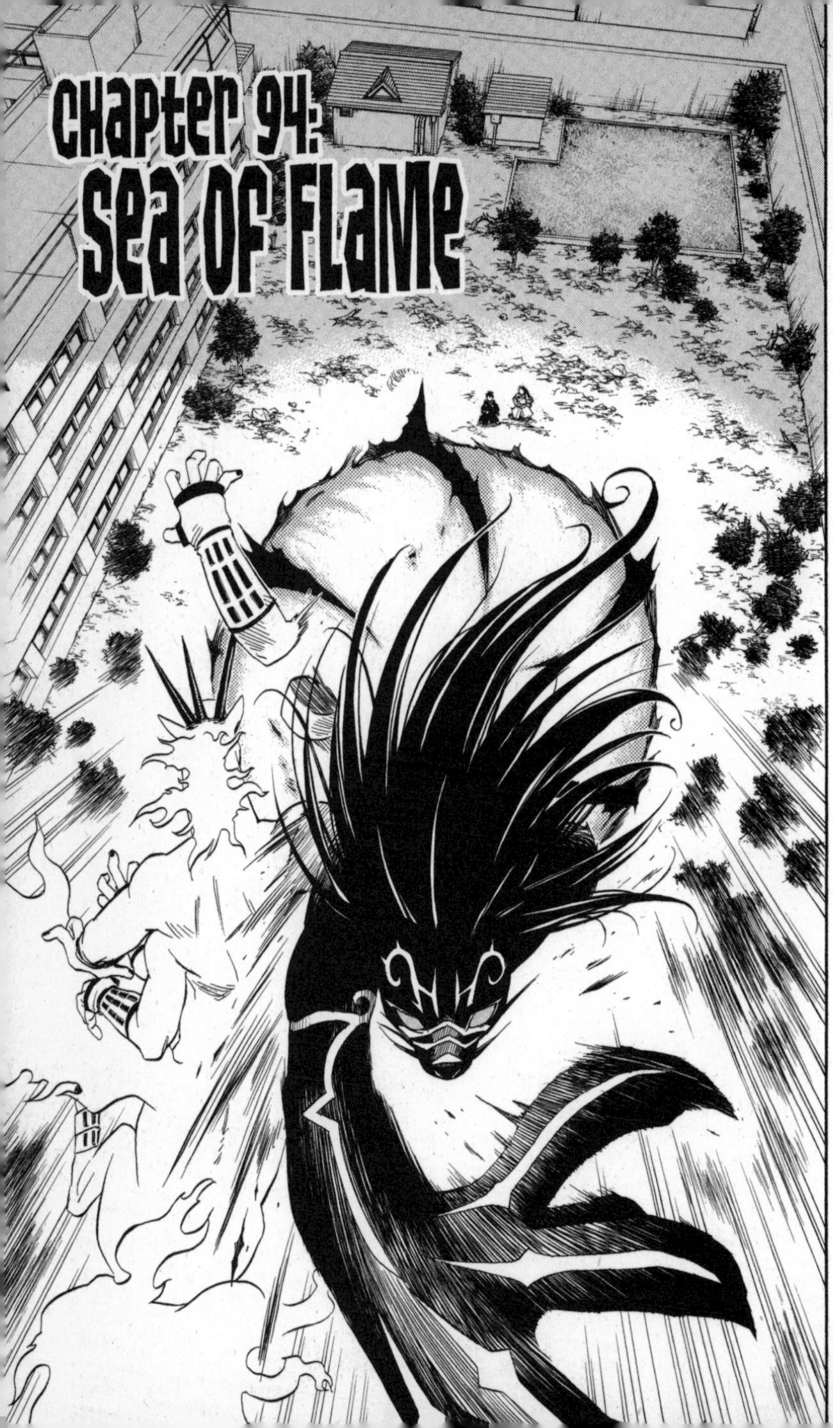
Chapter 94:
Sea of Flame

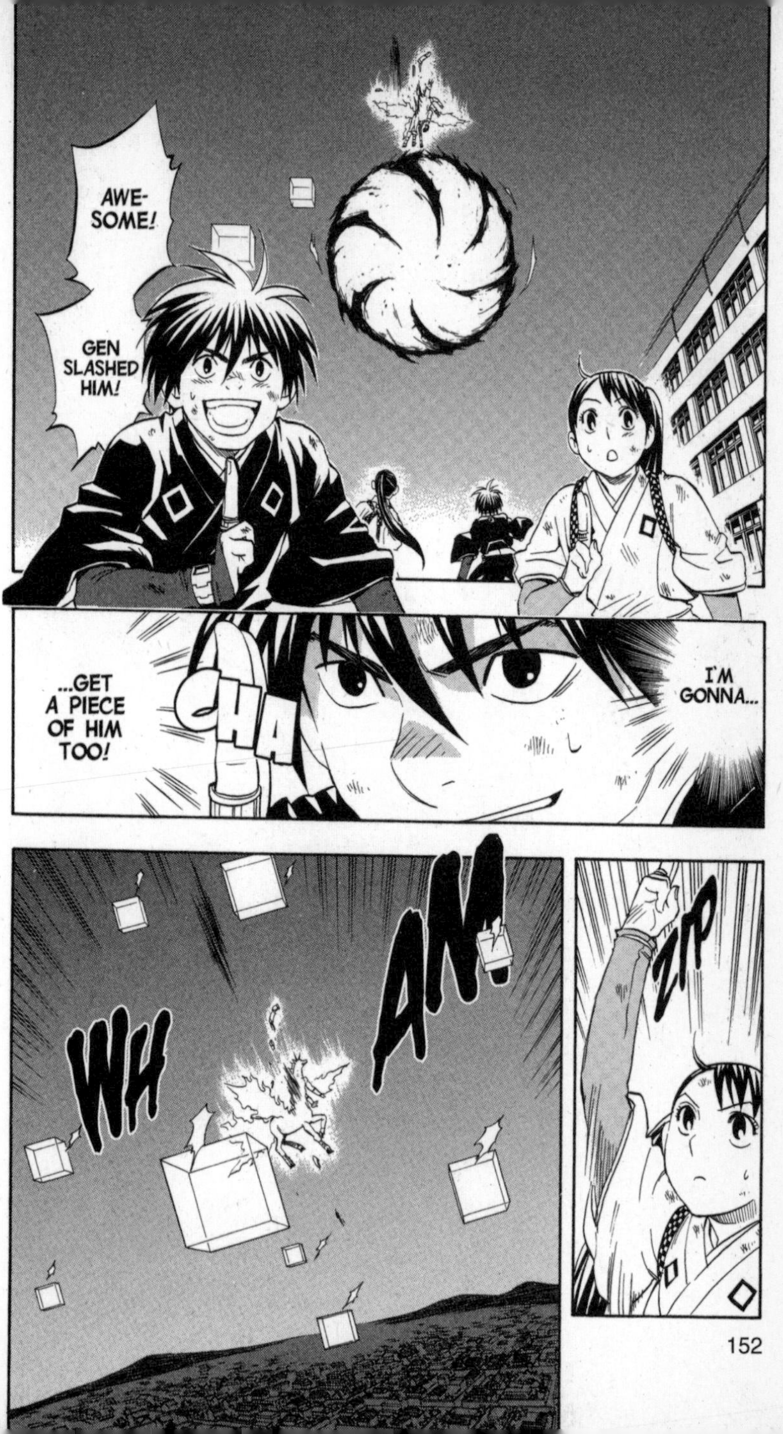
AWE-SOME!
GEN SLASHED HIM!
I'M GONNA...
...GET A PIECE OF HIM TOO!
CHA
ZIP
WH
AM

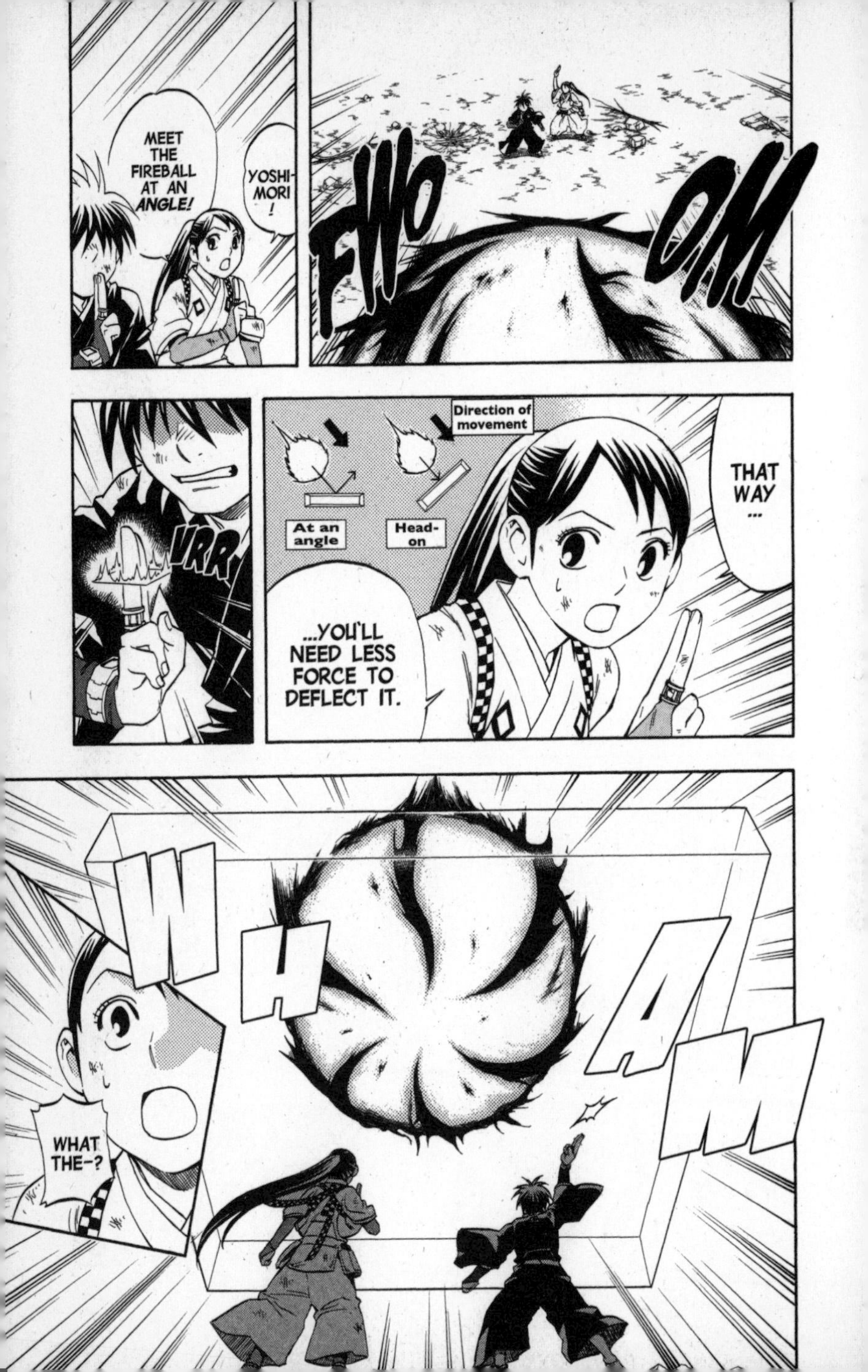
FWOOM
YOSHI-MORI!
MEET THE FIREBALL AT AN ANGLE!
THAT WAY...
Direction of movement
At an angle
Head-on
...YOU'LL NEED LESS FORCE TO DEFLECT IT.
VRR
WHAM
WHAT THE-?

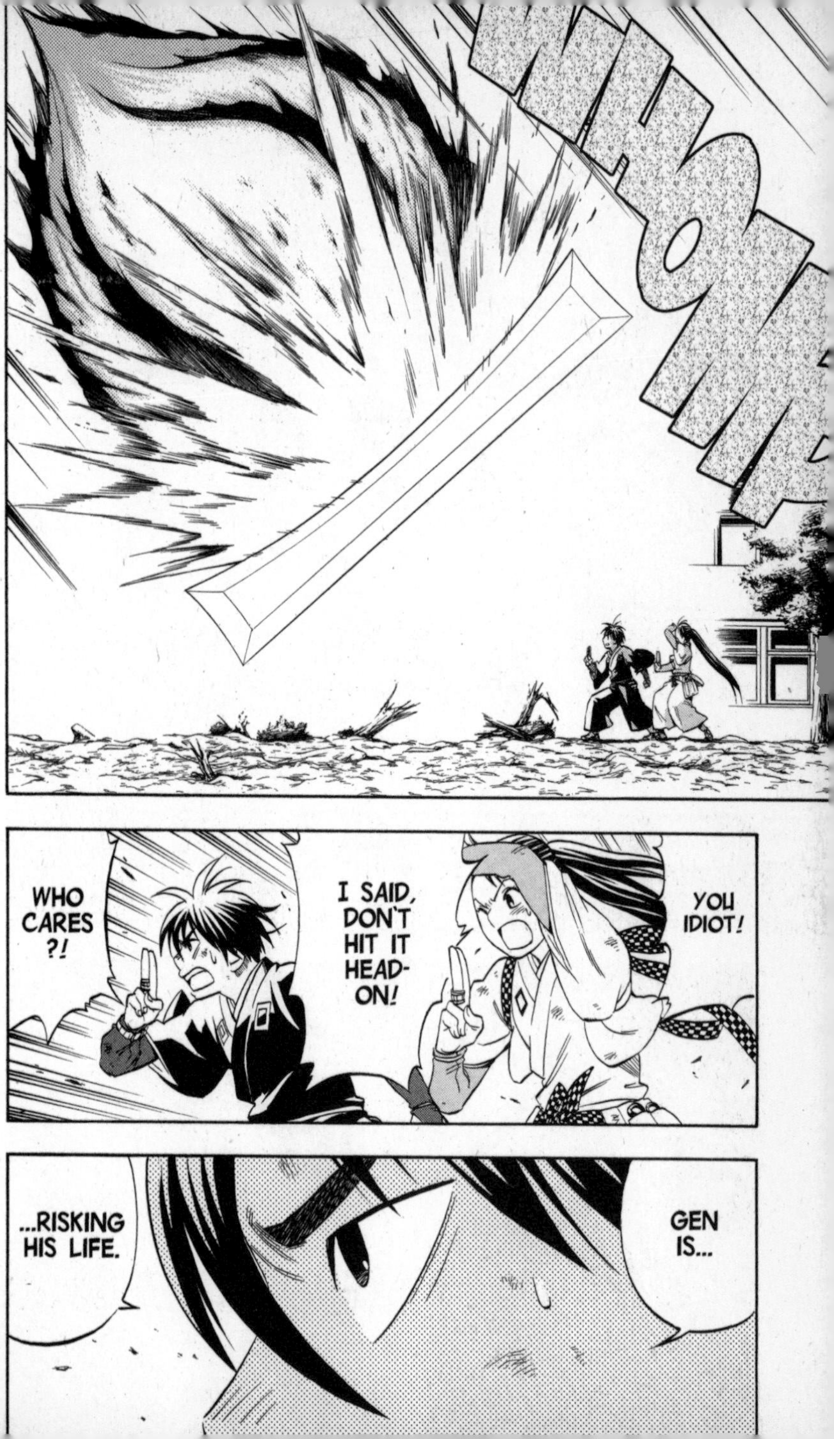
WHOOMP
YOU IDIOT!
I SAID, DON'T HIT IT HEAD-ON!
WHO CARES?!
GEN IS...
...RISKING HIS LIFE.

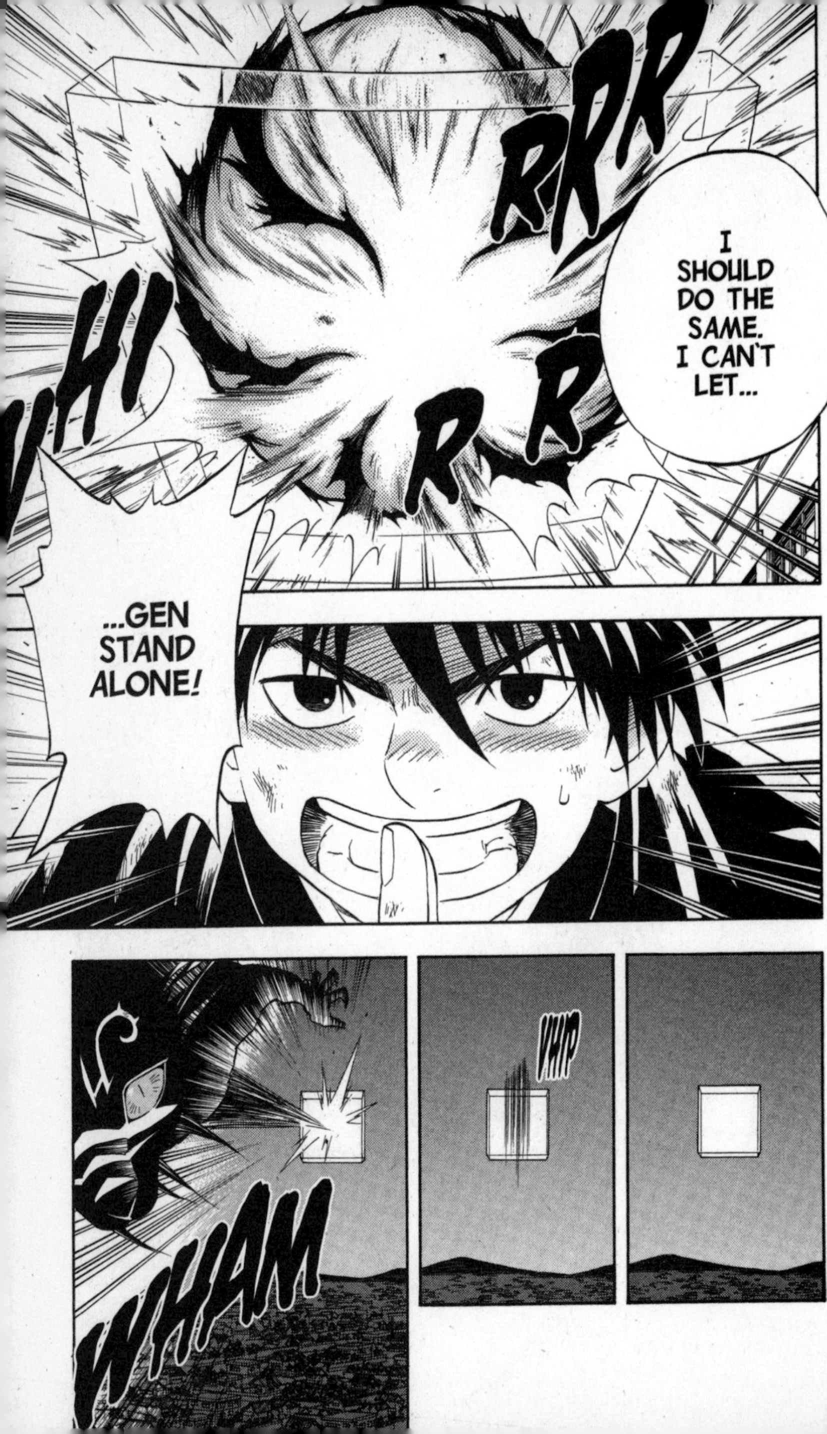
I SHOULD DO THE SAME. I CAN'T LET...
RRRRR
...GEN STAND ALONE!
VHIP
WHAM

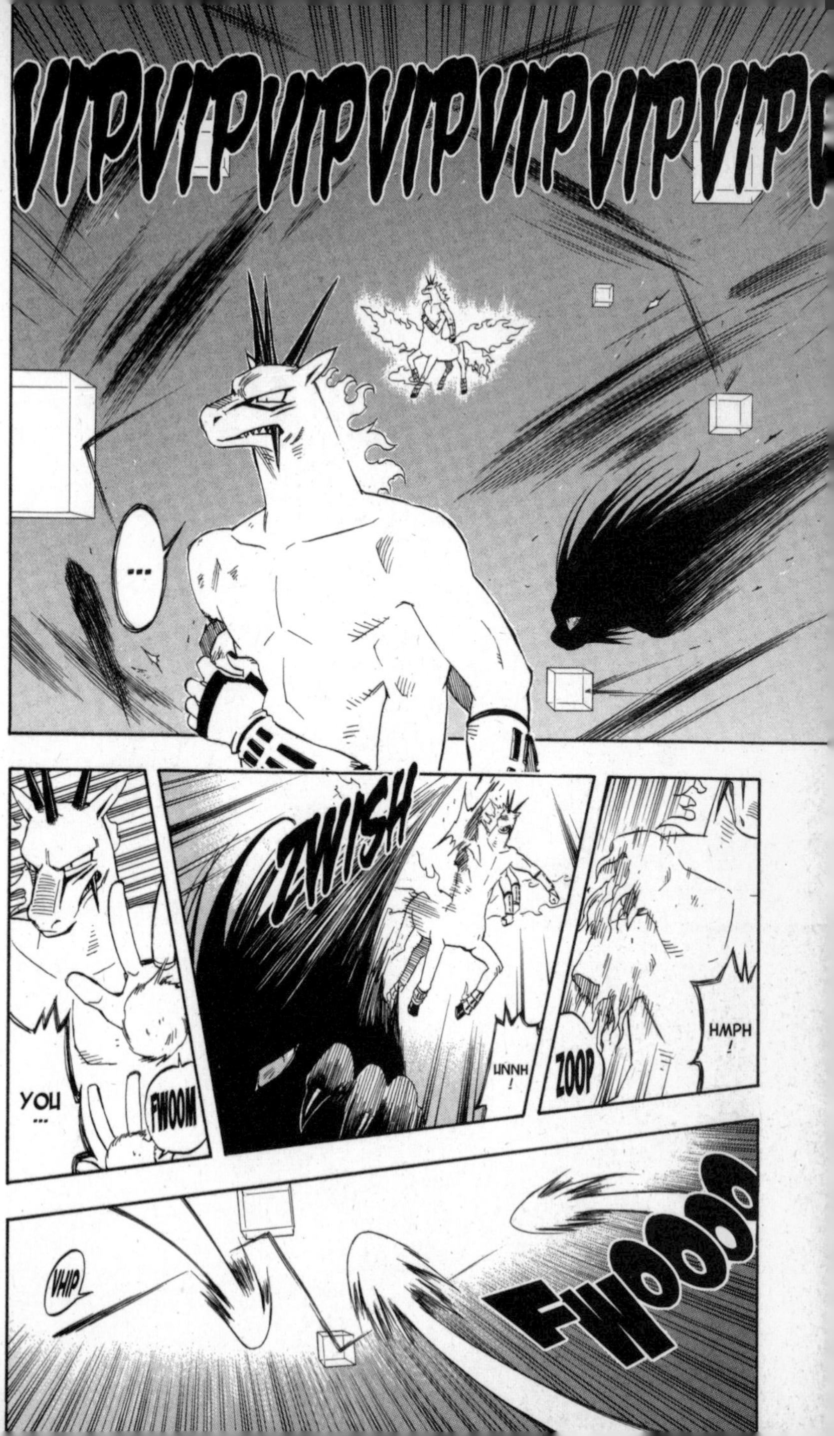
VIPVIPVIPVIPVIPVIPVIP
...
HMPH!
ZOOP
ZWISH
UNNH!
YOU...
FWOOM
FWOOOO
VHIP

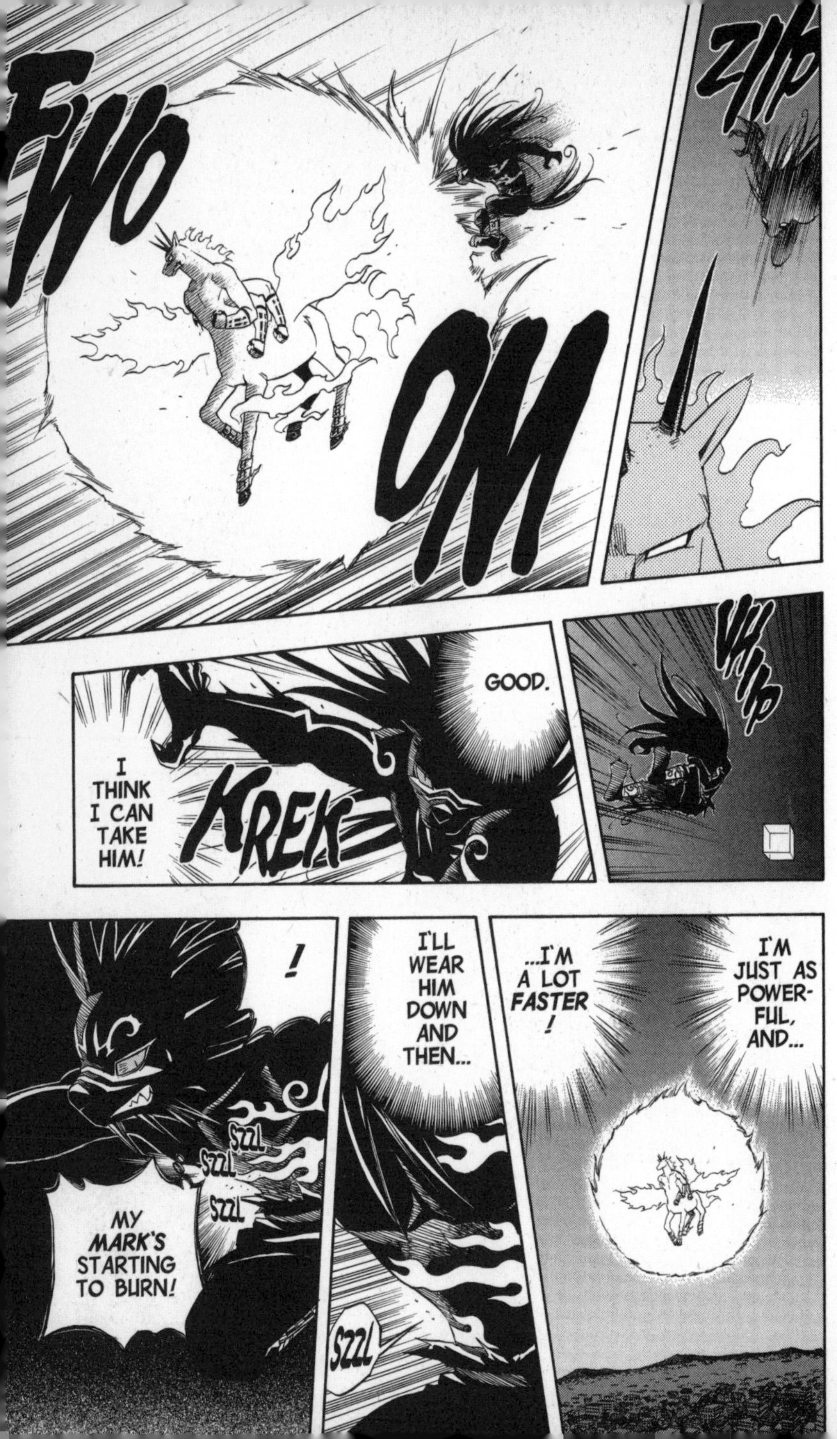
ZIP
FWOOM
GOOD.
I THINK I CAN TAKE HIM!
KREK
I'M JUST AS POWER-FUL, AND...
...I'M A LOT FASTER!
I'LL WEAR HIM DOWN AND THEN...
SZZL
!
SZZL
SZZL
SZZL
MY MARK'S STARTING TO BURN!

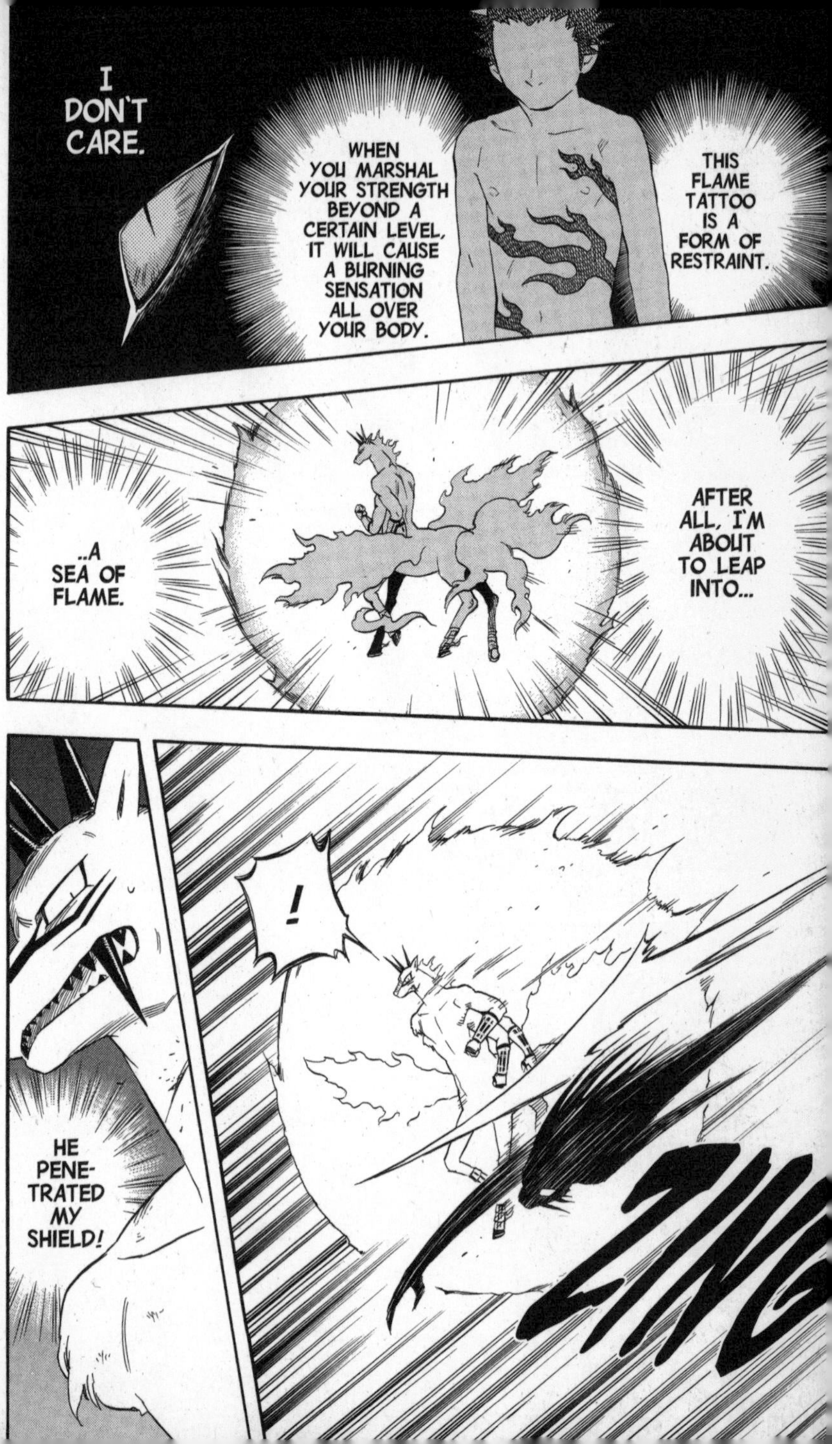
THIS FLAME TATTOO IS A FORM OF RESTRAINT.
WHEN YOU MARSHAL YOUR STRENGTH BEYOND A CERTAIN LEVEL, IT WILL CAUSE A BURNING SENSATION ALL OVER YOUR BODY.
I DON'T CARE.
AFTER ALL, I'M ABOUT TO LEAP INTO...
..A SEA OF FLAME.
!
HE PENE-TRATED MY SHIELD!

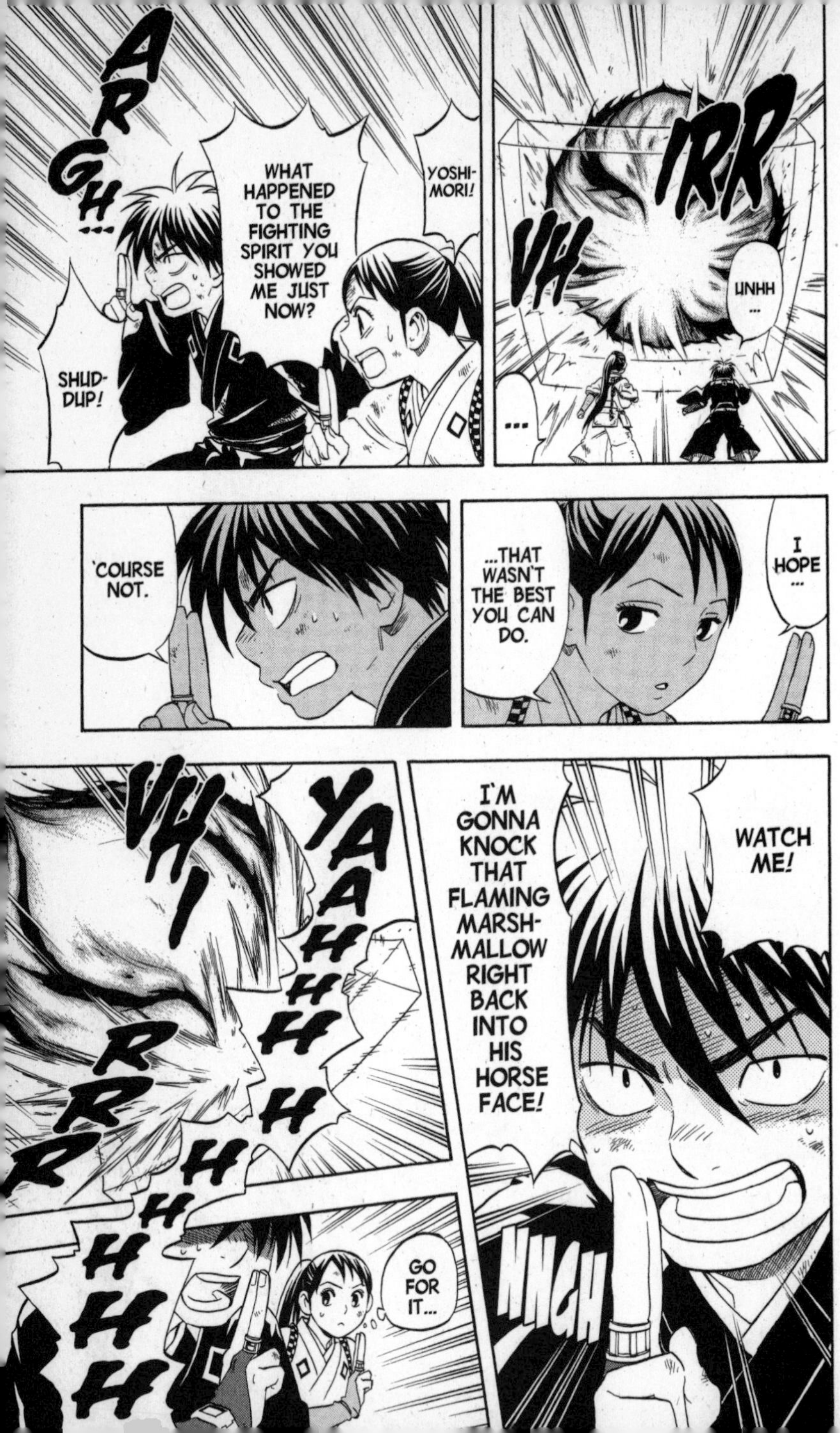
VH
IRR
UNHH ...
...
YOSHI-MORI!
WHAT HAPPENED TO THE FIGHTING SPIRIT YOU SHOWED ME JUST NOW?
ARGH...
SHUD-DUP!
I HOPE ...
...THAT WASN'T THE BEST YOU CAN DO.
'COURSE NOT.
WATCH ME!
I'M GONNA KNOCK THAT FLAMING MARSH-MALLOW RIGHT BACK INTO HIS HORSE FACE!
MNGH
YAAHHHHH
VHI
RRRR
HHHHHHHH
GO FOR IT...

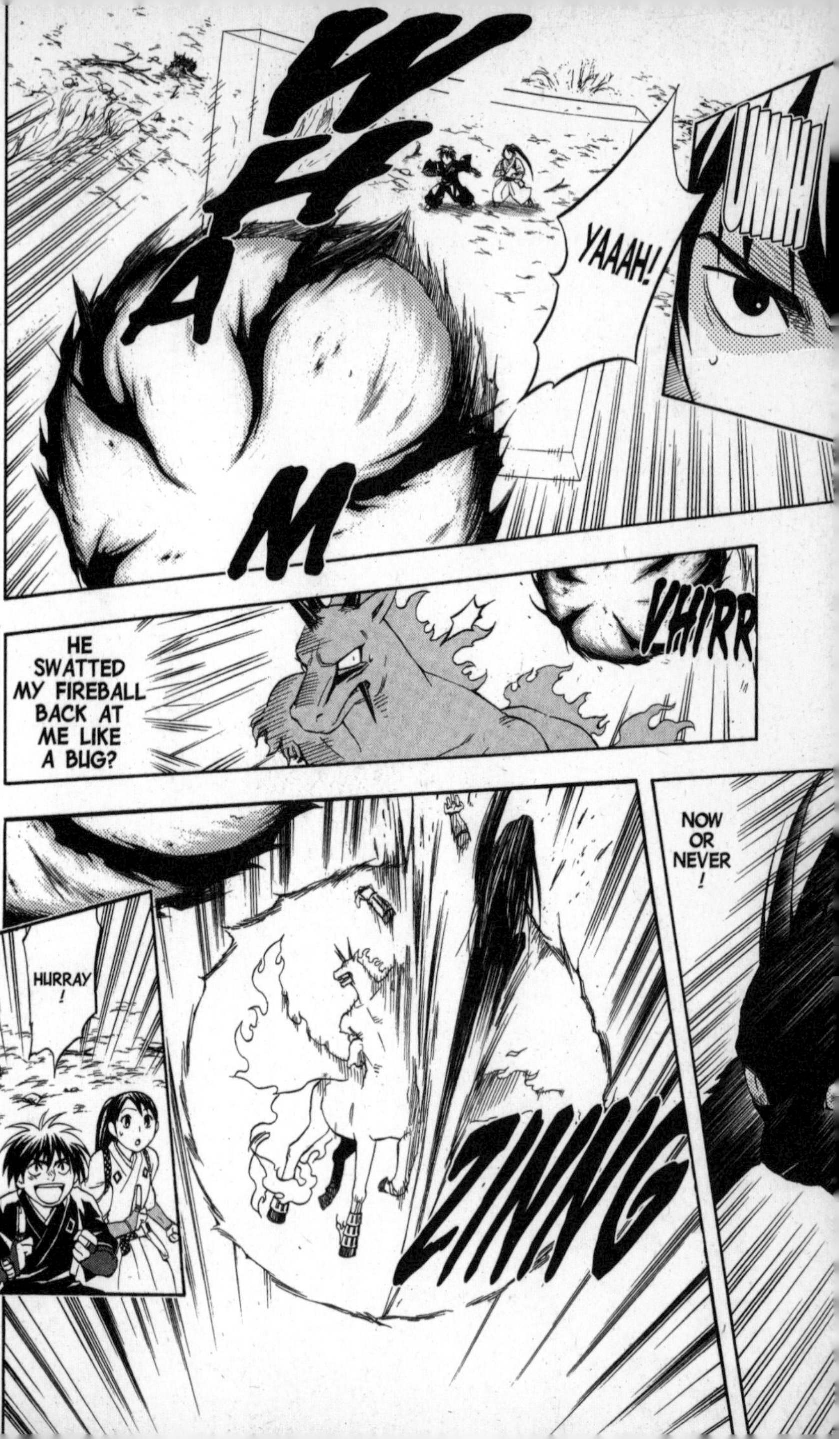
ZUNNH
YAAAH!
WHAM
VHIRR
HE SWATTED MY FIREBALL BACK AT ME LIKE A BUG?
NOW OR NEVER!
ZING
HURRAY!

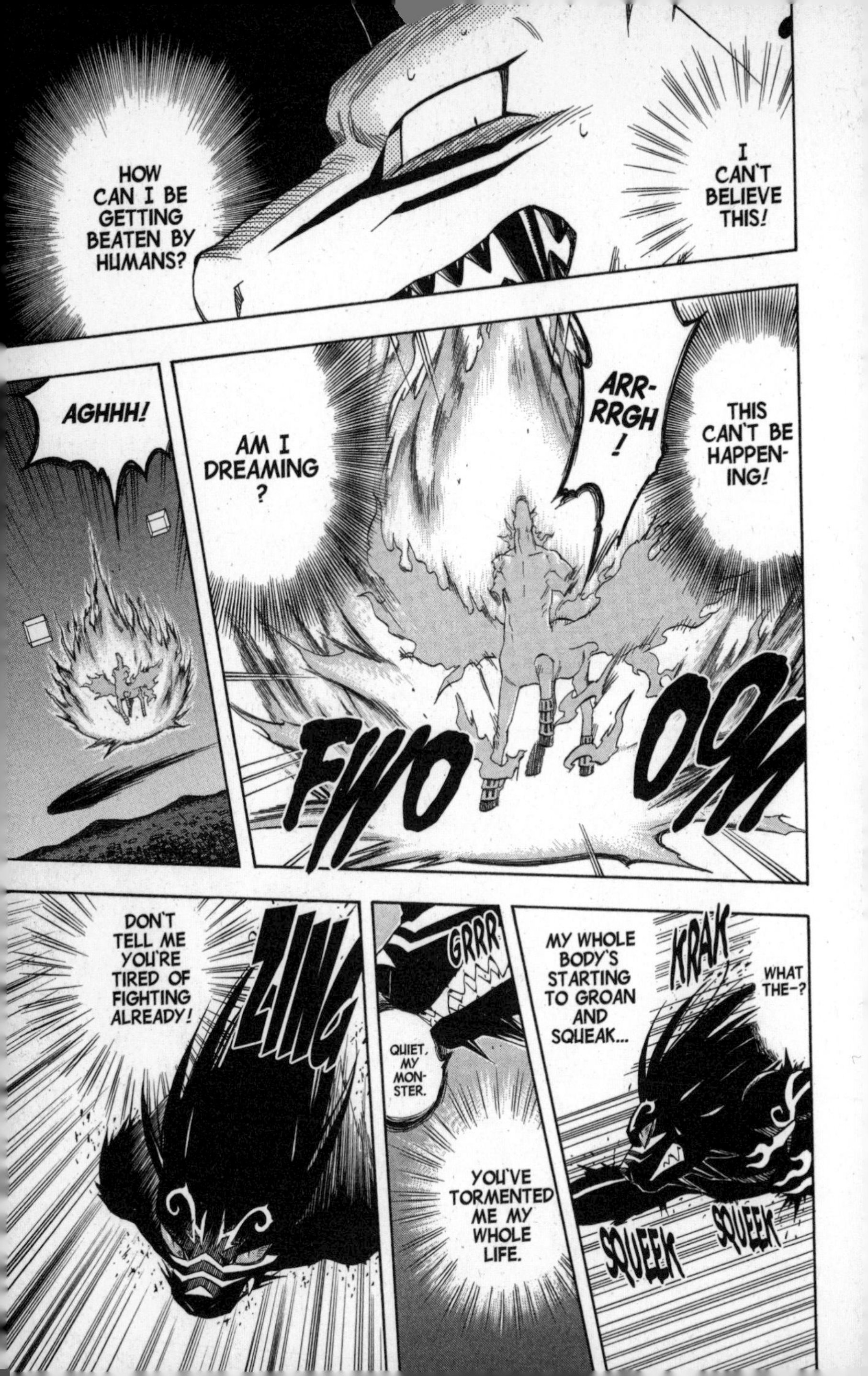

I CAN'T BELIEVE THIS!
HOW CAN I BE GETTING BEATEN BY HUMANS?
THIS CAN'T BE HAPPENING!
ARR-RRGH!
AM I DREAMING?
FWOOM
AGHHH!
WHAT THE-?
KRAK
MY WHOLE BODY'S STARTING TO GROAN AND SQUEAK...
SQUEEK
SQUEEK
GRRR
QUIET, MY MONSTER.
YOU'VE TORMENTED ME MY WHOLE LIFE.
DON'T TELL ME YOU'RE TIRED OF FIGHTING ALREADY!
ZING

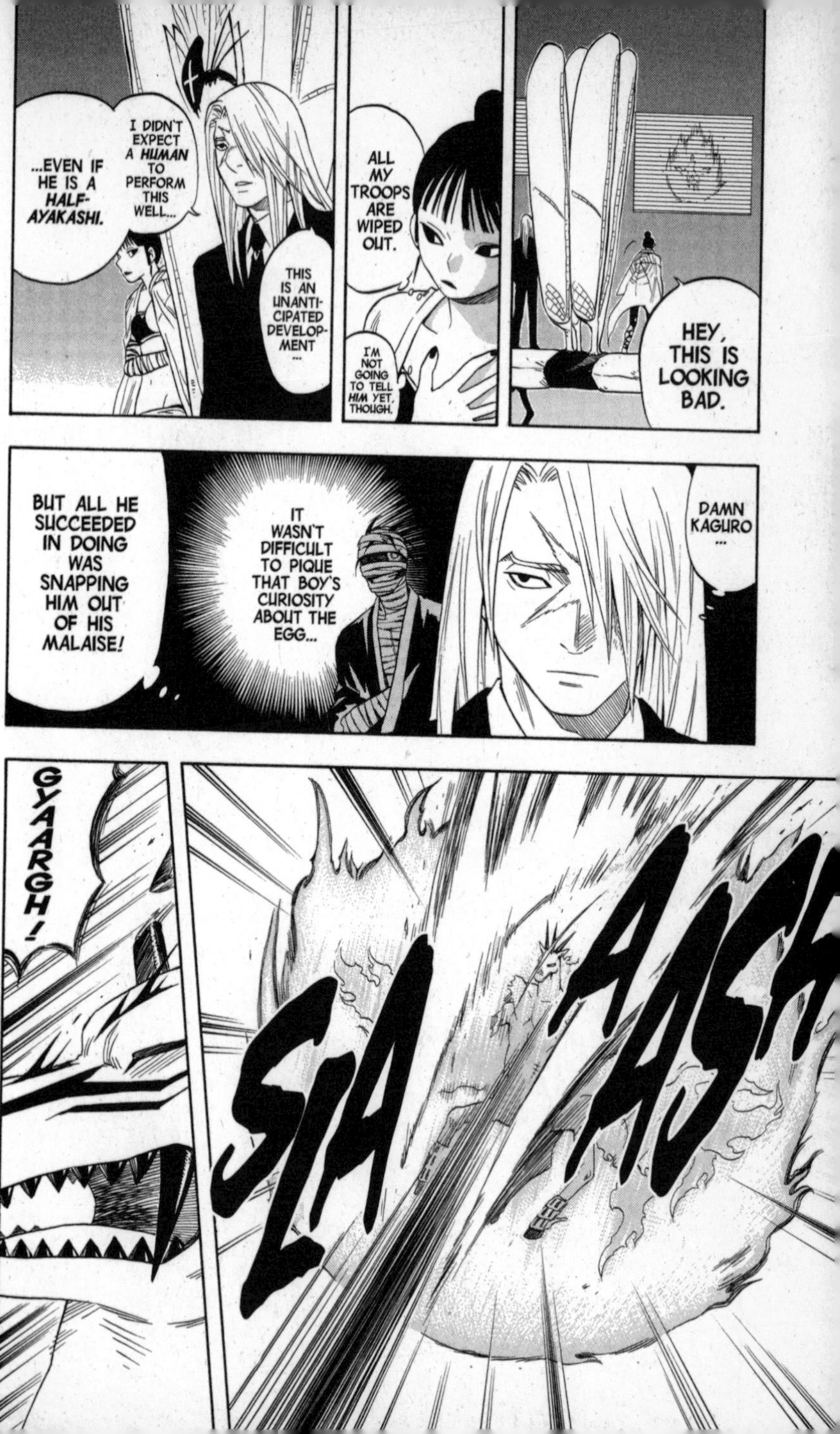
HEY, THIS IS LOOKING BAD.
ALL MY TROOPS ARE WIPED OUT.
I'M NOT GOING TO TELL *HIM* YET, THOUGH.
I DIDN'T EXPECT A *HUMAN* TO PERFORM THIS WELL...
...EVEN IF HE IS A *HALF-AYAKASHI.*
THIS IS AN UNANTICIPATED DEVELOPMENT...
DAMN KAGURO...
IT WASN'T DIFFICULT TO PIQUE THAT BOY'S CURIOSITY ABOUT THE EGG...
BUT ALL HE SUCCEEDED IN DOING WAS SNAPPING HIM OUT OF HIS MALAISE!
SHAAASH
GYAARGH!

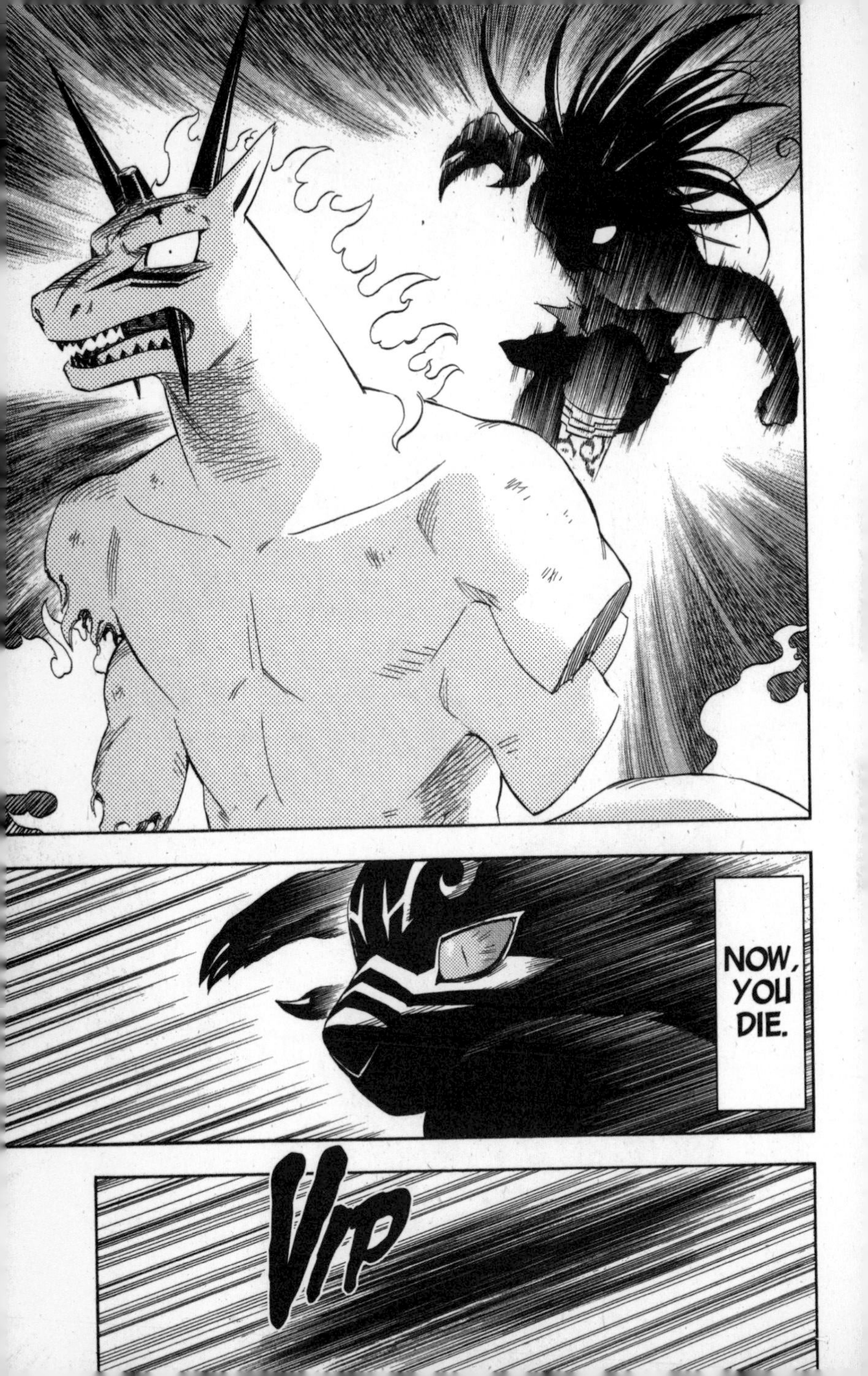
NOW, YOU DIE.
VIP

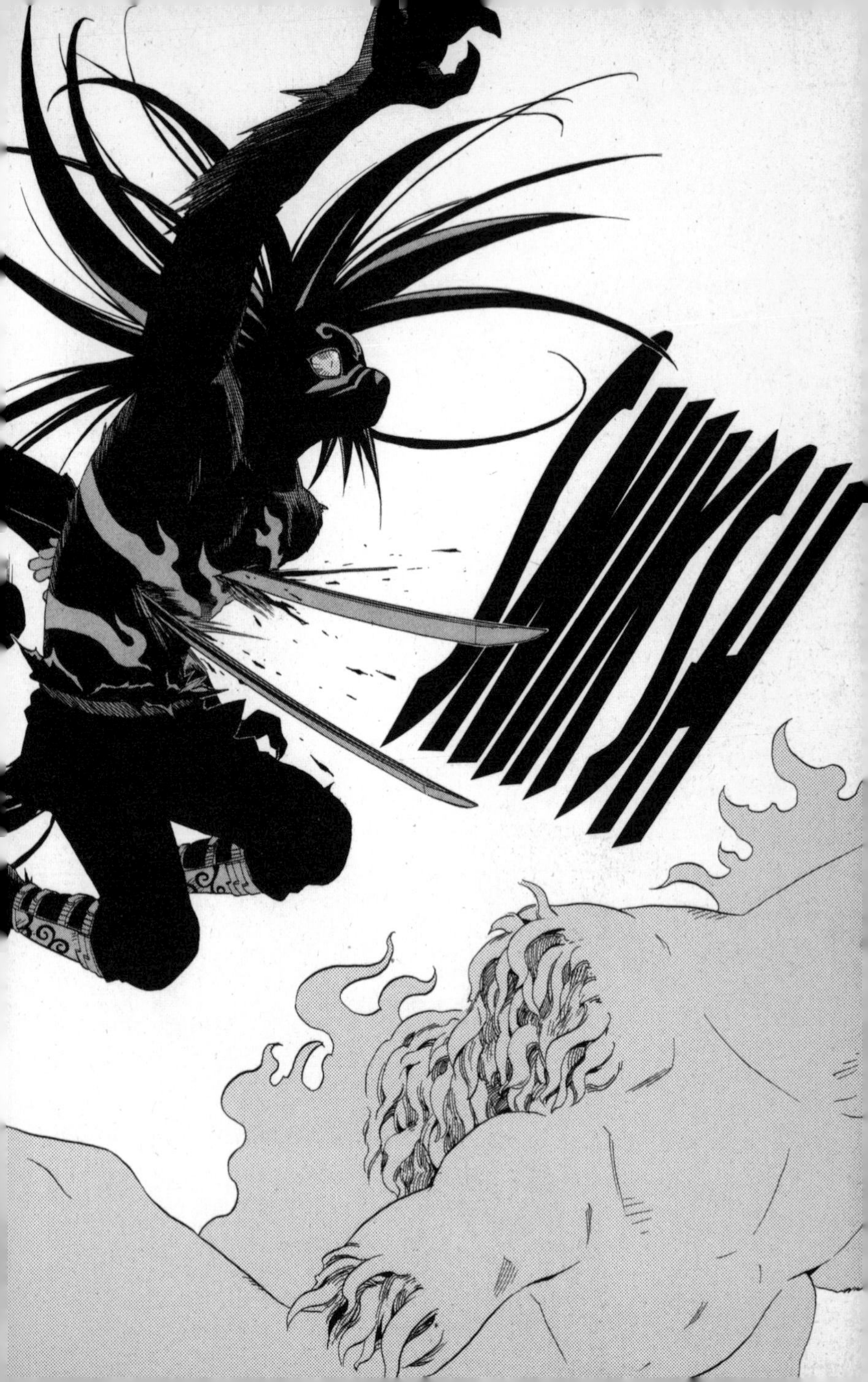

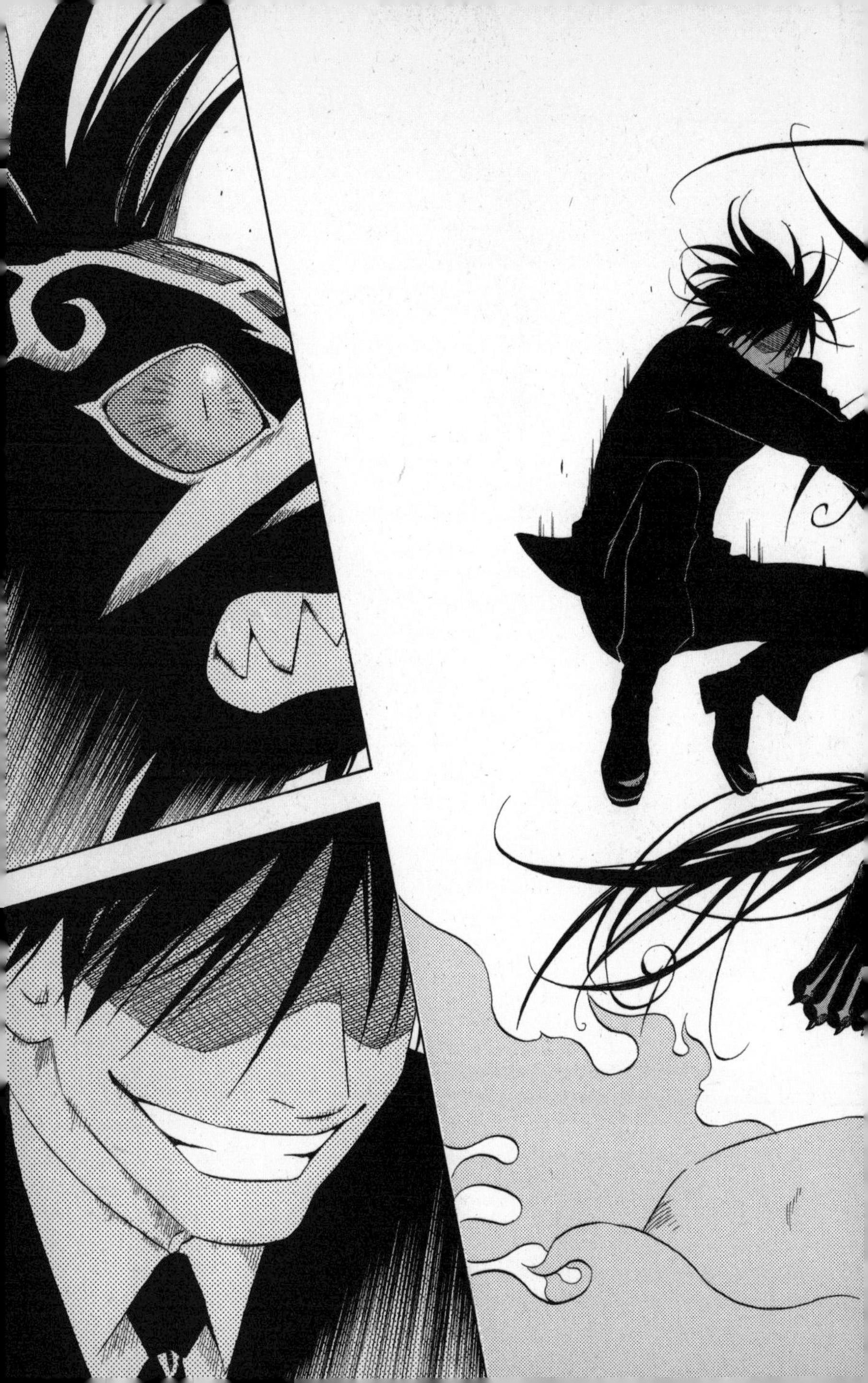

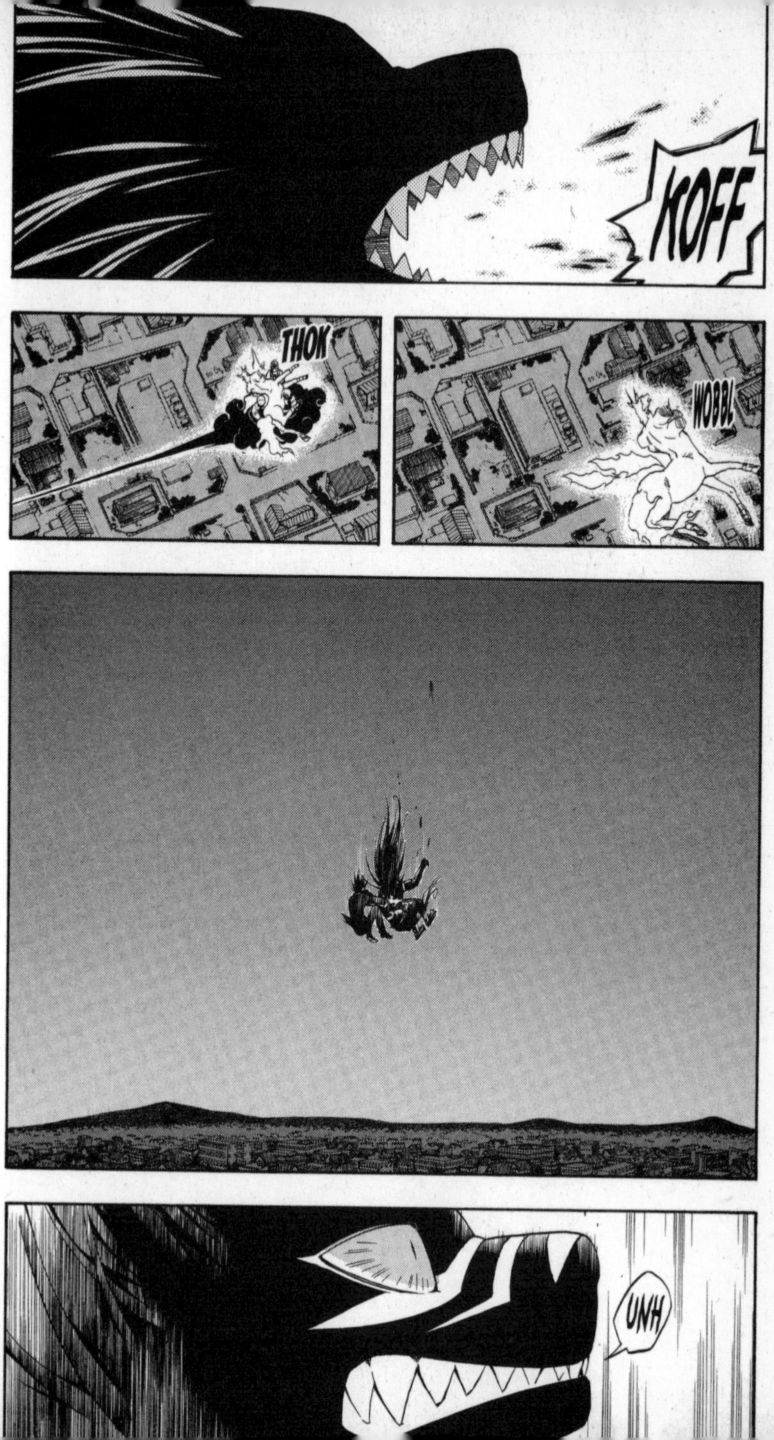
KOFF
WOBBL
THOK
UNH

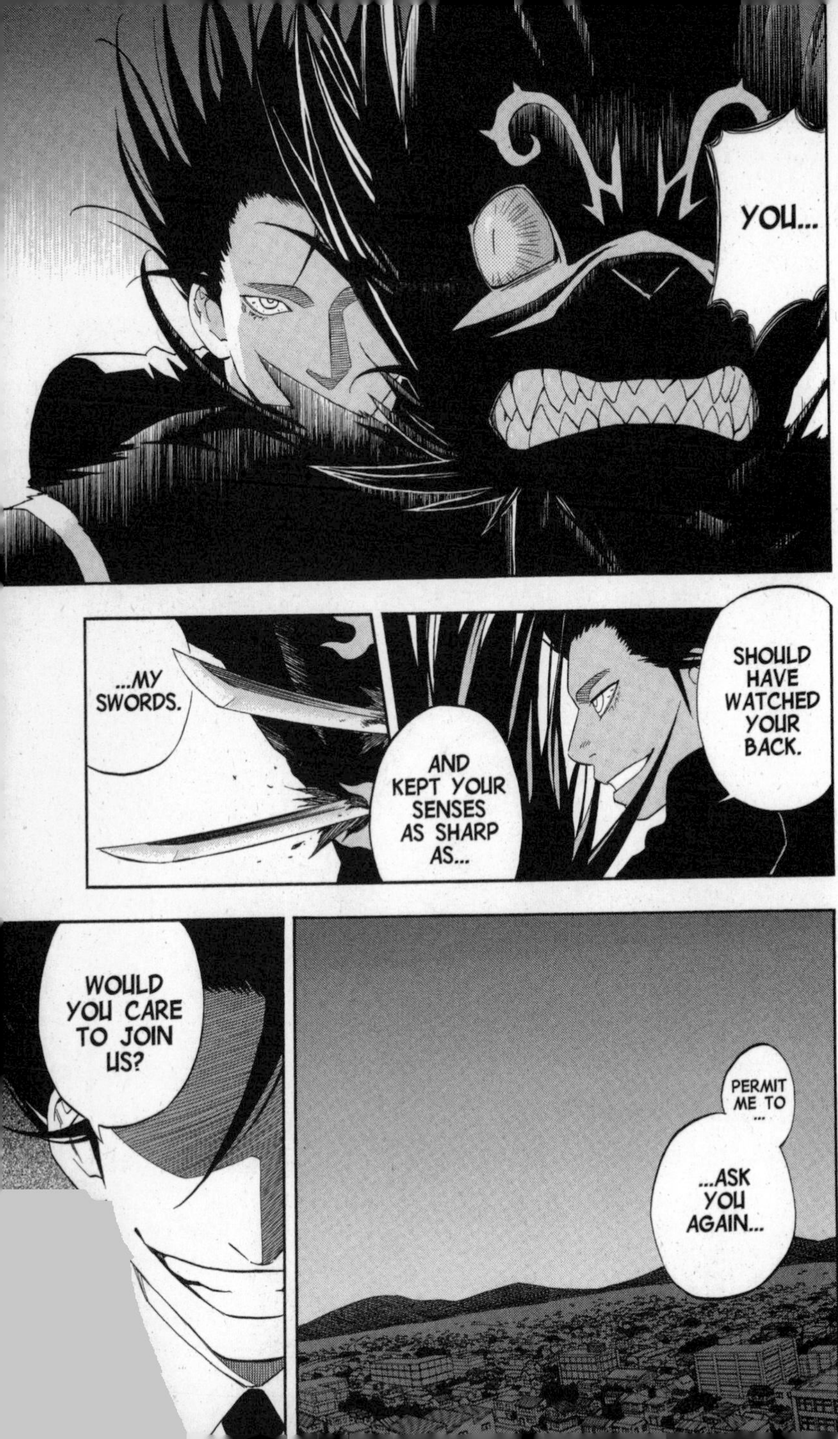
YOU...
SHOULD HAVE WATCHED YOUR BACK.
AND KEPT YOUR SENSES AS SHARP AS...
...MY SWORDS.
PERMIT ME TO ...
...ASK YOU AGAIN...
WOULD YOU CARE TO JOIN US?

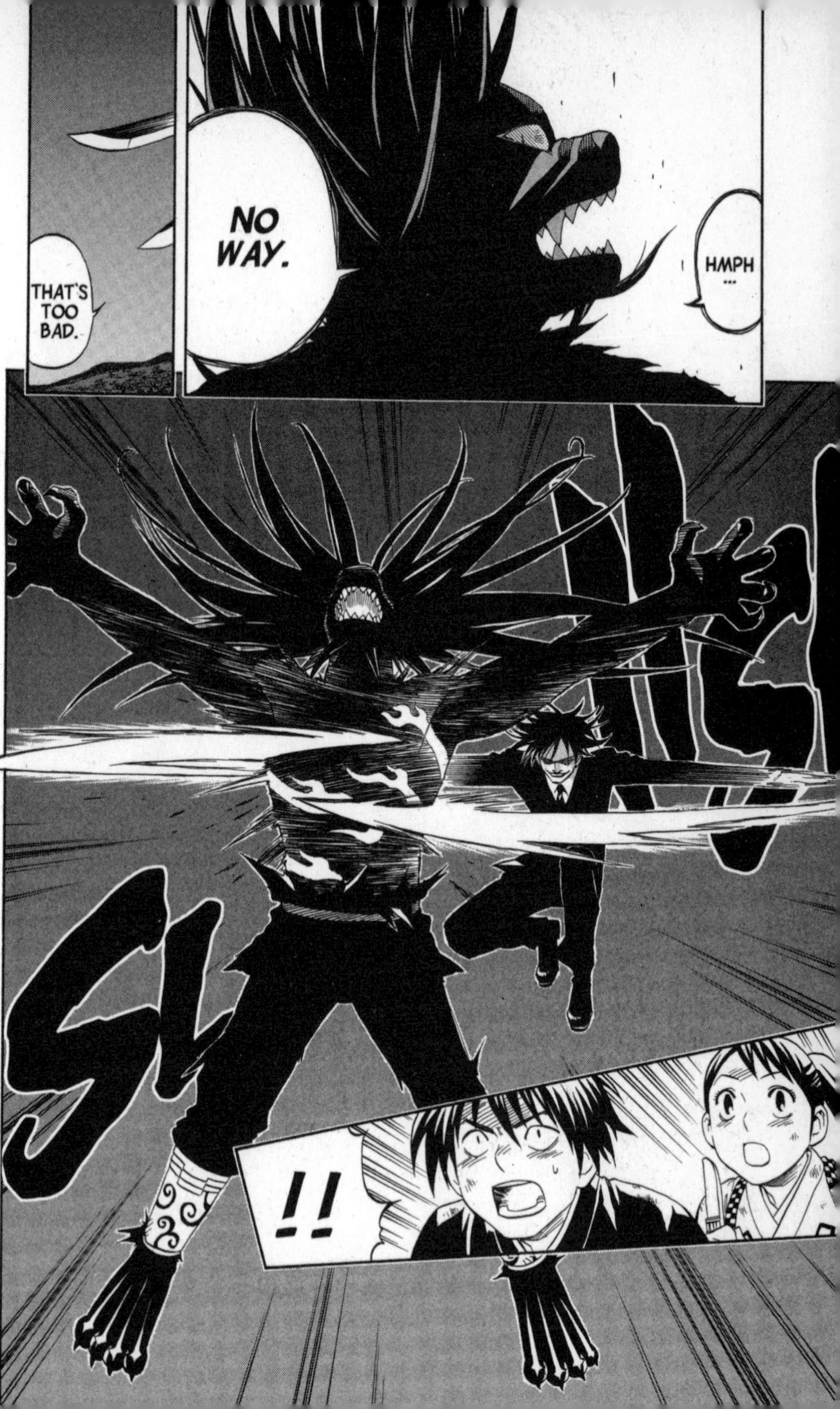
HMPH...
NO WAY.
THAT'S TOO BAD.
!!
SL

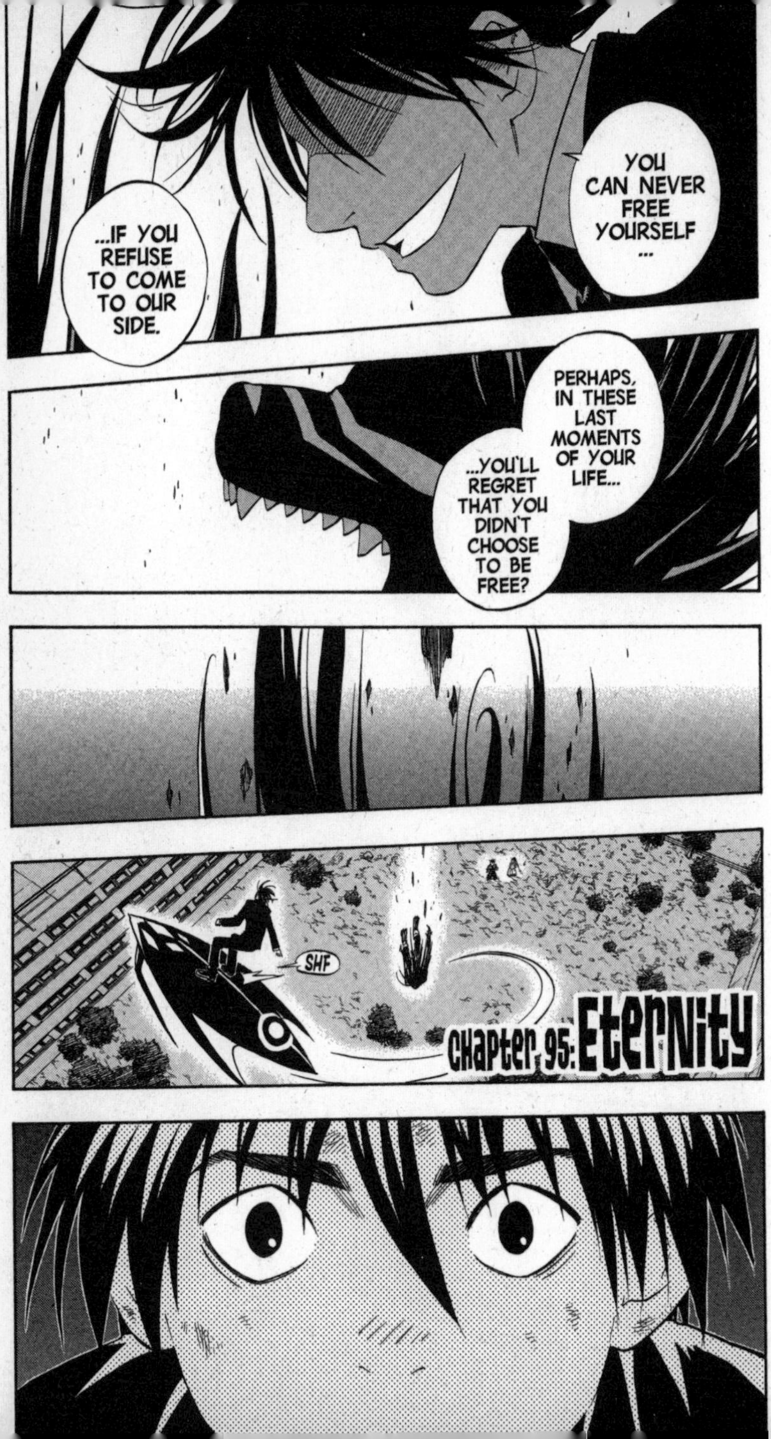
YOU CAN NEVER FREE YOURSELF ...
...IF YOU REFUSE TO COME TO OUR SIDE.
PERHAPS, IN THESE LAST MOMENTS OF YOUR LIFE...
...YOU'LL REGRET THAT YOU DIDN'T CHOOSE TO BE FREE?
SHF
Chapter 95: Eternity

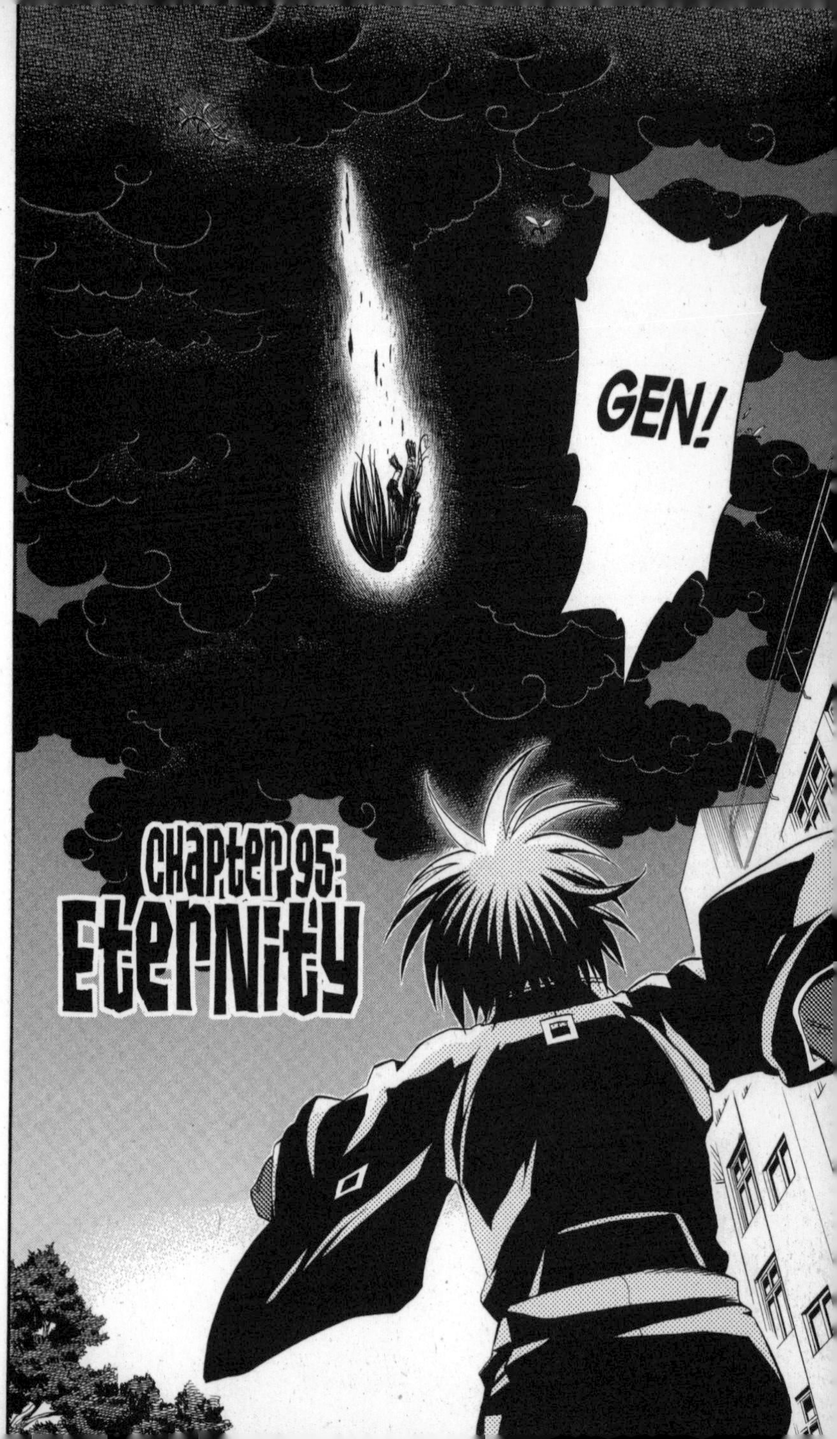
GEN!
Chapter 95:
Eternity

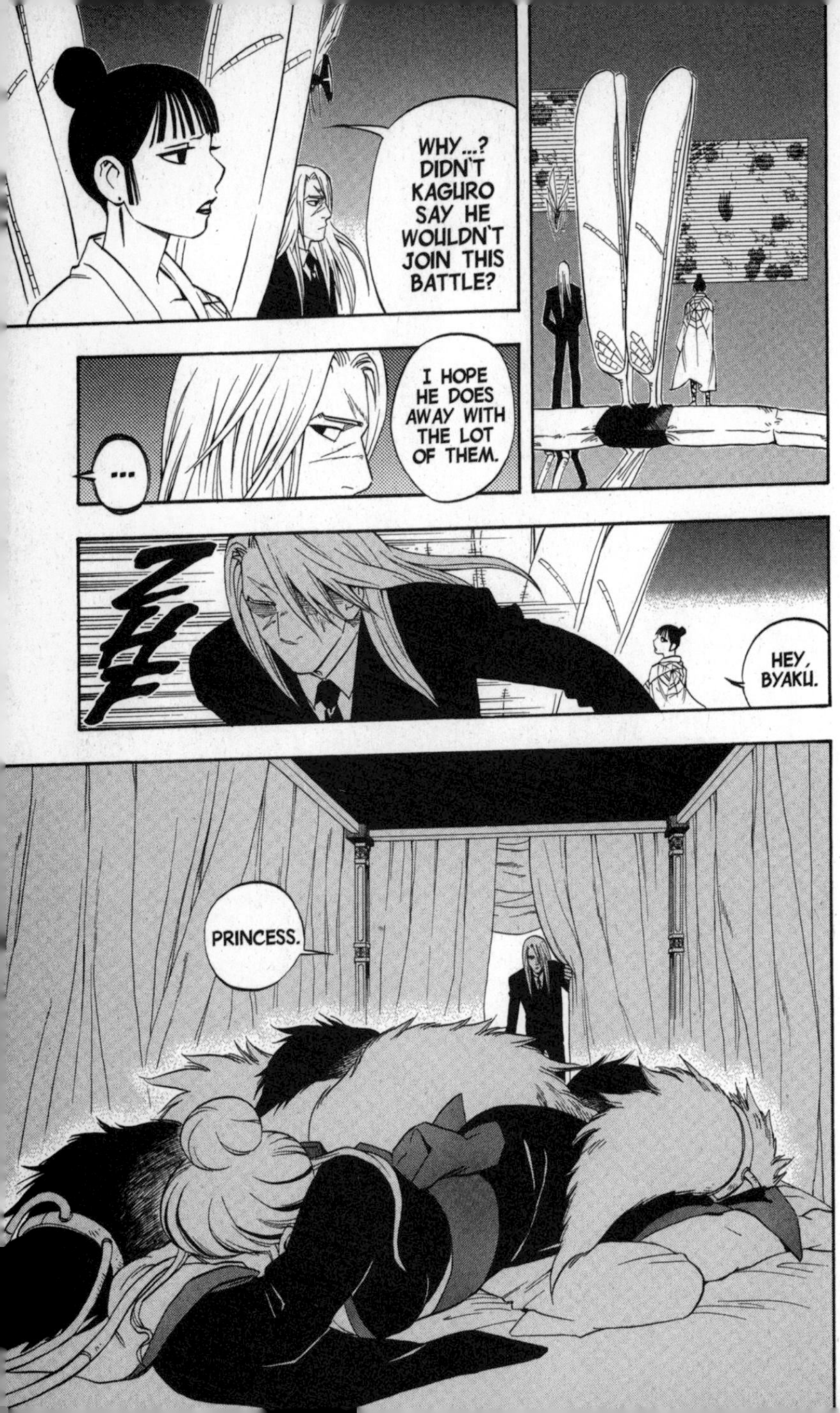
WHY...? DIDN'T KAGURO SAY HE WOULDN'T JOIN THIS BATTLE?
I HOPE HE DOES AWAY WITH THE LOT OF THEM.
...
HEY, BYAKU.
PRINCESS.

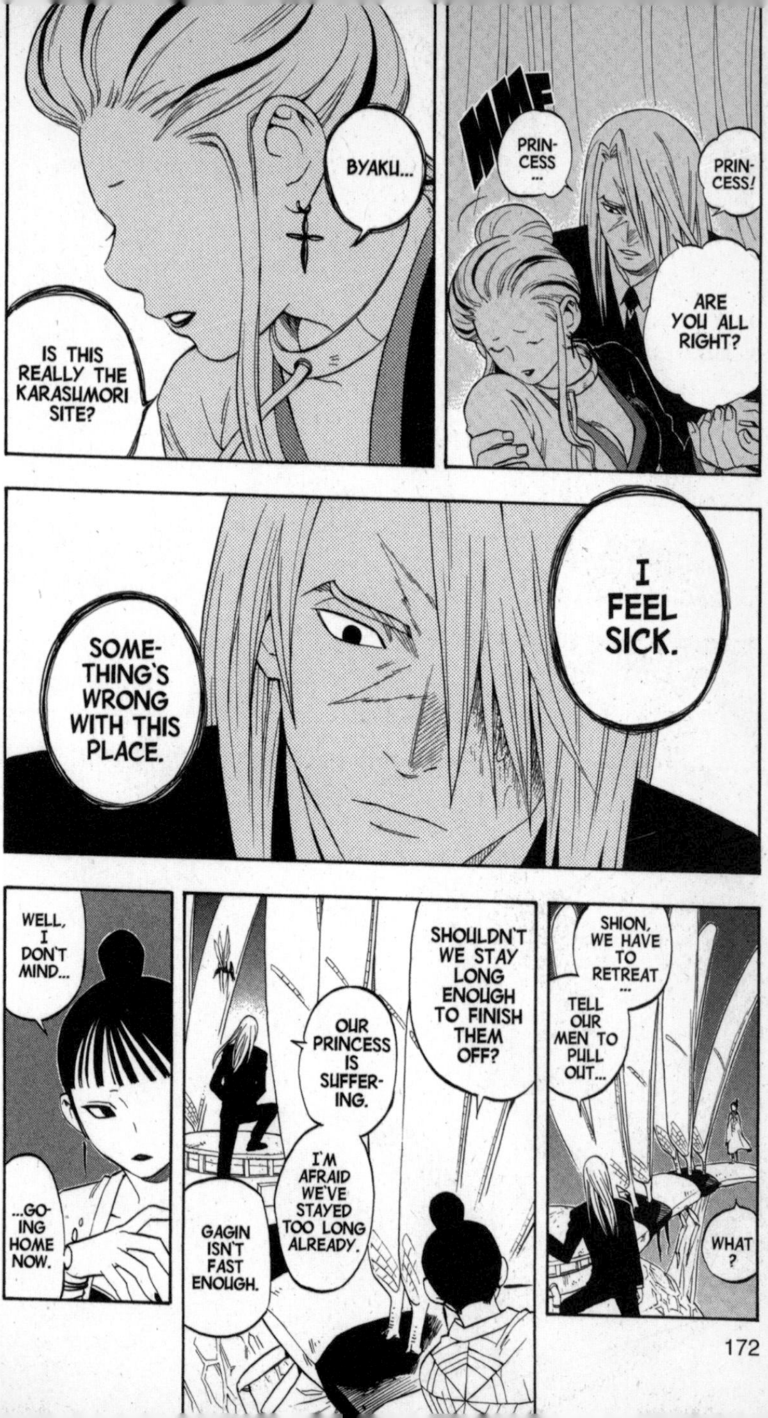
PRIN-CESS!
ARE YOU ALL RIGHT?
MMF
PRIN-CESS ...
BYAKU...
IS THIS REALLY THE KARASUMORI SITE?
I FEEL SICK.
SOME-THING'S WRONG WITH THIS PLACE.
SHION, WE HAVE TO RETREAT ...
TELL OUR MEN TO PULL OUT...
WHAT?
SHOULDN'T WE STAY LONG ENOUGH TO FINISH THEM OFF?
OUR PRINCESS IS SUFFER-ING.
I'M AFRAID WE'VE STAYED TOO LONG ALREADY.
GAGIN ISN'T FAST ENOUGH.
WELL, I DON'T MIND...
...GO-ING HOME NOW.

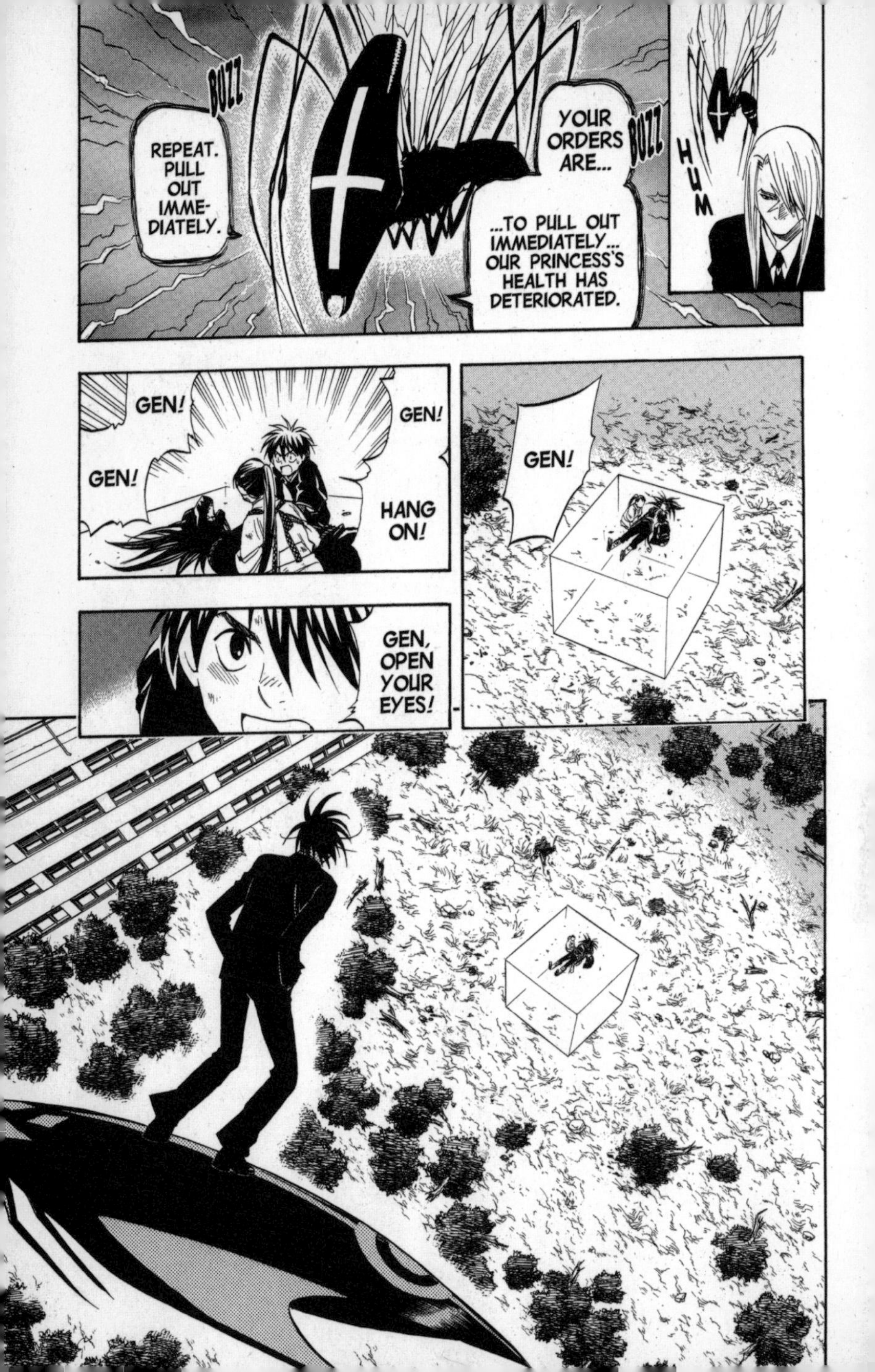
HUM
BUZZ
YOUR ORDERS ARE...
...TO PULL OUT IMMEDIATELY... OUR PRINCESS'S HEALTH HAS DETERIORATED.
BUZZ
REPEAT. PULL OUT IMMEDIATELY.
GEN!
GEN!
GEN!
GEN!
HANG ON!
GEN, OPEN YOUR EYES!

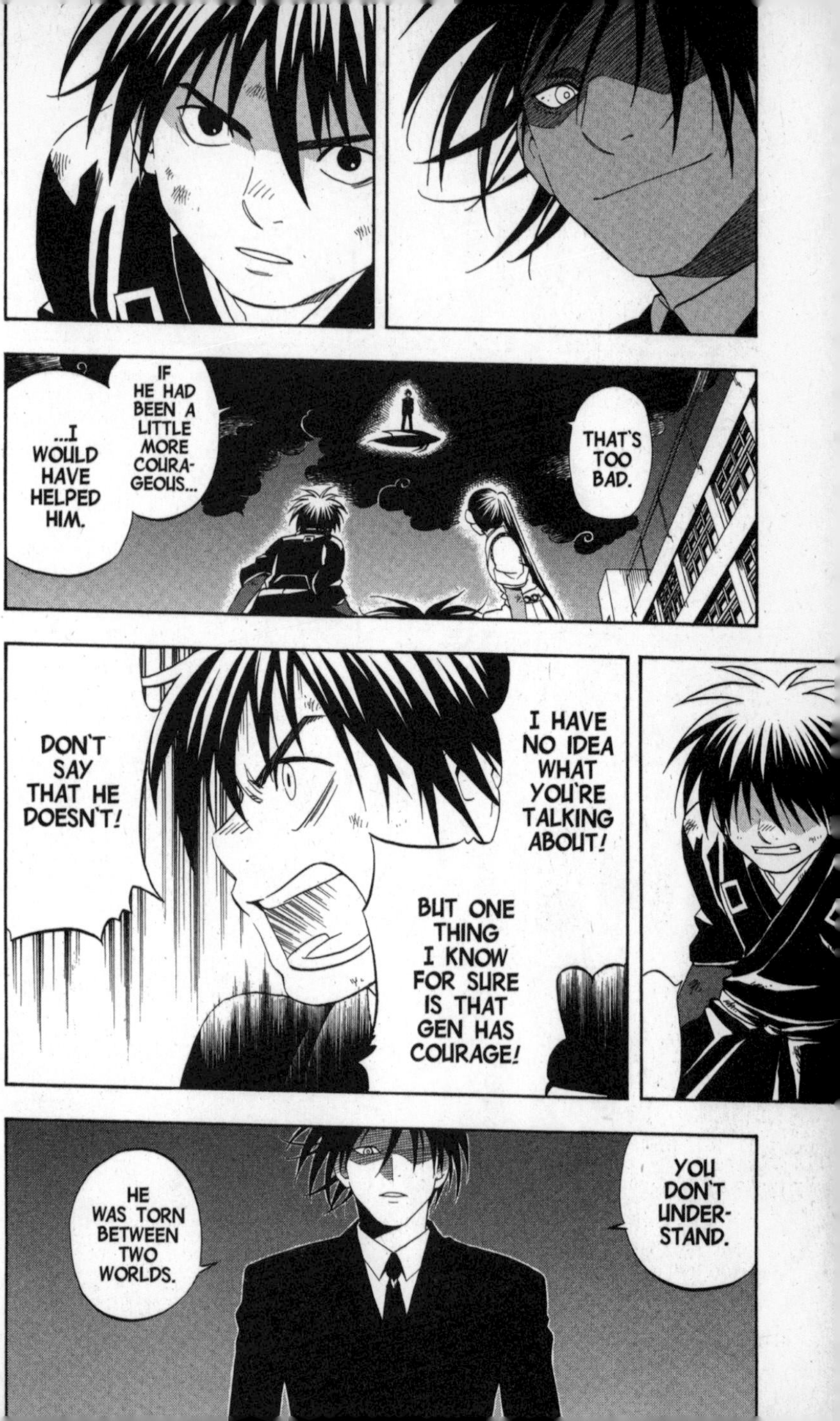
THAT'S TOO BAD.
IF HE HAD BEEN A LITTLE MORE COURAGEOUS...
...I WOULD HAVE HELPED HIM.
I HAVE NO IDEA WHAT YOU'RE TALKING ABOUT!
BUT ONE THING I KNOW FOR SURE IS THAT GEN HAS COURAGE!
DON'T SAY THAT HE DOESN'T!
YOU DON'T UNDERSTAND.
HE WAS TORN BETWEEN TWO WORLDS.

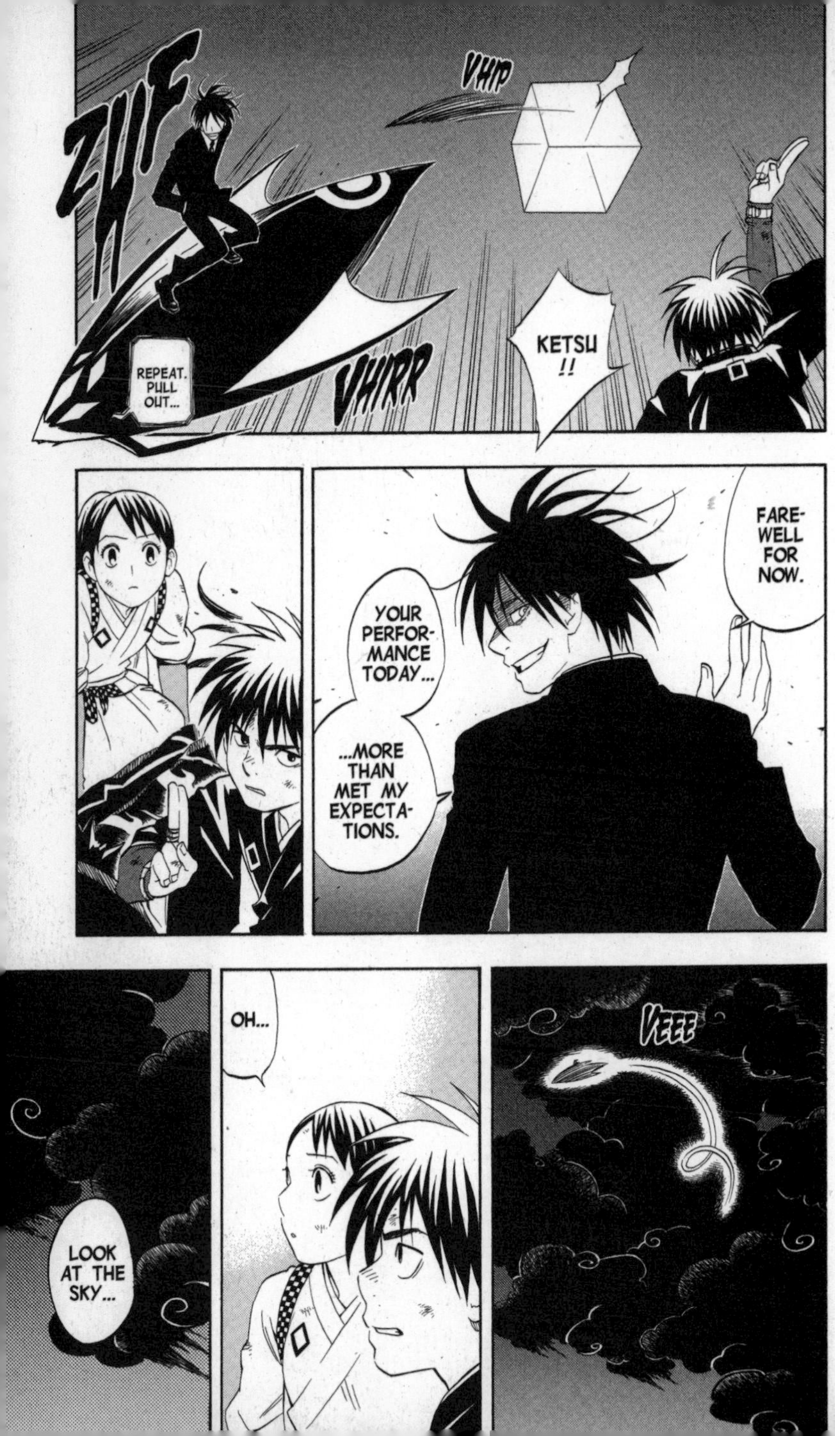
VHIP
KETSU !!
ZHIF
VHIRR
REPEAT. PULL OUT...
FAREWELL FOR NOW.
YOUR PERFORMANCE TODAY...
...MORE THAN MET MY EXPECTATIONS.
VEEE
OH...
LOOK AT THE SKY...

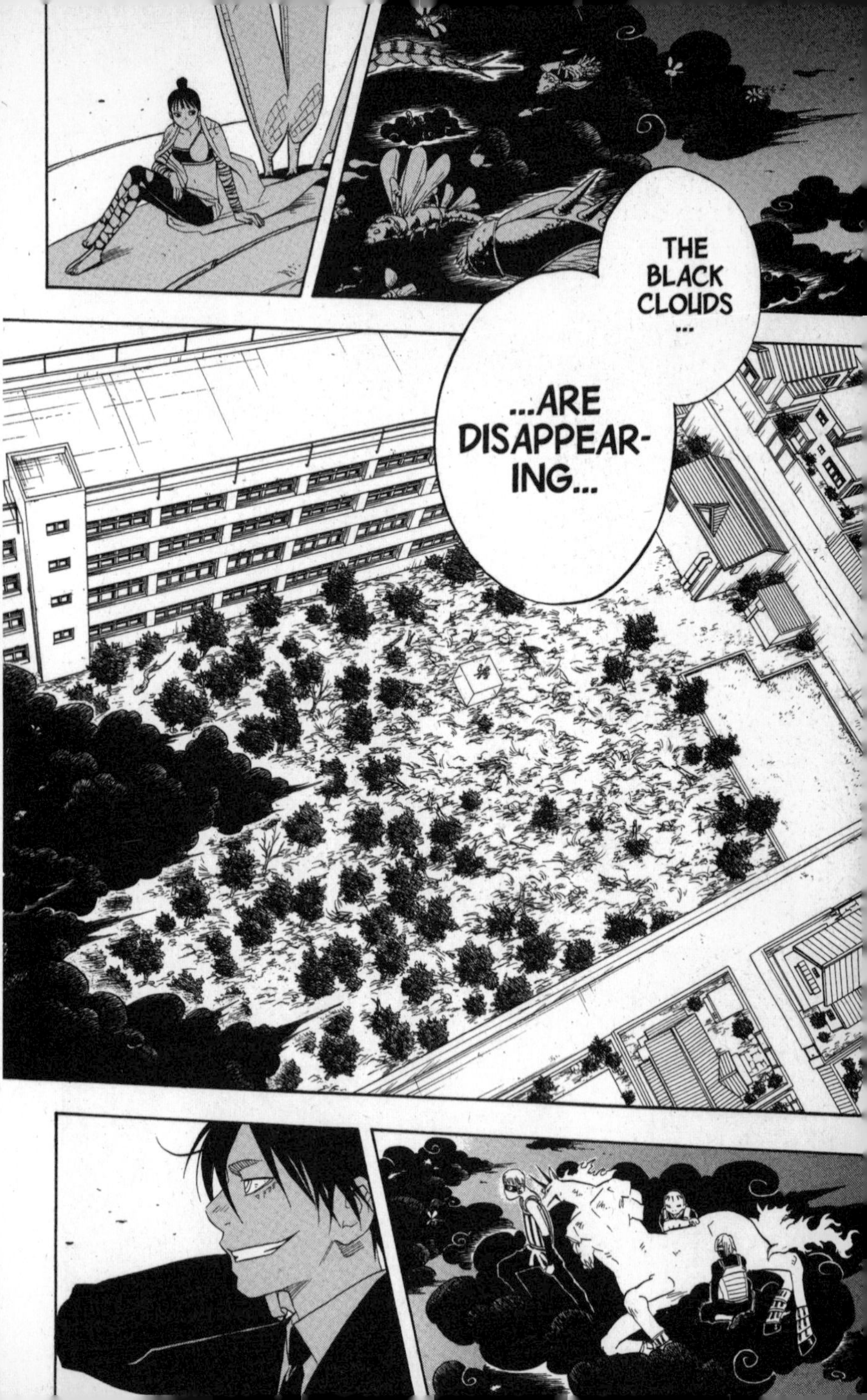
THE BLACK CLOUDS ...
...ARE DISAPPEAR-ING...

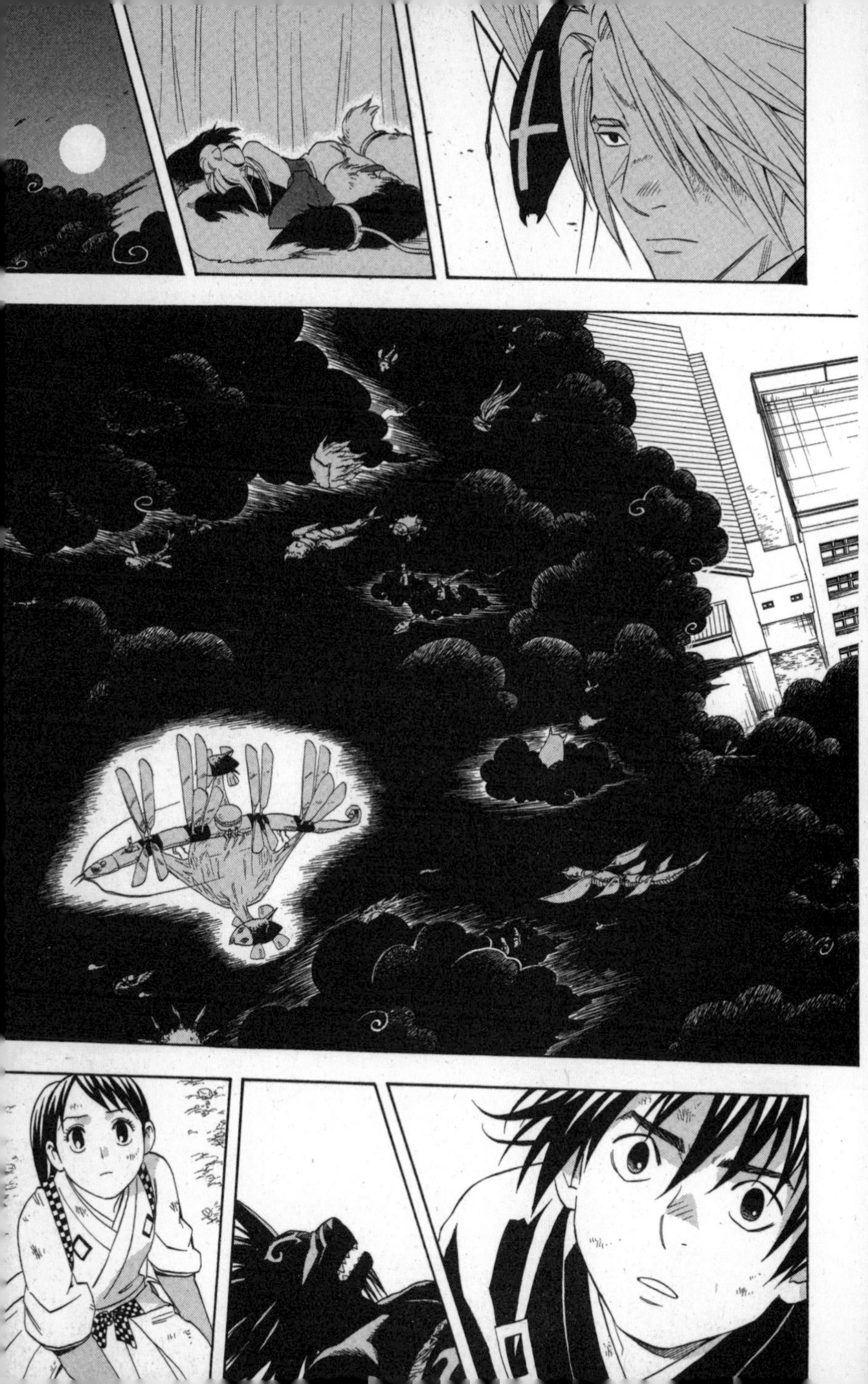

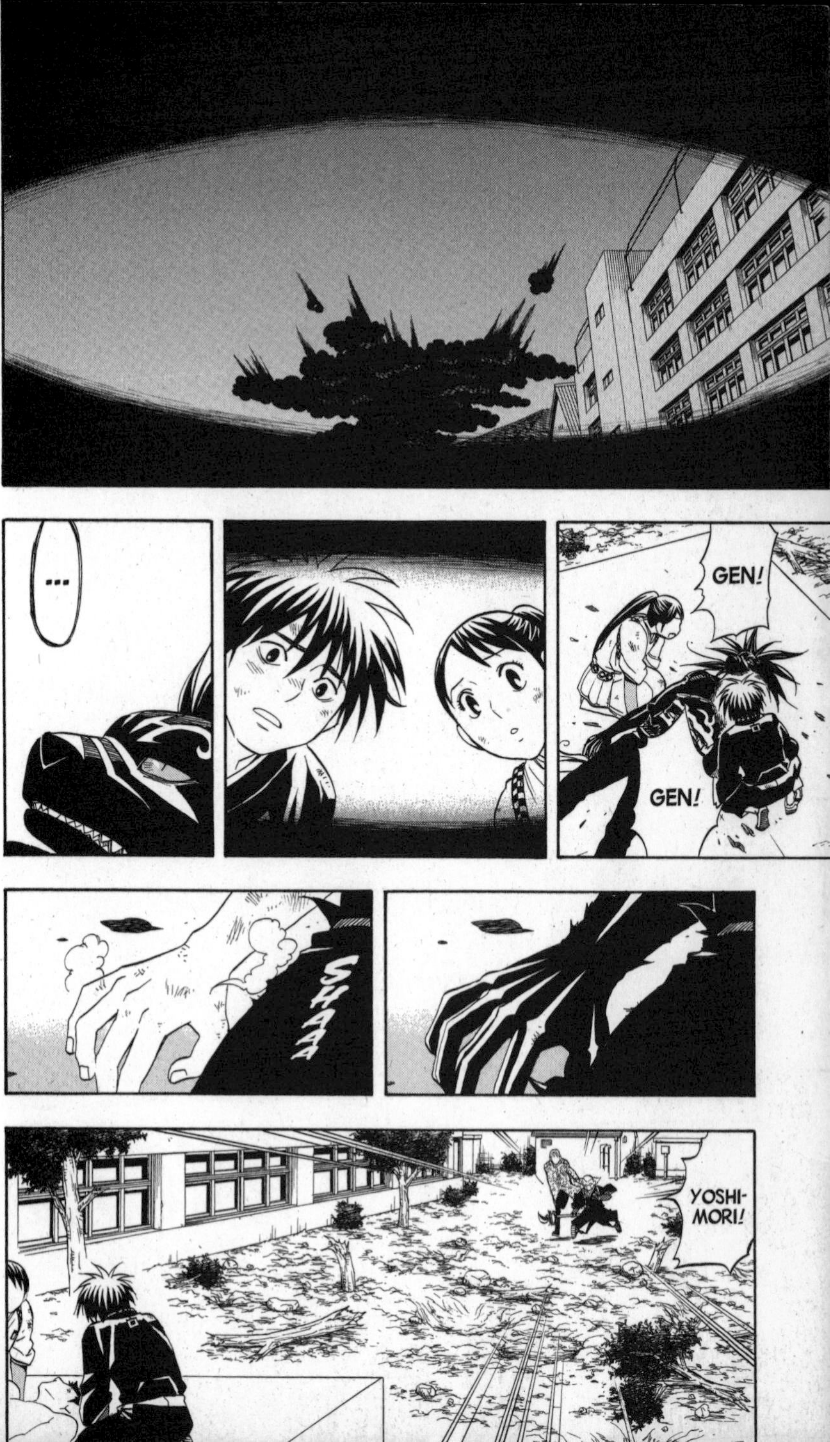
GEN!
GEN!
...
SHAAA
YOSHI-
MORI!

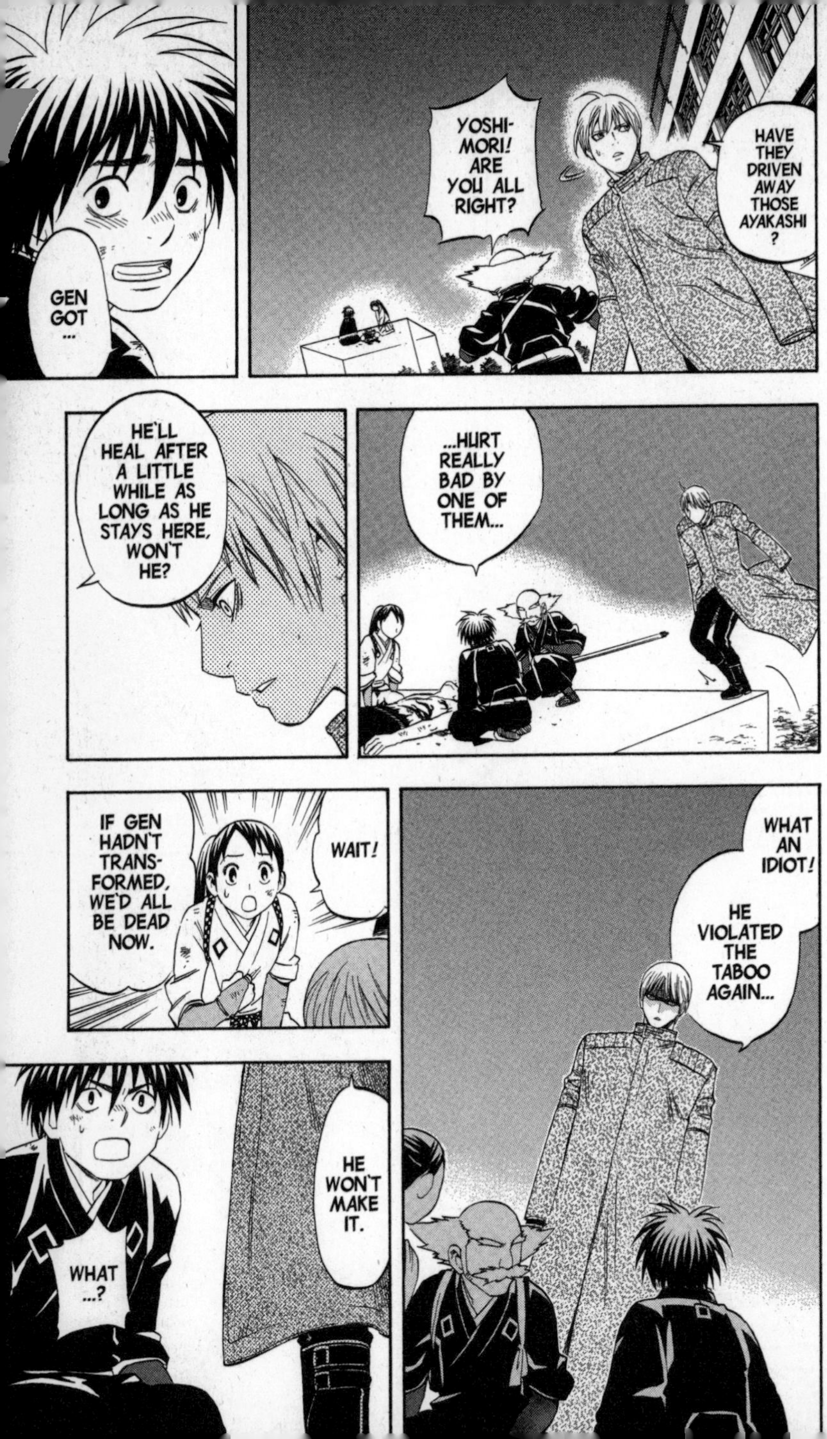
HAVE THEY DRIVEN AWAY THOSE AYAKASHI?
YOSHI-MORI! ARE YOU ALL RIGHT?
GEN GOT ...
...HURT REALLY BAD BY ONE OF THEM...
HE'LL HEAL AFTER A LITTLE WHILE AS LONG AS HE STAYS HERE, WON'T HE?
WHAT AN IDIOT!
HE VIOLATED THE TABOO AGAIN...
WAIT!
IF GEN HADN'T TRANSFORMED, WE'D ALL BE DEAD NOW.
HE WON'T MAKE IT.
WHAT ...?

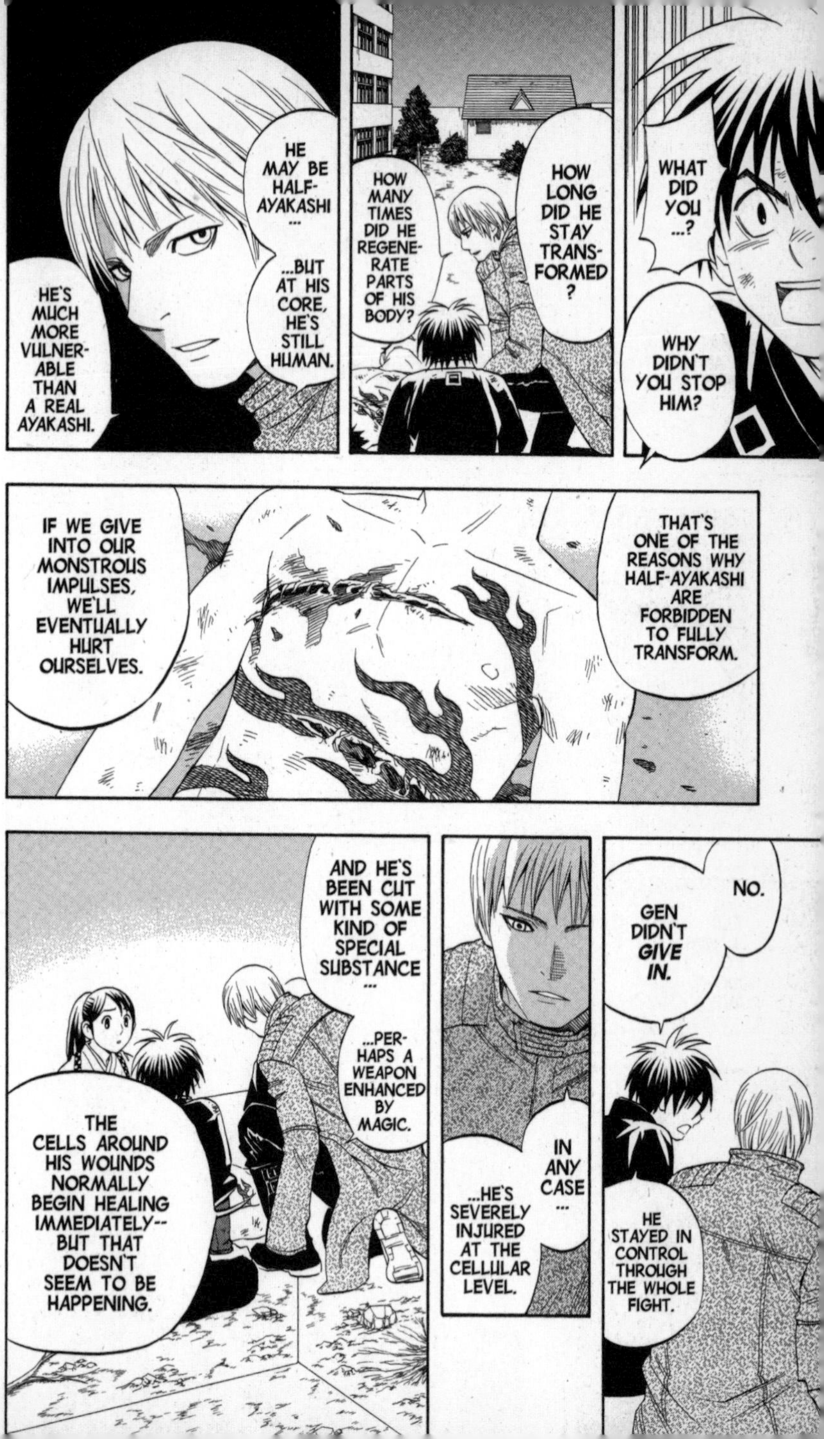
WHAT DID YOU ...?
WHY DIDN'T YOU STOP HIM?
HOW LONG DID HE STAY TRANSFORMED?
HOW MANY TIMES DID HE REGENERATE PARTS OF HIS BODY?
HE MAY BE HALF-AYAKASHI ...
...BUT AT HIS CORE, HE'S STILL HUMAN.
HE'S MUCH MORE VULNERABLE THAN A REAL AYAKASHI.
THAT'S ONE OF THE REASONS WHY HALF-AYAKASHI ARE FORBIDDEN TO FULLY TRANSFORM.
IF WE GIVE INTO OUR MONSTROUS IMPULSES, WE'LL EVENTUALLY HURT OURSELVES.
NO.
GEN DIDN'T *GIVE IN.*
HE STAYED IN CONTROL THROUGH THE WHOLE FIGHT.
IN ANY CASE ...
...HE'S SEVERELY INJURED AT THE CELLULAR LEVEL.
AND HE'S BEEN CUT WITH SOME KIND OF SPECIAL SUBSTANCE ...
...PER-HAPS A WEAPON ENHANCED BY MAGIC.
THE CELLS AROUND HIS WOUNDS NORMALLY BEGIN HEALING IMMEDIATELY--BUT THAT DOESN'T SEEM TO BE HAPPENING.

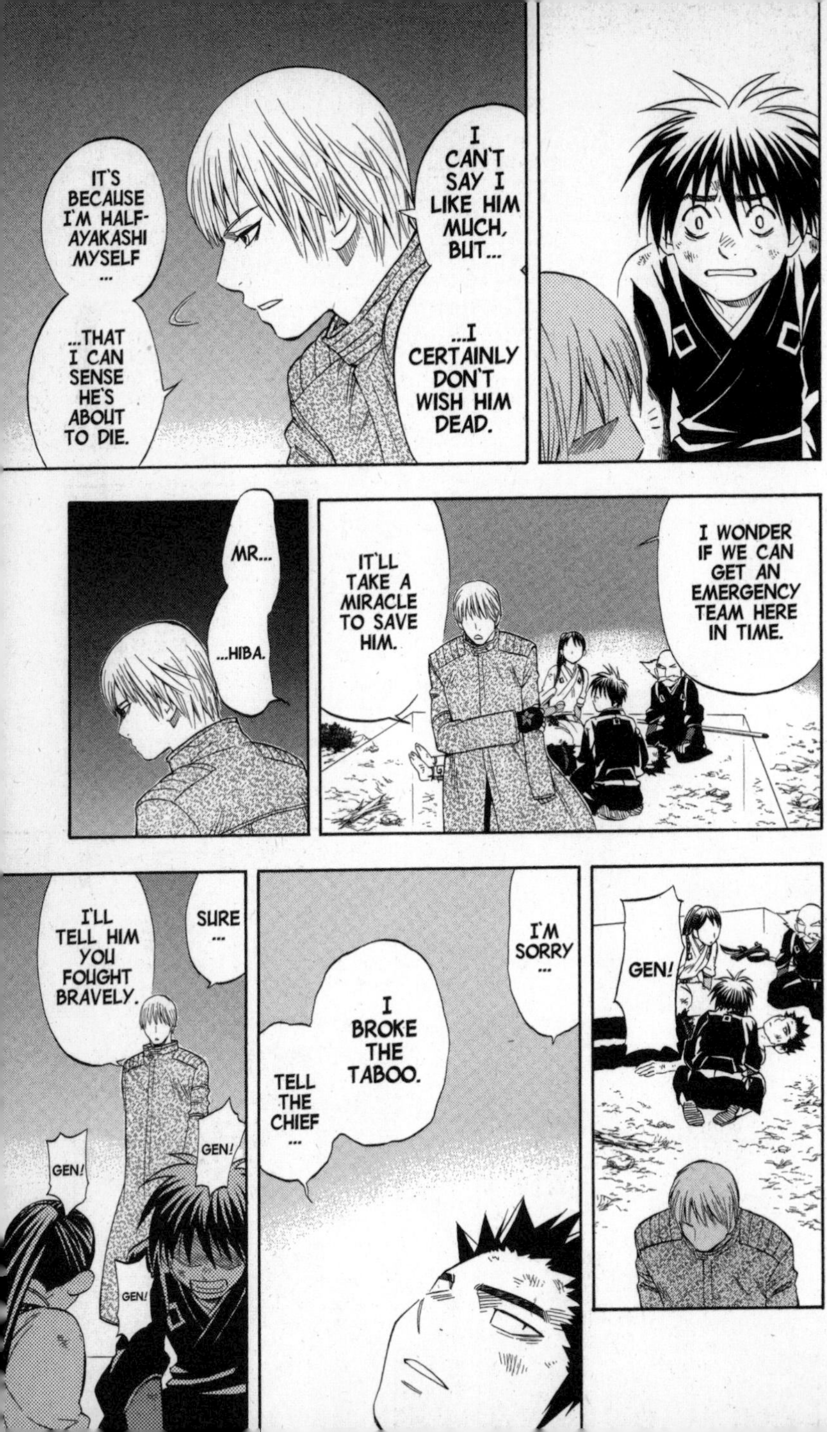
I CAN'T SAY I LIKE HIM MUCH, BUT...
...I CERTAINLY DON'T WISH HIM DEAD.
IT'S BECAUSE I'M HALF-AYAKASHI MYSELF...
...THAT I CAN SENSE HE'S ABOUT TO DIE.
I WONDER IF WE CAN GET AN EMERGENCY TEAM HERE IN TIME.
IT'LL TAKE A MIRACLE TO SAVE HIM.
MR...
...HIBA.
GEN!
I'M SORRY...
I BROKE THE TABOO.
TELL THE CHIEF...
SURE...
I'LL TELL HIM YOU FOUGHT BRAVELY.
GEN!
GEN!
GEN!

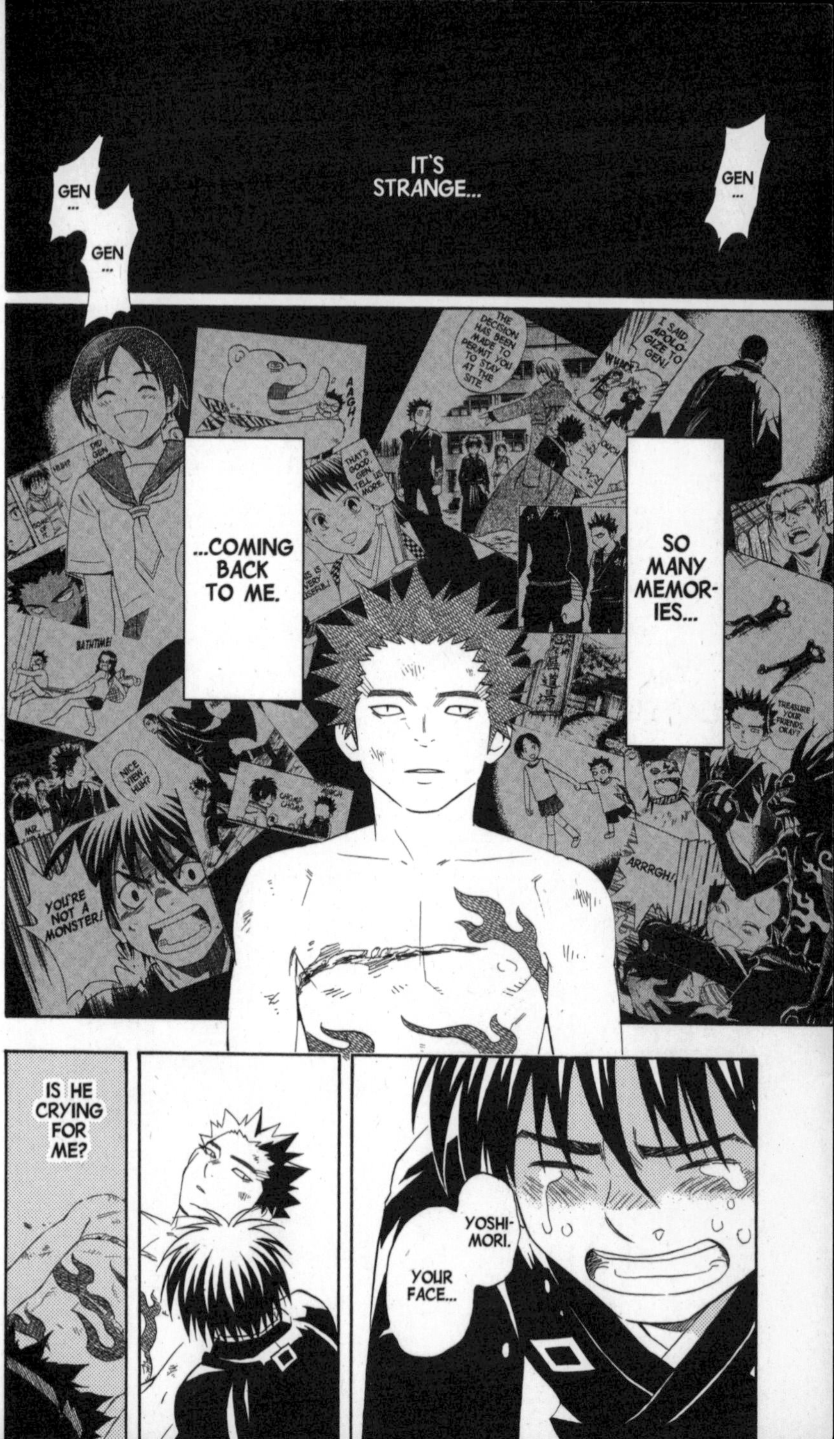
GEN...
IT'S STRANGE...
GEN...
GEN...
SO MANY MEMORIES...
I SAID, APOLOGIZE TO GEN!
THE DECISION HAS BEEN MADE TO PERMIT YOU TO STAY AT THE SITE
THAT'S GOOD, GEN. TELL US MORE.
AAGH!
...COMING BACK TO ME.
TREASURE YOUR FRIENDS, OKAY?
ARRRGH!
BATHTIME!
NICE VIEW, HUH?
YOU'RE NOT A MONSTER!
YOSHIMORI.
YOUR FACE...
IS HE CRYING FOR ME?

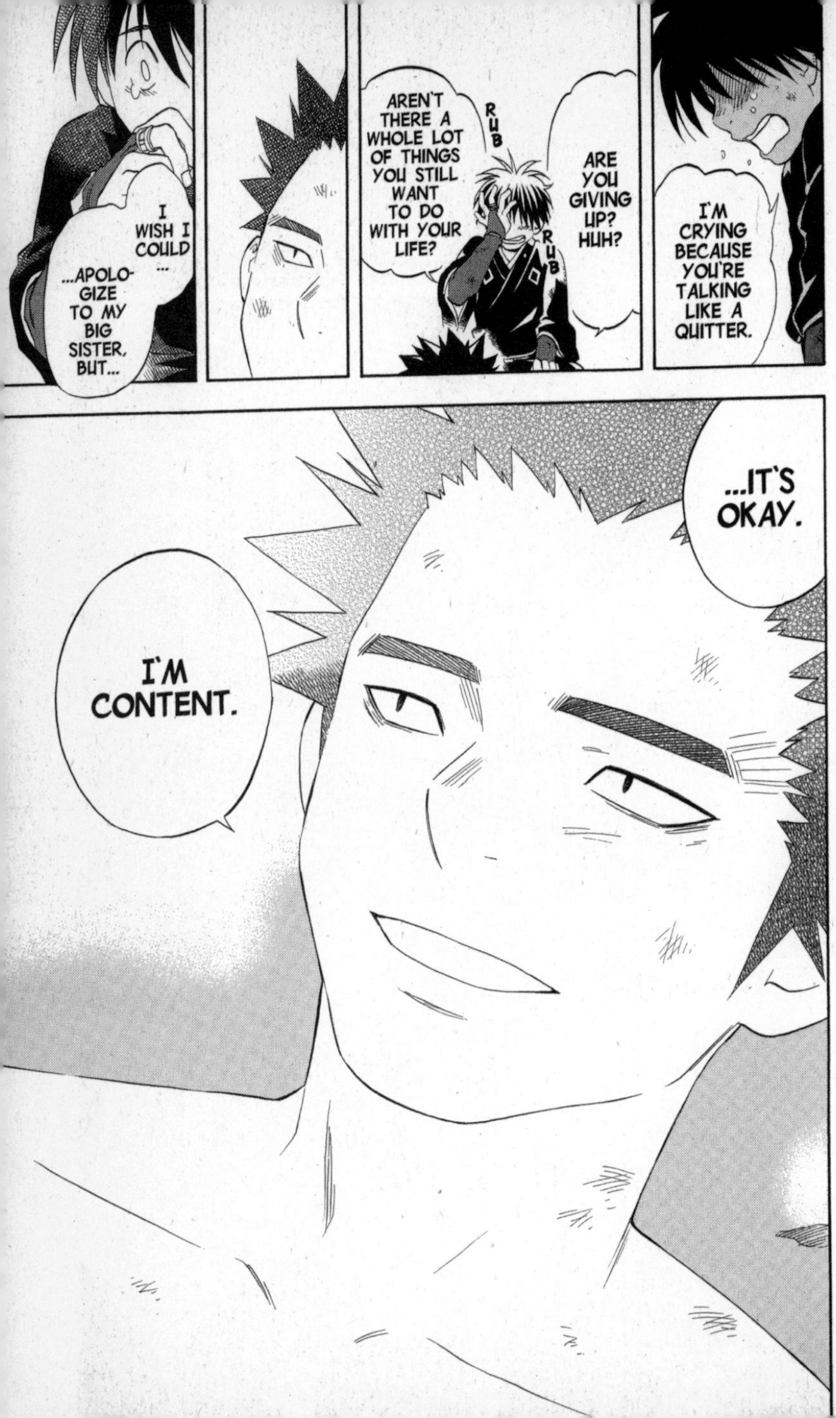
I'M CRYING BECAUSE YOU'RE TALKING LIKE A QUITTER.
ARE YOU GIVING UP? HUH?
RUB RUB
AREN'T THERE A WHOLE LOT OF THINGS YOU STILL WANT TO DO WITH YOUR LIFE?
I WISH I COULD...
...APOLOGIZE TO MY BIG SISTER, BUT...
...IT'S OKAY.
I'M CONTENT.

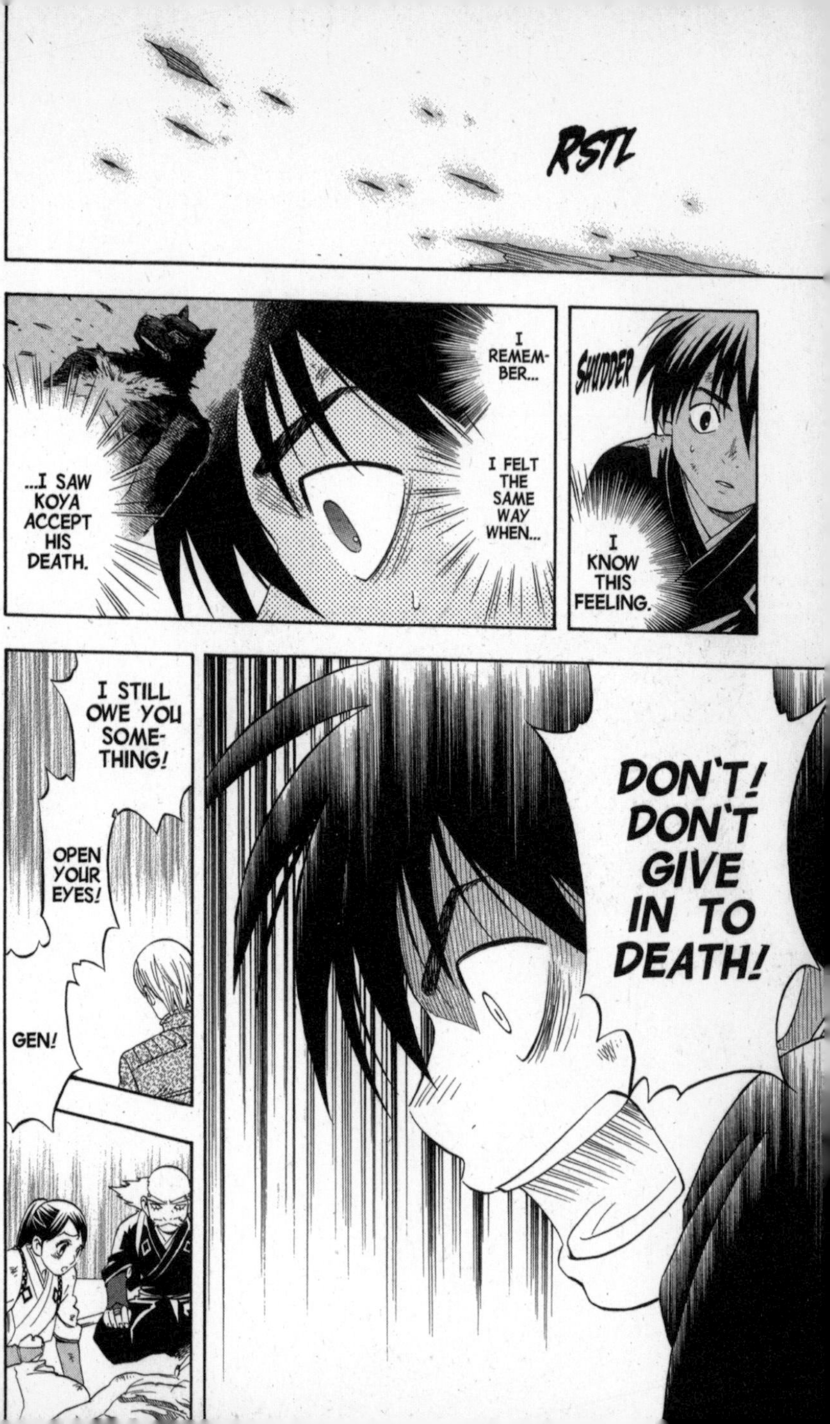
RSTL
SHUDDER
I KNOW THIS FEELING.
I REMEMBER...
I FELT THE SAME WAY WHEN...
...I SAW KOYA ACCEPT HIS DEATH.
DON'T! DON'T GIVE IN TO DEATH!
I STILL OWE YOU SOMETHING!
OPEN YOUR EYES!
GEN!

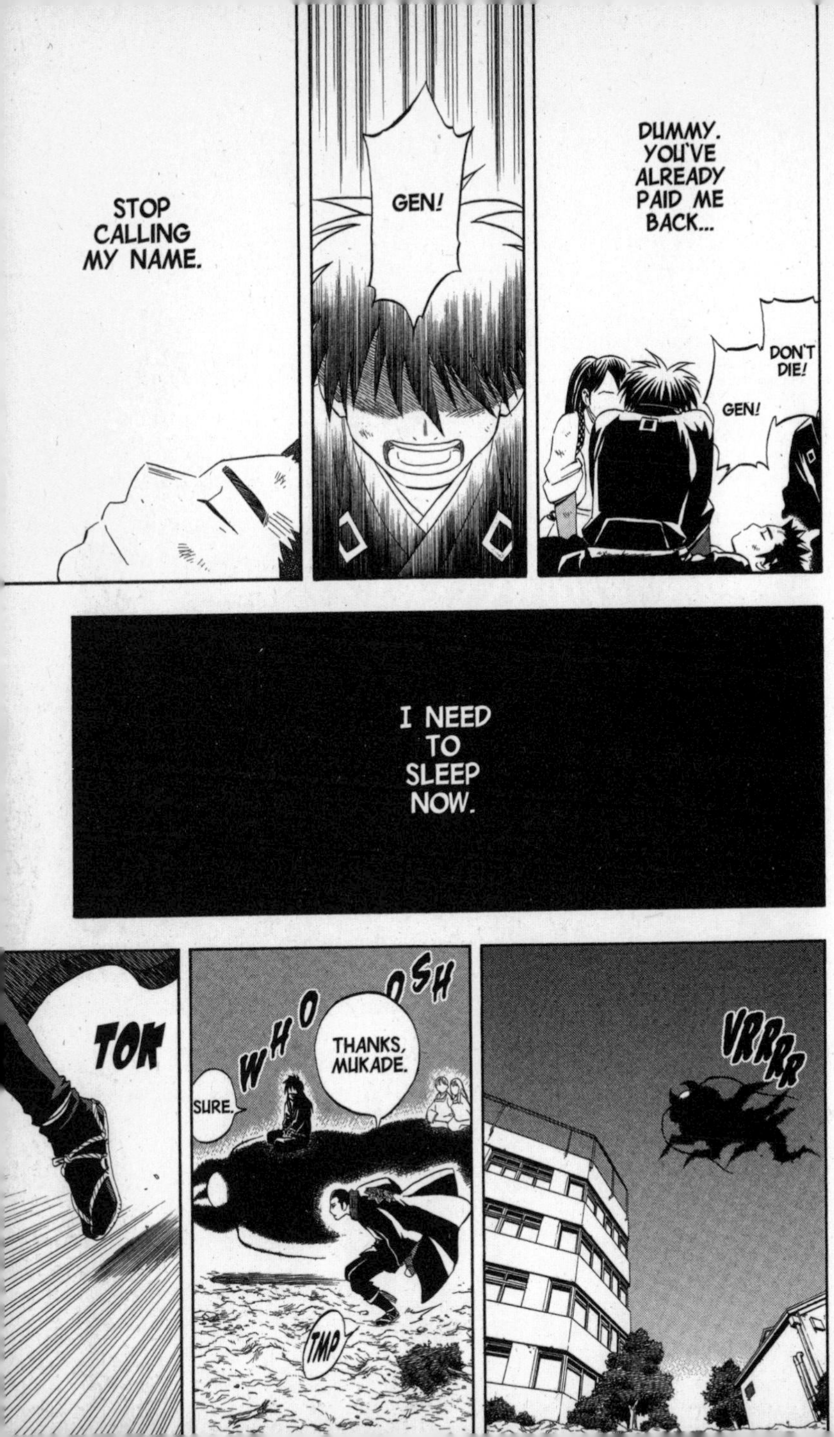
DUMMY. YOU'VE ALREADY PAID ME BACK...
DON'T DIE!
GEN!
GEN!
STOP CALLING MY NAME.
I NEED TO SLEEP NOW.
VRRRR
WHOOSH
THANKS, MUKADE.
SURE.
TMP
TOK

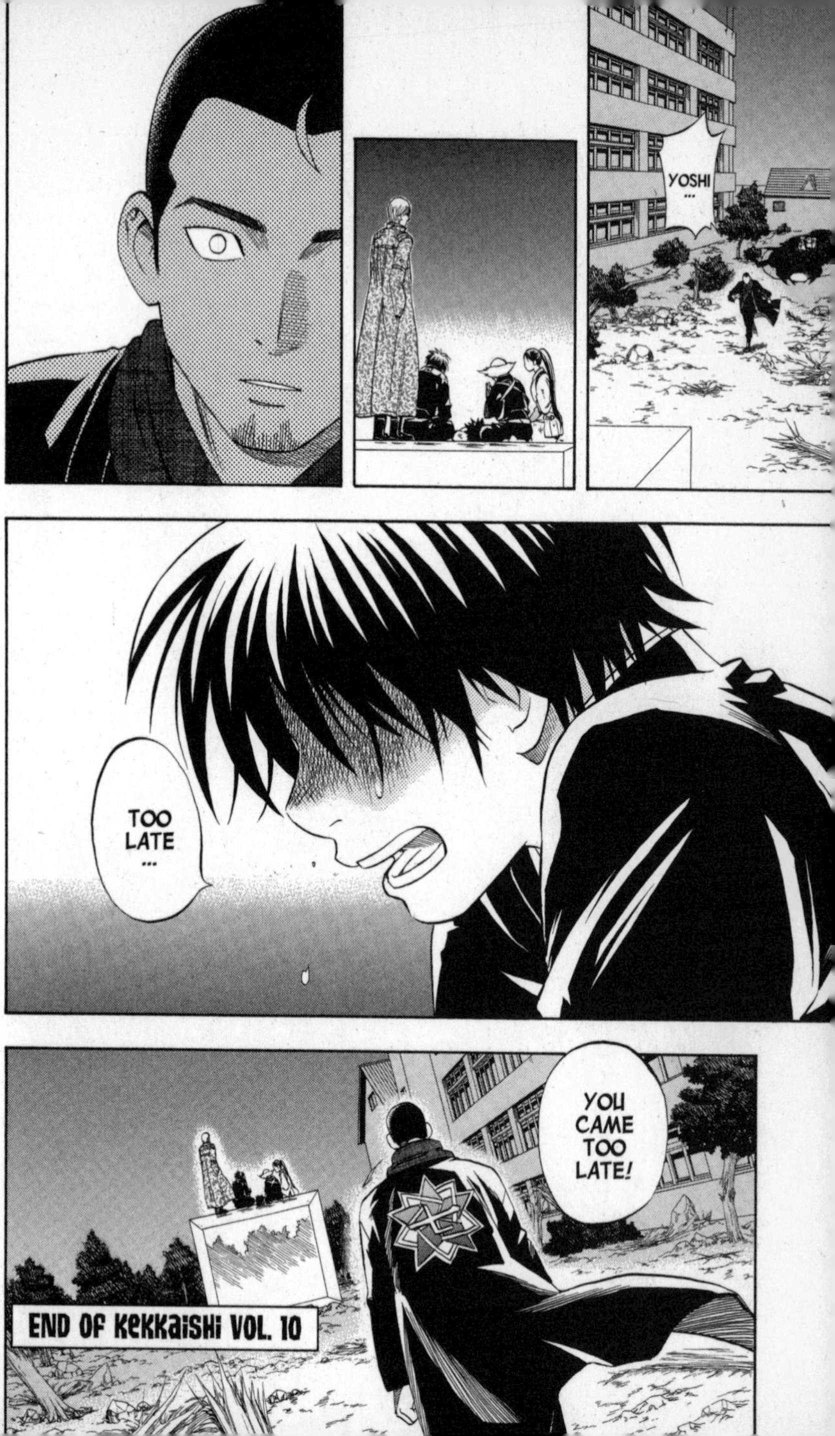
YOSHI ...
TOO LATE ...
YOU CAME TOO LATE!
END OF KEKKAISHI VOL. 10

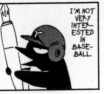

I'M NOT VERY INTERESTED IN BASEBALL.
ADDITIONAL EPISODE
ALL-OUT SPECIAL FEATURE: "EXPERIMENT"
OPERATION "MARSHMALLOW"
ONE NIGHT, MY NEW ASSISTANTS WERE TALKING ABOUT NOTHING IN PARTICULAR.
IF YOU MICROWAVE A MARSHMALLOW, IT'LL PUFF UP!
ACTING-ASSISTANT RACCOON
HMM.
ACTING-ASSISTANT FOX
HO.
TANABE
IT MAKES THE MARSHMALLOW VERY TASTY!
IT PUFFS UP LIKE THIS.
HE EVEN SHOWED ME A MOVIE OF IT ON HIS CELL PHONE.
HO.
I THINK SOMEONE GAVE ME SOME MARSHMALLOWS RECENTLY.
ALL RIGHT, WHY DON'T WE TRY IT?
SO WE DID AN EXPERIMENT.
YAHOO!
I'LL PUT THIS...
HEART-SHAPED GREEN MARSHMALLOW...
BOWL
...IN THE MICRO-WAVE!
MICRO WAVE
PRESSING START!
REFRIGERATOR
REHEAT
CLICK
VHIRRR

*IN REALITY, THIS STOOL WASN'T USED.

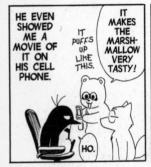

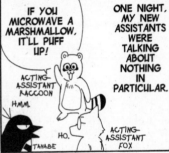

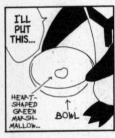

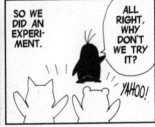

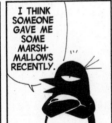

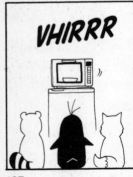

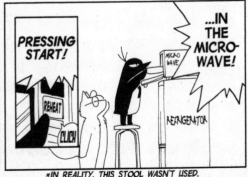

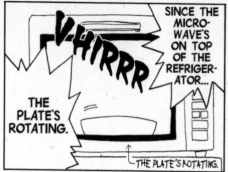

OH!
SINCE THE MICROWAVE'S ON TOP OF THE REFRIGERATOR...
V-HIRRR
THE PLATE'S ROTATING.
THE PLATE'S ROTATING.
DID IT PUFF UP?
VHIRRR
I WOULD SAY YES!
I CAN'T SEE A THING!
BOING
BOING
BOING
JUMPING SMALL ANIMALS
WE ZAPPED IT TOO LONG AND THE MARSHMALLOW TURNED INTO A STICKY GREEN GLOB.
IT DIDN'T LOOK TASTY.
...
SECOND-RATE SCIENTIST AND HIS ASSISTANTS.
WE LEFT THE DISH ON THE DESK OF ANOTHER ASSISTANT WHO WAS TAKING A BATH AT THE TIME.
WHAT'S THIS?
ACTING-ASSISTANT CANARY
"OPERATION MARSHMALLOW" FAILED.
END

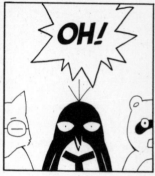

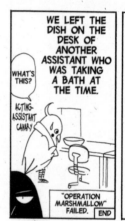

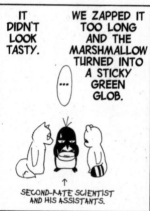

Next Volume...

Each of our friends attempts to cope with their grief at Gen's death alone. Tokine searches for a secret way into Kokuboro's castle, Yoshimori trains for an ultimate confrontation, and Masamori returns home with a regiment of his night troops, leaving his little brother with no room of his own. Unfortunately, before long, one of our three heroes is in need of a dramatic rescue...

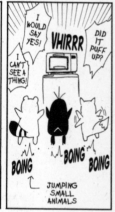

I wish there were a tunnel running straight from one ear to the other. That way, it would be so much easier to clean them.

MESSAGE FROM YELLOW TANABE

Very often, my ears get itchy when I'm working on a script and I lose myself in the act of cleaning them. Cotton-tipped swabs seem to be the best choice of equipment for the job, but personally, I prefer an ear pick. In the end, I wind up using both methods.

KEKKAISHI

VOLUME 10

VIZ MEDIA EDITION

STORY AND ART BY YELLOW TANABE

Translation/Yuko Sawada
Touch-up Art & Lettering/Stephen Dutro
Cover Design & Graphic Layout/Izumi Evers
Editor/Annette Roman

Editor in Chief, Books/Alvin Lu
Editor in Chief, Magazines/Marc Weidenbaum
VP of Publishing Licensing/Rika Inouye
VP of Sales/Gonzalo Ferreyra
Sr. VP of Marketing/Liza Coppola
Publisher/Hyoe Narita

Printed in the U.S.A.

Published by VIZ Media, LLC
P.O. Box 77010
San Francisco, CA 94107

VIZ Media Edition
10 9 8 7 6 5 4 3 2 1
First printing, August 2007

www.viz.com

store.viz.com

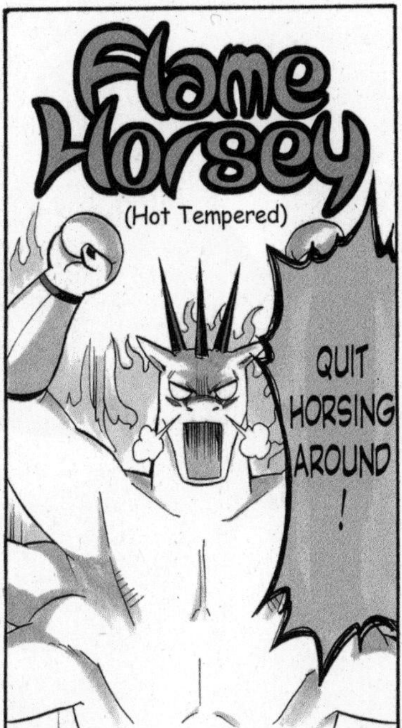
Flame Horsey
(Hot Tempered)
QUIT HORSING AROUND!

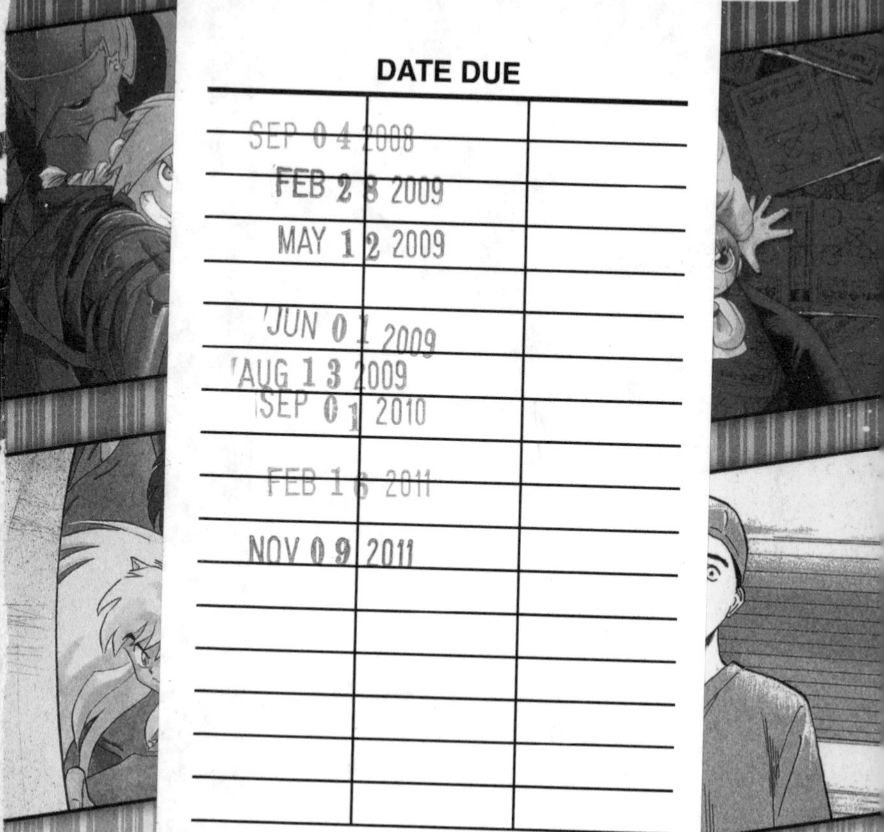